Sidney Lumet

Sidney Lumet

A Life

MAURA SPIEGEL

JESSAMINE COUNTY PUBLIC LIBRARY
600 South Main Street
Nicholasville, KY 40356

ST. MARTIN'S
PRESS
NEW YORK

First published in the United States by St. Martin's Press,
an imprint of St. Martin's Publishing Group

SIDNEY LUMET. Copyright © 2019 by Maura Spiegel. All rights reserved.
Printed in the United States of America. For information, address St. Martin's
Publishing Group, 120 Broadway, New York, NY 10271.

www.stmartins.com

Designed by Steven Seighman

Library of Congress Cataloging-in-Publication Data

Names: Spiegel, Maura, author.
Title: Sidney Lumet: a life / Maura Spiegel.
Description: First edition. | New York: St. Martin's Press, an imprint of
   St. Martin's Publishing Group, 2019. | Includes bibliographical
   references and index. |
Identifiers: LCCN 2019031704 | ISBN 9781250030153 (hardcover) |
   ISBN 9781250030146 (ebook)
Subjects: LCSH: Lumet, Sidney, 1924–2011. | Motion picture producers and
   directors—United States—Biography.
Classification: LCC PN1998.3.L86 S65 2019 | DDC 791.4302/33092 [B]—dc23
LC record available at https://lccn.loc.gov/2019031704

Our books may be purchased in bulk for promotional, educational, or business use.
Please contact your local bookseller or the Macmillan Corporate and Premium Sales
Department at 1-800-221-7945, extension 5442, or by email at
MacmillanSpecialMarkets@macmillan.com.

First Edition: December 2019

10 9 8 7 6 5 4 3 2 1

In memory

Justice Samuel A. Spiegel
Honorable Charlotte N. Spiegel
and
Ida White Gibbs

CONTENTS

ACKNOWLEDGMENTS

I wish to thank my agent, Don Fehr, for suggesting this project; Paul Lazar for his incredible support, and for opening countless doors; Daniel Myerson for the most extraordinary act of friendship and midwifery; Didi Heller, cherished friend for life; Michael Tencer for his excellent counsel and meticulous work on the manuscript; Mindy Fullilove, Ann Burack-Weiss, Lisa Heiserman, Gina Heiserman and Adrienne Munich, for wisdom, encouragement and crucial pointers. At St. Martin's, thank you to Hannah Phillips and Michael Flamini, my wise editor.

I am enduringly grateful to Sidney's family for allowing me access to his unfinished memoir. Special thanks for kindness and marvelousness to Mary (Piedy) Lumet, Jenny Lumet, Gail Lumet Buckley, the late Rita Gam, and to the late Gloria Vanderbilt for sharing memories and allowing me to reproduce Sidney's drawings. I am especially indebted to Lili Jacobs, who was a generous, invaluable, and delightful guide.

I want most urgently to thank Simon Fortin, Jim Gilbert, Helena Hansen, Kelli Harding, Craig Irvine, John Kavanaugh and Jack Saul, my very dear friends who read drafts endlessly and provided support in dark moments. Thanks also to caring colleagues and administrators Casey Blake, Rita Charon, Angela Darling, Andrew Delbanco, Margaret Edsall, Lisa Gordis, Peter Platt, Cindy Smalletz, and Danielle Spencer. For priceless help with research, Joan Cohen, Ido Levy, Megan Litt, Eric Monder, Oriana Gonzales, Felicity Palmer, Derick Schilling and Benjamin Jordan Serby. Thank you to Karen

Starr, Richard Fulmer, Elyse Goldstein, you know why. For generous help in countless ways, Kenji Fujita, Bob Milstein, Ilsa Klinghoffer and Lisa Klinghoffer.

I extend my sincere gratitude to all those belonging to Sidney Lumet's orbit who spoke with me and pointed me in the right direction: Ellen Adler, David Amram, Andrzej Bartkowiak, Walter Bernstein, the late Theodore Bikel, David Black, Boaty Boatwright, Stephen Bowie, Bobby Cannavale, the late Jonathan Demme, Brian De Palma, the late E. L. Doctorow, the late Bill Esper, Tom Fontana, Burtt Harris, Lisa James, Jane Klain, Geneviève LeRoy, Brian Linse, Gloria Loomis, Jenny Lumet, Kelly Masterson, Claudia Mohr, Chris Newman, Austin Pendleton, Martha Pinson, Amy Ryan, Theo Sable, Julie Salamon, Susan Scheftel, Stan Stokowski, Susanna Styron, John Tucker, Tony Walton and Treat Williams.

I wish to acknowledge the Margaret Herrick Library at the Academy of Motion Picture Arts and Sciences, the Warner Bros. Archive at USC, the Paley Center for Media, the New York Library for the Performing Arts, the Dorot Jewish Division of the New York Public Library, the Museum of the Moving Image, the Billy Rose Theatre Division of the New York Public Library, the YIVO Institute for Jewish Research, the UCLA Library Special Collections and the Kenneth Koch Literary Estate and Alfred A. Knopf, an imprint of the Knopf Doubleday Publishing Group, a Division of Random House LLC for permission to reprint an excerpt of "To Jewishness" from *The Collected Poems of Kenneth Koch,* copyright 2005. All rights reserved.

With very special thanks to Jill Spiegel and Phillip Robinson. To my inspiring family, to Katie, Sam, Taniya and my incomparable husband, Arthur, I love you so much. Thank you.

Sidney Lumet

PREFACE

Sidney Lumet would not have been crazy about the idea of a biography. "He erased his calendar after events," David Black, a writer and producer who worked with Sidney, observed. "This is gonna cause a problem for biographers." In fact, Sidney Lumet—pronounced "loo-*met*," with a hard T instead of in the French style, "loo-*may*"—left no diaries, no papers, no correspondence, no archive. His inclination was to keep moving forward and not to look back. Much of the work of this book, of necessity, involved entering the rich worlds Sidney inhabited by collecting memories from those he worked with and those who loved him. He attempted, in his sixties, to write a memoir, but could get no further in the narrative than his early twenties. When he opened the valve, painful memories flooded him; the effort was unsustainable.

Likely he preferred to let the movies speak for him. It wasn't just modesty—he wasn't exactly a modest man. What he valued most was what people did by choice, what they forged and made happen, rather than what befell them or where they fell short. His remarkable book, *Making Movies*, stands as a testament to this spirit.

He rejected the title *auteur,* insisting always on the collective nature and the "luck factor" of producing great work. He preferred the term "movie" to "film," retreating from anything he took to be fancy and unworkmanlike. He believed utterly in the value of working, in putting one foot in front of the other. He took on projects for many different reasons: because he adored a script or an actor, to learn a new aspect of his craft, to pay for a house—or just to be working. And he was hardly unmindful of the unevenness of his output.

He was not immune to praise or criticism, but he did his best to shrug them off equally. That thick skin would prove necessary for so much of his later working life, as Sidney was not canonized, was not lauded, wasn't even fashionable, despite his early successes. Critics complained that he was not edgy enough, and he was tarred with the "liberal conscience" tag, at a time, in the 1980s and 1990s, when the L word was reviled by both the left and the right. Some said he could never again hit the mark as he'd done in the 1970s with *Serpico, Network* and *Dog Day Afternoon*, that not only his politics but his cinematic language was out of date. Yet just as quickly as the critics abandoned him, they returned to praise him toward the end of his life, lavishly hailing his final film, *Before the Devil Knows You're Dead*, as "a return to form" by "a living treasure."

The fact is, though, Sidney never stopped experimenting. He was constantly working with new actors, new equipment, new genres, and new techniques. Throughout his career he drew upon his earlier experiences in radio, theater, television and film to expand beyond his comfort zones and break new ground as both an artist and a citizen. The proof of how fickle critical opinion can be, and how poorly it provides the measure of any film's enduring success, can be found in the ease with which Sidney was branded with that seemingly flattering phrase "return to form": Sidney's films had actually begun to receive that backhanded compliment no later than the early 1970s. *Serpico, The Verdict, Running on Empty, Q & A, Night Falls on Manhattan* and *Find Me Guilty* were at the times of their release all described as returning to form; indeed, with critics declaring so many returns, one has to wonder in retrospect whether half of Sidney's career might not ultimately be viewed as a return to the other half.

Over the course of fifty-five years, with a directing career spanning forty-three movies and more than seventy-five television episodes, movies, and plays for the small screen, as well as another dozen years before that devoted to acting in theater, radio, and film, Sidney strove to work constantly, to glean as many lessons as possible from past successes and failures in the cause of putting that knowledge into action. Even by his own estimation, some of those experiments failed, but for Sidney every one of them was worth trying, and each contained moments of truth.

The struggle was key: as with so many of the characters brought to life in unforgettable performances he directed, he believed that even a hopeless cause was worth fighting for if the cause was good and just. Sidney measured his own successes by how true he was to his characters, his craft, and himself. All other measures of success, like fame, wealth and accolades, were unreliable and often only tangentially related to the work.

I was drawn to this project for a host of reasons. At first it was his movies that attracted me, compelling me to get to know the life of a man I'd only distantly encountered a few times and never talked to. I wanted to understand the creator of movies I loved and to get to know the life behind those films that felt so legible to me. The tender treatment of flawed characters trying to be principled, the sense of irony somehow fused with genuine political engagement, his delight in urban characters and in the endless surprise of city life, all had for me an almost uncanny familiarity of tone and orientation. As I learned more about Sidney, I could attribute this sense of familiarity to a shared heritage; I had grown up on New York's Lower East Side, where Sidney spent some of his childhood, and where my family had roots. Indeed, I would learn that his family and mine shared roots in the old country too, in neighboring shtetls in Poland. Sidney's first language, Yiddish, the customs of his immigrant parents, his identification with the oppressed, and the curious amalgam of skepticism and magnanimity were familiar to me from my background; these elements are palpable throughout his work. Sidney left no road map, but finding him was a great joy and privilege.

Knowing, then, where Sidney came from, the causes he fought for and the principles he believed in has made it possible to elucidate themes running through his work and, I hope, to spark appreciation for some of his otherwise unacknowledged achievements.

What follows is my effort, despite Sidney Lumet's own attempted erasures of his past, to piece together the story of his life. As so much of that life was spent engaged in artistic work, this story contains a great deal of discussion of his art as well. I do not endeavor to judge here for posterity which of his works will speak most fully to viewers in the future, but I have no doubt that he will be revisited often.

1

YIDDISH ROOTS

Baruch Lumet . . . makes a full-blooded character of a familiar type, though he tends to overact discreetly . . . and Sidney Lumet as an alert and warm-hearted youngster is all of that and charming.

—FROM THE *NEW YORK TIMES* REVIEW
OF *THE BROWNSVILLE GRANDFATHER*, APRIL 19, 1935

He was heavy-handed and middlebrow—according to Pauline Kael, the formidable *New Yorker* film critic who never tired of panning Sidney's films. The first time she clobbered him was in 1968 when she was still establishing herself in New York, and her hostility baffled Sidney. Hadn't he welcomed her, a young writer from California, onto the set of his tenth film, *The Group*, for something or other she was writing for *Life* magazine? Sidney thought that nothing could be more instructive to a critic than to learn something about how a movie is made. In fact, he couldn't really fathom how someone could begin to evaluate a movie without knowing about film production. He hadn't expected she'd planned to make her name as a wisecracking detractor. Her barbs hurt: "The emphasis on immediate results may explain the almost total absence of nuance, subtlety, and even rhythmic and structural development in his work. . . . He seems to have no intellectual curiosity. . . . He'll go on faking it, I think, using the abilities he has to cover up what he doesn't know." But he wasn't about to change the way he worked in response to a critic—or to anyone. Well aware of his own shortcomings, Sidney liked to joke about his "bad taste," attributing it, more or less affectionately, to his background in Yiddish theater.

Sidney's father, Baruch, had been a Yiddish actor and had put his son on the stage when he was five years old. The young Lumet had served his apprenticeship in immigrant melodramas, where it was more than acceptable to commiserate with the struggles of the poor, to make social commentary, to allow yourself as an artist to teach and even to take to task.

Sidney's early apprenticeship in the Yiddish theater was, oddly enough, preparation for his career as a quintessentially American director. Its rough and ready atmosphere toughened him up. And despite Pauline Kael's disdain for his approach to storytelling, immigrant melodramas provided instructive models. A new phenomenon in Jewish life, Yiddish theater had arrived in New York in the early 1880s, finding a ready audience willing to spend as much as half a week's salary to get a seat at one of the lavish theaters built along Second Avenue between Houston and 14th Street on Manhattan's Lower East Side. Opening in 1911, the elegant 2nd Avenue Theatre held almost two thousand patrons, and other theaters on a similar scale soon followed. The "Yiddish Broadway," also called the "Jewish Rialto," was lined with costume houses, music and photography stores, and restaurants and cafés, where artists and intellectuals gathered with the theater crowd. They were considered the royalty of the Lower East Side. Actors hoping to

A film of Sidney singing the Yiddish song "Papirosen" [Cigarettes] was projected as a flashback during a Yiddish musical of the same name. *(From the Archives of the YIVO Institute for Jewish Research, New York)*

find work frequented these lively cafés—among them, Baruch Lumet, sometimes accompanied by his precocious little boy.

In one early performance, little Sidney, dressed as a beggar, sang a Yiddish ballad about an orphan whose sister, the only one who watches out for him, has died. Rain-drenched, he pleads to passersby to "take pity," to purchase his cigarettes, his *papirosen*, assuring them that, though he is soaked to the skin, his wares are dry. But pathos— usually seasoned with social conscience—was only part of what the Yiddish theater had to offer. There were Yiddish versions of everything from Shakespeare to Strindberg to Chekhov. For newly arrived im- migrants, it was a place where they saw their lives portrayed, where they received an education, were entertained and could let off steam. It was a rich emotional experience where ironies abounded and the sublime and the ridiculous lived side by side. Starving Jewish social- ists traded on their good voices and impersonated cantors, singing heartrending versions of Kol Nidre, the Yom Kippur prayer. Emotions were tossed back and forth from stage to audience and from audience to stage across a line that often disappeared. Even personal greetings were not out of place, with performers interrupting a scene to wave to friends and family.

The actors often had to appear in a new play every two weeks, and in addition they did benefit matinee performances of yet other plays simultaneously. They hadn't time to learn each part by heart, so hid- den at the foot of the stage was the prompter, called the *soufleur*, who whispered stage directions and lines to the actors. The Yiddish playwright B. Gorin (Isaac Goido) reveled in the mishaps and may- hem that sometimes occurred on stage as a result of the practice of "prompting." In a 1905 issue of the journal *The Menorah*, Gorin tells this story:

> *During a scene of a so-called "historical opera," a priest had*
> *to stab the king. The stage in that scene was packed with actors*
> *and actresses, chorus girls and supernumeraries, as in all the*
> *"thrilling" scenes of such performances. When the moment for*
> *the stabbing arrived the prompter said: "Stab!"*

The priest ran at the actor who stood opposite him and stabbed him.

"Not that one! Not that one!"

"Not him!" repeated the actor who had already lost his head, and not losing any more of his valuable time he stabbed another.

"Ah, not him, the king!"

The priest having parted with his wits altogether, stabbed whomsoever he could get hold of.

"The king! Stab the king!"

The priest ran up to the king and stabbed him, but this was the young king, the good king who should have remained alive, not the old, bad king whom the priest had to dispatch for his iniquities.

"Not him! Not him!"

The priest was now sure that the one whom he had to stab was not the king and he threw himself on everybody, stabbing without discrimination right and left the actors, supernumeraries and choristers, and hearing after each time the words "Not him! Not him!" he murdered everybody on the stage except the old king who remained alive after all others were slaughtered.

At the same time, Yiddish theater could be politically and aesthetically avant-garde, no matter how meager the production financing. For example, at a time when the Ziegfeld Follies and parlor dramas dominated Broadway, you could find the Sacco and Vanzetti story— of immigrant Italian American anarchists whose murder trial became a cause célèbre—staged on Second Avenue. It wasn't only the subject matter of the Sacco and Vanzetti story that was radical. The play was staged in an unconventional way. Since the theater was very small— actually there was no stage at all—the director created a sequence of forty-four brief scenes, illuminated by spotlights and separated by blackouts, that were staged on every side of the seated audience. Such a technique is frequently used today, but it was quite novel at the time.

It may have been the freedom of the Yiddish theater that taught

Sidney to experiment with so many different ways to tell stories. And this early exposure to Yiddish theater may have had something to do with his focus on characters from everyday life, his distrust of the idealized and the romanticized. In his movies, protagonists do extraordinary things like rob banks or expose corruption, but he emphasizes that they are just people, not so different from you and me, with recognizable emotions. You might encounter them any day on the street, especially the streets of New York.

As a child, Sidney did not much play with other children; he was too busy watching the adults play with great intensity and skill and learning from them. His father read him a Yiddish version of *Hamlet* when he was six, titled *Der Yeshiva Bokher*. An ardent spirit, Baruch, known to some by the nickname Bulu, threw himself into whatever he did, from the "high art" that was his calling to moneymaking ventures such as *Der Brownsviller Zeyde*, a Yiddish soap opera for the Brooklyn radio station WLTH in which the whole family performed beginning when Sidney was four. In daily fifteen-minute episodes, fifty-two weeks a year, the show related the adventures of the good-natured and charmingly disoriented immigrant *zeyde* (grandpa) who was trying to make sense of his new life in Brooklyn.

In the intense atmosphere of arguments over everything from stage timing to production costs to artistic shades of meaning, the boy underwent an apprenticeship. He became something of an *enfant prodige*, precocious, adult-oriented and serious. To everyone's amazement, six-year-old Sidney shouted at a stagehand who missed his cue, "Bring that curtain down!" Sometimes he would answer his parents strangely—until they recognized that his replies were lines from a play. He lived in the world of the theater so intensely that after a production was over he could still recite scenes and even an entire play by heart.

In summer the whole family decamped to left-wing Yiddish-speaking summer camps in the Catskills, where his father wrote and directed children's theater. According to Baruch, they alternated each year between Zionist and Bundist (anti-Zionist socialist) camps that shared a lake. The political, activist spirit of such places in the late

1920s and early 1930s was primed by Russian revolutionary, pro-union, Zionist and Territorialist (those who wanted to establish Jewish territories in Europe) ideas, as well as various utopian movements popular at the time. Camp photos include children waving flags that boast a hammer and sickle.

Added to the mix was an Orthodox religious background that encouraged the boy to think in terms of ethical paradoxes and moral riddles: "If I am not for myself, who will be for me? But being for myself, what am I?" Sidney cut his milk teeth on the contradictions and questions of Jewish thought. In an interview, he pointed to this early training as a major influence on his work. "And it comes back in a sense to the point of *12 Angry Men*: those who are bearing the legal responsibility of our lives are therefore in a way bearing the moral responsibility as well. And what are they like? Who are they?" When asked where his concern for these kinds of questions came from, Sidney answered, "Just from having been a good, solid poor Jewish boy. That gets you into it. I was brought up in an essentially Orthodox household. The Jewish ethic is stern, unforgiving, preaching, moralistic. And I guess it starts you thinking like that at an early age."

Sidney absorbed all kinds of influences, from the biblical to the Trotskyist, as well as the impact of the city, which Sidney was getting to know as a matter of necessity. To save a few dollars, the family moved from Manhattan's Lower East Side to Queens, to the Bronx, to Brooklyn, and then back through all the boroughs except Staten Island, because, as his father explained, "That's where the goyim live." As it happened, the neighborhoods were alive with fantasy. At Coney Island, a nickel subway ride away, it was Arabian nights, American style, complete with a flying car and an exhibit of premature babies in incubators brought straight from a local hospital.

In those early days he saw how the crowds loved fantasy and make-believe, from the illusionist ceilings of the movie palaces, with their moving clouds and stars, to their marble staircases, goldfish ponds, and Spanish troubadours. Such fantasies weren't too much for the crowds, working people or not. But the illusion never caught his imagination. His eye went to the people who craved the fantasy.

More American than his parents, he became part of his Brooklyn, Queens, and Bronx neighborhoods in ways they never did. His father resisted identifying with the working-class immigrant community, although he and his wife were themselves fresh off the boat. Baruch saw himself as an artist with a cosmopolitan background, and Sidney's mother, Jenny or Gittel—her birth name is uncertain—came from a well-to-do Warsaw family. Baruch spoke of the servants in her home and recalled that her father, a learned man, had owned so much property that a street was named after him. But apart from her affluent origins, Jenny never integrated into the community, in part because Baruch never settled his family in one place long enough for her to make friends.

A cousin of Sidney's, Henri Wermus, remembers Jenny's father, Abraham Izaak Wermus, as a wealthy landowner who had a library that was "filled to the ceiling with innumerable volumes." He taught the grandchildren lessons in literature at every holiday, and, taking them into his study, he would recount the family history. They got their name, he explained, from Worms, a town in the Rhineland, where their forebears had resided; it was an important center of study where the biblical interpreter Rashi founded a yeshiva in the eleventh century. The family fled the massacres that followed a blood libel in 1410 and had made their home in Warsaw since the sixteenth century. When Henri returned to Warsaw from Switzerland after World War II, he found not a single surviving member of his family.

Sidney never heard his grandfather's stories or learned those lessons. The lessons he was absorbing were about getting your foot in the door, getting what you need as an artist, asserting yourself and surviving. And he was learning that no circumstances are ever perfect, that you have to seize the moment and bend circumstances to your will. This came from his father.

Baruch's father—Sidney's paternal grandfather—had died when Baruch was only five years old, leaving the family in terrible straits. In their small town outside of Warsaw, his mother delivered milk door to door with a bucket and ladle, barely scraping by. Baruch was sent to live with his grandfather on a farm that consisted of a few cows, a horse and a wagon. Restless and unhappy, Baruch ran away to live in Warsaw with an uncle and became an apprentice to a tailor. Many days, Baruch took care of the tailor's baby, which allowed him to wander with the child around the corner and listen to rehearsals of the Warsaw Yiddish Art Theater. One day the stage manager asked him to be part of a crowd scene—and this was Baruch's beginning on the stage.

As he described in his memoir, Baruch learned to act by appearing before sometimes jeering audiences and by moving from theater to theater, place to place. With the exception of the acting studio operated intermittently by Michal Weichert, there were no Yiddish acting schools. Even in Warsaw, despite interminable efforts, Yiddish dramatic companies never managed to acquire their own theater and were forced to move from one locale to another at the whim of theater owners.

With a strange mix of nostalgia and abhorrence, Baruch painted a picture of the general tumult of Warsaw in those days, and his catch-as-catch-can existence there. In the opening decades of the twentieth century Warsaw had become home to the largest population of Jews anywhere outside of New York City. After the assassination of Russia's relatively tolerant Czar Alexander II in 1881, tens of thousands of Jews flooded into Warsaw, fleeing increasing persecution in the Ukraine and elsewhere in the Russian Empire. These newcomers brought secular culture and ideas—mostly socialism and Zionism—to that city's conservative, mostly Hasidic community. Yiddish arts and political movements flourished; creative energy soared with the emergence of a modern secularism that maintained Jewish identity without assimilation. The language itself had powerful significance for this left-leaning generation; as Isaac Bashevis Singer pointed out, Yiddish might have been "the only language on earth that has never been spoken by men in power."

For Jews and Poles alike, life in Warsaw was uncertain. The city had been under the control of the Russians for a century when Baruch watched the Germans march into Warsaw in 1915. "The Jews were happy," Baruch explained. "Things got better under the Germans. Theaters and vaudeville opened up, restrictions were lifted; you [meaning Jews] could travel anywhere." The renowned Yiddish theater troupe came from Vilna, a city with "everything of culture," and merged with Baruch's Warsaw troupe. Baruch reminisced, "That was beautiful, new life began."

Everything was great until the Germans lost the war and Poland gained its independence in 1918. A series of border conflicts escalated into full-scale war between Poland and Soviet Russia in 1920. "Everyone was impoverished again; no one knew what to do. Some volunteered for the army—as it was better for those who volunteered." For those who didn't volunteer, however, there were the press gangs that roamed the streets, grabbing men to dig trenches to fortify the city against the Bolsheviks. Baruch was picked up off the street by the "snatchers," or *khapers*, and put to work for two terrible weeks, "without so much as a change of shirt." There was no chance to tell anyone where he was. "That's where I was when my daughter Feiga was born," he explained, accounting for his missing the birth of Sidney's sister.

Years later, relocated in New York during the hardest Depression years, Sidney's father performed recitations in Yiddish for one or another of the Jewish fraternal organizations that sprang up on the Lower East Side, earning $15 for each performance. The recitations came from many sources in Yiddish literature, but sometimes Baruch wrote his own stories. In his unpublished memoir, Sidney recalled one of his father's original stories, *"Zwei Brudder"* (Two Brothers): the tale of a cruel and ambitious brother who torments his sensitive, gentle brother to make him weep, "because the tears of the innocent turn into diamonds." Baruch narrated the story, Sidney explained, dressed as a diamond-encrusted snake in an elaborate costume that he designed and sewed himself, "sequin by sequin, starting with a deep blue-green tail to a livid purple headpiece." Sidney watched his father rehearse: "I couldn't have been more than five, maybe less." At the end of the story, as the evil brother triumphs, the narrating snake begins to laugh. "The laugh grew to a maniacal pitch," Sidney re-called. "I was by now totally terrified. I screamed, got hysterical. No matter what my parents did, I couldn't stop crying." This ambivalent memory concludes, with an almost uncanny echo of the snake story itself: "Baruch was thrilled with himself." Sidney, shedding his tears, was living the story his father had just told.

In a happier memory from his early childhood, Sidney recalled standing in the wings watching his father perform in *Der Brownsviller Zeyde*, when "in the final scene, my father began to sing the theme song from the radio serial. He looked at me and made a slight mo-tion with his hands, and I went to join him as he started to dance. I simply followed his lead, doing every step he did." "I was adorable," Sidney admits. "The house went wild."

With all his faults and frailties, Baruch taught Sidney "about work and the discipline of work—and the lack of self-indulgence in work," as Sidney put it, and prepared him for "the trouble in show business." Most of all, Baruch struck the note that remained important to his son throughout his life: that the goal is not merely to survive. One could do that with a few cows, a horse and a wagon, as his grand-father had.

2

FAMILY STORIES

We live in a web of stories.

—CRAIG IRVINE

Sidney only spoke passingly of his childhood. He usually rolled out the same basic storyline: "My father played in the Yiddish theater back in Poland. From the age of eighteen, he belonged to the Vilna Troupe. He arrived in 1922 at the age of twenty-four. He put me on the stage when I was too young to realize it!" And often he would go on to say, preempting further questions, that he saw no downside to being put on the stage so young, to being exposed early to creative people: "It kept me off the streets"—and anyhow, "What's so great about playing stickball?"

In a different mood, he portrayed himself as a kid who'd learned the hard lessons of the city streets: "If I walked a few blocks one way or another into another neighborhood, I got beat up." Getting to know the streets also meant getting to know the cops: "When I was a kid pitching pennies on the sidewalk, a cop would come by to scatter us and he'd pick up the pennies."

Other times he noted that he was raised in what he described as a "more or less Orthodox" Jewish home, in an atmosphere where stern religious edicts were observed. And in yet another version, Sidney was the child of the Jewish left, attending socialist summer camps and Young Communist League meetings with his sister, and working at age fourteen with the Federal Theatre Project's "Living Newspaper," a form initially developed during the Bolshevik Revolution. Sometimes Sidney's childhood stories connected with the theme of his latest film. While these narratives don't sync up exactly, whose life actually does?

Every once in a while, Sidney let something slip in an interview, an unvarnished personal recollection: he refers to his "distant mother" and recalls "sitting and listening to Eddie Cantor with her and her laughing. And it was one of the few times I ever heard her laugh." Or he disparages his father's career: "In the Yiddish theater the best days were over; the great [actors], like Adler and Thomashefsky, were no longer around." The next generation's Maurice Schwartz, with whom his father performed, "was a pale imitation of the greats." Or regarding his own experience on the Yiddish stage, he noted, "I had no idea whether I liked it [acting] or not. I was just thrown up there . . ." and "There wasn't tremendous cultural stimulation. I was doing dopey musicals in the Yiddish theater."

Slipping the yoke of his official stories of little Sidney, son of a colorful actor, nurtured in the vitality and warmth of the Yiddish theater while holding his own on the unforgiving streets of New York, the adult Lumet cracks open a window into a complex home life, one he did not share publicly. When he was in his seventies, he made an effort to pen his memoirs; perhaps he was surprised by the unrelenting grimness of his recollections. In any case, he could not warm to the task. The narrative, in which he writes, "Had something finally caught up with me? Mama's madness? Papa's anger? My sister Faye's desperation?" breaks off abruptly, and its raw, unsparing pages were put away in a drawer.

Sidney's father, Baruch, unlike his reticent son, was an enthusiastic narrator of the events of his life. He left two accounts: a lengthy oral history undertaken by the American Jewish Committee in December 1976 and a memoir in manuscript, more than five hundred pages that Baruch began working on in 1977, a year after the oral history and a little more than a year after the death of his second wife, Julia. Mostly written by hand on yellow legal pads, the unfinished work is titled "Baruch Lumet: Who Am I? The Life Story as Told by Himself."

In the oral history, Baruch regales his interviewer with tales of his childhood in a small town outside of Warsaw, his first exposure to the stage, his journey to America, his struggles to make a living and break into the Yiddish theater, and his subsequent career on the American stage. Intermittently he answers questions about his famous son and provides details about the family. On the whole it is a bright, sunny narrative. Anita Wincelberg, who recorded Baruch in his "pleasant garden apartment" in West Hollywood, its walls lined with photographs of him in different characters, effuses that her subject is "completely free of the actor's ego which we have come to expect. Instead, he is a sweet, warm, kind and humorous person, and a pleasure to be with." In comparing this narrative with Baruch's written one, as well as with Sidney's, one can see many ripples in the smooth surface of the story, little and big untruths and inconsistencies regarding Sidney and his sister—and a bombshell or two. Taken together, the three narratives reveal the personality of Sidney's father and give contour and a sharp chiaroscuro to Sidney's childhood worlds.

A FAILED ABORTION

In 1921 Baruch traveled alone to the United States, leaving his wife and newborn daughter behind in Warsaw. His destination was Philadelphia, where he moved into a cramped apartment with his sister Esther and brother-in-law Willie, situated above Willie's bakery on Marshall Street, then Philadelphia's busiest Jewish marketplace. Willie, as Sidney later described him, was "an ox of a man . . . whose life consisted of getting up at 3:30 every morning, including Saturdays, to bake the day's bread." Baruch had no intention of ending up like Willie. Unable to find work on the Yiddish stage, Baruch began selling pianos door to door.

On her arrival in the United States, Sidney's mother, Jenny, and two-year-old daughter Fay (she would later add an *e* to her name) moved with Baruch into a one-room apartment on Marshall Street. Jenny was contending with the loss of her comfortable life in Warsaw, where she had had a nurse to care for her daughter. It was during this difficult transition that she realized she was pregnant with a second child. In the oral history, Baruch was unabashed about his reaction to the pregnancy: "I was very unhappy to have this second child, but it happened." There is no mention of any discussion with his wife about ending the pregnancy, but he recounts calling in "a man" to whom he paid $50 to perform an abortion. "What he did I don't know," Baruch writes, but a few months later he realized Jenny was still pregnant, and it was too late to do anything further about it.

It's conceivable that Jenny refused the abortion and sent "the man" away, or else he simply botched the job. Either way, on June 25, 1924, Sidney was born at Mount Sinai Hospital in Philadelphia. "I called him Shmul Hersh—in short, Sidney," Baruch said. "What do you think of that?" Baruch exclaimed musingly. "I didn't want him," he said, followed by a delayed "we"—"We didn't want him."

It's unclear if Sidney ever learned about the abortionist. He never spoke of it or mentioned it in his memoir. At age fifty-two, Sidney put his signature to his father's oral history, approving the transcription for his father, whose eyes were failing at the time. It's unlikely Sidney read the document before signing it. His relation to his father at that point in his life was near-estrangement, although he would continue to act as a dutiful son, bringing Baruch back east to be cared for during his final illness. If he didn't know about the attempted abortion, he knew well the strife in his parents' marriage.

A "LOVE MATCH"

We have competing stories from Baruch about his courtship and marriage to Sidney's mother. In his oral history he recounts a romantic tale of his first encounter with the lovely Jenny Wermus when, from the audience, she threw a delicate glove up on stage as he was taking a bow; when she ventured backstage to retrieve her glove, they fell in love. As he tells it, their love affair commenced in secret, Baruch never meeting her wealthy family. When her parents got wind of the

Baruch as he was photographed in 1921, the year he arrived in the United States. No photos of Sidney's mother or sister were among Baruch's extensive papers. *(Baruch Lumet Papers [Collections 1451]. Library Special Collections, Charles E. Young Research Library, UCLA)*

romance and attempted to separate them by repeatedly sending Jenny away, she refused to give him up. Baruch euphemistically explains that eventually her parents "became afraid something will happen to the girl that they will be ashamed of and they decided to make a wedding." In this telling, his father-in-law, in a gesture of acceptance, treated the newlyweds to a night at the fashionable Hotel Bristol, just around the corner from where Baruch was in rehearsal for a new play, *The Dybbuk*. It was May 1920.

Baruch's written account is less camera-ready. It begins, "We met secretly . . . she used to sit in at rehearsals. She claimed to be very much in love with me. In all honesty [crossed out: I could not fall in love with her too quickly.] I was not too pleased to see her although she had grown into a pleasant young lady." He goes on to note that she was three years his senior, and that he had to "work up" some enthusiasm for her. His reason for pursuing the match, given this lack of enthusiasm, remains unstated, presumably because he thought it was self-evident—that she belonged to a wealthy family.

In both Baruch's narratives of their courtship, Jenny was the initiator, and in each, Baruch cast himself as a theatrical character of one kind or another. Indeed, the flavor of the Yiddish theater almost always inflects his account. In one written episode, he appears as a lithesome young lad standing beneath the balcony of Jenny's affluent home on Rue Kaliska, listening to his betrothed play the piano; he says that he took her "banging" for good music, insulting her while presenting himself as a poor naïf who has mistaken this common girl for a person of refinement. Listening and waiting, he is stung when, instead of Jenny, her shrewish mother, described elsewhere by Baruch as unrefined and weighing three hundred pounds, appears on the balcony and shouts at him to "go back to where you belong." Some sixty years later he recalls this "humiliation" as one he "could not forgive or forget."

The matter of the "something" that "might happen" is repeated in the written memoir, with a significant difference. Unexpectedly, Baruch is invited to Sabbath dinner at the Wermus home. He is stunned when Jenny's father, a "nice, polite and quiet" man who "gave charity to many," takes him into his book-lined study and announces his intention to host a quiet wedding for the couple, preceded by an engagement party "at his club." Baruch is still reeling from this unanticipated development when Jenny jubilantly throws her arms around him. He stammers, "What did you do . . . tell a lie that you were pregnant?" Laughing, she says, "We're getting married, aren't we?"

Sidney, in his memoir, notes briefly his understanding of his parents' union: "[My father] had by now married my mother who was far wealthier than he. Her father kept warning her that she was throwing her life away (she was). But she loved the dashing young artist and would not listen. Her family lived in Warsaw, quite a step up from the shtetl existence of Baruch."

To these perspectives could be added the intermittent mutterings of Baruch's widowed mother, who at one point suggested the ruse of pregnancy to move things along with the wealthy girl's parents, and then, following the engagement party, confusingly advised her son to "stay away from the rich."

After the wedding, Baruch was disappointed that they were not housed in one of his in-laws' substantial properties. "Being married to the richest girl in Ochota" (a Warsaw district), he grumbles, "I never felt as poor in all my life." As he tells it, Jenny also quickly tired of her reduced existence, and, returning from her parents' house one evening, she produced a small bundle tied in a red handkerchief she unknotted to reveal a glittering jumble of her mother's jewels.

"Let's run away," she implored. "Take me to France, to Germany, anywhere." Baruch writes that he was adamant she must return the jewels: "They will send the police after us. They'll say I made you do it, and I'll be stuck in jail. Take it back." Jenny obeyed his wishes and returned the jewels, and here the story takes an unexpected turn, much in the style of a period melodrama: Jenny's parents were robbed at gunpoint in their home; all the jewels, along with the family silver, were taken. The episode concludes with Jenny berating Baruch for not allowing her to keep the jewelry: *they* would have had it instead of the thieves, and no one would have been the wiser!

The birth of their daughter coincided, Baruch narrates in his oral history, with his receipt of a draft notice. His older brother had died in the Russian Army in the First World War—the family was never notified where or how he had perished—and Baruch had no intention of giving his life to defend Poland against the Bolsheviks. Miraculously and just in the nick of time (or so Baruch's story goes in both versions), he received a ticket to the United States from his sister Esther, now married and settled in Philadelphia. Baruch needed no persuading to take passage. He knew that Yiddish theater was thriving in America. The renowned stage artists Boris Thomashefsky, David Kessler, and Molly Picon had traveled from New York to perform in Warsaw, and important plays were being written in the United States, including the work of Jacob Gordin, whose melodramas broke new ground by mirroring social reality. Unhampered by anti-Semitic laws or financial constraints, the Yiddish theater had made New York its capital.

Baruch boarded a train without a legal passport, risking the charge of desertion. He writes, "One thing you must remember, if something is wrong there is no court, there is no arrest, they just take you away and shoot you, court-martial you right there and then. That means a deserter."

Without bidding farewell to his wife or new baby daughter ("too risky"), he was gone in a flash. Baruch's subsequent journey to the New World does not conform to the familiar image of huddled masses crossing the ocean in steerage. Arriving in Rotterdam, he took one look at the vessel he was booked on and decided it was far too squalid. He wrote to his sister for money to book passage on a newer ship. Taking advantage of the delay, he visited Berlin and then spent six weeks in London, where he landed a role in a Yiddish stage production. His sister Esther ultimately coughed up the extra money, and he traveled to the United States in comfort.

REUNITED

Arriving in Philadelphia in September 1921, Baruch recounts that he was met not with welcome but with suspicion. Baruch's sister Esther wasn't certain he was her brother. He had been a boy the last time she'd seen him. It was not unheard of for immigrants to impersonate long-unseen family members in order to get a foothold in the new land. Baruch observes, "In those years many came to claim that they are relatives, you know, all kinds of fakes, I didn't know that, so they didn't trust me." If in fact Esther initially doubted him, she came around before long.

When Jenny and Faye were sent for, traveling with them was Baruch's mother, Sarah, who would remain with Esther and her husband in Philadelphia. Baruch writes, "During the time and the process of arrival, deep in my thoughts I hesitated." And then, in a crossed-out passage, he questions whether he is doing the right thing in bringing his wife and "the child I saw for about ten days before I left Warsaw." (It's notable that in his earlier account he claims he didn't even see the baby.) He contemplates married life, which he has come to consider in a new light: "It seemed to me that married life was a fraud. Maybe mine would be the same. However, I could not dismiss a wife and a child and say I made a mistake."

In this immigrant Jewish world, stories abounded of families unable to resume after these long separations. The divide between husbands and wives became too wide. The "greenhorn," the newest arrival, was seen as an embarrassment, a hindrance. Wife desertion, known at the time as the "poor man's divorce," was so common that the *Jewish Daily Forward*, the popular American Yiddish newspaper, printed the pictures of male deserters in a regular feature called the "Gallery of Missing Husbands" and established a special column to trace them.

Baruch comments that Jenny's "adjustment to a one-room apartment was not so easy." Adding to their travails, soon after her arrival she was hospitalized with typhoid fever. Her long hair was sheared "to the scalp," as was common practice with those suffering from high fevers. The shearing left her "inconsolable," he reports, and tensions between them mounted. Baruch describes a typical squabble:

> *The wife was jealous on one side and unhappy why she came to America on the other. After many conversations some of which were unpleasant ones, she said that a friend of ours who visited her at home in Warsaw was very interested to take her and the baby with him to South America. True he was a "bigger bargain" than I was. He was an engineer. "Well," I said, "too bad. It would've been so much better for both of us. Specially now. I will go to NY [from Philadelphia] if only I were single." This made her more jealous and we always ended up in bed loving each other.*

Although the passion had not entirely faded from the relationship, Jenny was frequently distraught by Baruch's choices and priorities. Unwilling to compromise his image of himself as an artist, Baruch turned down a lucrative job selling furniture, drawing the line at selling pianos door to door because "a musical instrument is different." He would later decide not to use his real name on his popular radio show *Der Brownsviller Zeyde*, though it could have led to more broadcasting work, because he felt it was "below my dignity" to be attached to such *haimish* (homey), unpolished radio hackwork. His family's comfort was not his priority, nor did he recognize the importance of stability for his children.

To relocate the family from Philadelphia to New York, Baruch arranged to share an apartment with a couple called the Gelhards. He described the apartment he rented on 11th Street between First and Second Avenues, for the six of them:

> *It was a long row of rooms downstairs, six steps up from the street—a front room leading to the kitchen (the kitchen had a stove, an icebox, a large tub for laundry, steam, hot and cold water), then a bedroom in the back facing other apartments. The toilet was right out in the hallway.*

That arrangement didn't last long. In fact, Baruch routinely moved them, sometimes several times a year to save a few dollars, since in those days the first month's rent was reduced or waived. As Sidney recalled them, the locations they lived in included, on the Lower East Side, apartments on Rivington Street, on 13th Street between First and Second Avenues, 2nd Street between Avenues A and B, 10th Street and Avenue A; and in Brooklyn, on Carroll Street and on Eastern Parkway; in Queens, "somewhere near 34th and Steinway"; and in the Bronx, near Broadway and 249th Street.

MEMORY AND COUNTERMEMORY

Baruch's two accounts of his wife in their married life don't line up at all. When his interviewer asked how his wife felt about his profession as an actor, Baruch promptly offered that she would not have wanted him to give up the theater: "This she liked of course, she fell in love with me because I was an actor and all that, and very loyal and very sacrificing I think, I would say." In his memoir, he claims that, rather than encouraging him in his career, Jenny grew resentful of his modest success with the radio broadcasts and of his popularity at the summer camps where children's plays were performed under his direction. Most of all, she was jealous of the attention he received from other women: "Some of my friends and [their] wives began to feel her hostile attitude."

When Sidney was six or seven years old, Baruch came up with a new idea to make some money; he would produce a stage show based on his successful radio program *Der Brownsviller Zeyde.* In the ongoing radio story, the widowed grandfather has made a pilgrimage to the Holy Land, where he has met a woman he wants to bring back with him to Brooklyn to marry. Baruch's plan was to stage their wedding. Jenny had had some experience acting in amateur theatricals in Warsaw, and she had been performing the role of Zeyde's daughter on the radio program, but Baruch did not want her to perform the role on stage. "I tried to talk her out of it, but it did not help," he writes. "The night of the 'wedding,' the hall was packed—hundreds of people—they sat two on one chair. The program was about to start but my wife was still at the beauty parlor. By nine in the evening a heavy rain came pouring down. She could not get a cab to take her to the hall." She didn't arrive until after the "wedding ceremony" was over. This was a turning point for Baruch, who writes, "I didn't realize, or maybe I did not want to realize, that I had a wife who was mentally disturbed."

Her jealousy escalated. She became convinced that Baruch was sneaking out at night.

> *She began to imagine things, such as, "Last night I saw you walk out of the house wearing your pajamas. Where were you?" I looked at her and convinced her that she imagined. It was not true. Later on I noticed certain marks on the door—pasted pieces of paper hardly noticeable on the door or window.*

She accused the neighbors' wives of sexual involvement with her husband, leading to more than one eviction, according to Baruch. One morning he woke to find she had tied his foot to their bedpost. He reports that she hired a detective to follow him. As her behavior grew increasingly erratic, there were "many unpleasant incidents in the family." She stopped looking after the house; her appearance deteriorated. "I begged her to have a talk with our family doctor. The answer was, I was the one who needed a doctor."

Baruch is adamant that Jenny's fits of jealousy were delusional.

But accounts of his infidelities turn up in the stories of family friends, suggesting that Baruch may have been gaslighting his wife. And there are his own unabashed admissions of afternoon trysts with the wealthy housewives on whose doors he knocked when he was selling pianos. He is shocked by "the hypocrisy of these women. . . . Having me in bed all of the afternoon, then asking me to stay for dinner, sitting at a beautifully set dinner table when the man came home." What can this tell us, he wonders, about the meaning of marriage? And we too wonder what marriage meant to this child of the shtetl, where matches were arranged by parents and matchmakers and companionableness and mutual attraction were often secondary concerns.

Among Baruch's many surprising and uncensored stories—including having been, at age fifteen, fondled by a gypsy fortune-teller from whom he withdrew, afraid she would bite his penis—is that of a German nun on the train he rode when he was fleeing Warsaw. Seated beside him, he writes, was "a very fancy lady—tall and beautiful . . . an elegant nun." Once they crossed the Polish border, Baruch relaxed and the two passed the hours in pleasant conversation as "she treated me to figs and pears from her father's garden." As the hour grew late, she leaned her head on his shoulder, and then unfolded a quilt from her basket, and with it she "covered her thighs and my thighs," and "her hands were very cozy . . . we rode the whole night." Arriving in Berlin, she persuaded Baruch to spend a few days with her there before continuing on. Months later, a letter from her reached him in Philadelphia: she wanted to come to America; she would marry him or do anything if he would let her come. Baruch could think of no way to reply: "After all, I was a married man."

The version of his escape from Poland that Baruch told Sidney—and that, perhaps unsurprisingly, Sidney never questioned—was quite different from the versions he recorded himself. Sidney writes, "With the Civil War between Reds and Whites in Russia after the Revolution, staying out of the Army was more and more difficult. So, finally, as so many before him, in 1922 [it was 1921] he fled. He hid inside an armoire that was being sent to Germany on a cart pulled by a donkey. He lived in it for four days, arriving finally in Kiel, where he found a ship to America."

WHAT CHILDREN KNOW

A final story about Sidney's mother underscores Baruch's priorities, and how he accounts for himself throughout his many pages. In the mid-1930s—when Sidney was about eleven or twelve years old— Jenny agreed to see a doctor, who in turn urged Baruch to place her in a sanitarium because of what he diagnosed as her "mental illness." Baruch acknowledged the wisdom of this: "She may do harm to some of us, or to herself." He then recounts what he claims is her family's history of mental illness, wondering why he hadn't paid more attention to it before: "Her older brother was freed from military service in Europe because of having fits. Her older sister has ruined her home life, and the two girls she had were both taken to a 'lunatic asylum.'" Baruch told the doctor to make the arrangements for "a very costly sanitarium" near New York City. "The children knew nothing about it at all," he writes. "Sidney went to school and at night to the show. Faye went to school, and I was trying to find a job in the English theater." Growing more and more focused on the cost, he ultimately changed course, deciding that, instead of paying for the sanitarium, he would keep Jenny at home—they were living on Central Park West and 103rd Street at this point, an upscale neighborhood—and "try to talk with her, tell her stories, be kind and get her to talk." He continues:

> I decided to save my family life and to save thousands of dollars in payments to a sanitarium. I desperately tried to talk to her—every day for weeks. This time I enrolled the help of both children—to watch her, at the same time not to anger her. It started to look different—she started to dress up and to take care of the house.

Over and over, Baruch's stories present his self-justifications, portray his pitiable victimhood, and often they contain sheer invention. He has no self-consciousness about his inconsistencies, his self-serving decisions, or how his stories sometimes mimic bits of theater of one kind or another, both high and low. In fact, one wonders if this tale of his wife's fragile recovery doesn't owe something to Sidney's 1962 screen adaptation of *Long Day's Journey into Night*, where the patriarch, James Tyrone, an aging matinee idol disappointed in his career, feels himself straddled with an unstable wife whose condition cannot be spoken of. The wife and mother, Mary Tyrone, has just returned from a sanitarium where she has been treated for morphine addiction. As the play begins, her family members are nervously hopeful; she looks healthier, is tending to her appearance and to the household.

The aspect of O'Neill's play that would have resonated with Sidney is the son Jamie's accusation that his father's miserliness—his unwillingness to pay for a good doctor—accounts in large measure for his mother's illness.

Baruch contends in his memoir that "the children knew nothing about" their mother's illness, but of course they did, as Sidney's memoir ultimately makes clear. Baruch's insensitivity to his children's experience is elsewhere expressed succinctly: "After all, what do children know? They feel, they hear, but they also forget."

RECKONING

After his 1995 book *Making Movies* turned out to be so successful—and it continues to be a standard text for film students—Sidney was urged to write his life story by his friend and literary agent Gloria Loomis. He'd begun to imagine a book about his lifelong involvement with acting: "I feel like John Gielgud in a way, who bridged from Ellen Terry to modern theater. I bridged from Jewish operatic theater (which is what it was—the style was operatic, the way of acting was operatic) to this extraordinary world I'm in now." But, he went on,

"I don't know if I'll ever do it, because it might take a degree of personal revelation that I may not be prepared to make."

In his friend Walter Bernstein's view, "It was too painful to go down into it. He kept making excuses. He put a lid on a lot of stuff. It enabled him to keep going. He lived totally in the present." Quoting the legendary baseball player Satchel Paige, Bernstein added that Sidney's philosophy was, "Don't look back. They might be gaining on you." Sidney's daughter Jenny observed, "He could put something in a drawer and never open that drawer again."

His memories were kept close, finding veiled release only in moments in his films, as Sidney acknowledged in one interview:

> *I know people who disguise their lives, and their* disguises *are more exciting and revealing than the lives of people who throw themselves at you naked. I mean, is there anything you don't know about George Cukor from seeing his movies? I hope some day it's apparent that there is a lot of me in* Serpico, *just as there is a lot of me in* The Sea Gull. *They don't have to be similar worlds for* me *to emerge. When I made* Long Day's Journey into Night—*which I happen to think is a perfect movie*—*I gave Katie that moment when Edmund says to her, "Mama, I'm going to die," and she hauls off and* whacks *him as hard as she can across the face. If you don't understand something about me from that scene, then you just don't* understand.

That slap that Sidney introduced to the play, as I understand it, is not only a mother's refusal to absorb information that is intolerable to her; it is also the gesture of a mother who hasn't the capacity to put her child first.

In an interview given in 2008, three years before his death, Sidney spoke about his childhood to Peter Travers of *Rolling Stone*. Travers approaches the topic this way: "Let's try an experiment: Pretend that you just got a script. And it's called *The Sidney Lumet Story*." Sidney laughs and replies, "I'm saying no right now." Travers persists, "I want to know where the movie starts. Do you paint a rosy picture of your life as the child of Baruch Lumet, a star of the Yiddish theater? You have a father, and then you have this guy who's also up on the stage. Is there a disconnect?" Sidney holds nothing back in his response: "He was no father figure," he says. "He was only a father up on the stage. It's the only time I liked him. He was a terrible man." Travers asks him if his father lost patience with him. Sidney answers, "He didn't have patience. He had a bad temper. He hit us. He was probably unfaithful to my mother all the time. I don't know. But she sure complained about him. I could hear the fights. Nothing admirable about him, until he went to work. And then he was admirable."

To this account of being hit, Sidney's widow, Piedy, recalled a story Sidney told her about a cold-bath punishment when he was nine or ten years old. For years in Sidney's immigrant household, disorder had prevailed, keeping everyone off-kilter, except perhaps Baruch. By constantly moving the family, pursuing his various schemes, not giving straight answers, Baruch managed to more or less follow his own inclinations and always find ways to rationalize them. Both of Baruch's accounts of his life—in different ways—are rife with narcissistic self-rationalizations, and with invention. When Sidney finally sat down to write about his life, he took great care with the past. In places his memoir reads more like a confession than a reminiscence; ultimately he found the introspection, the "degree of personal revelation," unsustainable. His father offered a countermodel for how to know oneself, how to speak about oneself. One cannot always select what one inherits, but Sidney tried hard to select only the good in his father as a legacy. The photographs of Baruch that Sidney kept on display in his home all represent his father in theatrical character, in full makeup, masked. Baruch at his best.

3

MOTHER AND SON

There was no familial life in the family. I have a picture of the four of us in the Bronx. My father is on one knee looking at the camera. Behind him my mother is standing, a face devoid of expression. To her right my sister stands stiffly, hands by her side. I'm on my mother's left squinting at the sun, my mouth turned down. I once brought the photo to an analyst I was seeing. He stared at it, then said, 'Nobody's touching anybody.' It was true. Each of us looked at the camera with no contact toward the others.

—SIDNEY LUMET, FROM HIS UNFINISHED MEMOIR

In life, Sidney's mother was a ghostly presence. "Who was she?" he wrote in the memoir he undertook in the 1990s. "Her name seemed a symbol of her life." He never knew for sure what her name was. Her family called her Gittel. "Perhaps Gertrude would have been closest in English . . . but," Sidney noted, "she insisted her name was Eugenia." To Sidney that sounded awfully grand. He wondered if she had been renamed at immigration, as many were, or if she renamed herself. Her immigration record lists her as "Eugenia Lumet," and the name on her gravestone is the same—although above it, in Hebrew letters, is inscribed "Gittel Lumet." Sidney mentions nowhere in his memoir that his father called her "Jenny," though that is what Baruch calls his wife throughout *his* memoir. Typically, Jewish women of that generation spelled that name "Jennie." In changing *ie* to *y*, Baruch, consciously or not, Anglicized it.

The frequent moves from apartment to apartment that Baruch orchestrated to save a month or two of rent meant that Sidney's mother, again and again, had to register the two children in a new school and find a grocer willing to give them credit. "No easy task for someone who never really learned English," Sidney wrote. It's hard to know what Jenny (we will use the name Baruch gave her) did with her days. She cared nothing for housekeeping: "The house was rarely clean . . . and the icebox was usually empty." Sidney, in his memoir, marvels at her "lousy cooking," recalling only one consistent meal, boiled potatoes with boiled beef shredded into it, "so that the quarter pound of meat would feed us all." There was no home life to speak of.

His fondest recollection of his mother was of her tenderness when he was ill, her "sweet care," although he offers no details. Once when *she* was sick in bed, Sidney, at eight or nine, was determined to make chicken soup for her. Buying a chicken was a special event—reserved for "when one of us was ill." Freshly killed, the chicken had to be gutted and plucked. He worked hard to remove the feathers, but "the hard little end bits stayed embedded in the bird," he remembers. Knowing no better, he tossed the innards into the pot with the rest of the bird. "It smelled awful and she got out of bed to see what was causing the smell. She looked at the pot and laughed out loud." He was startled: "I'd never heard the sound from her before." Twice more he recalls hearing the sound of his mother's laughter: once when they were listening to the Yiddish comedian Eddie Cantor on the radio, and once at a vaudeville show where a silent film starring Gloria Swanson played while a little Yiddish comic, standing beside the enormous images on the screen, pointed and mocked the glamorous star.

Mostly he remembers his parents' endless fighting—"She constantly berated my father for taking her away from her father's comfortable home"—and complained bitterly of Baruch's infidelities. "I have no idea whether he was unfaithful," Sidney wrote. "But they fought all the time, to a point where she'd smash things." Baruch's memoir leaves little doubt that her suspicions were founded. His discontent with his wife found further expression during the brief period that she performed on the family's radio show. Baruch persistently chided her when she sang. "She had a decent soprano voice but pitch was a problem," Sidney writes. Baruch was very musical, "and so, when she sang, he would constantly be calling 'Tainer, tainer' (Tones, tones) to her, indicating she was flat." This would have stung, as Jenny was proud of her voice, and had even claimed to her daughter, Sidney's sister, that she'd once been an opera singer. Pondering what his mother had hoped for and sought in marrying Baruch, Sidney writes, "She may have fancied herself an actress—no—more of what we called a soubrette," that is, a minor stock character in opera or comic theater, usually girlish, coy and flirtatious.

Recalling family train trips to Philadelphia to visit Baruch's mother, who lived with Baruch's sister and brother-in-law, Sidney considers that his mother "always seemed uncomfortable" around Baruch's family, but then he reconsiders: "She was uncomfortable everywhere."

Sidney was thirteen years old when one day he found his mother in the kitchen, moving slowly as if in a dream. They had recently relocated to an apartment on 103rd Street and Central Park West, following the windfall from the run of *The Eternal Road*, the show Sidney was appearing in. Standing at the sink, Jenny was filling glasses with water and slowly, carefully placing them on shelves in the cabinets above the sink. When Sidney asked her what she was doing, she said she was "warding off the *Malechamovous*, the evil one." Sidney gently assured her that there was no evil in the house and moved to pour the water out of one of the glasses. "Look, nothing bad will happen," he tried to console her. Tears pouring down her face, she grabbed his arm and pleaded with him not to touch them. His inclination was to convince her—and as he began slowly to empty the first glass, she suppressed a scream. When he finished emptying the glasses, she let go of his arm and slowly, silently left the room.

This memory resembles a scene in Sidney's 1962 adaptation of *Long Day's Journey into Night*, when Katharine Hepburn's Mary Tyrone floats in a morphine haze through the house, unmindful of the destruction she leaves in her wake. Her sons and husband stare after her in heartbroken mortification.

In his memoir, Sidney puzzles over his mother's mental deterioration: When did it begin? How long had she been so lost? When as a boy he asked his father about her condition, Baruch responded that the "fits" usually came upon her in the spring, around Passover; he proposed that they "might have to do with pogroms in Poland around Easter." Dr. Goldman, the white-haired physician who lived next door when they were living on Avenue A and 10th Street, and whom Sidney recalled as "the kindest doctor I ever knew," paid routine visits to his mother. His repeated assessment was that Baruch should place her in a sanitarium to recover her equilibrium. Baruch's answer this time was that "he would never deprive his children of their mother," a decision that Baruch again acknowledged was based in part on not wanting to pay the high cost of her hospitalization.

In his most trenchant and devastating assessment of his father, Sidney wrote, "As with everything else in his life, the story slowly turned from a discussion of her to his nobility and courage and sacrifice in the face of life's adversities. My lasting impression was the lack of any sympathy for her condition and the abundance of self-pity for the burden he carried." Of his mother Sidney wrote, "I have no memory of anything or anyone bringing her happiness. No real tenderness seemed to belong to her life." The only time he can remember her smiling "was when she told my sister and me that she was pregnant with the child that eventually killed her." Although she died in childbirth, of course it was not the child, as Sidney phrases it, who killed her.

The three accounts we have of Sidney's mother's death tell different stories. Two versions come from Sidney's father, and one from Sidney's unfinished memoir. This catastrophe was something Sidney never publicly spoke about—indeed, almost never spoke about at all. Baruch's accounts of his wife's death are muddled in both of his tellings. In the oral history, her death is first mentioned as an afterthought; he is discussing a later period in his life when he interrupts himself and doubles back, realizing what he's omitted, "My wife at that time before this happened wanted to have a baby after so many years." The story pours out in a few sentences: "One day she said she could not feel the baby." When the doctor came, "he started to take the baby because the baby is dead." Baruch continues:

> *A caesarean wouldn't help because she would really pass out. In those days they didn't have the medicines that they have nowadays. They said once in a million such a thing happens— the baby was strangled in the cord and she was poisoned and I lost my wife at that time. . . . She was forty-two I think or forty-three, and that was a tragedy. After that we moved out. Of course I left out a very important thing, that we were both engaged for a picture called* One Third of a Nation *for the Paramount people.*

Baruch's final comment, about the making of the film, "a very important thing" that he left out of the story of the death of his wife and baby, says so much about him.

In the amplified written account, Baruch explains that when Jenny's labor began he was away "meeting someone about business." When he got home, he "heard a scream which is still ringing in my ears." He summoned the doctor, who called for an ambulance. Baruch continues: "For two days they tried to take the baby. They could not make it come." Baruch is vague on the topic of why a caesarian section was not performed: "A caesarian operation they said meant losing her life as well. I did not know what it was all about. There were so many doctors there. Who am I, to give advice?" Given that we know Baruch had refused medical advice to send his wife to a sanitarium for her mental illness, at least in part because of the expense, we cannot rule out the possibility that cost may have been a factor in the decision to forego the caesarian section.

Baruch was not at the hospital when his wife passed away. He describes the baby girl lying beside his wife when he was taken to see her: "She looked so big like a year old." He notes the date of his wife's death as February 8, 1940, but on her gravestone the date is February 19, 1940. (Uncannily, Baruch would die on February 8, fifty-two years later.) Eugenia Gittel Lumet was either forty-two or forty-four; two different years of birth are documented. (Likely she changed her year of birth on her arrival to the United States, to eliminate the stigma of being older than her husband.) Baruch does nothing. No funeral is arranged. Two days pass before his wife and daughter "are taken" to the cemetery. He does not attribute his inaction to grief or shock; he says, "I felt cold and ashamed. Life insulted me. I was ashamed." A few family and friends appeared at the graveside, those Sidney and Faye had called, but Baruch "could not look at anybody to accept their sympathy." He reports little thought for his children, although he gives us this image: "The earth fell in to the grave and Sidney held on to me. He cried out daddy-daddy."

Sidney's account of these events in his memoir pages begins, "My mother was now in her ninth month. She was thirty-nine years old. She had taken to her bed the day before saying only that something didn't feel right. For some reason, Faye and I were not in school. Maybe it was a Saturday." His style of writing in this section is distinctly different from the rest of his memoir. The sentences are clipped, and details unfold without comment. He gets his mother's age wrong.

Sidney continues, "We were in the living room playing Monopoly. Baruch wasn't home. From time to time my mother would groan. One of us would go in, but she wouldn't want anything. Twice, we went downstairs to a doctor who lived on the ground floor. He wasn't in. We left messages for him." Contrary to Baruch's version, Sidney recalls that he and Faye went to fetch the doctor more than once, and he recalls, "We tried calling my father at every possible place. We couldn't find him anywhere." In the subsequent sentences, Sidney at last introduces some of what the two of them were feeling: "The moans went on for hours. Our fear rose but so did our irritation at her because she was ruining the game." Fear and irritation for "ruining the game." This is his first self-reproach.

"Finally," he continues, "when it grew dark, the doctor appeared. We led him into the bedroom. He pulled the covers back. A greenish liquid from between her legs had spread onto the sheets. The doctor ran to the phone and called an ambulance." Here again the story deviates from Baruch's, as Baruch claims that he was there when the doctor arrived, that he had summoned him. Sidney writes, "At that point my father appeared. Faye immediately attacked him. 'Where the hell have you been? We've called all over. No one knew where you were.' I thought of the years of fights about infidelity." Here again Sidney offers a glimpse into his internal state, his suspicion, shared by his sister, that while his mother was in labor his father was with another woman. "My father and the doctor looked pale."

"The ambulance arrived. As she was being carried out she reached for our hands. 'Goodbye, my darling children. I hope I see you again.' Faye and I smiled at her, blew kisses, and stood there terrified. Baruch went off with her in the ambulance. 'That son of a bitch,' Faye said." Her focus was trained on her father—as Sidney remembers it. Elsewhere in the memoir, when Sidney quotes his mother, she always speaks in Yiddish; here he delivers her farewell in English.

He writes, "I think it was a Friday. On Sunday we took a cab to the hospital. Baruch had told us nothing on Saturday other than the fact that the baby was dead." More deeply situated in the memory, Sidney corrects his earlier supposition that it might have been a Saturday.

"We knew something dreadful was up because we never took cabs. During the ride he told us that the cord had wrapped itself around the baby's neck and strangled it. It had been dead for a week." The baby remains genderless, an "it." She is never given a name.

When we arrived at the hospital we went up to a long hall. A doctor in a white coat came rapidly toward us. "I'm very sorry. She's dead." I don't remember what my father did, or Faye. I went into a corner and began to cry, long sobbing sounds like when you're two years old and have fallen and really hurt yourself. The pain seemed unbearable. I'd never felt anything like it. In the midst of it all, I remember thinking, "Remember this. You can use it someday."

More self-reproach, that in the midst of his "unbearable" pain he was thinking of how his grief might someday serve his acting. Such a reaction could have been produced by shock, depersonalization, or a loss of the sensation of reality in the moment, but Sidney chose a self-incriminating explanation.

> *The doctor asked me if I wanted to see her. I said yes. I walked into a room. She was on her back, mouth open. I saw only her profile. A single desk lamp behind her seemed to give her bluish skin. I stayed in the doorway for a second, then backed out.*

Sidney's image of the body is more specific than his father's—and the "large" baby Baruch described is nowhere to be seen. He concludes his account by imagining what his mother had experienced—something Baruch never does.

> *I looked around. I hadn't noticed when we came in that it was a Catholic hospital: crucifixes on the walls, saints in niches, stained [glass] windows. And nuns. Moving silently up and down the halls. Poor mama. What terror she must have felt being in such trouble among the goyim. February 19, 1939.*
> *Is that why I've always been uncomfortable with odd numbers?*

"Poor mama." Whatever pain it cost him to reenter this memory to write this, it was worth it in order to get there, to put those words down. "Poor mama." Sidney has the day of the month right, but the year is wrong; February 1939 was when *One Third of a Nation*, the film he starred in, opened, not when his mother died.

He closes this story with the comment about "odd numbers." This is an unexpected ending to this heartrending narrative. Nothing about Sidney suggests that he was superstitious; still, he did have a peculiar relationship with numbers. He writes in his memoir about his habit of counting: counting toothbrush strokes (392 of them) and the fourteen stairway steps up to the bedrooms in his East Hampton home. As a child he always counted subway steps; he notes that his rhythm for counting them was "one and"—so that if the steps were an uneven number he would land (preferably) on the number, not on the "and."

Sidney was a precise person who enjoyed working with numbers. Without consulting his watch, he knew when a live-television scene needed cutting by three seconds. He was happy to explain film ratios, and how the distance between where the image reverses itself and the recording surface (the film) is what distinguishes wide-angle lenses from long lenses, and he loved knowing those things. Still, the counting was different; it was a way to occupy his mind so that unwanted thoughts didn't intrude. He sometimes spoke openly about his need to keep his mind occupied: "I get in trouble when I'm not working." Counting was a kind of mental discipline—a way of coping; he turned to numbers, then, to conclude this most agonizing of memories.

Baruch reports the immediate aftermath of the deaths of his wife and child. That summer he rented a room for Faye and Sidney in a bungalow colony near the summer camp in the Catskills where he was running a drama program. With an icebox and a hot plate in the room, to fix breakfast and lunch, the two were left on their own. Baruch writes in his unpublished narrative, "I tried to visit when I could," and goes blithely on to describe the "honest, angelic face" of the mother of a camper. She is "divorced, with a good job as a hat designer . . . completely independent and ready to marry me."

Baruch's is an odd kind of exuberance. He is unable to refrain from celebrating his romantic conquests, even when they reflect poorly on him. Sometimes Baruch is mindful of the impression he is making, creating of himself a particular kind of character, alternately resourceful, overburdened, and pitiable. At other times his stories pour forth without a second thought. He soon decided against the marriage to the hat designer; he writes, "I was not quite ready for marriage. I wanted to travel and to see my son become the actor I was to become when I was his age."

Baruch notes, without any sense of why it might have been, "After coming home from camp [that summer] I watched some rehearsals and began to see a change in Sidney's behavior—disobedience and also revolt at times."

Following his mother's death in February 1940, Sidney's grades plunged. More telling, perhaps, than the Ds in French, algebra and geometry was that he stopped writing "Jewish" in the space for religion on his ID card; for the first time, he left it blank.

4

A BROADWAY EDUCATION

*I began on Broadway when I was eleven. . . . In six years or
seven years I did fourteen plays . . . you just do the work; you
just do the work. And it gives you the most terrific kind of
respect without putting you in awe of anything. You're not in
awe of anything.*

—SIDNEY LUMET

With all the moving from neighborhood to neighborhood, borough
to borough, Sidney didn't have an easy time getting to the public
school he attended on the Lower East Side. From the subway station,
he had a ten-minute walk. The wind off the East River could be friend
or foe, depending on the season. Less than a mile from his school
was the *other* Lower East Side, Second Avenue, where he performed
nightly on the Yiddish stage. The "Yiddish Broadway" was a place of
dreams and creative energy and homespun glamour, quite different in
feeling from the rough-and-tumble streets nearer the river where his
school was located. There were dreams and dreamers there too, but
the dreams were mostly of escaping poverty.

From those same streets emerged a generation of entertainers. In
Sidney's approximate generation, the list includes John Garfield, Zero
Mostel, Walter Matthau, Tony Curtis, Jerry Stiller and Lee Strasberg;
one generation earlier, those streets were home to Edward G. Robinson, Eddie Cantor, Jimmy Durante, Irving Berlin, George and

Ira Gershwin and James Cagney, one of Sidney's very favorites—neighborhood kids, all.

Sidney made his way daily between the two faces of the Lower East Side: the "abrasive, clamorous" neighborhood, as Irving Howe described it, and the cultivated, artistic Lower East Side of the theater world. Yet these two contrasting worlds of the streets and the arts were bound to one another by the deepest of ties—by religion, mutual need, and common experience. Playwright Tony Kushner observed that the Yiddish theater in its heyday was charged with a "profound and complicated need not to be elitist or removed. All people are smart and anybody with a good head can get a complicated entertainment." Sidney would adhere to this principle, never talking down to his audiences.

Sidney's pattern was and always would be to live amidst contrasts: at school he was ill-fed and poorly clothed, even as, at night, he took his bows to warm applause. A childhood classmate of Sidney's remembered him at PS 188 on the Lower East Side as "the kid in second grade who everyone pitied because he didn't have lunch money." Yet at nine years of age he often stayed up into the wee hours sipping tea Russian-style from a glass, at the Café Royal, where his father fraternized with the Second Avenue stars, the neighborhood aristocrats. Following those late nights, Sidney didn't always make it to school. The theater was where Sidney was most alive to learning.

DEAD END AS A BEGINNING

Sidney made his Broadway debut at age eleven in a hit show, *Dead End*, written and directed by the Pulitzer Prize winner Sidney Kingsley, who became a lifelong friend. Fresh from the Yiddish stage, Sidney had never performed in English, which was okay, since his role in *Dead End* had no speaking lines. It called only for him to deliver a "Bronx cheer," and he was good at sounds; in his radio debut at age four he convincingly impersonated a crying and hiccupping baby.

Dead End opened in October 1935, a New York melodrama about the clash of rich and poor, centering on Manhattan real estate. "For many years the dirty banks of the East River were lined with the tenements of the poor. The rich, discovering that the river traffic was picturesque, moved their houses eastward" reads the opening crawl of the movie adaptation of *Dead End*. Kingsley was inspired to write the play when he wandered one day onto the 52nd Street dock beside the newly constructed River House. Just yards from where the slum kids sought relief from the summer heat in the strong currents of the river, residents of the River House refreshed themselves in their private pool, played tennis in their private courts and moored their yachts at the residence's anchorage. The building would lose its yacht basin in 1940 with the construction of the East River Drive, which was soon renamed the FDR Drive. The 1946 novel *East River* by Sholem Asch presents a picture of the waterfront neighborhood that had only recently been an active shipping yard:

> *The streets ended in "dead ends." . . . In a couple of places, however, there was an old unused dock, the planks, water-soaked and rotted. From these docks one could hear the splashing of children swimming close to the shore . . . disregarding the perils of the holes and falling timbers.*

Asch doesn't mention the perils of the river itself, but Kingsley does, underscoring the filth and stench, the raw sewage and industrial waste that poured into it. By the late 1930s, the city health department began cracking down on kids swimming in the river, a common sight for generations. In 1936, eleven swimming pools, built by the Works Progress Administration (WPA), opened around the city. Sidney never swam in the East River, though many of the kids who performed with him in the show certainly did. He had only ever cooled off in open fire hydrants.

The river plays a big part in the production. In the original set design the water was placed upstage, but Kingsley worked with famed designer Norman Bel Geddes to turn the set 180 degrees, making the proscenium into a dock, with the orchestra pit functioning as the

A scene from the 1933–37 Broadway production of *Dead End*, in which Sidney made his first Broadway appearance. The monumental set was designed by Norman Bel Geddes.

river. The children would jump into it and climb out wet! The prize-winning set was modeled on the actual street corner where River House was built; it depicted the interface of the two worlds, the stately stonework and manicured shrubbery overlooking the begrimed tenements, with their fire escapes, waving laundry and garbage-littered street. *New York Times* critic Brooks Atkinson praised the set for being "solid down to the ring of shoes on the asphalt pavement." When the curtain rose, the audience gasped audibly, and often rose in applause.

A melodrama in the naturalist vein, the tale includes a checklist of stock storylines: Baby Face Martin, a gangster, returns to his old neighborhood to learn that his youthful sweetheart has become a streetwalker. His embittered mother wants nothing to do with him. Ultimately he is "ratted on" by his childhood friend, Gimpty, and gunned down by G-men. A second plot follows Gimpty, who escaped the neighborhood to become an architect but, unable to find work, has returned to his old haunts. His love interest, Drina, has a younger brother whom she supports—a brother-sister plot that will repeat—a good kid in danger of being lost to the streets.

Most prominent in the story—and stealing the show—are the young hooligans, originally dubbed the Second Avenue Boys, mostly nonactors whom Kingsley recruited from local boys' clubs. Kingsley wanted the voices he heard on the streets to deliver his New York dialect as scripted: "Tell yuh kid brudder tuh git da hell outa heah!" Kingsley recalled that "when the play opened, [the kids] were so good that a number of critics seemed to feel that I had just thrown a lot of kids loose on the stage and let them take over. Of course, nothing could have been further from the truth: I had to work twice as hard to discipline them and exercise great ingenuity to solve each one's separate problem." Their most famous members were Leo Gorcey and Huntz Hall, who became well-known in *Angels with Dirty Faces* (1938), the East Side Kids series and the Bowery Boys series. In *Dead End* and in their subsequent roles the gang members were unspecified "white ethnic" kids, interchangeably Irish, Italian or Jewish, which kept their appeal wide. That interchangeableness was not, however, how it worked on the real city streets. Sidney recalled the harsh ethnic divisions of his childhood: "If I walked a few blocks one way or another into another neighborhood, I got beat up."

At eleven years old and small for his age, Sidney was cast as the "kid brudder." As Sidney's father, Baruch, liked to tell it, he convinced Kingsley to add a few smaller boys to the scenario to trail after the big boys, trying and failing to be accepted—"a charming visual detail." Sidney is credited by name as "small boy." The second or third week of rehearsals, Baruch recalled, Sidney came home, "and this was an amazing thing, he recited practically the entire play by heart, the *Dead End*, all the characters."

Despite the cliché plot, the language and behavior of the street kids provided something new and a little daring. In one scene, taken from the playwright's own experience, the boys "cockalize" a new gang member in a hazing ritual of pulling down the boy's pants, rubbing dirt all over his groin and spitting on his genitals. The rough images and language didn't keep the show from being performed at FDR's White House, after First Lady Eleanor Roosevelt returned to see it three times, visiting with the cast backstage each time. Senator Robert Wagner cited the play as evidentiary support for the Wagner-Steagall Housing Act of 1937, the first major federal bill designed to wipe out urban slums and replace them with low-income housing projects, which at that time were the great hope, the progressive solution to housing the poor. This housing theme remained prominent in films and plays throughout the decade, perhaps most notably in *One Third of a Nation* in which Sidney made his movie debut in 1939.

Dead End ran for more than two years, from 1935 to 1937—a long run in those days, during which Sidney earned $55 per week. The family moved from the Lower East Side to Eastern Parkway in Brooklyn, a broad street with trees and places to sit. "It seemed rich beyond our wildest dreams," Sidney recalled. He rode the subway to Brooklyn by himself after the show. Like many New York City kids, Sidney felt at ease on the subway, even alone, late at night. He had his rituals: to head to the first car and stand at the front window where he could feel the propulsion of the train, watch the signals in the tunnels turn from red to green, and disappear into his own world. He remembered often singing to himself the 1930s Rodgers and Hart hit "Blue Moon," a love song that opens with a sad lyric about waiting for love with only the moon for company, and "Without a dream in my heart / Without a love of my own." The trip to Utica Avenue lasted about thirty minutes. It was Sidney's five-cent magic carpet ride.

Soon *Dead End* was adapted for the screen by a director Sidney would often mention among his list of favorites, William Wyler. Lillian Hellman wrote the script under instructions from Samuel Goldwyn to "tone it down." Samuel Goldwyn Productions wasn't taking any chances with *Dead End* after a prior screen adaptation of a

Kingsley play, *Men in White*, had been deemed "unfit for public exhibition" by the Catholic Legion of Decency—hints of an abortion in the film's subplot led to protests and censored screenings. For *Dead End*, Hellman removed the "cockalizing" scene and such moments as when a medical intern kneels beside the body of the dead gangster and remarks, "Phew! They certainly did a job on him! Nothing left to look at but chopped meat. God, they didn't leave enough of him for a good postmortem!" Hollywood films at the time were subject to far stricter censorship codes than New York stage productions. This was just one among many reasons New York theater people looked down on Hollywood.

BEFORE THERE WAS OFF-BROADWAY, THERE WAS BROADWAY

To me the sub-text of the Thirties was commitment, passionate, idealistic commitment to the best of all possible worlds. I felt it surging all around me—that emotion. Everything contained the excitement of commitment.

—SIDNEY LUMET

Nowadays on Broadway, approximately 33 shows run at any given time. In the 1930–1931 season, the number of productions was 187. The Depression had actually downsized Broadway, as 250 shows had run yearly before the 1929 crash. The cutbacks led to more daring, experimental and openly political dramas. The Group Theatre (1931–1940) and the Federal Theatre Project (1935–1939), part of the WPA, were two of the most influential forces on the scene. Young Sidney was in both their orbits. The Group Theatre's aim was to bring "real life" to the stage, to get away from the Broadway star system with an ensemble approach based on Stanislavski's Moscow Art Theatre. Members of the company produced and financed their plays and shared profits. With Clifford Odets' 1935 working-class drama *Awake and Sing!*, the group found their voice and announced a truly American theater, introducing an acting style that would ultimately become famous as the Method.

The Federal Theatre Project had a different mandate, but more than just providing theater workers with jobs, it shook things up. It introduced stage innovations and launched the careers of young directors. Its Negro Theatre Units in New York City, Los Angeles and eleven other cities across the country staged some thirty productions, the most famous of which was the "voodoo" Macbeth directed by Orson Welles. Tickets were priced between fifteen and forty cents. The hugely popular Living Newspapers were inspired by Bolshevik artists of the 1920s; they dramatized such current issues as labor union disputes (*Injunction Granted*), corruption in the electric utilities (*Power*), STDs (*Spirochete*) and substandard housing (*One Third of a Nation*); the film adaptation of the latter play would be Sidney's movie debut. Amid charges of communism and subversion, the Federal Theatre Project worked steadily and defiantly for five years.

The political punch and variety, and the rapidity with which Broadway shows went up and came down, was unlike anything seen today. It imprinted on Sidney a model of creative productivity. "If you had a flop you'd be back the next season with another play," Sidney reminisced. "There was a kind of rhythm to a career on Broadway then. . . . The meaning of work in these people's lives was very clear to me at a very early age. The workers in the theater dealt with it as craft. . . . No sitting around waiting for inspiration or what have you. No fear." He noted, "I think the biggest single influence that [the theater] had on me was this faith in quantity, that we really don't know what the result is." This "respectful work, meaningful work" was the thing in his life that never let him down, even though some shows ran for only seven nights or less.

Along with teaching him to become a professional, and not to be in awe of anything or anyone, the plays were opportunities for him to explore his own worlds and himself. Several of the fourteen Broadway shows he appeared in before he was seventeen years old had an almost spooky resonance with his lived life, in one way or another. The make-believe helped make his life more real to him, helped him to know himself within the instabilities of his childhood.

FROM *DEAD END* TO *THE ETERNAL ROAD*

As a child I was exposed to Maxwell Anderson, to Kurt Weill and to Sidney Kingsley. Believe me, worse things can happen to a child. So what if you don't get to see kids your own age— all that means is you don't learn to pick your nose and scratch your butt the way they do.

—SIDNEY LUMET

Less than a year into the run of *Dead End*, Sidney, still eleven years old, auditioned for a role in *The Eternal Road*, a production that brought together two of Europe's most esteemed theatrical talents, director Max Reinhardt and composer Kurt Weill, both eager to leave Europe following Hitler's rise in Germany. Of the two, Weill was less recognized in the United States, as his *Threepenny Opera* (1928), created with Bertolt Brecht, had bombed on Broadway in the spring of 1933, closing after twelve nights.

Sidney's father chose "The Charge of the Light Brigade" for Sidney's audition piece—"with gestures," as Sidney recalled:

On the day of the audition, I walked onto the stage of an enormous theater. I could vaguely see a group of people out in front. With no nervousness, I took off, filled with confidence. When I finished, Reinhardt came down the aisle to the stage and said in German, "Come here." It was close enough to Yiddish that I understood him. He was a small man, with gray and white streaks in his hair. He had a tender, compassionate face that could turn frighteningly fierce in an eyeblink. He reached up to me. I knelt on the stage.

"Schprechen sie Deutsches?" he asked.

"Nayne. Uber ich farshtayzie." I replied in Yiddish. (No, but I understand you.)

He beamed and hugged me to him very tight.

. . . I was hired on the spot.

In this great big biblical pageant, Sidney was offered the role of Isaac, the sacrificial son of Abraham. Baruch saw an obvious advantage in the move from *Dead End* to this higher-profile production, and Sidney would graduate from his Bronx cheer in *Dead End* to a speaking part, albeit of just one word, "Father," called out as Abraham lifts his knife above him. But things did not go smoothly in this storied production, with its massive investment of half a million Depression-era dollars, its 245 actors, singers and dancers, its massive sets and 1,772 costumes.

The Eternal Road was not just a show, it was a cause—the brainchild of Meyer Weisgal, whose day job was executive director of Zionist activities for the Midwest, and who would later become private secretary to Chaim Weizmann, the first president of Israel. Weisgal had a passion for theater, or, more properly, for pageantry. He had scored an enormous success with a musical pageant at the 1933 Chicago World's Fair, celebrating the history of the Jews and their aspirations for a homeland in Palestine. Set against the accession of Hitler to chancellor of Germany six months earlier, "The Romance of a People" featured six thousand performers, including three thousand schoolchildren and seven hundred and fifty dancers. Following the World's Fair, he then managed to take the pageant on tour around the nation, raising large sums. Nearly a million New Yorkers made their way to the Kingsbridge Armory in a remote corner of the Bronx for the show, raising almost $500,000 toward resettling German Jews in Palestine. Weisgal's promotional skills were formidable: Mayor John O'Brien declared a "Jewish Day" for the pageant's opening, and volunteer pilots flew twenty-five airplanes in formation over City Hall in celebration. At the armory, anti-Nazi leaflets were passed out. One of the guests of honor toward the end of the pageant's monthlong run was refugee Albert Einstein, who had only just arrived in New York.

Pageants like "The Romance of a People" were prominent in the first half of the twentieth century, combining mass spectacle with ritual toward political ends of one kind or another. Popular in both the Soviet Union and Nazi Germany, the pageant-spectacle, with its enormous cast of performers, aimed for audiences to feel like part of a new collective identity. Typically these mass performance events extolled humble folk battling oppressive forces and enduring sacrifice for the benefit of "the people," shown emerging with renewed faith in their communities and fortified for the challenges of the future. Meyer Weisgal brought the pageant form to the cause of creating a Jewish homeland.

Following the success of "The Romance," Weisgal was determined to produce a more *artistically* ambitious pageant, a "theatrical answer to Hitler" that would draw on the Old Testament and the cultural heritage of the Jews. He sought the renowned Max Reinhardt, famous for his colossal stagings of classic dramas, performed in circus arenas, vast exhibit halls and outdoor venues, to create what he called the "Theatre of the Five Thousand."

Reinhardt initially turned him down, writing, "I'm not going to deny my Jewishness, but I can't put on a biblical variety show" that, as he put it, takes "us from the creation of the world via the dance around the golden calf to every well-known alpine peak of kitsch." This project, he concluded, was "an opportunity for [Cecil B.] deMille which I could not seize for all of De Millions in the world."

But Weisgal managed to win Reinhardt over, promising any composer and any writer Reinhardt wanted and offering significant financial relief to the soon-to-be displaced director. Along with Kurt Weill, Reinhardt requested Austrian author Franz Werfel, whose most recent book, *The Forty Days of Musa Dagh*, had brought the Armenian genocide of 1915–1917 to public awareness. That same year, 1933, Werfel watched his works being heaved on the Nazi bonfires, along with those of Einstein, Freud and others, as Germany's propaganda minister, Joseph Goebbels, announced that "Jewish intellectualism is dead." At the very same moment in the United States, Werfel's *Forty Days* had rocketed to the top of the bestseller list.

The three artists convened for the first time in 1934 at Reinhardt's Austrian castle-home, Schloss Leopoldskron, the former residence of the prince-archbishop of Salzburg and later the location used for Captain von Trapp's villa in the 1965 film *The Sound of Music*. Reinhardt had refashioned the residence into a breathtaking performance space, where writers, actors, and composers gathered. Planning their New York production, which they dubbed their "theater in exile," they sat within sight of Berchtesgaden, Hitler's mountain retreat in Bavaria.

In a matter of months the three artists were in New York developing the production. Eleven-year-old Sidney was in their midst, eyes wide open. It was far from the Yiddish theater world, but there was *something* familiar about these inspired European men.

Proximity to the world-famous Max Reinhardt, a household name in those days, left its mark on Sidney. Although Reinhardt spoke almost no English and few of the actors spoke German, as Sidney recalled, "his intensity and conviction made everything clear." To Sidney he was an "angelic demon," more than a little bit otherworldly. Sixty years later, Sidney recalled, "I'd never smelled cologne on a man before. It gave him an unreal quality. But most glamorous of all was his jacket. It was cashmere. I'd never felt anything like it. It wasn't only the softness of it. It felt rich beyond richness; not in money but in other-worldliness, as if not human hands had made it." The creator of the magical 1935 Warner Bros. movie production of *A Midsummer Night's Dream* was, for Sidney, glamour incarnate; he cast a spell. This kind of allure would reach its apotheosis for Sidney in his marriage to Gloria Vanderbilt. Drawing a connection between the two, he writes:

> *Years later, when I was married to Gloria, she gave me a gray cashmere suit, tailored by Knize, at that time a great New York tailor. I wore it until the seat and elbows were worn through. It's unwearable but I still have it. When I touch it it becomes Reinhardt to me.*

But Reinhardt meant more than cashmere and cologne to Sidney. "Though not needed much, I came to rehearsal every day to watch Reinhardt creating a miracle before our eyes." Sidney saw Reinhardt as an artist whose "effort and dedication instilled in me a work ethic that is still a mainstay of my life more than 60 years later."

Werfel's pageant tells of a "timeless community" of Jews huddled together in a synagogue where they've taken refuge from a pogrom. To give courage as they await their fate during an all-night vigil, the rabbi recounts stories from the Old Testament, which are enacted on-stage: Abraham's sacrifice of Isaac, the marriage of Jacob and Rachel, Joseph in Egypt, Moses and the Exodus, the loyal Moabite Ruth, tales of the reigns of Saul, David and Solomon and more. As the stories unfold, the watchers in the synagogue, identified as the Rich Man, the Pious Man, the Adversary (a skeptic), the Estranged One (an assimilated Jew) and the Estranged One's Son (played by Sidney), ask questions and share their woes and fears.

Staging this gigantic affair was more challenging than any of them imagined, especially once they brought Norman Bel Geddes aboard to design the set. Vetoing Reinhardt's idea of staging the show in a giant tent in Central Park, Bel Geddes chose the Manhattan Opera House on West 34th Street as the venue. He gutted the building to accommodate the five-story set that covered a full acre. Along with twenty-six miles of electrical wiring for a thousand stage lights, the scenery included a movable mountain rising from below the orchestra to thirty feet above it; the temple of Solomon with forty-foot columns and Joseph's Egyptian palace with its own thirty-two-foot statues. How to pay for all this? "There hardly existed a Jew in New York with a dollar to his name on whom [Weisgal] had not drawn his Zionist pistol," recalled Max Reinhardt's son Gottfried.

Sidney was enthralled by every aspect of the show and its production, including the raising of funds. For years he had watched his father figuring costs, worrying over every penny for his radio and stage productions. The boy caught many of the goings-on among the artistic giants and their financial backers. And he was as curious about what the electricians were up to; he watched with fascination as seven hydraulic elevators were installed at the back of the stage to move the massive sets up and down. During rehearsals, Sidney rode one of the elevators "up to the mountaintop" with Abraham, played by Thomas Chalmers, whom Sidney would direct on television years later. While they rode up, Abraham and Sarah's tent would be descending on another elevator.

Sidney had the kind of mind that needed to know exactly how things worked, all the parts and pieces. *The Eternal Road* offered a lifetime of lessons. For example, when Reinhardt became unhappy with the placement of the synagogue in a small space far above the audience, Bel Geddes hit on the idea of deepening and expanding the orchestra pit—a solution that had the unfortunate effect of absorbing three hundred orchestra seats, the most profitable tickets. Sidney recalled this detail in later years, and what happened next.

> *So they began to dig, and in Manhattan when you dig you hit rock. So they blasted into the rock—right into the rock—water. We had to stop rehearsal and the entire summer was spent with pumps, pumping the East River into the Hudson River.*

The flooded sets had to be entirely rebuilt. This and other technical disasters brought about a fifteen-month delay in the production that wreaked havoc with union employees and actors, many of whom had to be replaced. Sidney was among those losing wages, and Baruch urged the boy to try to retrieve his role in *Dead End* in the interim. Sidney staunchly refused, not willing to unseat the boy who had taken his place in the show. As Baruch tells it—in his accented English—Sidney responded, "Oh no! Because I went out of the play to better myself, and another little boy took my place, I should come back and say, 'Oh, you get out'?" Baruch proudly lingers in his memoir over this memory: "This is something that I will never forget, a beautiful feeling in a child, a consideration, and he refused to go back."

During the delay in *The Eternal Road*'s production, Sidney appeared in an all-Yiddish Federal Theatre Project production of Sinclair Lewis's *It Can't Happen Here*. When *The Eternal Road* got back on track, Baruch was able to secure a small part for himself, and one for Sidney's sister too. This was the only time the three of them appeared together on stage; it was Faye's only theatrical work. The income set them up for another move—also temporary—this time uptown, to "a small apartment in a small apartment house" on Central Park West and 103rd Street—an address that signified "arrival" for Jewish New Yorkers.

As opening night finally approached, Sidney was thrilled by the increasing intensity. The more than two hundred performers and stagehands basically lived in the theater for the weeklong technical rehearsal. "Cots were brought in for sleeping; food, coffee . . . people went home only to bathe and change clothes," Sidney recalled. While Reinhardt was making drastic changes to the sets, including relighting each scene to give it the feel of a different time and place, Kurt Weill was revising his music; "his perception changed because of the actors," Sidney noted. During the "nightmare of the technical week" Weill continued to revise, "with love and no temperament which he would have been entitled to." For Sidney, the memory of Kurt Weill "on hands and knees downstairs in the men's lounge, the score spread out before him as he recopied orchestrations, will always be with me."

Weisgal described the opera-oratorio's opening night:

> We had no curtain, all the effects were based on
> lighting—$60,000 worth of it. When the first lights went on
> dimly they revealed only the small synagogue, and the Jews, men,
> women and children, huddled together in fear—nothing more.
> Then the chazzan [cantor]—a marvelous singer—began to
> chant "And God said 'Abraham . . .'" Slowly the stage began to
> light up, revealing the depth and height of five broad ascending
> tiers, and, finally, at the top, the choir—one hundred singers
> in the robes of angels, a heavenly host. The audience caught its
> breath and one could hear a collective "A-ah."

Sidney's role was significant. For his original part of Isaac, Reinhardt had worked with him to get just the precise combination of confusion and terror into his one line, "Father!" As a result of the production delay, however, Sidney not only outgrew his costume, but his voice changed. Seeing something special in Sidney, Reinhardt recast him in the major role of the thirteen-year-old Son of the Estranged One, a character whose father has chosen assimilation in the hope that it might save them both from persecution. Throughout the night's vigil, the child listens closely and comments on the biblical stories, until finally he expresses a wish to "join those men, father, from whose voices arise the beautiful visions."

Reviewers were bowled over by the pageant, and repeatedly they singled out three sequences for praise: the sacrifice of Isaac, the golden calf dance sequence, and Sidney's final speech, which never failed to draw a huge response from the audience. It went like this: after the sequence representing the sacking of the Temple by the Babylonians and the subsequent enslavement of the Jews, the boy, spotlighted alone on the vast stage, with arms stretched wide, declaims:

> *Messiah . . . where art thou? Hearest thou not our mother Rachel? She mourns for her children. She has been waiting so long, so very long. . . . Why does she receive no answer? Her children are being destroyed. . . . Why did the Temple have to be burned? Why do we experience nothing but sorrow . . . and forever sorrow? Why just we . . . ?*

In response to his plea, "an incorporeal image of mere light," as the stage direction describes it, appears above the sleeping congregation. Ecstatically, the boy rouses the sleepers to deliver the Angel's message of redemption—their return to Zion:

> *Wake up! I see . . . I hear . . . I have my answer . . . Wake up! . . . Why do you lament? . . . Are you weary after this night? . . . I am not weary. . . . Come, father, come all of you, and follow our Rabbi. . . . I have seen the Messiah. . . . He is even now on his way. . . . We must set out to meet him.*

The child then leads the congregants in procession out of the synagogue to make their winding way up the five levels of the stage to join the succession of biblical characters, marching onward to where the angelic choir sings. Sidney's ardent speech and the show's climactic imagery brought down the house. Max Reinhardt was said to weep openly night after night. One evening the president's mother, the reserved, socially correct Sara Delano Roosevelt, broke down and solemnly kissed Sidney on the forehead as she congratulated the child. If the Christian-inflected redemption imagery troubled some Jewish viewers, others saw in this conclusion a Zionist parable, the boy representing idealistic youth leading the Jewish people to the Promised Land. Sidney himself recalled, "All of us discussed this ending tirelessly. What was it meant to signify? Both Werfel and Reinhardt were, as Sidney described them, *"Geshmatteh Yiddin"* (literally, destroyed Jews); though born Jewish, they had converted to Catholicism." Half a century later, he wondered, "Did the final scene represent the Second Coming? Was the twelve-year-old boy really Jesus? I never asked Reinhardt; I was just thrilled to be playing a big part." Sidney remained convinced that Reinhardt's conversion to Catholicism was merely a rumor.

Theater critics praised the pageant for its appeal to both Christians and Jews, its "universal message." This entirely missed Weisgal's intended message, to call attention to Jewish persecution in Europe. Only *Time* magazine's reviewer extracted an anti-Nazi theme, "a symbol of solidarity to rally World Jewry to the defense of their fellow Jews suffering the lash of Nazi persecution."

The lack of an explicit anti-Nazi message in *The Eternal Road* resulted in part from the different orientations of the three "most famous non-Jewish Jewish artists," as Gottfried Reinhardt described his humanist father, Max; Werfel, "a zealot of the Roman Catholic Church"; and Weill, a "Marxist-oriented atheist." There was also the influence of Norman Bel Geddes, Reinhardt's collaborator in designing the Christian pageant *The Miracle* in 1924, described by Gottfried as a "Waspish American anti-Semite" unable to conceal his dislike of Jews. Observing a slowdown in ticket sales, Max Reinhardt's business manager, Rudolph Kommer, hypothesized, "It is perhaps too artsy for New York; for the little Jews it is perhaps not obvious enough, for the big Jews—too Jewish. The Catholics are crazy about it."

Yet the show's clouded message accords in some respects with the alloyed responses of American Jews in 1935 to the predicament of their coreligionists in Europe. That was the year Hitler enacted the Nuremberg Race Laws, depriving Jews of their German citizenship. American Jews were unsure how to plead for special attention from an America that didn't much like Jews to begin with; they feared that calling too much attention to the plight of European Jews would backfire. A majority of Americans opposed opening the country's doors to Jewish refugees, and a 1938 poll found that 65 percent of Americans believed that European Jewry was at least partly responsible for its own persecution. Growing louder still was the claim that the Jews were dragging the country into another war in Europe, a staple of isolationist rhetoric. American Zionists contended that Nazism was proof that Jewish nationhood—not assimilation—was the only strategy for survival. The message carried by Sidney's character in the play was that assimilation did not protect Jews from persecution.

Young Sidney took a different message from the show, as he watched it hemorrhage money, leaving Weisgal penniless and the backers filing for bankruptcy. They were forced to close in May 1937 after 153 performances. As a movie director, Sidney became famous for bringing movies in on or under budget—and on or ahead of schedule.

There's a Broadway bookend for Sidney to this show's failed alarm bell. Almost ten years later, after the war, after the revelations of the death camps, Sidney starred in *A Flag Is Born*, a play excoriating the British for not allowing a greater number of Jews into Palestine during the war, and also pointing the finger at American Jews: "Where were you?"

LEARNING AND DOING

After *The Eternal Road*, Sidney became a go-to child actor on Broadway, earning enough to keep the family afloat. In December 1937 he entered, at midyear, the small private Professional Children's School, where he was awarded a full scholarship. Despite many moving parts in his life, including his peripatetic family, Sidney happily remained at the school, located then on the eighth floor of a commercial building on Broadway and 61st Street, for four full years.

The students were a motley crew; along with child actors, there were child models, figure skaters and even a vaudeville specialty act. To give the theatrical children a chance to catch up on sleep, the school day began at ten in the morning, and it ran until three in the afternoon—except on matinee days, when the children could leave at one o'clock. Under the caring gaze of the tall, elegant principal, Mrs. Nesbitt, the children were well looked after. Sidney remembered her fondly. "She understood what these children were carrying on their shoulders. Many, like me, were supporting their families. Others, coming from show business families often had one or sometimes both parents on the road. Others came from homes broken by divorce because the strains of careers played hell on home life." The theater kids stuck together—created a family of sorts. They founded an organization in 1937 called Footlight Juniors, consisting of Equity actors between the ages of seven and sixteen. Their aim: to raise money for ice-cream parties. Sidney is quoted in a *New York Times* article as an organizer negotiating rent for a meeting room at the Hotel Piccadilly and organizing a kids-only benefit performance.

The students frequently met for dinner at a restaurant between matinee and evening performances. "It never occurred to us that we might look strange, seven or eight teenagers sitting around a table eating dinner around 5:30, some still in make-up. This was during the Depression. Kids were not eating out in cafeterias." Everyone at school was mindful of the fact that the children were earning almost double what their teachers were taking home. Central Park was just a few blocks from the school, and the kids sauntered over on nice

Sidney, in a jaunty beret, waves in front, exiting the office building of the school with his classmates. *(Courtesy of the Professional Children's School Archive)*

afternoons. One fall Sidney organized a football team, but he realized it wasn't going to work out when one player, Frankie Thomas Jr., moving up the field, yelled, "Watch out for my face, fellas. Watch out for my face." Their good looks were too valuable to risk.

While Sidney was settling in and making friends at his new school, he was aware that many of the young performers from *The Eternal Road* had gone off to Spain to fight the fascists as part of the Lincoln Brigade. Moved deeply by the political passions around him, twelve-year-old Sidney packed a bag and tried to sneak out of the house, determined to join the fight. His father caught him before he got far, but something new and lasting had been stirred in him. With all the excitement of the moment, it was often hard for Sidney to become invested in his schoolwork. In his first grading period he received Ds in all subjects except geography, where he earned a B+. The report card notes that he "does not attend class and turns in no correspondence," but by the end of the school year he managed to pass all his classes by scoring 80s and 90s on his final exams.

In ninth grade he encountered Mrs. Livewright—really her name—an intense, diminutive history teacher. He remembered his very first class with her; it was on Edmund Burke's "conciliation speech" to the British Parliament, in which he argued against a war in America. "Not one student knew who Edmund Burke was, what Parliament was or what conciliation meant," he recalled, but by the end of the session "her class meant as much to me as work did." Which was certainly saying a lot! Indeed, Sidney earned a 96 on his history Regents exam that year, by far his highest grade in school.

Despite his spotty grades, the principal, Mrs. Nesbitt, recognized something special in Sidney and recommended him for a highly selective summer camp called Rising Sun. Founded in 1930 by George E. Jonas, whose family had made a fortune in felt hats, the tuition-free and invitation-only camp sought to cultivate leadership skills, recruiting children from around the world. Sidney would attend the camp in Rhinebeck, New York, for part of the summer of 1939, crossing paths with another camper, Pete Seeger. He was never at a loss for educational experiences, especially when they took place outside of school.

Sidney's third Broadway show, *Sunup to Sundown*, was a flop, playing only seven nights in February 1938. It was a "protest play" about child labor abuses set on a tobacco plantation. Its author, Francis Edward Faragoh, had been nominated for an Oscar for the screenplay of the classic 1931 gangster movie *Little Caesar*, and he co-wrote the screen adaptation of *Frankenstein* that same year. Despite its short run, the play won awards from the National Child Labor Committee and the International Ladies' Garment Workers' Union. The story was of a seventeen-year-old laboring boy who is prohibited by his employer from marrying the fifteen-year-old Mexican girl who is pregnant with his child. The director, Joseph Losey, had worked with Bertolt

Brecht, directed political cabaret and the Federal Theatre Project's Living Newspaper series and would soon be hounded out of the country by the House Un-American Activities Committee (HUAC). In England, where he relocated, he went on to become a major film director (*The Boy with Green Hair*, *The Servant*, *The Go-Between*, *Galileo*, *Mr. Klein*). Sidney remembered him as a "very nice, very concerned, and very talented man but also as pompous then as he is now."

Sidney appeared next in a comedy, *Schoolhouse on the Lot*, which spoofed the behind-the-scenes tantrums and shenanigans of Hollywood's child actors—emphasis on tantrums. It had a good run, fifty-five performances, but is little remembered. It was Sidney's next play, in which he had a leading part, *My Heart's in the Highlands*, written by William Saroyan and produced by the Group Theatre, that would have the greatest consequences for him.

My Heart's in the Highlands was a stylized production under Bobby Lewis' direction, with music by Paul Bowles, who would become well-known for his fiction, especially *The Sheltering Sky* (1949). A poetic piece in a mythic-feeling rural landscape, Saroyan's set description reads, "An old white, broken-down, frame house with a front porch, on San Benito Avenue in Fresno, California. There are no other houses near by, only a desolation of bleak land and red sky." Critic Joseph Wood Krutch noted of the set's surprising whimsy, "[It] looks as though it might have been conceived by Mr. Dali in a mood of unwonted cheerfulness." It centered on a penniless poet and his nine-year-old son, Johnny, who, despite their harsh circumstances, celebrate the pursuit of artistic expression and the gifts, given and received, of community. The production was controversial among the members of the Group because it deviated from the hard-hitting, message-carrying stories—what Sidney later called "the-fried-eggs-on-stage realism"—that the Group was known for.

The play opened with the father kneeling on an upper platform of the stylized house, muttering words in search of a rhyme; below the porch, his son, played by Sidney, tries to do a headstand. As Group Theatre historian Wendy Smith notes:

*Each attempt and fall of the son's is synchronized with the
discovery and discarding of a new rhyme by the father. . . . Just
as the poet finds the perfect rhyme, his son manages to stand on
his hands. In another scene, to make the point that people are
nourished by art, Lewis arranged the villagers bringing food to
an old man playing the trumpet to create the image of a plant
blossoming as it is watered.*

Sidney found the story and staging a bit mystifying. "I must say it
struck me as very odd! It excited my imagination enormously, but it
was very surprising," he recalled. His character, Johnny, is described
by Saroyan:

*JOHNNY, aged nine, but essentially ageless, is sitting, dynamic
and acrobatic, on the steps of the porch, dead to the world and
deep in thought of a high and holy order.*

Playing Johnny, the good-natured "ageless" son (Sidney was thirteen, not nine) on whom the father relies to use his honest charm to
obtain food from the local grocer on credit, Sidney was even then
mindful of the parallels to his own life. "One of the points of the play
was that my father is a poet, and I'm the kid . . . and I'm taking care
of him, 'cause he can't do squat about life. I'm the one who gets us
through it."

The insolvent poet, Johnny's father, was played by Philip Loeb,
who became another important figure in Sidney's life. "He taught me
tenderness more than anyone else," Sidney later commented. Loeb's
own son suffered from schizophrenia and was hospitalized, and Loeb
took a fatherly liking to Sidney. "He took me to the Museum of Modern Art for the first time, taught me about art." Sidney recalled Loeb
introducing him to the work of Marc Chagall—and then, unforget-
tably, to Chagall himself.

Loeb was beloved for his sense of humor. At the Group's summer camp, during baseball games, if he didn't like the umpire's call
he would take off his pants and wave them in the air. At a birthday

party in his honor, he delivered a sincere thank-you speech while absentmindedly smearing birthday cake all over his body. Loeb became well known in 1949 for his role as Mr. Goldberg on the television show *The Goldbergs*. Despite the show being a hit, however, it was abruptly dropped by CBS in 1951 when Loeb was blacklisted: a right-wing tract, *Red Channels: The Report of Communist Influence in Radio and Television*, labeled him a communist, along with 150 other actors, writers, and broadcast journalists. The TV show reappeared without Loeb the following year. For years afterward he was unable to find work, and in 1955 he checked into the Taft Hotel in midtown Manhattan under a false name and took a fatal dose of sleeping pills. This tragedy was later memorialized in *The Front* (1976), written by Sidney's dear friend Walter Bernstein, about the blacklist, in which a Loeb-like character played by Zero Mostel takes his own life. Loeb's suicide would have a far-reaching impact on Sidney, affecting political choices he would make as a television director during the HUAC hearings.

My Heart's in the Highlands, originally scheduled for five performances as part of the Group's seasonal program, was a surprise hit that ran for six weeks, launching Saroyan's career as a playwright. Sidney, by this time, was about to enter the most event-filled year of his life.

These were the creative and learning arenas of Sidney's childhood and early youth. He was always on the move, always negotiating different worlds. From play to play, from theater to school, from family to stage, from stage to street. Each of the shows he was part of took up a significant theme in his own life: urban poverty, religious identity, political activism and, finally, a son's role in the life of his artistic father. He could feel, early on, how personal and real art could be, how it could give shape and meaning to experience. At the same time, he was finding in the work an escape from family troubles, an atmosphere where everything was urgent and in the moment, where the personalities were larger than life and where, in the shared high stakes of a production, an alternative theater family could offer temporary emotional shelter.

Sidney's father thought what Sidney loved was acting, but what he loved was the theater, where there was life, laughter and the gladness of make-believe and creativity. With a precocious sense of professionalism, Sidney took his successes and failures in stride. But he would also recall absorbing at times the sting of the adult actors' judgments and skepticism, and how painful it could be to expose himself to audiences night after night.

The 1930s theater world Sidney knew was charged with idealism, with people who were committed to a common purpose. The theater probably saved his life. It certainly taught him a lifetime of lessons. What he hadn't yet learned to think about was acting. He'd been running on boyish charm, intelligence and an unshakeable, unselfconscious confidence. His growing involvement with the Group Theatre would open to him the deep resources of technique, method and introspection, and introduce him to the gratifications of analyzing and developing character and story.

5

BROTHER AND SISTER

What is this strand of DNA between
us, unconnected to & of the shadows parading past, our
outlines already chalked into the earth?
—"If This Is Your Final Destination" by Nick Flynn

A little more than halfway through the 1983 film *Daniel*, adapted from E. L. Doctorow's novel *The Book of Daniel*, a sequence unfolds in montage, a technique rarely used by Sidney. A brother and sister, the young children of the fictionalized Ethel and Julius Rosenberg, have managed to slip away from the Bronx shelter where they've been placed while their parents are in prison awaiting trial in the early 1950s. The children begin their long walk home through a gray and indifferent New York City. Daniel, the older child, grips his little sister by the hand and instructs her not to run, not to draw attention. The music picks up: Paul Robeson's mournful rendition of "This Little Light of Mine." Through much of the sequence the camera keeps its distance, emphasizing how small, vulnerable, and isolated they are as they make their way through varied neighborhoods, some crowded, some deserted. Beneath the music, we hear six-year-old Susan ask her brother to slow down; she crouches to pull up a white ankle sock that has slipped into her Mary Janes. Further along, we hear Daniel's whispered questions to her, "Are you tired?" and then later, "Why are you crying?"

Doctorow, who adapted his novel for Lumet's film, recalled that the song was Sidney's choice. Robeson's deep tones conjure a surrounding darkness against which the "little light" has scant power. As the children are unknowingly and inevitably carried toward the gravest personal catastrophe, the execution of their parents, their somber progress grants the viewer time to ponder the lyrics. Has Susan become Daniel's little light? Does their shared act of defiance in running away represent a flicker of hope? Robeson's voice grounds the scene in history. He was a political and cultural icon of the beleaguered American left of the late 1940s and early 1950s, and a personal one for Sidney. The songs he recorded were sung around the campfire at the socialist and Zionist summer camps Sidney and his sister attended during the 1930s.

With the Rosenberg story, Sidney felt that Doctorow had chosen "the most unimaginable situation, the most bizarre and horrendous removal of parents to explore whether children can pull themselves out of their own graves," and, likely thinking of his own sister's recent premature death, he wondered "why one might survive and another not." It took time and hard work to get *Daniel* funded; the story must have taken on greater personal urgency after Faye's death in 1980, when she was fifty-nine.

When Faye died, they had not seen one another for years. Nobody is quite sure what came between Sidney and his sister. Sid and Faye, Shmul and Faigele. They could not have been closer when they were young. They shared a bed until Sidney was eleven—a fact startling today but less surprising in those times. After the war, their relationship began to wane, and over time they all but lost contact. For many years they lived only blocks apart in Manhattan. Their daughters, first cousins, never met one another.

"ORPHANS IN THE STORM"

Faye was almost four years older than Sidney. She was born in Warsaw just ten days before her father, Baruch, left Poland for the United States. Baruch didn't see her again until she was a two-year-old child, when she arrived with her mother and grandmother in Philadelphia. Faye grew up watching her father focus his attention on and delighting in her little brother. Of Sidney's precocious success at age four on their Yiddish radio show, Baruch wrote, "My little son Sidney became a favorite as my grandson over the radio." And elsewhere: "He had a terrific will, will power; for acting he was never tired." Throughout his memoir, when Baruch talks about little Sidney, he *kvells*, bursting with pride over the child's talent, intelligence, and upright character. But his tone is different when he writes about Sidney's sister: "My daughter Faye was not interested to act in [the radio show], so she was out." In his memoir, Sidney wonders about it: "I don't know why he [Baruch] didn't write a part for Faye. I'm sure she resented it."

Buried among Baruch's many stories extolling Sidney's precocity, discipline and charm, there is just one story about Faye as a small child. When she was three years old, her first summer in the United States, the family managed to decamp to a modest working-class bungalow colony in the Catskill Mountains. Venturing to the lake with her father, Faye sat dangling her feet in the water. She didn't know how to swim, and Baruch didn't take her into the water with him, as many fathers would have. Instead, he gave her a nickel and told her not to move while he swam out into the lake. "Keep still and play with the nickel," he instructed her. When he returned she was not where he had left her. Standing in the water, nearsighted without his glasses, he called and shouted for her but got no reply. Suddenly he felt something catch hold of his leg. Frightened, he kicked the "object" away, then bent down to realize that his half-drowned daughter was tugging on him. Lifting her out of the water, he suffered some anxious seconds before she began to cough and cry. The nickel had fallen into the water, she explained, and she had tried to retrieve it. Had he been gone a few seconds more, Baruch realized, he would have lost her.

We can imagine that Baruch puzzled irritably over why his daughter didn't listen to him and why she was never satisfied with what he gave her. Baruch's manipulative charm worked for years with Sidney, who was his apt and ready pupil, but it had never worked on Faye, who was, after all, the recipient of so much less of it. Perhaps because their relationship had begun belatedly, the father and daughter never properly bonded. In any case, Baruch did not disguise the difference in his feelings toward his two children. Recalling his thoughts about ending his unhappy marriage, he writes in his memoir:

> *Many times we wished we could separate, but I never allowed it to go this far. Not when two children are involved. I also thought of the way Sidney's life would be broken, when his home would be broken. He was a sensitive boy with artistic tendencies. I felt him to be part of me. Not so much the girl but the boy.*

Baruch concludes this passage with an optimistic flourish: "And besides, we have [*sic*] a radio feature still going and everything could be so glorious." Opportunity was never far from his thoughts when it came to Sidney. Along with his sense of Sidney's financial promise, the boy's talent served other, narcissistic, needs that his daughter did not: "to see my son become the actor *I was to become when I was his age*" (emphasis mine).

Asked in an interview in 2008 if he had any siblings, Sidney replied, "A sister, older, and I think she probably had some resentment because, among other things, I got all the attention." Later, in his unfinished memoir, Sidney wondered about his own inattention to Faye. Recalling the family's efforts to stage their radio serial, he considers: "During all this time it never occurred to me to think of how Faye was doing," since she was not included in any of these theatricals. His mother alluded to Faye's "sweet singing voice," he recalled, and his father had encouraged Faye until Sidney's talent began to reveal itself. "But after I started working for him, he dropped Faye. . . . If she resented me, she never let me see it. In fact, she seemed devoted to me." He details a memory of Faye coming to his rescue at an early age when he got into one of many fistfights on the street:

> *The kid I was fighting landed a solid shot to my nose. It began to bleed. For some reason I'll never understand I decided to*

dramatize everything. I wasn't hurt at all, but letting out a moan, I fell to the ground. . . . I could hear the gasp of onlookers, young and old. Suddenly, this virago burst from the crowd. It was Faye. Arms flailing like windmill blades, she beat the kid silly. He would end up running up the street crying, having borne the worst possible shame: being beaten by a "goil."

Adding to the mystery of what later came between them, Sidney concludes, "Her protectiveness of me stayed well into our adult lives."

In the confusion and upheaval of their home life, no one seemed particularly alarmed by what Sidney at first described as Faye's "strange habit," when all of a sudden, "for no apparent reason, she'd start to skip around the room. She couldn't hear anybody during . . . the attack [that] seemed to last about 30 seconds [and] then would subside as suddenly as it came." His parents were, he said, "so ignorant . . . that no one ever checked or had her examined by a doctor." Indeed, Baruch would tell her to "'cut it out' as if she had any choice." Sidney hypothesized that these "fits"—as they were called—must have been partial seizures of some kind, and that perhaps such a seizure accounted somehow for her early death.

BREADWINNER

Sidney and Faye "clung to one another. They were like two orphans in the storm," recalled Ellen Adler, Sidney's first girlfriend and daughter of the legendary acting teacher Stella Adler. Given their father's pattern of moving them from place to place, it is easy to imagine the two children walking the streets, like Daniel and Susan in Lumet's film, trying to find their way in a new neighborhood. A quick glance at Sidney's school address card for 1936, when he was twelve years old and entering eighth grade in the middle of the school year, gives an idea of the frequency with which they moved and their rapid shifts of fortune:

1369 St. John's Place, Bklyn (crossed out)
3162 29th Street, Astoria (crossed out)
Hotel Woodrow, 35 W. 64 Street (crossed out)
115 W. 86th Street, NY NY

Four months, four moves, three boroughs, from a Crown Heights tenement to a pleasant apartment house in Queens, then on to a quasi-bohemian Manhattan residential hotel, and finally to a canopied building on a fashionable uptown street.

In Sidney's busiest professional year, 1939, he lists on his school record an address in Coney Island, but soon that address is crossed out and a second address appears, this one in Astoria, Queens. Before the year is out, he relists the prior Coney Island address. This was when he and Baruch had moved to 33rd Street in Queens to be close to the Astoria Studios, where they were shooting the film *One Third of a Nation*. The father and son had left the mother and daughter in their Coney Island apartment while they made the film. That is, they left Faye alone to contend with their lonely, aggrieved, and unstable mother.

Just as Sidney's star was rising, his father's was sinking. By the early 1930s New York Jews were increasingly assimilated, and the restrictive Immigration Act of 1924 had drastically reduced the number of newly arriving European Jews. The Yiddish stage was quickly becoming a relic, with performances put on only twelve weeks during the year, "leading up to and immediately after Passover," Sidney recalled.

There was little work for Baruch. He hired a speech coach but could not manage to unthicken his Polish accent, which precluded Broadway roles. As Sidney later put it, "When I worked, we ate." Sidney was fourteen years old and playing a lead role in William Saroyan's first Broadway production, *My Heart's in the Highlands*, with the Group Theatre. The reviewer for the *New York Times* noted, "Lumet, as the boy, was charming and showed a manly technique." In a 2008 interview, Peter Travers asked Sidney what "manly things" he was doing in the role. "I was acting the part," he replied. "One of the points of the play was that my father is a poet, and I'm the kid, thirteen, and I'm taking care of him, 'cause he can't do squat about life. I'm the one who gets us through it." Travers pressed, "Just like at home?" and Sidney replied, "Exactly."

That same year, at age fourteen, Sidney began supplementing his Broadway income by doing radio work. He appeared on several shows, including *Let's Pretend*, a Saturday morning children's program; *The Theatre Guild on the Air*, which produced a radio version of Sidney's first Broadway show, *Dead End*; and *The March of Time*, where actors reenacted news stories of the day. For the latter show, Art Carney played Franklin Delano Roosevelt, Orson Welles played Sigmund Freud and Dwight Weist, known as "the man of a thousand voices," impersonated Adolf Hitler, Joseph Goebbels, William Randolph Hearst, Fiorello La Guardia, George Bernard Shaw, John Barrymore, Lionel Barrymore and Ethel Barrymore, among others.

Sidney looking bored, sitting with actor Myron McCormick for a CBS Radio drama, *One More Free Man*, broadcast in 1941 on the series *The Free Company*. (*CBS Photo Archive / CBS / Getty Images*)

Sidney's most lucrative radio gig, at $85 per episode, was a soap opera aptly titled *Big Sister*. Because magnetic recording tape wasn't used in the United States until after World War II, every show was live. As Sidney explained it, "You always did a repeat. You would do the show and then you'd come back three hours later to do the repeat for the West Coast."

The soap opera was about a young woman who devotes herself tirelessly to her orphaned younger brother and sister while being repeatedly betrayed by her alluring love interest.

This theme of an orphaned boy cared for by a selfless older sister was a well-worn formula in popular entertainment at a time when as many as one hundred and forty thousand children lived in more than twelve hundred orphanages throughout the country. We see the selfless older sister, typically portrayed as a virginal "little mother," in two other productions Sidney was part of: *Dead End* and *One Third of a Nation*. The orphan plotlines may also have expressed a first-generation American fantasy of being released from the thrall of immigrant parents, leaving the children free to invent themselves.

Sidney's first wife, actress Rita Gam, held the view that Sidney's sister had raised him. She said Sidney never talked about his mother, and Rita was actually convinced that their mother had died when he was a baby. But given that Sidney was the breadwinner for the family, it's not so easy to say which sibling parented the other.

ON THEIR OWN

Friends from their youth describe Faye as "strong, aggressive, tough," "adorable, a charmer," "cozy, *haimish*." "She was a real 1930s, 1940s political animal," Ellen Adler recalled. "I mean, she was for the common man. She was the typical rah-rah girl for the liberals." She went on to say, "She was very touching, and Sidney loved her."

Faye was to the left of liberal, and she took Sidney with her to May Day marches and meetings of the Young Communist League. He got thrown out of one meeting for disputing a speaker's claim that the

Soviet Union was a classless society. Sidney objected that he knew for a fact that artists lived better than other people, a situation that he found appealing. He was promptly ejected, but Faye stuck around, "an attractive blonde, fiery, political cause kind of girl." Here is another link to the siblings in *Daniel*—the sister wed to political causes who will later lose heart.

The frayed thread holding the family together snapped with their mother's death. All that was left, it seemed, was the financial arrangement between the father and his children, and Faye figured out a way to dissolve that last tie. Her plan was for the two siblings to move into a hotel until they could rent their own apartment, then to consult a lawyer and legally emancipate Sidney from their father. After that summer left alone in the bungalow, what was holding them back? The last straw was that Baruch had begun talking about marrying a widow named Julia, a dancer with a four-year-old daughter, Claire, whom Baruch was thinking of adopting. Faye was deeply stung by this development.

One night Baruch returned home to find the children packed and gone. Among those he phoned while looking for them was Stella Adler. She wasn't a great fan of Sidney, according to her daughter Ellen, but she had no reason to take Baruch's side. Baruch eventually tracked them down to a hotel on West 61st Street. His story is that he offered them the keys to their apartment, saying he would move out, but Faye wasn't interested. Faye rented a costly apartment on Lexington Avenue and ordered furniture for it, but Baruch managed to sour the deal, telling the rental agent that Faye was underage. Later Faye called Baruch and defiantly claimed she was glad he had interfered; the place had been too expensive anyway. Next Baruch tried to communicate with Sidney, waiting for him outside his stage door. When Sidney saw his father, he looked away and kept walking. Baruch later recalled thinking, "You'll come back kid, if you ever find me."

Baruch blamed Faye for everything: "It came down to plain figures in money. The boy makes now 150 a week. The girl, who never earned or cared to learn how to earn a dollar, found it easier to convince the boy to live away from home." But in a different mood he would take a modest measure of responsibility: "I had no prospects for acting jobs or movie jobs. It seemed I lived off the boy's earnings. It also seemed that I may get married again. I didn't know what it seemed to my kids—but dissatisfaction took over instead of concern for one another."

In 1939 the Child Actor's Bill, also known as the Coogan Act, was passed in California. Named for Jackie Coogan, the child actor whose mother and stepfather had burned through almost his entire earnings, the law mandated for the first time that a percentage of a child actor's income be set aside in trust. But no such law yet existed in New York. After consulting with their lawyer, Faye and Sidney decided to offer Baruch 25 percent of Sidney's earnings until he came of age. It was likely Sidney's idea. The money, Baruch understood, was to acknowledge what he had done for his son's career. Baruch didn't like it: "I'm his father. I'm not his agent." Baruch turned for advice to the celebrated trial lawyer Louis Nizer, whose client list at the time included Charlie Chaplin, Mae West, and Salvador Dalí. At first Nizer couldn't believe the story; he knew Sidney, and Sidney could never do such a thing to his father. But then Nizer urged Baruch to change his mind and take the money. It would be a way of keeping in touch, he advised, and Baruch could save the money for Sidney, who might need it one day. Clinging to his pride, Baruch refused the offer. He soon remarried and began a new chapter in his life, seeming not to look back.

Seven years would pass before father and son resumed contact. Those years included Sidney's military service. In the theater of war, Sidney received no letters from his father.

MAKING THEIR WAY

Sidney and Faye, ages sixteen and nineteen, settled briefly in the Great Northern Hotel on West 57th Street, moving soon to the Edison, a large art deco hotel near Times Square (and still in operation today), which was closer to the theater district and to the Professional Children's School. Midpriced New York residential hotels were, at the time, often the province of writers, composers and actors. S. J.

Perelman described the interior of one such establishment, the Sutton Club Hotel on East 56th Street, where Perelman's brother-in-law Nathanael West once served as the manager:

> *The décor of all the rooms was identical—fireproof early-American, impervious to the whim of guests who might succumb to euphoria, despair, or drunkenness. The furniture was rock maple, the rugs rock wool. In addition to a bureau, a stiff wing chair, and a lamp with a false pewter base and an end table, each chamber contained a bed narrow enough to discourage any thoughts of venery.*

Domestic life, a home, continued to elude them. Sidney lugged along in every move his phonograph and the classical music recordings he had bought with carefully saved coupons when he was younger. Most mornings the siblings went out together to a coffee shop for breakfast, and then Sidney took himself to school—sometimes. His attendance remained spotty, but he got by, preparing for his exams backstage.

By that time the William Morris Agency had signed Sidney. With his father out of the picture, he was making his own professional decisions. Not following his agent's advice to only accept ever-larger roles that would bring more money, he was happy to go from a leading part to a smaller one and take the corresponding decrease in pay. As would be his policy throughout life, his first priority was to keep working. After several major roles, he took a small part in the hit comedy *George Washington Slept Here* by George S. Kaufman and Moss Hart. It turned out to be a consequential choice, both for the warm friendship he established with Moss Hart and for his sister's future.

How did Selwyn James, foreign news editor for the left-wing newspaper *PM*, make his way to Sidney's dressing room? It might have been the work of their mutual friend Ellen Adler, who'd met James in London and found him "terribly impressive." Faye was in Sidney's dressing room that evening, keeping him company as she often did, when Selwyn came to interview the sixteen-year-old actor. Something clicked between Faye and the Englishman, who "looked like Leslie

Howard," with fine features and dusty blond hair, and who shared her political views. Educated at Brighton College, an elite public school founded in 1845, and the London School of Economics, Selwyn James had covered the Spanish Civil War for *The Manchester Guardian* and served as its Moscow correspondent before spending a year writing for the *Rand Daily Mail* in Johannesburg. He had just recently arrived in the United States, where he would rapidly become a radio commentator and lecturer. At *PM* he wrote about the war in Europe while also working on a pathbreaking study, *South of the Congo* (1943), which recorded both the historical and contemporary horrors and injustices of white rule in southern Africa. In his book, James made connections between colonial racism and contemporary fascism, recounting, among many atrocities, the extermination in 1904 of the Herero and Nama peoples in German South West Africa (now Namibia). Among his readers was Hannah Arendt, who would later cite his book in *The Origins of Totalitarianism*.

Selwyn's newspaper coverage of the plight of Jews in Europe led to speaking engagements at Jewish organizations around the country, and in 1941 he intervened with the chief of the British Information Services in New York on behalf of eighty-six Jewish refugees onboard the Spanish ship *Cabo de Hornos* who had been refused entry to Brazil, Argentina and Uruguay. *PM* reported that Selwyn James and others had persuaded the Dutch government-in-exile to allow the refugees to land in Curaçao. Selwyn's effective activism on behalf of Jews imperiled by both fascist and apathetic governments may have contributed to Sidney's decision to enlist in the U.S. Army at age seventeen.

Selwyn and Faye were married in March 1941, and they lived together with Sidney until he left for the service some months later. Sidney was stationed at a signal corps training camp in Florida in October 1942 when Faye gave birth to Leslie, the first of her two daughters. Sidney would call her "Lulie."

When Sidney returned from the war, he remained close to his sister, enjoying boisterous evenings at the Russian Tea Room in midtown Manhattan, where "everybody knew everybody." Faye would hand little Leslie to the maître d' to keep her amused for an hour or two while the grown-ups ate, drank, talked politics and the arts and gossiped about the New York theater world. Faye's second daughter, Debra, was born in 1955. Soon thereafter, Faye's marriage to Selwyn began to fray. According to one friend, the crisis occurred when Selwyn was "caught" in Central Park with another man.

By the time Faye's marriage ended, Sidney was married to his second wife, Gloria Vanderbilt. Leslie (now known as Lisa) recalls brunches and holiday visits at Sidney and Gloria's apartment on Gracie Square: "The Christmas tree—it felt like Rockefeller Center." Lisa recalled the elegance of the powder room off the apartment's entry foyer—her favorite spot in the lavish residence. One birthday, Gloria gave her a precious opal–covered compact. Faye used to say that Gloria was "my rock" after she and Selwyn divorced. But sometime during those years, Sidney broke with his sister.

Although Gloria said she did not know Sidney's sister Faye very well, she had a vivid memory of rushing with Sidney to Bellevue Hospital, where Faye had been hospitalized for a breakdown. Gloria thought it might have been connected to the dissolution of Faye's marriage to Selwyn James, with whom Faye had been deeply in love. If the divorce didn't cause the breakdown, Gloria reflected, "it surely didn't help." Something was, as Gloria put it, "medically wrong" with Faye; in a later phase of her illness she developed an obsession with Leonard Bernstein, becoming convinced that he was in love with her and that they were to be married. Gloria noted that Bernstein "didn't even know who she was."

DETACHMENT

She added an 'e' to her name. Faye. Where's the sense in that?
—SIDNEY LUMET, FROM HIS UNPUBLISHED MEMOIR

Some say the siblings drifted apart; others are convinced that Sidney abruptly turned on his sister and cut her off completely. Faye's daughter Lisa insisted there was no rift between brother and sister: "The family just wasn't close." Apparently, Sidney's capacity to seal off painful memories could extend to sealing off people as well. Old friends comment on his capacity to terminate relationships without looking back. His first wife, Rita Gam, tells of her amazement when one day she ran into Sidney walking with his fourth wife, Piedy, on 57th Street: "He didn't know who I was." Piedy, who had immediately recognized Rita and had prompted Sidney to say hello, also described this encounter as unsettling.

One theory offered by a friend of what went wrong between the brother and sister is that, when he returned from the war, Sidney discovered that Faye had spent all the money he had been sending her over the past four years—every one of his army paychecks. She was married, but she still needed the money—so she spent it.

As a far-too-young breadwinner, Sidney hadn't had time to have a life of his own. It would take years for him to figure out how to be close to people—outside of work—without feeling he would have to give all of himself away, preserving too little for himself.

One could also speculate that as Faye got older and started to show signs of her mother's depressive illness, Sidney experienced it as a form of abandonment. Or perhaps, as Rita Gam observed, Sidney simply could not deal with mental illness. Nothing in Sidney's unpublished memoir indicates a definitive cause for the rupture.

Faye's daughter Lisa described her mother as "a great artistic soul . . . brilliant tipping over into crazy." As an older woman, Faye had relayed to Lisa bits and pieces of her own childhood; she said she had adored her mother, who was, she claimed, an opera singer. Telling me the story, Lisa interjected, "Mummy might have embellished a bit." Faye told her that her mother, Jenny, had had a "breakdown." She had also said they had moved around a lot and spoke proudly about their radio soap opera that she said was "the cat's meow."

Over time Faye's relationships with Sidney's friends faded. For years Faye spent her days at the Art Students League on 57th Street, painting and drawing. Ellen Adler recalled seeing Faye on a crosstown bus in her later years: "Something about her made me realize I couldn't be around her anymore. . . . She seemed a little crazy."

Eventually Faye joined her daughters in Los Angeles after they both moved there. She regularly looked in on Baruch after the death of Julia, his second wife. Nothing in Baruch's memoir, though, suggests a softening of his feelings toward her. Among his papers, there is not a single photo of Faye alone, or of Sidney's mother. There are several of Julia and her pretty daughter, Claire, and many professional shots of Sidney in different roles. Near the end of his manuscript Baruch wrote, "The psychological damadge [sic] done by my daughter Faye to me, to Sidney and to herself never healed. Faye was unhappily married. Sidney who so easily won friends didn't learn how to keep them. His brain became a 'casting office.' He began to see pictures instead of people, including his father."

In the early 1980s when Sidney was working on *Daniel*, he, like the film's main character, was the surviving brother of a troubled sister. He never ceased to wonder "why one might survive and the other not."

6

A SECOND HOME:
THE GROUP THEATRE

*I don't want life reproduced up there on the screen. I want life
created. The difference lies in the degree of the actor's personal
revelation.*

—SIDNEY LUMET, *MAKING MOVIES*

Baruch kept a watchful eye on Sidney as he was emerging from childhood. Or, more accurately, he kept a critical eye on Sidney's acting.
He recognized that Sidney had by now become "the most intelligent
young boy actor for better plays," but he worried that he might not
survive the "in-between age," when the "natural charm of the young
child" begins to wane. In this delicate time of transition, Baruch
felt that Sidney's talent especially needed his skilled ministration.
More and more, Baruch pointed out to Sidney weaknesses in his stage
presence—a clumsy delivery of a line, an unintended tension in a part
of his body, even the unconscious wiggling of a toe. And more and
more, Sidney was becoming less responsive to his tutelage.

As Sidney matured and gained a wider experience of their shared
theater world, his father appeared to him in a new light. Baruch's
bad temper was nothing new, nor his habitual arguments with their
mother, but for Sidney, he was no longer *the* creator of magical
make-believe worlds or *the* authority on Sidney's artistic potential.
And he was no longer his champion, shuttling him to auditions and
bathing him in the warm light of fatherly approval—and narcissistic

gratification. Sidney began to observe Baruch's professional interactions. "My father always had very stormy relationships with other Yiddish actors," Sidney once remarked. He understood that Baruch's career would have gone very differently if, when he first arrived in New York, he had been admitted to the Yiddish Actors Union, where he had applied and auditioned three times and three times been rejected. Something "political"—as Baruch described it—kept getting in the way. In his memoir, Sidney recalled the line from *Death of a Salesman* in connection with his father: "liked, but not *well* liked." Then he reconsidered: "Even the 'liked' may be inaccurate." Throughout his career, Sidney would operate with his colleagues in a very different fashion, drawing far more on the congenial spirit of Harold Clurman, the much-loved cofounder of the Group Theatre.

His father's churlishness and bluster—and pathos—came into sharp focus when Sidney's success on Broadway attracted attention from Hollywood. As Sidney told the story in *By Sidney Lumet*, directed by Nancy Buirski in 2015, "I was appearing in a play [*The Eternal Road*] that had gotten wonderful reviews and I was summoned to meet the great man . . . [Louis B.] Mayer. 'I saw you in the play last night and you were marvelous,'" Sidney mimicked in a commanding voice. Mayer offered him a contract on the spot.

But there was a troublesome backstory to this dream scenario, as both Sidney and his father were aware. MGM was just then renegotiating a contract with their number-one child "property," Freddie Bartholomew, who had starred in such prestige pictures as *David Copperfield* (1935), *Captains Courageous* (1937), and *Kidnapped* (1938). The offer to Sidney was primarily intended to put pressure on Bartholomew. Still, the negotiations proceeded in earnest, and Sidney was offered a seven-year contract with graduated raises to $750 per week, a massive sum at the time—at the peak of his Broadway career he was receiving $150 per week. But Baruch wanted to hold out for more. "My father kept upping it," Sidney recalled. "Whenever they'd offer a new contract he'd agree and then just before signing he would say, um, 'NO, I want some more.'"

The negotiations ended abruptly when Freddie Bartholomew finally signed his contract, and "we were dropped the next day," Sidney explained. Sidney had no lasting regrets about Hollywood. The part he found excruciating was what happened about a year later, one night at the Cafe Royal on Second Avenue where many of the by-then aging Yiddish actors gathered, and where Sidney still sometimes went for a late-night bite with his father.

> *A bunch of men were seated at another table. Remarks started back and forth, and finally he [Baruch] got up, walked to the other table. . . . Mind you, this negotiation had been dead for a year now . . . he pulled Metro's last offer from his pocket and said, "Listen you bastards, we've got this. I can go to Hollywood any time with my son." . . . By now it was a sheer figment of his imagination. I don't know if he imagined it was still on. He couldn't have, because it would've been insane. But the humiliation that I felt for him in having to do that was uh . . .*

Sidney's story broke off in midsentence, but then writing about the event in his memoir, he adds, "The idea that he'd been walking around with that deal memo in his pocket filled me with the first real sympathy I ever felt for him. . . . And with the sympathy for him a feeling of total humiliation for myself rose in my throat because in a way he was including me in whatever lie it was important for him to manufacture for the world." Years later, Baruch claimed it was his wife, Sidney's mother, who had refused the contract.

Meanwhile, things at home continued to deteriorate. His mother's instability, what Sidney would eventually acknowledge as her "madness," was becoming less deniable.

Sidney turned to the world outside for nourishment, literally. He relished his restaurant meals. His favorite eating place was the Horn & Hardart Automat on 47th Street and Eighth Avenue. Later he would pay tribute to it, featuring it in two of his films, *A View from the Bridge* and *The Group*. With its spacious art deco design and decor and its democratizing spirit, it had looked great on film as a setting in many movies of the 1930s and 1940s. In his memoir pages he enthuses about the "magic" of the automat, with a rare injection of sensorial recall: "the way the nickels landed on the marble counter silently, well worn from the coins landing and hands picking them up. The slots with the sandwiches, the door popping open as you turned the brass handle. . . . Milk or hot chocolate came pouring out of the lion or dolphin's mouth as you pulled the handle, always to the brim of the glass or cup, never spilling over." For Sidney, the reliable fare of endlessly replenished sandwiches, pie and strong coffee served on china and available to anyone with a nickel was consolation for the wear and tear of urban life.

Sometimes Sidney's schoolfellows, those who were also performing on Broadway, would gather there for dinner between matinee and evening shows on Wednesdays and Saturdays. Still wearing their theater makeup, laughing and talking shop, "The feeling around the table was familial." Sidney reflected, "I think for most of us it *was* family." He then added, "Even when I ate alone it was more familial than eating at home."

Another favorite place to go when he was by himself was Canton Village on 49th Street and Seventh Avenue, where future restaurateur Pearl Wong was hostess. No matter how crowded the place was, Pearl, as he called her, always gave the boy a booth to himself. Unfamiliar with Chinese cuisine, Sidney always ordered the same meal—wonton soup (which to him was just chicken soup with *knaidels*, or dumplings), breaded veal cutlet, and pistachio ice cream, all for fifty-five cents. One evening Pearl brought him a metal-covered dish, saying, "Try this. It's chicken chow mein. If you don't like it, I'll take it back." He did like it, and from there Pearl encouraged him to try different foods. One day she introduced him to lobster, which gave him his first tremulous taste of *traif*—nonkosher food. Years later, in the mid-1960s, Sidney wisely invested $1,000 when Pearl went out on her own; her hit restaurant became a New York hot spot popular with celebrities. Looking back, Sidney observed that what might have appeared a "pitiful sight, a kid eating alone in Times Square rather than with a family, turned into a tender, nurturing experience provided by a stranger."

Surrogate fathers were also sought and cultivated by Sidney. Performing in the Group Theatre production of *My Heart's in the Highlands*, Sidney found perhaps his most influential paternal figures. In addition to Sidney's costar, the kindhearted Philip Loeb, the play's director, Bobby Lewis, who had cast Sidney in this leading role, took a liking to the precocious, good-looking child, and invited him to attend the Group Theatre's "summer camp," their annual retreat. Escaping his father's increasingly complicated scrutiny and his mother's bottomless unhappiness, Sidney set off for Lake Grove in the beautiful farmland of Long Island, where the Group had taken over a capacious Christian Science children's school for the summer.

Sidney knew exactly how lucky he was to be there. The Group Theatre was considered by many to be the most significant experiment in American theater to date, a permanent paid repertory company that would function as a collective, not driven by producers or by the Broadway star system—or by money. These values and aspirations were formative for Sidney. The Group's summer camps were legendary, then in their ninth, and it would turn out, final year. "Everyone was there except for Lee Strasberg who had already left: Elia Kazan, Bobby Lewis, Sandy Meisner, Stella Adler, Harold Clurman, Lee J. Cobb, Morris Carnovsky," Sidney recalled forty years later. Each of these personages would play a part in Sidney's life and work in one way or another.

The Group Theatre, established in 1931, was the brainchild of Harold Clurman, Lee Strasberg and Cheryl Crawford, who had until then been working at the distinguished Theatre Guild, an organization remembered by playwright Clifford Odets as having "created the American theater . . . put it into long pants." The Guild had "raised the I.Q. of Broadway plays," producing most of the works of Eugene O'Neill, Maxwell Anderson and Philip Barry, "all of the great playwrights of the Twenties. And to get any part with the Theatre Guild was an actor's dream," said Odets. But to Clurman, Strasberg, and Crawford, the Guild lacked a distinctive theatrical style or vision; it had grown stuffy, its audience was too narrow and, most significantly, it was politically out of sync with the times. Of New

York in the early 1930s Harold Clurman wrote, "It seemed as if the color of the city had changed—the afternoons had grown haggard, the nights mournful. We could smell the Depression in the air. It was like a raw wind."

Along with a group of idealistic actors, assorted spouses, and children, the Group, as it would soon be known, set out to establish a new kind of American theater that would for the first time affirm the "dignity," in Elia Kazan's words, "of the feelings, experiences and emotions of the common man." They would perform only new American plays, *political* plays about "the poetry of ordinary life."

Sidney drank in the political passions of the group. Clifford Odets' 1935 play *Waiting for Lefty* was centered on the question faced by taxi drivers of whether to stage a strike. With the news delivered at the end of the play that their leader, Lefty, had been shot dead, one of the drivers, played by Elia Kazan, stepped out into the audience and screamed "STRIKE!" The audience rose up in response, shouting, "Strike, Strike, Strike!" As Clurman remembered the moment, "The audience and the actors had become one." Some historians claim the Group had plants in the audience; nevertheless, the effect was electrifying. Many of the plays produced by the Group stayed alive in Sidney's memory, but Clifford Odets' work would have the most lasting influence; his rendering of ordinary people, with ordinary but poignant aspirations, in such plays as *Awake and Sing!* (1935) would directly inspire Arthur Miller, Paddy Chayefsky and David Mamet, all writers Sidney would later work with.

REVOLUTIONIZING ACTING

The Group's new kind of theater would demand a new kind of acting. They drew on the work of Konstantin Stanislavski and the Moscow Art Theatre. Lee Strasberg had seen this renowned Russian company when they toured the United States in 1923–1924, when he was twenty-two years old. They performed only in Russian, but the power of their technique was clear to Strasberg. Philosopher J. M. Edie writes, "Reacting against the histrionics, the poses, the tricks, and the false emotivity of the traditional dramatic theater in which he was educated, Stanislavsky attempted to make theatrical acting true . . . by bringing . . . real emotions to life on the stage." Many critics also caught on and raved that for the first time they were watching "real people on-stage."

Stanislavski's ideas and the man himself caught the public's imagination, becoming the subject of Sunday articles and popular jokes alike. Like another recent import, psychoanalysis, Stanislavski's ideas tapped into a particularly American appetite for self-discovery, and they offered what appeared to be a procedural how-to for deepening one's creative potential.

Strasberg, future guru to Marilyn Monroe, Montgomery Clift, James Dean, Jane Fonda, Dustin Hoffman and many others, was moved to study under two of Stanislavski's famous adherents, Richard Boleslavsky and Maria Ouspenskaya. This would be the foundation of the Group's method.

At the summer retreat, Group members practiced and built on Stanislavski's exercises to teach performers to "live" onstage, to reveal a character's embodied experience, and to work from the inside out. The acting exercises Stanislavski and his students developed ranged widely. Some were designed to promote concentration and relaxation; yoga was among Stanislavski's practices. Other exercises were devised to quicken the actor's imagination to elaborate biographical details beyond what was supplied in the text, or to cultivate affective and sense memories, working with what Stanislavski called the "magic if," which required the actor to begin by asking, "What would I do if I were in these circumstances?" The "believable truth" he sought to create onstage called for actors not to imitate or pretend but to find their own deeply personal connection to the character, to *emotionally experience* the character's feelings.

For Sidney, who'd had only his father's guidance as an actor, the Group's evolving method was a revelation. Years hence, as a director,

Sidney would place more emphasis on the deep character analysis he learned that summer than on the personally introspective aspect of the work, which in his own experience he found prohibitively painful.

The aura surrounding Stanislavski spilled over onto the Group; from the very beginning the Group received a surprising amount of media attention, especially their summer retreats where attractive young actors worked and lived together in what was perceived as cult-like seclusion. Rumors of harsh, personally invasive teaching methods added to the mystique.

That final Group Theatre summer of 1939 that Sidney attended was a little different from prior years. Bobby Lewis had an idea to raise money for the strapped company with a summer theater school. Twenty full-paying students at $100 tuition apiece could support a ten-week semester; the Group could offer some scholarships and still make a little profit. Sidney would go along for free. He attended Lewis's class for the younger actors. Occasionally Stella Adler and Sanford Meisner would step in and co-teach. There were classes on speech, movement, poetry, and improvisation and lectures on various political and social matters, including a series on current labor disputes delivered by a labor organizer. Of all the fertile theatrical experiences of Sidney's young life, this would be the most transformative. He later noted, "It was very exciting for the young man that I was. It was during this 'summer school' that I really learned the acting trade."

The acting exercises devised by the Group that Sidney encountered that summer were themselves works of ingenuity. Roman Bohnen described some basic exercises in a letter to his father:

> We feel various materials, cotton, silk, etc., and sensitize ourselves to it; then in pantomime, without the material, we learn to suggest to the onlookers by the way our fingers move what kind of material it is. . . . We also learn to pound a nail into a wall so that in pantomime we really feel the weight of the hammer and every detail. Then we do it without the nail and hammer. Then we take an "adjustment," which means

*we assume there is someone asleep in the next room; another
adjustment is to pretend we have hit our finger the time
previous . . . there are a million ways to pound a nail into
a wall.*

In a two-person adjustment exercise, the actors created the following
scene: a man enters a room as a woman cleans. The man says, "Hello.
I didn't expect you to be here. How have you been? Would you like
to do something? How about taking a walk?" The actors then under-
take these "adjustments":

1. The couple is engaged to be married. The man has just
   learned that he was fired that day.
2. The couple is engaged; the man has just received a raise.
3. The couple was engaged to be married sometime in the past.
   The man was sent to prison and the woman moved to another
   town to avoid him.

They also practiced communication exercises, like taking a scene
from a given play and attempting to make it understood without speaking the words of the text, using only gibberish sounds and fluctuat-
ing tones. Maria Ouspenskaya's sense memory exercises were adapted
by the Group. She instructed students to listen to imaginary sounds,
such as a mouse scratching in the corner, a foghorn, the approach of
a subway train; or to feel a localized pain in your stomach, then in
a tooth, then in your hand; or, while seated in a circle, to pass from
person to person an imaginary pigeon with an injured wing, and then
to pass an imaginary pot of hot tea.

Ouspenskaya's "memory of feeling" exercises included simply taking yourself under observation and discovering the mood or emotion
you were currently in. Another was to bring a special garment to
class, to reanimate the event for which you wore it and the past emotion associated with the event. Designed to develop spontaneity over
artifice, such improvisatory work built confidence as well as skills.

Strategies for building confidence resonated deeply with Sidney. A crucial lesson of that summer was Harold Clurman's rule "to let your actors feel your confidence in them." Authority doesn't come from shouting; rather, "Authority comes from the confidence you arouse in people." Sidney's exposure to the deep, introspective work of the Method helped him throughout his career to recognize and respect the profound vulnerability actors experience. "I was an actor myself," Sidney often commented. "The process of acting is extremely painful. I know that doesn't sound logical to most people, but all good work is self-revelation. . . . If I can help them to feel any more secure, and any more unafraid of releasing whatever part of themselves they have to, I understand that I can help them that way. They feel that. I don't even have to articulate it." Actors who worked under Sidney's direction invariably expressed their gratitude for the confidence Sidney instilled in them that strengthened and sometimes transformed their work.

What eventually would be as important to Sidney as these insights into acting was the collaborative spirit of the Group, including in their approach to a theater piece. Group actor Ruth Nelson recalls how it worked: "No one knew what part they were going to play," the idea being that this would allow the actors to focus on the whole piece, not just their part. "Then Harold [Clurman] would discuss the spine of the play, then the spine of each character." For Clurman, the "spine" meant "the progress of the play's inner action: how each segment and scene reveals the development of the characters' and the play's continuing action so that the pattern of the play as a whole becomes evident." Years later, Sidney would follow this pattern. His actors would know what role was theirs during rehearsals, but he adhered in other ways to this rehearsal mode, specifically in discussing the spine of the film's story and the arc of each of the characters. "Because I came from the theater—it's where I start—[I make my] dramatic selection in advance: this piece is about this," Sidney observed of his own process. "You don't do the piece and discover what it's about . . . you do it in advance." Here Sidney distinguished himself from movie directors who forego rehearsals and choose to "find" the film in the editing process, or through multiple takes, providing options to think the scene through in the editing room. In contrast was Sidney's relatively unusual procedure of two to four weeks of rehearsals, held in a rehearsal room, usually located on the Lower East Side of Manhattan. "Rehearsals are very much like a play, breaking down the characters, breaking down the scenes, talking through it," Sidney explained. Given that most films are shot out of sequence, the rehearsals allowed actors to place themselves in a scene with the full confidence that they knew precisely where they were in the arc of the story.

SUMMER'S END

While most members remember the Group's final summer of 1939 as one of contention and heated disputes, Sidney's recollections are warm and fond. He wasn't aware of the strife or that things were falling apart. What he experienced was a dedicated company of artists "who took their work, but never themselves, utterly seriously." They were, he recalled, "some of the funniest people in the world."

Sidney was too young to have run into one of the inciting issues at the camp, although he would later on. Troubling the waters was the intrusive psychological probing of the actors by some of the directors; some felt their judgments bordered on cruelty. Clifford Odets recalled:

> Very early, and perhaps wrongly, the Group Theatre directors began to call us in, one by one, and—I'd almost forgotten this— make rather keen, but perhaps harmful, analyses of each person's personality, their character defects, what they had to work on, where their problems lay. They wanted to create the "new theater man." But—not that they were incorrect—I think this was done a little carelessly. Emotionally and psychologically some of these things were quite damaging.

This kind of scrutiny and appraisal to heighten a performance was originally associated with Strasberg and Kazan, and over time it contributed to deep divisions. Additionally, Strasberg's affective memory exercises were highly prescriptive: he required, for example, individual actors to privately relive a memory of a time they received extremely bad news. "Close your eyes and begin to recall the room you were in, the time of day, the voice of the person who brought you the message, the fullest possible sensory history of that event." Stella Adler was the most vocal opponent of this practice: "Drawing on the emotions I experienced—for example, when my mother died—to create a role is sick and schizophrenic. If that is acting, I don't want to do it."

The tensions that developed in the early days of the Group Theatre were still very much at play as, years later, Sidney was beginning to work as a director. Sidney would eschew any techniques he found to be manipulative, despite his awareness that, especially in the hands of Kazan, they could produce thrilling effects. For Kazan, a director was someone who, as he put it, trains himself to be "a hypnotist who works with the unconscious to achieve his ends."

Burtt Harris worked with both Sidney and Kazan as assistant director. In his view, Sidney was analytical—"He could make actors think"—while Kazan made actors, "even Deborah Kerr," *feel*. Kazan was, Burtt explained, "a wonderful manipulator, to make great work. It wasn't to reduce anybody." Sidney wasn't interested in "triggering emotion." He might instead suggest an action, "to twist your body on a certain line," in order to help an actor locate an emotion.

Sidney shared an example of this in his book *Making Movies*, regarding a scene in *Network* (1976). William Holden was having trouble with an intensely vulnerable speech to Faye Dunaway. Sidney realized that Holden wasn't looking into Dunaway's eyes. "He looked at her eyebrows, her hair, her lips, but not her eyes," Sidney writes. After a dreary first take, Sidney asked him to try again, but this time looking nowhere else but directly into Dunaway's eyes. It worked. "The emotion came pouring out of him. . . . Whatever he'd been avoiding could no longer be denied." Sidney goes on to note that, unlike some directors, he always respected the actor's right to privacy, and so he never queried Holden about the emotions he had been trying to avoid.

Creating a collaborative atmosphere for the work, plenty of rehearsal time for identifying the spine of a story and enthusiastic support for his actors were some of the lessons Sidney learned from working with the Group. These contributed to Sidney's reputation as an "actor's director" with whom actors were always eager to work, and played a part in fostering performances that earned his actors eighteen Oscar nominations over the years.

That said, Ethan Hawke did share a story that suggests that by the time of his last film, at age eighty-three, Sidney had resorted to a bit of actor-handling and director chicanery in directing Philip Seymour Hoffman and Hawke, who were playing brothers in this film. Ethan Hawke recounted what he playfully described as Sidney's Machiavellian machinations:

> *Every day on the set Sidney would take me aside and say, "I watched the dailies last night. Philip is f—ing unbelievable. . . . Not since Marlon Brando . . . I remember directing* The Fugitive Kind *with Marlon Brando, and watching Phil I got that same buzz." When we wrapped I gave Phil a big hug and said, "It's been great working with you. I'm so glad it's over because if I've got to hear Sidney tell me how great you are one more time, I'm gonna kill myself." And Phil says, "Does he say I'm like Marlon Brando?" I said, "Yeah." "He says that about you!" The guy'd been playing us both the whole time—got us both like keyed up. Every time Phil came to set I'm like—"He's not like Marlon Brando. I'm* like *Marlon Brando."*

FIRST LOVE

Sidney's rose-colored recollections of the summer of 1939 may have owed something to the fact that he was falling in love for the first time. His first girlfriend, Ellen Adler, was the only child of resident diva Stella Adler and grandchild of the great and beloved Yiddish actors Jacob and Sara Adler. In her early teens, Ellen was cosmopolitan, intellectually curious, and perfectly lovely. (Author Terry Southern would later dub her "the most beautiful girl in Paris.") She had been sent off to boarding school at a very young age; had lived abroad in Paris and London with her mother; and on returning to New York, had attended the small progressive private City and Country School in Greenwich Village, where Pete Seeger taught music, Jackson Pollock was the janitor, and *Eloise* illustrator Hilary Knight was a fellow student. This worldly bohemian girl must have been quite a revelation to Sidney.

It began as a summer-camp romance—"Sidney was still wearing short pants," she said—but it continued until Sidney enlisted in the spring of 1942. "We were sweethearts. It was fun," Ellen reminisced. "What did we do? We went to the movies. I remember we liked a restaurant that served Danish food." Ellen became close friends with Sidney's sister Faye. The three of them palled around. Ellen recalled that Faye took her to see the film *One Third of a Nation*, and when they got in their seats Faye covered Ellen's face with a handkerchief, pulling it away to surprise her when Sidney appeared on-screen. Ellen puzzled over the fact that Sidney didn't much like her mother, Stella—perhaps, she hypothesized, because "she was fancy." And she reflected that, although he was a good actor, she suspected he hadn't *liked* acting much. "He had to be in the theater," she allowed; "he didn't know anything else."

Sidney and Ellen remained friends throughout Sidney's life. "Over the years when we got together," Ellen recalled, "we would sing some of the four hundred leftist songs we knew from those days. Here's one: 'One, two, three, pioneers are we / Working for the working class against the bourgeoisies / Four, five, six, little Bolsheviks . . .'" Sidney's daughter, Amy, "hated it when we got started with those songs." Amy's response is noteworthy, given that she later defected from her family and became an ardent Republican.

Sidney and Ellen's youthful romance ultimately dissolved when Ellen fell hard for her mother's most famous and devoted student, Marlon Brando. She said, "I did tell Marlon when I first met him that I had a boyfriend—Sidney."

As Ellen remembered it, Bobby Lewis "really was Sidney's mentor."

Lewis was an intense, moody and, some say, "impossible" man. As Ellen described him, "Bobby was mean—very fun—but mean." His tight connection to Sidney made it all the more painful when, almost ten years later, soon after the creation of the Actors Studio, Lewis was responsible for disinviting Sidney, or "pruning him" out of the Studio's first class.

Among Sidney's strongest memories of that summer with the Group was the moment on August 23, 1939, when news arrived of the Treaty of Nonaggression between Nazi Germany and the Soviet Union. The adults, Sidney recalled, had been rehearsing Chekhov's *The Three Sisters* under Clurman's direction, with Stella Adler playing Masha and Luther Adler playing Chebutykin in a production that never came to fruition. Sidney heard a commotion and stepped onto the dining room porch to see Clifford Odets looking shocked, standing stock still, "tears rolling down his face."

Harold Clurman contended, though, that the Group members weren't really "political animals." As he saw it, "they were all sentimentalists." Whether they were political animals or not, after World War II most of the Group Theatre members were investigated by the House Un-American Activities Committee. Elia Kazan, Clifford Odets and Lee J. Cobb testified and offered up names of members of left-wing organizations. Those who refused to name names, including Stella Adler and John Garfield, were blacklisted.

By the end of Sidney's magic summer of 1939, the Group Theatre, what Clurman had called "a theater of hope in a hopeless time," was coming to an end. It had lost its cohesiveness, fractured by financial problems, disputes about the Method, defections to Hollywood and plenty of plain old personality conflicts. But despite its relatively short nine years, the Group Theatre had an impact on American acting that continues to be felt. Many of its members became renowned acting teachers and directors, passing on the spirit and principles that had originally drawn them together. In 1947, the Actors Studio would be the first of several major acting schools to emerge from the Group, headed by Bobby Lewis, Elia Kazan, Cheryl Crawford and, later, Lee Strasberg.

Sidney's summer with the Group Theatre far exceeded his previous experiences of the temporary community created by theater work. The Group was more like a family, one whose squabbles barely registered on the boy, accustomed as he was to harsher registers of contention. In Yiddish theater, on Broadway, and on radio, he'd found escape, solace, and inspiration, but among these driven and introspective artist-intellectuals with whom he shared political passions and, with most, an ethnic and cultural background, he'd found a new orientation, a way to be in the world.

When Sidney returned to the city from camp, things at home had taken an unexpected turn. In his memoir pages Sidney writes, "The last time I saw [my mother] smile was when she told Faye and me that she was pregnant. Faye asked her if she was gaining weight. Her smile appeared gently. '*Ich shvin zack.*' (I'm pregnant). We were both very pleased, I think. It's hard to tell since what happened later was so complicated."

7

WHAT THE CAMERA SEES

Sidney in his only major movie role, in *One Third of a Nation*. He stares in horror as he hallucinates that the tenement he lives in is literally taunting him.

Almost exactly a year after Sidney's first and last performance in a movie, a leading role in the 1939 tenement drama, *One Third of a Nation*, his mother died in childbirth, and with her the baby girl. This was in February 1940, when Sidney was fifteen years old. Sidney played Joey, a Lower East Side slum kid. The story is set on the very streets Sidney knew from his early childhood.

BREAKING INTO AND OUT OF THE MOVIES

One Third of a Nation was adapted from the Federal Theatre Project's most successful Living Newspaper production, a theatrical agit-prop written by Arthur Arent on the topic of slum housing. The published play includes footnotes citing sources, statistics, and indications of which characters are "fictional," since many of the actors played historical and living people, delivering their actual speeches. Among the then-current politicians portrayed are Mayor Fiorello La Guardia, Senator Robert F. Wagner and some of the Republican senators who opposed the Wagner-Steagall Housing Act, the first federal effort to address dangerous urban living conditions. The play took its title from Franklin Delano Roosevelt's second inaugural address:

> *I see millions whose daily lives in city and on farm continue under conditions labeled indecent by a so-called polite society half a century ago. I see millions denied education, recreation, and the opportunity to better their lot and the lot of their children. . . . I see one-third of a nation ill-housed, ill-clad, ill-nourished.*

In the theatrical version, the curtain rose on a night scene of crumbling and tangled old-law tenements, apartment houses constructed before 1901, all of which were exempted from the health and safety laws that were being introduced in the early decades of the twentieth century. Old-law tenements were the cheapest housing to be had in New York, and, in Mayor La Guardia's words, they were "rotten antiquated rat holes." Reviled as breeders of crime and disease, they were most notorious for being firetraps.

The play's action begins with a little girl fetching water from a tap in the cellar and then lugging the heavy bucket up the stairs, as was standard in these apartments that had no running water—or toilets, only outhouses in the backyard. Within minutes the audience detects smoke filtering up from the cellar, and, as the fire begins to rage, the tenants scramble to wake neighbors and grab possessions. As a crowd gathers outside the building, a fireman works a searchlight, revealing a man hanging perilously from a broken fire escape. Cries from the crowd of "Look! Look!" compete with screaming sirens and clanging bells. Just as the man is about to fall, the stage goes black.

The opening scene of the original Federal Theatre Project's stage version of *One Third of a Nation. (Federal Theatre Project Collection, Music Division, Library of Congress)*

The following scene opens at an investigative hearing into the cause of the fire. Before the action begins, a loudspeaker, "the voice of the Living Newspaper" that is heard throughout the play, announces details of the real fire on which this scene is based: February 19, 1924, at 397 Madison Street on the Lower East Side, when "thirteen persons lost their lives . . . four men, two women, and seven children."

In the film adaptation by Oliver H. P. Garrett, whose credits include the melodramas *Night Nurse* (1931), *The Story of Temple Drake* (1933) and *Manhattan Melodrama* (1934), the tenement fire remains central to the story, and portions of the investigation are also preserved. We find the same weary commissioner and inspectors from the Fire Department, the Building Department and the Tenement House Department. In both the play and the film, these public servants pass the buck to another bureaucratic entity. Asked by the commissioner if the tenement was a firetrap, the housing inspector replies, "If that building is a firetrap, then so is every old-law tenement in New York City; and there are 67,000 of them." He goes on to explain that the city hasn't got the manpower to keep track of the conditions in these decrepit buildings. Dismally, the commissioner concludes the hearing: "According to your testimony there were no violations, and all the laws were scrupulously upheld," which was word for word the judgment of the real commission that investigated the Madison Street fire.

The theatrical version of *One Third of a Nation* traces the history of slum housing from New York City's earliest days. The historical background begins with a landlord remarking to a slum tenant:

> *If you can only afford to pay $24 a month you'll have to live in my house or one just like it—and you cannot blame me. You'll have to go back into history and blame whatever it was that made New York City real estate the soundest and most profitable speculation on the face of the earth.*

Beginning in 1705 with an English governor's land grant of 63 acres to Trinity Church, the theater piece instructs us that over time the church became one of the city's most egregious slumlords. We are presented with a lesson in Manhattan's population growth and private investment in land, and the decades of failed efforts by legislators, the courts, and private citizens to address dangerous slum conditions. Sanitary reforms go unenforced. Court battles by tenant groups fail. And when progressives in the legislature finally attempt to allot money to the construction of public housing, their efforts are met with Republican opposition. The play's final scene presents a rousing appeal to the audience to fight against a hundred years of inertia and demand more public housing. And the show concludes with a grim "or else," a reprise of the opening scene of a deadly tenement fire.

The film adaptation is not nearly as didactic or politically explicit as the play, but it nevertheless lands a punch. Hollywood-style, the film introduces a romantic plot in which a handsome, well-meaning millionaire named Peter Cortlant (played by Group Theatre actor Leif Erickson) takes a fancy to the spirited tenement-dwelling Mary Rogers, the older sister of Sidney's character, Joey. Unbeknown to Mr. Cortlant, his old-money family owns the slum where Joey and his family live. Mary (played by Sylvia Sidney), struggles to be true to her class, and to resist the millionaire's charms. Notably, the film refuses the attractive couple—the tenement girl and the millionaire—a happily-ever-after. The film's message is unambiguous: there can be no real love match between rich and poor, a point that Mary's class-conscious and less picture-perfect boyfriend, Sam, states explicitly. Mary will instead marry Sam, toward whom, again contra Hollywood, she feels no romantic attraction. In place of romance, the couple share values and modest, *realistic* aspirations.

Although distributed by Paramount Pictures, *One Third of a Nation* was independently produced on a budget of $200,000 by a few wealthy investors, including Broadway producer and songwriter Harold Orlob, who had purchased the screen rights for $6,000. In the 1930s, few movies were independently produced outside the studio system. A significant exception was the genre of "race films," produced by black filmmakers with all-black casts for segregated black audiences. Famed producer-director Oscar Micheaux, whose studio was in Chicago, worked within standard Hollywood genres such as westerns and gangster films, mostly steering clear of issues of social and racial injustice or depictions of poverty. A smaller, left-leaning industry in New York was producing less conventional stories on modest budgets, pointedly rejecting Hollywood glamour and glitz and relying on Broadway talent. But while resisting Hollywood's market control and its enforcement of status quo social messages, these moviemakers still had to rely on big studios like Paramount for distribution, as most movie theaters at the time were studio-owned.

A handful of New York–made movies were among the most politically radical feature films ever released by a major American studio. In one such project, photographer Paul Strand paired up with Elia Kazan to make an anti-fascist film, *The Spanish Earth*, narrated by Ernest Hemingway. Sidney was a part of another production by this group, the documentary *The 400 Million*, in which he narrates an account of the Japanese invasion of China, the theater of war where Sidney would soon find himself. These New York–made films offered a model Sidney would one day follow—in his own way.

One Third of a Nation was one of the final two features made in

New York before the war. The other, *Back Door to Heaven*, was also a tragic slum story. *One Third of a Nation*'s director, Dudley Murphy, is now most well known for the classic 1924 Dadaist film *Ballet mécanique*, made with Fernand Léger and Man Ray, but he also directed Bessie Smith in the short *St. Louis Blues*, and Paul Robeson in *The Emperor Jones*.

For *One Third of a Nation*, Murphy had hoped to emphasize the story's gritty realism by filming on location on the Lower East Side, but the film's backers opposed the plan. Instead, an entire tenement block was built on the Astoria Studios back lot. In the original cut, the film opened with a newsreel clip of Roosevelt delivering the "one-third of a nation" portion of his second inaugural address, but again the backers objected to this "New Deal propaganda." Still, the company asserted its independence in small but noted violations of the Motion Picture Production Code, as when one tenant in the building, Myrtle, is unambiguously shown as a prostitute conducting business out of her apartment. The movie also contains dialogue that would have been too provocative for a studio film in 1939, the year that *Gone with the Wind* was released, winning the Oscar for Best Picture. One example: at the hearing investigating the fire, Mary Rogers reacts when her love interest, the millionaire slum owner, offers smug answers to the questions put to him by the commissioner. She bursts forth:

> *Breeding, that's pretty important to you. You're pretty proud*
> *of your own breeding. . . . You come from one of our oldest and*
> *finest families but your lousy tenements breed criminals and sick*
> *people, and you don't know what kind of women—that's where*
> *some of your rent comes from Mr. Cortlant, women like that.*
> *If you don't believe me, come down and see for yourself. Stop off*
> *sometime on your way to your yacht in the East River. Use your*
> *eyes and your ears and especially your nose.*

Pushing limits further, during the tenement fire scene a burning body is seen falling from the building, and the camera sweeps over several bodies lying on the sidewalk, lined up in a row. Later in the film the camera takes in the piles of garbage that clutter the tenement hallway, focusing in on swarms of cockroaches. Such graphic images were not created on Hollywood soundstages. *The New York Times* offered a mild commendation, calling the film "an interestingly presented editorial for slum clearance."

A detail of tenement life that resonated with Sidney's own story appears in both the play and the film, although differently dramatized. The play presents a vignette to demonstrate how the slums foment violence and cruelty: one tenement boy bullies another, mocking him for sharing a bed with his sister. When the bully suggests that the boy must get a "feel" in once in a while, and that he'd like to take the boy's place in bed with his sister, they begin to brawl. In the film this topic is echoed when Joey's sister excitedly explains to him that Mr. Cortlant, her millionaire friend, is going to "give this whole block to the city, and they'll knock these old buildings down," to replace them, she enthuses, with houses "that have air and sunlight and playgrounds." Joey's only response is, "And I won't have to sleep with you no more?" Sidney did sleep in a bed with his sister, Faye, until he was about eleven and she was fourteen or fifteen.

When the film begins, we hear Joey, Sidney's character, shouting animatedly in a game of kick-the-can, a combination of tag and hide-and-seek. Joey undergoes a major transformation in the course of the story when a tenement fire breaks out. He hangs from a broken fire escape, gripping his roller skates. In the movie, unlike the play, we see his fall. His life is saved, but he is left crippled, only able to tentatively maneuver with crutches. Once a popular, lively child, he is isolated by his infirmity and grows increasingly withdrawn. He begins to exhibit an obsessive hatred of the tenement building where the fire occurred and where he still lives with his older sister and his out-of-work immigrant parents. Indeed, he begins to go mad. The boy's dread of the decaying tenement gives rise to the film's most surprising element: when alone at night, Joey heaves threats at the hated structure, and the building answers him back. The tenement speaks in a jeering voice, boasting to the half-mad boy of its malignant history. Scenes unfold before him, and us, from the building's past, of families undone by cholera, tuberculosis, poverty, and squalor.

Ultimately Joey sets fire to and destroys the structure once and for all, losing his life in the process. His sacrifice becomes the catalyst for slum clearance and the construction of a city-funded housing project. The film ends with actual documentary footage of tenement houses being torn down, followed by a shot of neat, newly constructed housing units, on which, in a final image, Joey's face is superimposed. The new units are likely the Vladeck Houses, put up in 1939, which still stand at Corlears Hook on the Lower East Side.

Most of the movie was filmed at Astoria Studios in Queens in the summer of 1938. For convenience, Sidney and his father, who had a small role in the film, temporarily took up residence near the studio. The tenement-fire scenes, however, were shot on location. "It was the first time that the NYC Fire Department had ever cooperated officially in the making of a film," director Dudley Murphy explained. "Mayor La Guardia was greatly interested in the subject."

Sidney's father had one scene in the film, playing Mr. Rosen, who loses his wife and children in the fire and is called to testify at the hearing. Baruch's thick Polish accent lent authenticity to the scene, but he played the role like a theater actor, too big for the camera.

Sidney was also unsure how to respond to the camera. Everything he knew about acting was based on his stage and radio experience. He was still a year away from his training at the Group Theatre summer camp, which likely would have led to a more internal, nuanced performance, conveying more through his eyes and less through his facial expressions and body gestures. Years later he reflected bitterly that the director, Dudley Murphy, "knew nothing about working with actors."

Making matters worse for Sidney on the set, the film's star, Sylvia Sidney, who played his protective older sister, was "terrible" to him: "When it was time for my close-up, the director said, 'Sylvia, please give him the lines, instead of the script girl.'" She so resented feeding lines to a child that she sat rigidly and unresponsively, "clicking her knitting needles. She was a great knitter," Sidney recalled. "Not one look at me, just mumbling." Sylvia Sidney, then married to Luther Adler, Ellen Adler's uncle, was famous for playing sympathetic urban working girls in progressive films such as *Street Scene* (1931), *Fury* (1936) and *Dead End* (1937), a film adaptation of Sidney's first Broadway show. In real life she turned out to be neither progressive nor sympathetic.

When Sidney was asked years later why he had not pursued a career as a movie actor, his go-to explanation was that, although he'd been "a pretty good-looking kid," as he put it, he "hadn't grown up to be Clark Gable," and didn't want to make a career of "being the little ethnic guy" who gets rescued by the movie's star. Many factors contributed to his move away from acting, but one of them was surely how he felt about his performance in *One Third of a Nation*. "I *hated* acting in the movies. . . . That glass has a psychic and spiritual thing about it. The third eye. It's going to see something you don't want seen."

Making the film had been "a lousy experience," but it's hard to say when exactly he started feeling spooked about what the camera had detected. Over time, this film and seeing himself on the screen at that age may very well have become linked in Sidney's mind with the worst trauma of his youth, the deaths of his mother and baby sister almost exactly a year after the film was released. In the roller-coaster ride that was Sidney's life, the excitement and scrutiny that attended the opening of the film became in some way conflated with the tragedy that followed.

Sidney was partnered with his father for the filming of *One Third of a Nation*, prompting the two to move temporarily away from his mother and sister. The excitement he shared with his narcissistic, philandering father at their appearance in the movie likely came to feel like collusion. One of the things that the movie camera—that third eye—had seen was Sidney's enthusiasm for what he was doing; it is palpable to the viewer. What's more, in the summer of 1939, shortly after the film was released, Sidney, age fifteen, had become involved with his first girlfriend, Ellen Adler. His youthful buoyancy would likely have become associated with the weight of guilt and remorse he felt about his mother's death. Falling in love for the first time, performing, going to school (and supporting the family), he hadn't devoted much of himself to his needy, unstable mother in the months preceding her death. His performance in the movie seemed to document his filial neglect.

While he found the movie camera unnerving, acting onstage was second nature to him, and he continued to work steadily in the theater. His next show, the comedy *George Washington Slept Here* by George S. Kaufman and Moss Hart, was a big hit. It was followed by a short-lived succès d'estime by

Sidney posing in his role as the young Jesus in Maxwell Anderson's *Journey to Jerusalem* (1940). *(2018 / Alamy Stock Photo)*

Maxwell Anderson, *Journey to Jerusalem,* an invented tale based on a fragment from the Gospel of Luke about the child Jesus traveling to Jerusalem with his parents for the feast of the Passover. Sidney played Jesus, although his character was renamed Jeshua because at that time it was technically not legal in the state of New York, based on an obscure statute, to mention Christ's name on stage. Playing Jesus's mother, actress Arlene Francis complained that whenever she embraced her "son" on stage, she couldn't help but detect that Sidney had an erection.

His final show, *Brooklyn, USA,* concerned the efforts of a group of Brooklyn longshoremen to thwart a fifth columnist, the owner of a shipping company committed to aiding the Nazis. Warner Bros. was eyeing the play, but it was never picked up because it was deemed too radical in its representation of "national disorder, disloyalty and dissension." Further, it highlighted the failure of the forces of law and order and suggested the existence of "class struggle" in America— altogether an appropriate show to precede Sidney's induction into the army. All in all, Sidney appeared in fourteen Broadway productions before he enlisted in early 1943.

Many factors contributed to Sidney's turn—years later—to directing. His hatred of acting in front of a camera was not a matter of vanity; Sidney was not a vain man. His dislike of the camera convinced him that he could "never be a really good screen actor." Yet his negative feeling about the camera also gave him one of his greatest assets as a director: "I've understood all about actors ever since." Of the actors he directed, Sidney often said, "That's *them* up there," and "the process of self-revelation is extremely painful." As a director he sought always to help his actors feel more secure, to make them "unafraid of releasing whatever part of themselves they need to."

8

GI JEW: EATING HAM
FOR UNCLE SAM

In outline, Sidney's war years were not so bad. He was well trained in a highly technical field, and he was assigned to teach at a secret military camp in Florida before being deployed to northern India. He never saw combat. But his wartime experiences left their scars. Nothing in his hard upbringing prepared him for the brutality and moral injuries of the army. A central theme in his work in later years would be the brutality of men—often in uniform—in their institutionalized treatment of one another.

Sidney didn't like to talk about his nearly six years in the military. His daughter Jenny reflected that she had never heard him talk about any of it; nor had his first wife, Rita Gam, whom he married not long after returning from the war. Unaware of his nightmares, she thought that his time in the service had "passed through him, like everything else." It's a conventional truth that men of his generation kept silent or shared their memories only among themselves; Sidney kept no friendships from his nearly five years in the Army Signal Corps. Even with friends who had also served overseas, like Walter Bernstein, for example, no stories were shared. It was only toward the end of his life that he shared a few stories, and all of them were dark. In his unpublished memoir he gave voice to some of the pain he'd carried through the decades.

Early in those pages Sidney contemplates his fascination with the numbers 7, 2, and 1. "It occurred to me, one day, that I had enlisted in the Army at 17 and gotten out at 21." He reflects: "The Army. The source of a recurring dream for over 40 years." The dreams varied as to specific circumstances, but they always followed a single pattern: "I'd be notified I had to report for duty by midnight of a certain date. My protest was always the same, changing only by the length of time the dream had been recurring: 'I've served already.' 'I'm over 40.' 'I'm past 50.' 'I'm over 60. It can't happen to me.' But there I'd be—midnight approaching, and reporting for duty. And I would awaken, tears on my cheek, the pillow also wet, and a deep blue day ahead of me."

It wasn't the war but the army that Sidney found crushing, a cauldron of brutality, bigotry, and boneheadedness. What could be further from the world of sensitive and idealistic artists and intellectuals he'd left behind? Just prior to enlisting he'd been taking courses in French literature at Columbia's extension school. Like so many, he'd signed up with a full heart. The army taught him technical skills he would value throughout his career, but it tore the idealism and youthful zeal out of him, and he suffered a disappointment in himself—perhaps even, for a time, a loss of self.

SIGNING UP

As soon as the United States entered the war, Sidney scrambled to find a way to enlist. He was seventeen years old, a year too young for the army. He found his way to a navy recruiting station where boys were accepted before their eighteenth birthday. He was promptly turned down because of his poor eyesight. He then learned that a new radar training program in the Army Signal Corps was looking for recruits and would take boys at age seventeen, though "not into the army," Sidney explained. "You would still be a civilian. They would train you for six months—at the end of the six months, when you were 18, you went into Basic Training, then into the Signal Corps as a radar repairman." To qualify, he was required to score at least 110 on the Army General Classification Test, the same as officer candidates. The high standards led to a low acceptance rate; Sidney sailed through.

Sidney was soon stationed at Camp Murphy, a top secret school located in southeast Florida, just north of Palm Beach. Beginning in June 1942, radar training in the United States took place at this five-mile-long encampment, which was covered in dense forest and invisible from the air. Designed to be unrecognizable as a military site, its roads crisscrossed the base in a haphazard pattern rather than in the grid typical of military facilities. The buildings, almost a thousand of them, were painted a dull green for camouflage and scattered on the grounds in a nonuniform pattern. Secrecy and urgency ruled; classes were held around the clock for some ten thousand men between 1942 and 1944, with Sidney among them.

"The science courses were particularly intense," Sidney recalled, "cramming the equivalent of a Bachelor of Science degree into 6 months. It consisted of math, physics, electronics and, believe it or not, machine shop," because "the antennas on some of the radars were huge, perhaps 20 to 30 feet across and had to spin at a fairly rapid rate. The whole structure was metal. If anything happened in the field, we might have to repair these giant parts ourselves. So we had to learn to operate lathes, acetylene torches, soldering, etc." Seeing himself with an acetylene torch repairing a gigantic moving machine struck him as so unlikely as to be comical. He prided himself on his technical know-how, and was always determined to understand how machines work, but he never saw himself as the hands-on guy.

Radar was new, or new to warfare. During the 1930s the British built Chain Home, a series of radar stations along their eastern and southern coastlines designed to provide early warning of German air attacks. In 1940 Chain Home would prove essential to the defeat of the Luftwaffe in the Battle of Britain. According to historians, the continuing development of radar was, for Britain and the United States, the central technological project of the war, more important even than nuclear weapons or code breaking, and radar repairmen were the elite of the Signal Corps. "He's a *radar* man" was the caption under a cartoon depicting an enlisted man strutting between two high-ranking officers.

Sidney was surprised by how much he enjoyed learning science, a neglected subject in his education up till then, and how good he was at it. He would be promoted to radar instructor upon completion of the course, but first he had to complete basic training. He was sent to Fort Monmouth in New Jersey, a contrast to attending classes as part of an elite program next door to Palm Beach.

BASIC TRAINING

His life thus far had been one of extremes—poverty and stardom, misery at home and camaraderie and nourishment in the theater—but nothing had prepared him for boot camp. If Sidney's artistic milieu had been devoted to aesthetic cultivation, self-expression, idealistic political views, collaboration and esprit de corps, boot camp was its perfect antipode. Sidney writes about reporting for duty in December 1942:

> *A group of us had been driven by bus to a camp in Red Bank, New Jersey. It was one of those cold December nights when your knuckles hurt if they brush against anything. We arrived close to midnight to face an infuriated staff sergeant. We were the last group in that day and had kept him and the Quartermaster people from getting off early. He kept thrusting his head in front of each of us and screaming, "Fuckhead! Faggot!" He stopped in front of me, his head thrust forward, as if he were literally going to bite my head off. "What kind of fucking start is that—showing up at ten to twelve!" I put on my most conciliatory smile. "Well, Sergeant, it's close to the holidays—I wanted to spend time with my family." "Spend time with this, you faggot cocksucker" he said, grabbing his crotch. "What holiday? You're a Hebe."*

Although it was—and still is—routine for new recruits to be met with taunts and insults, an initiation to military authority, Sidney could not help taking it personally. He was again a vulnerable child, without safe haven; his charm and intelligence could mitigate nothing.

He understood the rationale behind the mindless, repetitive drills, and why everyone had to look the same and sleep in identical beds. He probably also understood the intentionally demeaning aspects of boot camp, but he found them harder to tolerate. He writes in his memoir about his mystification that the toilets had no stalls, no dividers separating one from the next. Its purpose, he concluded, was "to destroy any sense that you're an individual." For Sidney, this strategic degradation tore at his self-worth. Even more frightening to him was that, as he writes in his memoir, the army encouraged "mob mentality."

As his description of his arrival at Fort Monmouth—the origin of his decades of nightmares—continues, it grows more dreamlike, written in the present tense:

> We're herded into a line and marched out. Rain and sleet have begun to fall. My foot slips off the duckboard walkway as we head for another building. Water is oozing into my civilian shoes. The cold rain hits my neck and runs down my back. We enter a hut. Two privates and a corporal are behind a long counter. They throw each of us two blankets and a pillow as we pass. Out into the night again and we are walking toward a barrack. This time there are not duckboards and my feet are sinking into the cold wet mud. I stumble up three steps and into the warmth of a barrack. Twenty upper and lower cots run down each side of the room. The heat is welcome but the smell is awful; coal gives off a sweet acrid odor unlike anything else. Now it's mixed in with the smell of wet wool, farts and unwashed bodies. Most of the bunks are occupied by earlier new arrivals. Two 25-watt bulbs at either end of the barrack provide the only light. I stumble into a lower, shaking now with cold. I kick off my shoes, throw my wet coat over my feet and wrap myself in one blanket, covering myself with the other. A muddy shoe lands on my cot as someone heaves himself onto the upper. I'm exhausted. Just before I fall asleep I think, "Is this how I'm going to fight fascism?"

He concludes the story of his first night in the army, "I *wanted* to enlist in the Army. And yet the first night filled me with a sweating dread that stayed with me for decades. The next morning I was awakened by wet drops on my arm. It was blood. The guy in the bunk above me had slit his wrists during the night." He writes nothing further about the soldier who slit his wrists, whether he lived or died.

BACK TO CAMP MURPHY

Basic training behind him, having become an army signalman in uniform, he returned to Florida to become a radar instructor. The tenor of his daily and psychic life was again reconfigured. Following the devastations and depersonalization of boot camp, he found himself back in an elite training camp, in a position of authority, teaching highly technical skills to smart men. Reveling in again feeling recognizable to himself, he spent his free time writing a musical, three acts with six original songs, that would occasion his directorial debut. He called the show *On the Ball.* He may have been emboldened to take on this endeavor by the meagerness of the entertainment on the base, which included a "demonstration by a champion billiardist," as well as Carmelita Mullis, a "lady wrestler," known as the "Amazon Bone Crusher," or, as she was promoted at the camp, "A female flounderer of feminine pulchritude." From the Camp Murphy newspaper (and only from that source, as no one in Sidney's life seemed to know a thing about it) we learn that Sidney's show opened on July 2, 1943. The camp newspaper raves, "It brought down the house. About a thousand GIs jammed the hall, sitting, standing and hanging from the rafters!" Sidney had just turned nineteen.

But Sidney hadn't joined up to be an entertainer, and he wrote disparagingly about his friends who took jobs in *This Is the Army,* a show directed by Moss Hart that toured bases in the United States. "He [Hart] had asked me to be in it . . . I refused because it was not my idea of fighting fascism." He adds, "Most of my friends were pulling tough duty in the Russian Tea Room on 57th Street."

The Signal Corps itself offered many opportunities for someone with Sidney's theater and film background, as it was responsible for producing training and propaganda films for army personnel and civilians, many of which were made at the Astoria Studios in Queens, where Sidney had acted in *One Third of a Nation*. Some of these films were produced by major Hollywood figures, including Darryl Zanuck, Frank Capra, John Huston and George Stevens. The most famous of these include Capra's series, *Why We Fight*, and John Huston's *San Pietro*.

Sidney's focus remained fixed on radar. "I knew electronics as well as anybody could," Sidney boasted, uncharacteristically. "At one point I was teaching a specific radar circuit, I think I was 18 years old, in the Philco Radar laboratories in Philadelphia, to professors, to guys who had their masters in many other sciences. But I knew that particular circuit better than anyone in the world."

OVER THERE

He found the technical work agreeable, but, he writes, "I desperately wanted to do more than I was doing: teaching Radar Repair in Camp Murphy, Florida, a cushy job anyone would have given their right arm for." The problem was his poor eyesight: he had been classified as "limited service," which meant he would never be shipped overseas. Just as he'd found a way into the army at age seventeen, Sidney found a way around this obstacle; indeed, clearing obstacles was surely one of his greatest gifts, confirmed throughout his career. "The chance arose," he writes, "when the Army asked for volunteers for a mission overseas. No details were given." In other words, it was a blind assignment—he didn't know what he was volunteering for. "I and five of my buddies at Camp Murphy raised our hands and we were off within days. All of us were thrilled." He soon learned that he was to be dropped into Yunnan Province in southwest China:

We were to link up with Chinese Regular Army units to teach
them radio communications and Radar, which the U.S. was
now beginning to supply to the Chinese troops. We would also
set up direct communication with the U.S. forces in India, who
were now arriving in greater numbers. The whole operation was
called the "Y Forces."

An interpreter would need to be somewhere on the scene for this training to succeed, but the radar men would be equipped with a booklet the U.S. Army had devised for communication between Americans and Chinese, called *Pointie Talkie*. English words and Chinese characters were placed side by side, allowing communication between speakers of one language and the other by pointing. Service men were also provided with a list of do's and don'ts for this part of the world. It included tips on dealing with the climate: "Avoid mosquito bites. Treat all cuts and scratches promptly, no matter how trivial. Drink only sterilized water or a beverage known to be safe. Take extra salt."

The booklet also offered guidance on behavior and social interaction: "Respect the Buddhist monks—the religious leaders and wise men of the country. Learn the Hindu caste marks—they are the insignia of the people. Be generous with cigarettes and tobacco. Salt is an excellent trading medium. Don't confuse the customs and religions of the different peoples. Don't gamble with the Burmans; they're poor losers. Don't argue with Hindus about caste. Don't touch the food of Hindus or allow your shadow to fall across it. Don't stare at a Mohammedan woman or try to remove her veil—her male relatives may kill you both."

Sidney was on his way to this almost-forgotten corner of the conflict, the China-Burma-India (CBI) theater, known to many Americans only from a handful of later movies, the most famous being *The Bridge on the River Kwai*, directed by David Lean in 1957, about British POWs forced to build a railroad bridge along the Siam-Burma Railway for the Japanese. Another film closer to Sidney's experience,

Objective Burma!, directed in 1945 by Raoul Walsh and starring Errol Flynn, contained actual combat footage filmed by U.S. Army Signal Corps cameramen in the CBI theater. Aptly enough, the story, based loosely on real events, follows a group of paratroopers, dropped to locate and destroy a camouflaged Japanese Army radar station that was detecting Allied aircraft flying into China. The mission is neatly accomplished, but the Japanese then capture, torture and kill several of the Allied group; the survivors are forced to retreat into the enemy-occupied jungle, where they manage to distract the Japanese from a successful British aerial invasion. *The New York Times* praised the film: "There are no phony heroics by Errol Flynn or any of the other members of a uniformly excellent cast. These boys conduct themselves like real soldiers and even the newspaper correspondent is a credit to the craft." But in a turn of events that speaks volumes not only about the CBI but about the war effort more broadly and the Hollywood films that portrayed it, the film infuriated the British prime minister, Winston Churchill; he had it withdrawn from release in the United Kingdom, complaining of the Americanization of an almost entirely British and Commonwealth mission. An editorial in a British daily complained, "It is essential both for the enemy and the Allies to understand how it came about that the war was won . . . nations should know and appreciate the efforts other countries than their own made to the common cause."

In his memoir Sidney takes us through the procedure of shipping out on his way to the CBI. His leave-taking was not at all as it appeared in so many World War II movies, with wives and mothers waving handkerchiefs from crowded docks. "Before shipping overseas, you were sent to a replacement Depot," Sidney explained. "Here, units were formed by the shipload. When a unit was formed for a particular destination that filled a ship (about 7,000 men) we'd be loaded on a train and sent directly to the ship at whatever port it was leaving from. The whole process took about two weeks." The next leg of the trip was far longer; Sidney's urgent secret mission seemed to be taking forever to reach.

We had left the U.S. in February, crossed the Atlantic to
Casablanca, then overland to Oran. It was the time of the
landings in Anzio. Twenty-four hours after landing in
Oran, the six of us were the only ones left in camp. Our entire
boatload of 7,000 troops had been shipped out for the collapsing
beachhead.

Chafing to do his part, Sidney was in a holding pattern, while the others on board were heading into a consequential battle, a landing in Italy that didn't work out the way it was supposed to—it lasted four months and resulted in more than forty thousand Allied casualties. Where he was headed, the CBI theater, was considered by many a mere sideshow, not the *real* war.

Sidney arrived in this theater having voyaged through the Suez Canal and across the Indian Ocean to Bombay, where a train took him across India to Calcutta. The entire trip was four months long, by which time the Japanese had overrun the Yunnan Province, which meant Sidney's mission, the Y Forces, was canceled. "There was no place for us to move out to," he recalls. Eventually, Sidney was deployed to northern India.

The theater's acronym, CBI, to American troops over there stood for Confusion Beyond Imagination. Although the stated primary mission was to support the Chinese in their fight against the Japanese invaders and to protect India from invasion by supplying military equipment and improving the efficiency of the Nationalist Chinese army troops (as Sidney's Y Forces mission was meant to do), as well as bombing the Japanese who had conquered Burma and were threatening India, the actual mission in the CBI was a mosaic of competing projects. Americans, with various Allied partners, were brought in to accomplish several vast engineering projects, carried out under persistent Japanese attacks and baneful jungle conditions. These projects included building the Ledo Road, from Ledo, Assam, in India to Kunming, Yunnan, in China—more than a thousand miles of construction across the eastern Himalayas and through Burmese swamps and jungles; laying pipelines to run from India through Burma to China to supply oil and gasoline to the Chinese; and creating the Assam airfields for landing transport aircraft delivering supplies to China and Allied soldiers in Burma and along the Indian border. Transport planes were also tasked with air-dropping supplies to Allied forces who were working on these enormous projects.

These missions were hampered by sweltering heat, monsoon rains, impenetrable mountains and dense, impassable jungles and swamps, as well as by tropical diseases like malaria, typhus and dengue fever. In fact, Sidney contracted dengue fever, a horrible experience that his wife Gail recalled him telling her about. She said that he remained ever wary: "Mosquitoes never got near him in East Hampton."

The efforts of the Allies in the CBI were further compromised by the conflicting interests of the British and the Chinese. The British were concerned with restoring their empire, reclaiming the Japanese-occupied territories and protecting their prized colony, India, from invasion. The Chinese Nationalists welcomed Allied nations to the fight against Japan, but they were equally focused on preserving as much of their own power as possible in preparation for a postwar attack on their internal enemies, the Communists. Gail recalled Sidney telling her that Chiang Kai-shek, the leader of the Chinese Nationalists, was a thief; when shipments of supplies were flown "over the hump," as they called it, into China, one planeload would be just for him personally.

Sidney's duty was again radar training rather than *using* the radar, since, as he explained, "radar couldn't work because the mountains in Burma wrecked the echoing blips." He remained for two years stationed in the eastern Himalayas' intense heat and cold, a radar expert where radar was useless.

THE WAR WITHIN

Of course humiliations are par for the course. They keep increasing as one ages. But you get used to them as a normal part of life. When you're young, however, they burn holes in you.

—SIDNEY LUMET, FROM HIS UNFINISHED MEMOIR

Before ending up at the Burma border, Sidney and his small group of highly trained radar men were temporarily assigned to a camp outside Calcutta. "The six of us who had volunteered in Camp Murphy were now hopelessly stuck in what the GIs called Camp Shapiro. The camp's name was actually Conchiappara [Kanchrapara], a suburb of Calcutta." Sidney described Calcutta as "a dreadful city in 1944," crowded and ill-smelling, with bodies mounting in the streets from famine.

Always unhappy when he was inactive, he was languishing. "I get in trouble when I'm not working," Sidney once remarked. "Depressed, hot, irritated by another useless day"—and, with nothing else to do, he decided to take the train into Calcutta on a day's pass. On the return trip, Sidney encountered an act of violence by his fellow soldiers that would haunt him for the rest of his life.

The story, one his family had never heard, is recounted in his memoir, and he spoke about it for a documentary film a few years before his death. He recalled that the train, like English trains, had compartments with separate doors onto the platform. He was looking out the window as the train was pulling out of the station when he saw "a girl, a beggar who looked about 12, who was suddenly swept off her feet and pulled onto the train by an American GI." He knew instantly what he was seeing. "I immediately started toward the car behind mine. I stepped into the car. There were four or five GI's with the waif. She was seated on a Sergeant's lap. He had her dress up around her belly and was fingering her. I heard him say, 'Ooh, look at her little pussy—it's got hair growing on it.'" There he stood, a slender, bookish young man of nineteen, five foot, six inches tall, in the door of the compartment. "I don't think I have ever dealt with a situation of that brutality . . . it was a kind of descent into bestiality," Sidney writes. One of the GIs pushed him out of the compartment and said to him, "If you want in, it'll cost you."

What happened next was that Sidney said "No," and returned to his compartment. Fifty years later he still wrestled with that moment, of returning to his seat. "When you are standing there and there are 8 men around or 9 men all of whom are in one stage or another of sexual anticipation or sexual completion and if you think you're going to make a dent in that without getting thrown off the train—while it's moving. You have to be ready to give up your life in a moment like that—and I wasn't going to do that." Telling the story more than fifty years later, he was left with "a whole kind of self-loathing . . . I think that is probably about as bad as anything I've ever done, when I went back into my compartment and sat down."

But another note enters his reflections when he reasons, "I think that kind of heroics belongs in a movie like *High Noon*—that's a romantic version of real life." Here in his attention to the disparity between how things play out in real life and their portrayal in movies is a theme that will become fundamental to his greatest films—a number of which are based on real events. Sidney commented once that he'd always wanted to make "a real war movie, because I've never seen one that I found convincing." For a time he'd hoped to adapt (or readapt) the "best novel on the subject, *The Thin Red Line* by James Jones, but today it would be too costly." Terrence Malick pulled it off in his superb 1998 remake of the 1964 Andrew Marton film.

Sidney's recollections of that day continue: as they neared the camp the train slowed to a crawl. "A GI standing on the exterior steps of the compartment gently deposited her on the ground beside the tracks. I guess I was glad they hadn't thrown her."

And right here, at the end of this horrifying story, is where Sidney's memoir pages break off. With this story his effort to reenter his past abruptly ends. Unlike memoirists of a later generation, he finds no benefit, no release or revelation, in revisiting old pain.

SIDNEY'S WAR MOVIE

Sidney never completed his memoir, but, like so many of his deepest experiences, his wartime years found their oblique expression in his highly regarded and little-known 1965 film, *The Hill*. He acknowledged that the film drew on his army experiences. He made *The Hill* the very same year he directed *The Pawnbroker*, one of the first American films to delve into the story of a Jewish death-camp survivor. Both films took him into the heart of the war, some twenty years after he'd returned home.

The 1960s saw a spate of Hollywood movies that celebrated American actions in World War II. A short list includes *The Longest Day* (1962), *Battle of the Bulge* (1965), *None But the Brave* (1965) and *Von Ryan's Express* (1965). One of the most popular of these films, *The Great Escape* (1963), tells the story of Allied prisoners of war held by the Germans, and their ingenious efforts to break out and return to the fight. Sidney's film, *The Hill*, released two years later, is also about prisoners, but not POWs. From a semi-autobiographical screenplay by Ray Rigby set in a British military prison in the North African desert during World War II, the film centers on a group of five British soldiers imprisoned for such offenses as drunkenness, insubordination and profiteering. In a dramatic break from his star turn as 007, the film featured Sean Connery as a former squadron sergeant major from the Royal Tank Regiment convicted of assaulting a commanding officer who had ordered him to lead his men in a senseless suicidal attack. Connery himself had hated the military, the discipline, the officers and, most of all, the class distinctions. He had been conscripted after the war by the Royal Navy but had managed to be "invalided out" due to ulcers.

The film exposes the demeaning cruelty and physical sadism to which the men are subjected, and the absolute power over others sometimes placed in the hands of brutal or stupid men. For Sidney there was a fascist dimension to military discipline, designed to crush the individual. He recalled a brief exposure he'd had to an American wartime prison:

*When I was in North Africa during the war, I was stationed
for a few days outside of Oran, and there was a prisoners'
enclave for American prisoners—[used for] everything from
murder to getting drunk in Oran, drunk and disorderly. And
there was a Moroccan band, we used to call it "music hill"—on
the top of the hill in the middle of the camp. And they played all
day. I don't know how the band stood it, the guys in the band,
but I sure don't know how the prisoners stood it. That's all you
have to know to do that movie. Somebody could think of that.*

In the tagline for *The Hill*, "They went up like men! They came down
like animals!" one hears echoes of Sidney's experience on that train
in Calcutta.

Shot by Oswald Morris (whose films as director of photography
include *Look Back in Anger, Lolita, Oliver!, Fiddler on the Roof* and,
with Sidney, *The Wiz*) in stark black and white, a choice Sidney often
made in the age of Technicolor, *The Hill* was filmed on a 20-acre set
constructed in the Spanish desert near Almería, where *Lawrence of
Arabia* and several Sergio Leone westerns, including *The Good, the
Bad and the Ugly*, were shot. "The physical hardship of the actual
shooting is something that coincides with the physical hardship that's
necessary for the film," Sidney told an interviewer on the set, "and
through it all—the caked sands, the windstorms going on while we
were shooting, the cracks in the lips—those were all for real." Of the
arduous making of this film, he commented, "I find that the harder
the work is, the easier the communication gets. You start picking up
energy and keying from each other so that a mutual excitement de-
velops so it goes up and back." With a large cast and crew, requiring
22,000 gallons of water to be shipped in, Sidney recast his own military role, from victimized enlisted man to competent commanding
officer. He took charge, but in a spirit of creative collaboration.

Connery's character, Joe Roberts, puts up the noblest fight against
the indignities and injustices of the prison, but the film does not reward
his effort. Ultimately, Sidney acknowledged, the film is "about the
hopelessness of fighting authority for anything other than your own

conscience." The perennial Hollywood lure into a story, "Who-do-you want-to-see-killed-and-who-do-you-want-to-see-kill-'em," is upended here. In this film as in so many that will follow, Sidney does not portray triumphant heroism; rather, he affirms those who stubbornly persist.

The Hill is a British story, but in Sidney's hands it references the segregated American army Sidney was part of and the bigotry he knew firsthand. The character of Jacko King (named Jacko Bokumbo in the screenplay) is played brilliantly by the great American actor Ossie Davis. At the time of filming, Davis was already a noted civil rights leader—an organizer and emcee of Martin Luther King Jr.'s 1963 March on Washington. With Ahmed Osman, Davis delivered the eulogy at the funeral of Malcolm X. This was in 1965, the same year the film was released.

Throughout World War II, most black enlisted men were not allowed on the front lines. Unofficially designated "unfit for combat," they were relegated to support services such as quartermaster, supplying troops with rations, clothing, fuel and other supplies, or transportation units, driving trucks, or they were sent to remote corners of the world to build roads and airfields. In the China-Burma-India theater where Sidney was stationed, more than nine thousand black soldiers worked beside Indians and other Allied troops building the thousand-mile-long Ledo Road and driving supply trucks across dangerous mountain passes. According to an official army history of the Signal Corps, prepared in 1957:

> *Negroes in foreign theaters posed problems. Australia wanted none of them. They were not acceptable in China. In Africa itself the economic status of the United States Negro bred discontent among the native blacks. There were of course problems in the United States, too: segregation in some states, and strong local prejudices in some areas, notably in the vicinity of Camp Crowder, Missouri, where the Negro construction units trained.*

The Signal Corps history notes that at Fort Monmouth in New Jersey, where Sidney began his service, "the situation was quite different.

The few Negro officer candidates who were in school there studied and lived among the white trainees and there was no race problem." Military segregation was shocking to many white northern soldiers, Sidney included. Racial segregation remained official armed forces policy until Truman's presidential order in 1948, although blacks and whites had fought together in a few instances in the Pacific. In the face of segregation, the Tuskegee Airmen, the all-black 332nd Fighter Group and the 477th Bombardment Group of the United States Army Air Forces, distinguished themselves in their deployment to Europe and North Africa.

In *The Hill*, Ossie Davis plays a West Indian imprisoned for stealing three bottles of whiskey. When the racist prison officer in charge tells him he cannot be exercised beside the white prisoners, he points out that he is a British subject from the West Indies. He is then "granted equal privileges" by the regimental sergeant major (RSM). Despite this concession, Jacko is subjected to persistent racial abuse by this same RSM that is far more explicit than anything seen in American films of this era. Finally, Jacko reaches his limit, and in an unforgettable scene he tears off his uniform and rips it into pieces, yelling, "I quit your stinking army. . . . This is what I think of British justice." Bursting into the commandant's office, he gives him a piece of his mind, wearing only his skivvies. As Davis recalled, that was Sidney's idea: "You know what you ought to do—go ape . . . go jungle," Sidney suggested, and persuaded Davis to tear off his clothes.

The film is a devastating commentary on the cruel exercise of power. The British Board of Film Censors expressed concern about the film's "dangerous influence . . . for the young aggressive adolescent type in the presentation of authority as ineffectual, weak and not really caring." In the United States, after a tussle over censoring the film for its "over-emphasis on brutality and sadism that we feel . . . could not be approved under Hollywood Code requirements," *The Hill* was ignored by the American Academy of Motion Picture Arts and Sciences. It was, however, nominated for the Palme d'Or, the Cannes Film Festival's highest award, and won several awards in England.

In *The Hill*, Sidney indirectly addressed the bigotry he witnessed in the segregated U.S. Army, and, even more indirectly, the bigotry he himself experienced. One feature of army life that Sidney did publicly remark on through the years, without providing any specifics, was his experience of "a lot of anti-Semitism." Polish, Irish, and Italian Americans all experienced bigotry, but blacks and Jews seemed hardest hit. Years later, when he learned of the killings of civil rights workers Michael Schwerner, James Chaney and Andrew Goodman in Mississippi in 1964, he remarked that in the army he'd known people capable of that.

Over the years, stories from Jewish World War II veterans about their experiences of anti-Semitism have emerged in bits in pieces. In Deborah Dash Moore's 2009 book on the subject, from which this chapter draws its title, the stories share some basic features, attributable in part to what was then a far more homogeneous and segregated Christian nation. Jewish soldiers shared accounts of being treated by their fellow soldiers as curiosities, as if their existence was presumed to be mythical. Jews made up a small number of the more than half a million men and women in uniform, and the oft-reported sentence "I never saw a Jew before" did not have a friendly ring to it. In one report, from a New Yorker in basic training in Florida, a Memphis boy asked him for his signature to send home, "to show them how a Jew signs his name." In November 1944 the army magazine *Yank* decided not to run a story about Nazi atrocities against Jews; the author was urged to do "something with a less Semitic slant."

Sidney had been accustomed to being surrounded by an almost protective web of talented Jewish men. As was not uncommon for urban Jews of that time, his friendships did not often cross ethnic lines. Anti-Semitism was not unfamiliar to him, but the New York City version wore a different aspect from the kind encountered in the barracks. Childhood brawls between ethnic groups on the city streets were between members of groups equally dispossessed. The use of racial epithets by people with tangible power over every aspect of daily life was a disorienting experience for Sidney.

Adding to his culture shock was the contentious urban-rural divide.

In the 1930s, 30 percent of young Jewish men in New York went to college, usually to a free city university, while among white Southerners, 30 percent could not read or write.

Jewish soldiers were commonly confronted with anti-Semitic stereotypes: they made poor warriors, were cowardly and manipulative, couldn't tolerate physical labor, lacked leadership skills. The military had its own hand in this: a World War I manual of instructions for medical advisory boards noted, "The foreign born, especially Jews, are more apt to malinger than the native born." Many of the ranking officers in World War II had come up through a military in which anti-Semitism was based in racialist scientism. "The military regularly scoured its ranks for potential officers—but the widely held view that Jews would not make good officers exempted them frequently from consideration," Deborah Dash Moore notes. "The 'less Jewish' one looked or sounded, the less different from other Americans, the more chance of consideration for elevation." One anti-Semitic canard was that Jews avoided combat by seeking placement behind combat units, in the supply lines, a story that accorded with the stereotype of the Jewish shopkeeper. Moore quotes an excerpt from a work by the Jewish poet Kenneth Koch entitled "To Jewishness":

> *You went with me*
> *Into the army, where*
> *One night in a foxhole*
> *On Leyte a fellow soldier*
> *Said Where are the fuckin' Jews?*
> *Back in the PX. I'd like to*
> *See one of those bastards*
> *Out here. I'd kill him!*
> *I decided to conceal*
> *You, my you, anyway, for a while.*
> *Forgive me for that.*

Along with this, many gentiles could not conceive of why a Jew would have any patriotic feeling or want to fight in the first place, since he was not a "real American." And in a further turn of this screw, the Jew's willingness to enter combat was viewed as motivated by a need to prove himself *as a Jew* rather than out of a sense of duty or loyalty to his fellow soldiers.

In 1945, Arthur Laurents (*West Side Story, The Way We Were*) made his Broadway debut with *Home of the Brave,* a play about a traumatized young Jewish soldier. Under attack, the Jewish soldier must abandon his best buddy who has been fatally shot in order to deliver reconnaissance information. In psychiatric treatment for his trauma-induced paralysis, he reveals that his friend had uttered an anti-Semitic slur just as the enemy was firing on them, and the Jewish soldier was momentarily gratified when his buddy was shot. His guilt for that feeling has caused his paralysis. When the play was adapted for the screen in 1949, the central character became a black GI, but the story was unchanged.

Sidney—short, bespectacled, brainy, and designated "limited service"—puzzled over how to react to being called a "Jew boy." Should he try to be more inconspicuous? Should he shrug it all off as "guy talk"? Was it possible, he wondered, to correct their misperceptions?

It was a moral conundrum, and it left him angry, full of shame and confusion. Such feelings and questions would come, directly and obliquely, to permeate many of his films, from his first, *12 Angry Men*, to his last, *Before the Devil Knows You're Dead*. They all feature men being bullied and humiliated by other men. "The worst humiliations took place in the Army," he writes in his memoir, and he drew upon his memories of those experiences throughout his career.

Not once is the term "anti-Semitism" mentioned in the memoir, despite the many times Sidney had remarked on it in conversation and in interviews over the years. The humiliations that he does describe—often in detail—carry transferred feelings from what he could not bring himself to write about. One particular story describes the kind of double bind he often experienced:

It was February 1944. The entire camp was on parade for a visiting three star General. Standing in ranks in mud and snow, we could see the General approaching. He stopped in front of me. "How's it going, soldier?" "Fine, sir." "Food okay?" "Yes, sir." He seemed kind and genuinely interested. "Plenty of hot water in the shower?" It was the one agony of the place. The showers were always ice cold. But I was terrified that if I told the truth, the camp personnel would be so angry at me, they'd screw me out of going overseas. "Yes, sir." The last thing I wanted was to make waves. "Really?" he said. "Plenty of hot water?"

"Yes, sir." I said. "You kidding me?" "No, sir." He shook his head in disbelief and walked on. Obviously he'd heard differently earlier down the line.

I could feel thousands of pairs of eyes boring into my neck. I swear I heard snorts of contempt. Even the Camp Commander, moving past me behind the General, gave me a look that made me wish I could sink into the mire I was standing in.

Trying not to lose his chance finally to be shipped overseas, he is perceived as a "suck-up," playing into yet another stereotype. That thousands of ears would have heard his exchange with the general is impossible, but Sidney felt thousands of eyes "boring into" him. He was the object of contempt with no way to refute the unspoken accusations.

The reasons Sidney didn't write openly about the anti-Semitism he encountered are nowhere articulated. We know that American Jews of his generation were taught from childhood not to speak about anti-Semitism, not to call attention to it for fear of inflaming it. More significantly, after the revelations of the death camps, how could an American Jew harp on his mistreatment in the army?

9

COMING HOME

We are back
but not back all the way.
 —"Coming Home" by Vern Rutsala

At war's end, Sidney was among the 7.6 million U.S. men and women returning from military service abroad, and one of 700,000 New Yorkers coming back to their city. Drifting back into civilian life, Sidney, like so many, would need some time to find his bearings. He'd left New York a beautiful Broadway child star, but the twenty-two-year-old man who returned was no longer precocious or quite as handsome as his youthful looks foretold. Bespectacled now, and, absent the anticipated growth spurt, he stood at five foot six. That his confidence was in some ways badly shaken was perceptible to very few, since his outward style was always upbeat, whatever was going on inside.

It was to be a time of hard transitions. After the massive victory parades through Manhattan and the slow process of demobilization, the number of the war dead had yet to be contended with: more than 400,000 American lives lost. On October 26, 1947, the bodies of 6,248 Americans arrived in New York Harbor, and a single symbolic coffin was carried to Central Park for a funeral service with a crowd of 400,000. Worldwide, there were 15 million battle deaths, 45 million civilian deaths. New York's 2 million Jews would learn in detail of the systematic extermination of European Jewry. For many, this meant members of their immediate families had perished; this included Sidney's mother's Warsaw family, the Wermuses. A cousin whom Sidney never met, Henri (Hershel) Wermus, later provided a partial list of his maternal family members murdered by the Nazis: Aunt Sarah and Uncle Léon, cousins Jehuda, Hania, Josef, Chaja, Sura, Micia, Berek, Ida, Jakub, Samuel and Eli Wermus. Henri, who became a professor of mathematics at the University of Geneva, was the only European survivor of his extended family.

Sidney moved in with his sister Faye, her husband Selwyn and their little girl Leslie, or Lulie, as Sidney called her, in their downtown Manhattan apartment. It wasn't just the postwar housing shortage that drew him to Faye; she was home to him. Through those long years, most of Sidney's modest wartime correspondence had been addressed to her, and he'd sent her his army paychecks to save for him.

THE SIX MILLION . . . AND BROADWAY

Although now a trained engineer, Sidney's first move upon his return was to the theater, his world. His agent greeted him glumly, not having seen Sidney since he was seventeen years old: "Too bad you didn't grow taller." Sidney got the message, that he would not likely be cast in leading roles. But Sidney's old Group Theatre crowd reached out to him, tapping him to replace nineteen-year-old Marlon Brando in a show called *A Flag Is Born* that was underwritten by the American League for a Free Palestine. The production was aimed at raising funds for a ship to carry Jewish refugees from Europe to Palestine. The left-leaning theater world was turning its focus on the revelations of the death camps, a subject Hollywood wouldn't touch directly for years. Sidney's 1965 film *The Pawnbroker* became one of the first American films to portray a concentration camp survivor.

Sidney took over Brando's role as David, a fiercely embittered young survivor of the Treblinka death camp. The long one-act, set entirely in a cemetery "somewhere in Europe," was written by the Oscar-winning screenwriter Ben Hecht (*Scarface*, *Nothing Sacred*,

His Girl Friday, Spellbound, Notorious, and *Gunga Din*). Kurt Weill composed the music; Luther Adler, a Group Theatre alumnus, directed; and film star and former Yiddish theater actor Paul Muni joined Brando and then Sidney in the cast. The play is an undisguised political intervention, castigating Britain for permitting only eighteen thousand Jewish refugees to enter Palestine each year (the actual number was fifteen thousand), interning the rest in camps in Cyprus. Hecht's fury had been exacerbated when the British foreign secretary, Ernest Bevin, made the claim that Truman and the Americans favored allowing one hundred thousand Jews into Palestine because "they did not want too many Jews in New York."

The play's narrator was Quentin Reynolds, a radio correspondent whose voice was immediately recognizable to the audience; he had broadcast from London during the Blitz. In the play he approvingly recited a list of recent anti-British attacks, analogizing the Zionists in Palestine to the American revolutionaries. But Hecht did not hold only the British to account. The show's most devastating moment was a reckoning with American Jews. Sidney's character, David, stepped each night to the front of the stage and under the blaze of three spotlights confronted the audience:

Where were you—Jews? Where were you when the killing was going on? When the six million were being burned and buried alive in the lime pits. . . . Where was your voice crying out against the slaughter? . . . You Jews of America! You Jews of England! Strong Jews, rich Jews, high-up Jews, Jews of power and genius! Where was your cry of rage that could have filled the world and stopped the fires? Nowhere! Because you were ashamed to cry out as Jews? You would rather let us die than speak out as Jews! A curse on your silence! . . . We heard your silence in the gas chambers . . .

The play's story line, such as it is, unfolds as an aged couple, Tevye and Zelda, played by Paul Muni and Celia Adler, also survivors of the Treblinka death camp, are making their weary way on foot to

Palestine. They encounter young David when they pause to rest in a cemetery. In an echo of Max Reinhardt's *The Eternal Road*, the elderly Tevye has visions of biblical sages and kings which are enacted onstage. Each figure speaks to Tevye, offers solace and faith and affirms the reestablishment of a Jewish homeland. King Solomon urges Tevye, "Be not afraid of mighty councils," and in response a UN-style tribunal appears on the stage, before whom Tevye pleads the case for a Jewish homeland. The council votes unanimously to open the doors of Palestine to the Jews, but in the next breath an English statesman expresses second thoughts, proposing that they "consult the Arabs," at which point Tevye beseeches, "No, don't go away! . . . If you go you will forget again! Great statesmen, Kings . . ." And the tribunal vanishes.

Sidney's character, David, berates Tevye for "holding out his heart like a beggar's cup," but their debate is cut short when Tevye realizes that his aged wife, Zelda, has collapsed. He discovers she is dead. As Tevye begins to recite Kaddish (the prayer for the dead), the Angel of Death appears, and as Tevye dies beside his wife he urges David to go on alone to Palestine. With yet another loss, another elder vanquished, David lifts a knife, preparing to end his own life, when in the distance the somber notes of "Hatikvah" are heard—the song, meaning "The Hope," which would become the national anthem of Israel. Soon the marching feet of soldiers become audible along with their chant, "We're the Hebrew army of Palestine. . . . We speak to [the British] in a new Jewish language. . . . We fling no more prayers or tears at the world. We fling bullets. . . . We're waiting for you. . . . Help us give birth to a flag." Finding a new resolve, David gently lifts Tevye's prayer shawl from his body and raises it above his head as a homemade flag, then joins the men and women marching off to fight. "When the Zionist flag was raised in the final scene, with Kurt Weill's music in the background, it sent a chill through the audience," recalls an audience member. After each performance, buckets were passed for contributions. "The buckets were always full," recalled one of the teenage ushers, young Victor Navasky, later the publisher of *The Nation* magazine.

Sidney as David in *A Flag Is Born*, with dying Tevye, played by Jacob Ben-Ami, who replaced Paul Muni in the role. *(Lucas-Pritchard / Museum of the City of New York)*

The $400,000 raised by the show went to refitting one of sixty-six illegal immigration ships that attempted to penetrate the British blockade between 1946 and 1948. On March 8, 1946, British destroyers intercepted a vessel filled with refugees who had boarded near Marseilles. The ship, named the SS *Ben Hecht*, was impounded and the refugees were sent to a detention camp in Cyprus; the American crew was imprisoned for a month at the Acre Prison in northern Palestine.

In a newspaper interview Sidney gave at that time, he observed, "This is the only romantic thing left in the world, the homecoming to Palestine, the conquest of a new frontier, against all obstacles." Indeed, in the post-Hitler moment, the back-to-the-land socialist model of Zionism taking shape held a lot of romance for leftist Jews. As Zionism changed, so too did that view.

Sidney went on the road with *A Flag Is Born* to Philadelphia, Boston, Chicago, Detroit and Baltimore. In Baltimore, on the eve of their opening night, the company learned that the National Association for the Advancement of Colored People had been picketing theaters throughout the city where black audience members were restricted to the last two rows of the balcony. Hecht and the cast joined the picket line outside their theater, and the owner gave in and suspended their Jim Crow policy. Years later, Sidney remarked that he was "very proud" of the protest and "pleasantly surprised that it was so successful." He was unaware that the theater reverted to its segregation policy once the play moved on. Many Baltimore theaters were not desegregated until 1952.

The play would be personally consequential: It was during this run that Sidney met his first wife, Rita Gam. It was also during the play's run that Sidney and his father had a reunion after a seven-year hiatus. Baruch had not reached out to Sidney while he was overseas, not a letter or a phone call. As Baruch tells it in his memoir, he and his second wife, Julia, were visiting New York from their home in California, when he read in the paper that Sidney was replacing Brando in the play; they extended their stay in New York to see it. When Sidney stepped onstage, Julia, who'd never met him, pointed and said, "There's your son." Baruch asked how she could tell. "He looks exactly like you. His movements are yours." "I bet he knows I am in the theater," Baruch responded. "He seems so tense—his performance is strained." He was convinced that somebody had tipped Sidney off. "When we went out with the crowd, I saw him standing at the stage door, his eyes searching on all sides. He noticed me and cried out, 'Daddy!' He jumped on top of me, nearly keeling me over, then kissed Julia." The three went into Sidney's dressing room and sat together when, "several minutes later, a young girl knocked on the door. He introduced Rita Gam, 'my girlfriend.' He ordered a sandwich and coffee and asked whether we would like to eat with him." Baruch recounts that they spoke about Sidney's five-year service in the Signal Corps. "They offered me service in the USO," Sidney told his father, "but I didn't want to entertain, I wanted to fight Hitler." Baruch notes that Sidney talked about resuming his acting career, adding his own undercutting assessment: "But Sidney was not that 'charming little boy' anymore. He was twenty-two. Now he had to be the 'type,'" meaning the type to be a leading man.

It might have been in defiance of his father's belittling assessment that Sidney quietly urged his agent at William Morris to get him a screen test for the lead in a film at Warner Bros. titled *Rebel Without a Cause*. This first incarnation of that classic movie was an adaptation of a nonfiction book by that title about a sociopath being treated with hypnosis. The studio furnished Sidney with "the cost of first class round-trip transportation, including Pullman [train], between New York and California" for the test to play the disturbed Harold Kempter. Also tested for the role of Harold Kempter was Marlon Brando. The adaptation, written by Theodor Seuss Geisel (Dr. Seuss), was eventually put aside, and nothing but the title remained by the time James Dean took the lead in 1955.

Sidney's next and final Broadway appearance was almost two years later, and although he was the lead, he was still playing the part of a youth. *Seeds in the Wind* opened in May 1948. The production had begun as an experimental piece off-Broadway. Sidney played the leader of a group of children who had survived the horrific Nazi massacre at Lidice on June 10, 1942. A reprisal for the assassination of SS Obergruppenführer Reinhard Heydrich, the Reich Protector of Bohemia and Moravia, the massacre was carried out against the village, which was indirectly linked to the assassination plot. The event was described at the Nuremberg trials in 1946: the village of Lidice "was erased from the face of the earth. Even its cemetery was desecrated, its 400 graves dug up. Jewish prisoners from the camp at Terezin were brought in to shift the rubble. New roads were built and sheep set down to graze. No trace of the village remained." Eighty-two of the Lidice children were transported to the extermination camp at Chelmno and gassed in trucks.

Set in the Carpathian Mountains in Czechoslovakia in the summer of 1945, the play imagines a group of Lidice children who survived. During three years in hiding, they have concocted plans to create a postwar world in which the young take charge and make things right. When a kindly old Czech patriot finds his way into their communal cave and raises practical concerns that complicate their utopian vision, conflicts in the group erupt, casting a shadow over the long-held aspirations that have given them a reason to survive. The *Billboard* magazine reviewer quipped that Sidney Lumet, as the leader of the children, is "heroically tortured . . . and has quite a time for himself being intense." The play ran for only seven performances, whereupon the curtain fell on Sidney's professional acting career.

Sidney's confidence in his acting had taken blows from this reviewer and from his father, and more of the same was to come from his old mentors at the Group Theatre, who, with Sidney's participation, had recently established the Actors Studio.

Years later, thinking back on this period, he sometimes considered what his career might have been if he'd left the Broadway stage and gone to Hollywood to become a movie actor. His thoughts returned to his only movie appearance, as the "crippled little kid, Joey." "When I got out of the army, and I'd been in it five years, and there I was—I hadn't grown much," he commented. "And I figured a part like Joey, that's what I'd be doomed to, the little Jewish kid from Brooklyn who'd get shot—and Clark Gable would pick me up in his arms and wipe out a German machine gun nest—so that didn't seem very promising." These conjured images of himself as a helpless object of pathos stand in dramatic contrast to the dynamic in-command director he would become.

He was in for another unpleasant surprise when he learned that his soldier's pay, all of which he'd sent to Faye to save for him, was gone, spent. All of it. Baruch recalled that at their reunion at the theater, Sidney "admitted that he was without funds. . . . He came home and found nothing." Baruch writes, "I could see that he was adamant to talk about her [Faye]." Given the history of the tensions between father and daughter, Baruch would relish Sidney's complaining to him about his sister, especially on the theme of money. It was a small victory in the battle between father and daughter over Sidney, and over the earnings that had supported them both.

"Perhaps Sidney's thinking was that she would use what she needed and save the rest for him," pondered Ellen Adler, who was still very much on the scene at war's end, although preoccupied with her new sometime-beau, Marlon Brando.

Faye's husband, Selwyn, handed Sidney the keys to his sports car, a bright red MG, likely as a gesture of compensation. And soon Sidney was happily buzzing around town in it with his glamorous girlfriend, Rita. All in all, despite the hard knocks and the lack of acting prospects, Sidney felt it was good to be home.

10

MARRIAGE TAKE ONE: A SEASON IN BOHEMIA

The highbrow meets the lowbrow; sweet meets hot; uptown, downtown, all around the town.

—MARGO JEFFERSON

"Sidney was still beautiful when I first met him," recalled Rita Gam, Sidney's first wife, but she noted that it wasn't his looks that drew her. She rather liked the fact that "he didn't give a shit about how he looked. No, no, no. He didn't have any ego. No personal ego." His intensity and confidence were energizing. "There was nothing negative about Sidney, and I was attracted to that. . . . He had no doubts about where he was going, what he was, what he was doing." But it wasn't that simple—as Rita went on to ponder. He had no doubts about himself, but he wasn't exactly "happy with himself." "No," Rita corrected herself, "in a funny way, he was very happy with himself. No. He didn't have a demon in his head. He really didn't. You felt like he was a person who had been loved. You didn't feel like he was a person who had been abandoned. Although he had been."

Rita was nineteen when she and Sidney met. She had replaced her brother in a minor role in *A Flag Is Born*, just when Sidney had replaced Marlon Brando in the leading role. Rita's was a "trouser role," playing King David, her first professional shot after a stint in acting classes. They had friends and ambitions in common.

Born in Pittsburgh to wealthy parents, Rita, like Sidney, had had a bumpy childhood. "My real father was a strange man named Milton Mirkich. He owned property all through Pennsylvania. He was very rich, and very crazy, and very dead when I was four." Somehow, inexplicably, her mother ended up empty-handed following her husband's death. Rita thought over her childhood predicament while sitting across from me at a restaurant famous for its caviar and borscht, south of Central Park. In her eighties, and still beautiful, her bright blue eyes skillfully mascaraed, she spoke with the perfect diction of an old-school actress, and with the fluid and distinctive way with words that I'd learn was a beguiling feature of each of Sidney's wives. She told me the family moved to the Bronx and lived in modest circumstances for six or seven years until her mother remarried. "My stepfather had made a lot of money in the garment business, in the war—you know, war money." They relocated to a stylish apartment on Riverside Drive overlooking the Hudson River, and young Rita was enrolled in a Manhattan private school. She described herself as "an expensively educated girl."

When she and Sidney got together, Rita had no interest in marriage; she was interested in running away from home and discovering where her brains and looks might take her. Sidney was possibility incarnate, tireless and "insatiably curious," Rita said. Her parents were doubly disappointed by her "shacking up," as she put it, and doing so with a lowly actor. "They thought Sidney was a lousy idea to begin with."

Rita moved in with Sidney and his sister's family. She liked Faye very much, describing her as "strong and aggressive and tough." Before long, she and Sidney took a room at the Great Northern, a residential hotel on West 57th Street, where Isadora Duncan had once lived, and where Sidney had stayed with Faye when they ran away from their father. Eventually, they landed in an apartment just north of Greenwich Village, on 15th Street west of Seventh Avenue: "It was an in-between neighborhood, commercial, factories. There was a school just opposite, and a Laundromat where we did our laundry.

The lobby of the Great Northern Hotel, 118 West 57th Street, where Sidney and Rita lived briefly in 1947.

Our windows overlooked the backyard where a tall tree stood." They shared their one room, and bathroom in the hall, with a black pussy-cat named Electra.

DRIFTING IN THE VILLAGE

Sidney had been away from conventional life expectations for five years. Still in his early twenties, he was performing again, on and off, but he wasn't sure where his future lay, and that was okay for now. In Rita he found someone he could talk to and share his enthusiasms with. When I asked Rita what she thought Sidney loved about her, she said, "I had no natural tendency to gloom and doom," a quality of sparkle and lightness shared by all the women Sidney loved, in vivid contrast to his mother. He would by nature go toward what was nourishing and away from what was painful or too needy, as Rita would find out.

"We had a terrific time. We just loved theater, and never thought of the big picture. Making it wasn't in our mind. In our mind was, what wonderful work can we do?" Rita said. They "talked a lot," went to the movies a lot. "It was a terrific reading time . . . drifting in the Village . . . " Rita took a job as a hatcheck girl at the Copacabana, a celebrated nightclub that was a prominent feature of New York's posh postwar scene; it drew Broadway and Hollywood celebrities along with high-profile gangsters.

Sidney and Rita are posed practicing lines in their apartment for a *Life* magazine spread about the noteworthy New York couple. *(Yale Joel / The LIFE Picture Collection / Getty Images)*

AN END AND A BEGINNING

In the fall of 1947, less than a year into his relationship with Rita, Sidney joined Elia Kazan and Bobby Lewis, two of his teachers from the magic Group Theatre summer of 1939, on a new project: "I helped found the Actors Studio," Sidney later declared, a fact no one seemed to remember because his relation to the Studio was brief and ended unhappily. Kazan and Lewis were, as Sidney put it, "*the* most successful producer/directors on Broadway" at the time. Kazan had directed the hit play that put Arthur Miller on the map, *All My Sons*, and had won his first Oscar for *Gentleman's Agreement*, a bland exposé of white-shoe anti-Semitism. On the heels of these two triumphs, Kazan directed the original production of Tennessee Williams' *A Streetcar Named Desire* that made Marlon Brando a star.

For the Actors Studio's first class, Kazan and Lewis selected a small roster of actors to audition; those chosen attended tuition-free. Sidney was pleased that he'd been asked to join the advanced class for "experienced" actors taught by his mentor, Bobby Lewis. That class met in an abandoned church in the West 40s, and it included Marlon Brando, Montgomery Clift, Maureen Stapleton, Eli Wallach, Jerome Robbins, Anne Jackson, Karl Malden, Patricia Neal, Beatrice Straight and E. G. Marshall.

Sidney was thrilled being in this mix. Rita recalled that "Sidney was always slightly jealous of Marlon. Who wasn't?" What happened next was one of those mettle-testing moments for Sidney. Bobby Lewis decided that the class was too large, so "Gadget [Kazan] and I pruned it after the Christmas break, with loud protestations from all, pruned and unpruned alike." Sidney was among the pruned.

Sidney's ejection from the Actors Studio was the subject of multiple interpretations. Rita's view was that it was because Sidney hadn't grown up "being beautiful," and, she noted, Bobby Lewis cared a lot about looks. What was worse, she said, was that "nobody defended him—nobody came in for him, nobody, nobody."

Sidney's account was different. As he put it, "Very quickly I began to disagree with [Kazan and Lewis]. I had the impression that instead of performing really for yourself, you were auditioning for them." What's more, Sidney went on:

We were sticking to the realist tradition in which we all excelled. I wanted to try my hand at something different, play Ostrovsky, Sheridan, Farquhar, and not stage Waiting for Lefty *for the umpteenth time, not to mention all the social theater from the 1930s that I could have played perfectly fine even if I had been woken up by surprise at four in the morning without any preparation! Some of us discussed this orientation, and we were thrown out.*

Ellen Adler recalled that Sidney was stunned and heartbroken that Bobby Lewis, "who really had been Sidney's mentor," had not invited him back. She said he wept openly to her. Years later, she asked Lewis why he'd eliminated Sidney; his answer was that Sidney was "too needy." If this assessment ever reached Sidney's ears, it would have stung, echoing, as it does, Sidney's withering description of his father: "His desperation showed. A too eager smile played around his lips. You could sense his desire to please."

Sidney's relationship with Bobby Lewis ended then and there. He would never become personally close with Kazan, who was fifteen years his senior, even though they both worked in New York with many of the same actors and crew—but they were curious about each other, as reported by Burtt Harris, who'd worked with them both. Sidney's dazzling record of eighteen Oscar nominations for his actors was topped by Kazan's twenty-four.

After this painful rejection, Sidney turned to another great acting teacher he'd known from the Group Theatre, Sanford Meisner. Meisner's instructional focus was on making the actor into a "spontaneous responder," as part of developing an authentic onstage *relationship* between actors. The relationship was for Meisner the essential thing, what he called "the glue" holding two characters together. His exercises also sought to "eliminate all intellectuality from the actor's instrument." For Sidney, perhaps aware of his tendency to intellectualize, Meisner was "the best acting teacher I ever saw. I studied with a great many teachers, but nobody like Sandy." Sidney adopted another dictum of Meisner's: "Acting is doing . . . and, assuming that you've chosen the proper action, the feeling will be stimulated in you to communicate itself to an audience." Meisner's principles would guide Sidney throughout his career. Years down the road, Sidney referred to Meisner as "my rabbi."

Always finding relief in activity, Sidney promptly got busy forming his own theater group, which he called the Actors Workshop. "There were thirteen other people who were let go [from the Actors Studio]. I took those and also invited about twenty other people . . . and formed my own group downtown," Sidney explained. Rita Gam's brother, Alex, helped get it off the ground, setting up in a downtown loft.

"I joined the Actors Workshop, along with many of those who

didn't make the cut for the Actors Studio," recalled Richard Kiley. "It was a wonderful little group, with people like Yul Brynner, Marty Balsam, Ossie Davis, Ruby Dee and Sidney Lumet, who was just a kid then but very interested in directing. We had a loft on 4th Street. I was good with carpentry and helped to build a stage."

They sketched out a three-year teaching program. Sidney outlined the curriculum: "For two to three months we did modern realist theater, which was what we knew best, in order to set down a 'common language.'" Then they delved into different acting styles, working their way backward from contemporary realism and naturalism to Chekhov and Ibsen, to Shaw and Wilde, then to Restoration comedy, Shakespeare, and finally Greek drama. "We could make it run on about 200 bucks a week," he recalled, so the members each contributed a weekly five dollars. As Sidney explained it, they were all actors; nobody had the job of directing. Sidney began by just staging scenes, and "that's how I began directing."

Sidney's father was witness to this endeavor, writing in his memoir:

We went to the first performance of the [Actors Workshop], three one-act plays—one of them directed by Sidney. The "stage" was nailed together with beer and milk boxes. There were several seats. Others had to stand after climbing up three flights of stairs. It was worth it. These were a group of talented young men and women. For years now, the members of that group have achieved names in the profession, names too many to mention.

STEADY WORK

If Sidney and Rita hadn't yet locked into their professional grooves, they were both striving to achieve something artistically, working and enjoying the insouciant poverty of bohemia. "When I say we were broke, we were *broke*," Rita recalled. At Workshop rehearsals, Sidney recounted, "Yul and I had been literally sharing canned spaghetti." Being broke, Sidney discovered, was a lot better than being poor, but he knew he needed to earn some money. A member of the Actors Workshop, Ted Post, told him about a teaching job at a new high school in Manhattan, a "trade school for actors, musicians, and dancers," one of the first arts-oriented public schools in the nation. As Rita remembered the moment, "Sidney said, 'Hey what should I do, become a teacher?' And I said, 'Sure, why not? To hell with it.' So he started teaching at the High School for Performing Arts and loved it."

Rita's going steady

Better taste Luckies...LUCKIES TASTE BETTER...Cleaner, Fresher, Smoother!

Described by Hollywood columnist Louella Parsons as "the Hedy Lamarr of television," Rita pulled her weight, doing TV commercials and posing for print ads.

Sidney's salary was $40 per week; Rita was pulling in a little more, modeling and doing television commercials. They kept afloat; they kept working on their craft, and Sidney took to teaching. Sidney, she said, created a bubble of enthusiasm, whatever he was doing. "We had these twelve-to-fourteen-year-old kids over," Rita remembered, "and they adored him, and he loved them and our life was really full of his teaching and his directing." In a rare convergence of memory, Baruch observed, "In a short time he developed a rapport with the kids. He was a successful teacher."

Many decades later, one of Sidney's students recaptured her first encounter with Sidney:

At the beginning of one term, I was the first one to arrive. No, there was one student who had preceded me. I had not seen him before, so I assumed that he was a new student. I told him that I had heard that this new teacher was very good and that he was

professional. We chatted a while, standing, while the class filled.
I felt that I had better take my seat. He strode to the front of the
classroom and introduced himself: "My name is Sidney Lumet,
but you may call me Sid."

Looking back sixty years, another recalled:

I liked Sidney very much. He made us aware of everything.
He'd ask us, "Who was sitting opposite you on subway? Did
you notice anyone with a strange walk?" He identified us all
as animals, by our physical traits. I was a mongoose. "Silent,
quick, and deadly." My friend Eddie Leisner was a fluffy panda
bear. I learned a lot from him—in many subtle ways, the way he
introduced things, brought them to our attention.

Yet another of his students told me about a time Sidney was eating a
Baby Ruth candy bar while he was teaching. He was eating it with so
much pleasure—whether as an acting lesson or not, she wasn't sure—
but when the class ended, all the kids rushed to the vending machine
for Baby Ruths.

For the new school's first senior production, Sidney chose a hit
show that had just closed on Broadway, *The Young and Fair*, which
had been directed by Group Theatre cofounder Harold Clurman. Rita
had a small role in the Broadway production, as had her good friends
Julie Harris and Doe Avedon, then married to photographer Richard
Avedon. For the high school girls, the all-female play was a perfect
choice (there were only two or three boys in the class). Rita and Julie
Harris attended the student rehearsals to support Sidney.

The play, set in a fashionable junior college, is the story of a popular and villainous rich girl who attempts to frame two students and
a servant as thieves. In the end those who have stood up for what's
right are cast out, but they grow closer to one another and go forth
with hope. The play's class critique is not nearly as bold as the plays
of the 1930s, but what each character chooses to do—the stand
she takes or doesn't take—for advantage, out of intimidation, or

for a principle, spoke directly to the pall the House Un-American Activities Committee was just then throwing over the artistic community.

TAKING THE LEAP

Rita explained the practical impetus behind their decision to marry: if they were married, her parents would help them move to a nicer apartment. According to Rita, Sidney had no objection: "He said, 'Sure why not.' I mean we were that totally connected and crazy. We were crazy." The wedding was held in Rita's parents' Upper West Side apartment. Rita's stepfather now owned a high-profile dress line, and a little help from him came in handy for the newlyweds.

The little wedding was "lavish," by Sidney's father's estimation: "From her side, wealthy dress manufacturers, from our side, actors, directors, mostly from the Group Theatre." Baruch goes on to note, "Her parents strongly objected to the marriage, but the 'kids' lived together anyway, so why wait?" Baruch contends that a rabbi performed the ceremony, but when asked if they were married by a rabbi, Rita replied, "Certainly not." Of Sidney's four wives, Rita was the only one who was Jewish; like Sidney, she kept faith with her background in her own fashion, although she had little attraction to religious practices. Recalling the wedding pictures, she laughed: "Sidney looks like a fourteen-year-old. I had a gold dress on and high high heels." Baruch's recollections contain some familiarly self-serving amplifications:

> I tried my best we should not look poor. I bought a full-length fur coat for my wife, a suit for Sidney and myself at Brooks Clothier. I bought two wedding rings for Rita and Sidney. Her mother paid the first month's rent on a yearly lease. Her parents bought some pieces of furniture. One room and a kitchen, called a "studio apartment," did not need much furniture. The presents from the guests filled the rest.

"It was a pretty little place in a white stone house on Riverside Drive and 103rd Street," Rita recalled, "just a little bandbox place, but really it was home, with all this lovely furniture. He was a lousy cook, but I was worse. It was a young, fun marriage . . . without Hollywood money and all that stuff."

As he would for the rest of his life, Sidney surrounded himself with his type of artists—New York theater people, actors, writers, composers, and visual artists who shared his assumptions about the world, about theater and the arts, and about New York. In what would become for Sidney a lifelong delight in dinner parties, he and Rita began to entertain. Their professional and social worlds were one and the same. A perhaps unlikely frequent guest in this period was the legendary Marlene Dietrich, who at the time was romantically involved with Sidney's close friend and fellow member of the Actors Workshop, Yul Brynner, nineteen years Dietrich's junior. "Dietrich would cook us Sunday night supper," Rita recalled. "Marlene just adored Sidney. She thought the world began and ended with him."

Although most of their theater friends and colleagues were holding fast against the increasingly magnetic pull of Hollywood, many were making professional (and financial) headway, leaving *la vie bohème* for uptown and more settled arrangements. Rita's best friend, Grace Kelly, who had been getting by, like Rita, doing some modeling and a little TV, soon went west to co-star with Gary Cooper in *High Noon*. Times were changing and their ambitions were ignited.

Rita recalled how Sidney's career in television directing began. She ran into Yul Brynner while doing a toothpaste commercial at CBS Studios. Yul had been dabbling in television since 1946, when only a couple of thousand television sets were privately owned and shows were broadcast only two hours per day twice a week. Yul had been urging Sidney to join him, having found that TV was working out far better financially than playing and singing "gypsy songs" at society parties, but so far Sidney hadn't shown much interest. For one thing, Sidney didn't own a TV set. He couldn't afford one and knew almost nothing about television. That day at CBS, Rita urged Yul to try again to persuade Sidney, and this time it worked. "Nobody here knows what the hell they're doing," Yul told him. "We are making it up as we go. Anything is possible." This sounded good to Sidney, right up his alley. Director Arthur Penn's description of the TV world at that time offers a similar glimpse into the emerging medium:

> *In live television: most of the directors were veterans. . . .*
> *There was a certain kind of—I don't know what—I would*
> *characterize it as "It doesn't scare me." Here we were in a new*
> *medium, inventing it every day. As a new piece of technology*
> *came in, we would then utilize it. And that was true, as well,*
> *in the ineffable aspect of actors' talent.*

DIVERGING PATHS

Sidney would soon be on a sure footing and forging ahead; Rita, however, wasn't so sure which way she wanted to go. She was still serious about her acting and, like other New York actors, she continued to pick up work on television. Soon Sidney was able to cast her in episodes of the shows he was directing. But her career was tilting in the direction of glamour-girl starlet—and tabloid fodder.

In 1952 she was featured on the cover of *Life* magazine, leading the pack of "six top TV actresses." Seen by some as an Ava Gardner look-alike, she caught the attention of movie producers. She had her start in *The Thief,* a B film with a Red-scare spy plot, starring Ray Milland. Shot in New York and Washington, DC, the film had a gimmick: no dialogue. None. It got noticed and so did Rita. She landed a leading role in *Saadia,* with Cornel Wilde and Mel Ferrer, both major heartthrobs at the time. In this tale of a "strange Arab girl whose life has been dominated by a local sorceress," she was cast as a sultry exotic, a type she would often portray. Shot in Marrakech, Morocco, with three thousand Moroccan extras and camels aplenty, this MGM spectacular, while notable now for its sympathetic representation of Islamic religious fervor, got hammered in reviews. *The New York Times* opined that the direction was so flat and monotonous that "the actors do not perform. They pose or walk through their scenes like zombies."

Rita's next venture, a spy caper set and filmed in Germany called *Night People*, starring Gregory Peck, was more profitable, but Rita's part, as Peck's "slinking secretary (and mistress, it certainly appears)," was second tier. Although none of her films really hit the big time, not even when she played a "fiery brunette Indian princess" in *Mohawk*, the tabloids loved her, and she and Sidney became favorites of the gossip columns:

> *"A picture of Rita Gam (the baddie in* The Thief*) was ordered out of the Roxy lobby. Too sexy . . ."*

> *"She wears such a low necked gown that two Air Force generals refuse to pose with her at the opening of* Breaking Through the Sound Barrier.*"*

> *"You know who will reign as queen of the Art Students League's Gala Dream Ball in New York City—the fabulous Rita Gam. Will her TV producer hubby (*You Are There*) be there? Or will he be sulking as a little birdie told us he was after last night's bash?"*

Ultimately, this down-market notoriety began to ripple and trouble the waters of their marriage. It's hard to say whether such notices were reporting or causing tension between the two. Gossip columnist Earl Wilson's spin: "Gam and her hubby, a New York video director, are in a hassle. She's twice postponed leaving him for Hollywood. It's one of these career-or-marriage things." Some gossip sheets portrayed their marriage as a test case for the epic battle raging between New York and Hollywood: "She still hasn't reported to MGM to start her much-ballyhooed contract. Now it's agreed she can remain in New York with her hubby until the studio has a definite role for her." Rita's recollection was that it wasn't all smoke; Sidney had worried. "'If you do this Hollywood thing,'" Rita recalls him saying, "'it's going to be the end of us.' He had enough sense to know that."

At the premiere of yet another sandal-and-sword epic, *Sign of the Pagan*, starring Jack Palance as Attila the Hun, we can picture Sidney sinking down in his seat, watching Rita stare lovingly at Palance adorned with a "Fu Manchu mustache" and with whip in hand, declaiming, "An enemy who remains alive will always be an enemy, unless she's a woman. If she bears me a son, she will be my favorite wife. Take her away—and kill the others." The *New York Times* reviewer included this in his shellacking: "Poor Rita Gam truly rates sympathy as Attila's sister [actually his daughter], a strutting Annie Oakley type."

Some felt that Rita's good looks could get in the way of her acting. As one old friend put it, "Rita was beautiful; it was a bit of a handicap with her. She couldn't talk to you without thinking about how she looked."

Contrary to media speculation, it wasn't career versus marriage or Hollywood versus New York that did their six-year marriage in. The biggest trouble spot in their marriage, according to Rita, involved her brother, Alex, who'd been a member of Sidney's original downtown theater group. "My brother had emotional problems, and unfortunately Sidney was very tough. He decided to cut off from Alex for no good reason except that he didn't want to be responsible anymore. And so I too cut off, which is something I've always felt guilty about my whole life long. Of anything I've done, I've felt guiltiest about that. But that was Sidney. He would make up his mind and he would stick to it like glue." This pattern would hold, his ability to seal himself off from intensely difficult feelings, especially those aroused when he was called upon to be responsible for someone struggling with "emotional problems." His mother's illness and his family's financial dependence on him had left their marks. "Sidney simply could not and would not be around mental illness," Rita attested.

The death blow to the marriage, Rita said, was a Frenchman who caught her eye when she was away on a shoot: "Having been a good girl and a virgin when I met Sidney, I'd never known another man. There I was, the star of this big picture, and I got involved with a

French assistant director—an *assistant* director." When she got home, it didn't occur to her to hide what had happened. "I told him and Sidney moved out. It was just like that. He walked out and didn't look back."

"The thing about Sidney and marriage," Rita considered, was that "he wasn't much on romance. It was really more like wham-bam-thank-you-ma'am—but he also made you feel you were *it*—and 'I'm sticking with you.'" She concluded, "His feeling about women intellectually and in general was like any other man of that time. But personally, he wasn't like that. He didn't expect any womanly duties to be performed, but he expected a companion. It was loyalty he wanted."

There were two sides to Rita: the one who a bit later wrote fine books on movie acting and the other who enjoyed the attention of gossip columnists and wrote beauty advice. One side would write:

> *We know more about the fifties because of James Dean.*
> *Humphrey Bogart told us about the forties, Nelson Eddy the*
> *thirties, and John Barrymore about the twenties. It's all there—*
> *manners, morals, and the psychological gestures. Actors are*
> *litmus paper upon which the smallest mannerism reveals an age.*

While the other side would write:

> *Do you wear your hair in an up-sweep? Rouge your earlobes,*
> *by all means. Illness or too much dieting can sometimes make*
> *earlobes pale and waxy looking, which suggests ill health. A touch*
> *of pink and you're not only glowing but your earrings, should*
> *you wear them, will be more dramatic.*

Rita had a "huge breakdown" over the divorce. The ending was so severe. "When we got divorced, not for one penny did I ask, did I take, not one penny. Not even the rent," Rita said. She was remarried before long to Thomas Guinzburg, cofounder of *The Paris Review*, and president of Viking Press.

"Sidney fell into the first bed he was attracted to" was Rita's part-ing shot. He became engaged to Gloria Vanderbilt before his divorce from Rita became final.

Rita and Sidney sometimes ran into each other over the years—once on 57th Street, Rita recalled, "He really had to stop and think about who I was . . . but that was very Sidney; he closed doors." But there was one time, Rita remembered, "Many years later when I was getting a divorce from my second husband, I called him. I think I called him at twelve o'clock at night. I was so miserable. And we hadn't seen each other in years and years. And he said, 'Come on over,' and I went, and we talked in the middle of the night for a couple of hours, and then I went home."

11

TELEVISION: WORLDS WITHIN WORLDS

There was a saying, "You play to Mrs. Lutz in the Bronx."
—TELEVISION ACTRESS MARIA RIVA

If this were a movie—instead of being Sidney's actual life circa 1952—this is how it would open:

FADE IN:

INT. GRAND CENTRAL TERMINAL MORNING, 1952

Crowds of people hurry in every direction.
Typical commuter rush. The camera singles out
an interesting, bespectacled, not-tall YOUNG
MAN making his rapid way up the subway steps
and through the hubbub. CLOSE UP. His casual
attire contrasts with the black-suited, white-
shirted, fedora-wearing commuters he weaves
among. He is somehow both lost in thought
and keenly alert. In an out-of-the-way ramped
passage of the station, he waits impatiently
for one of four inconspicuous elevators.

Greeted familiarly by the uniformed ELEVATOR
MAN, he is taken up to the fifth floor, where
the doors open on a blank silent hallway that
contrasts dramatically with the noise and
bustle, the pink marble and limestone landscape
below. YOUNG MAN opens an unpromising door,
marked number 42, and enters a different kind
of hubbub altogether. Television cameras,
lights, and heavy wires are being pulled into
place around the set of a sixteenth-century
Spanish town; costumers and makeup artists
are preparing the actors, BORIS KARLOFF as Don
Quixote and GRACE KELLY as Dulcinea. Without
taking a breath, the twenty-seven-year-old
SIDNEY LUMET—our Young Man—dives in. He is
"merry as a bee," as Ralph Richardson would one
day describe him.

Hidden away above Grand Central's main waiting room, CBS
had set up their first television studios in 1939, when a shift from
radio to the new medium was beginning to look inevitable. Sidney's
1952 studio was a room of about 40 feet by 60 feet, and its windows were visible below the statue of Mercury that stands atop the
southern façade of Grand Central. Everything was jammed in there:
three cameras, three or four sets, the actors and the props, the prop
table with two prop men who handed props to the actors, the floor
manager, sometimes fifty or sixty extras, and often an ad executive
or two. The commercial advertisement setup was also in there; if the
show's director filmed the commercial, he got paid extra. It was next
door to the studio from which Edward R. Murrow reported the news.

Shortly before Sidney joined his good friend Yul Brynner as his
assistant director, Brynner had been doing daily broadcasts from the
newly established United Nations, and directing a live show from the
Stork Club, a café society hangout on East 53rd Street. The chit-

chat between diners and the club owner, Sherman Billingsley, was stilted and dull, but it gave viewers a glimpse of the New York elite. They really were making it up in this new medium as they went. Sidney joined Yul to work on yet another show he was directing called *Mama*, the TV adaptation of the radio classic *I Remember Mama* (and also a 1948 George Stevens film), a nostalgic look at the daily joys and sorrows of an immigrant Norwegian family. Television work was so plentiful—there were no reruns to fill airtime—that it was not unusual to be employed by more than one show at a time. Directors, writers and actors migrated from show to show and network to network. Some of the shows migrated too: *Kraft Television Theatre* aired on Wednesday nights on NBC and on Thursday nights on ABC, because they were produced by sponsors or ad agencies rather than by the networks. Along with *Mama*, Yul and Sidney ran two weekly detective shows, *Man Against Crime*, starring Ralph Bellamy—which had originally run on the short-lived DuMont Television Network—and *Crime Photographer*. Brynner's most successful series was a half-hour live dramatic anthology called *Danger*. Within months of Sidney's arrival, Brynner shaved his head to take the starring role in the Broadway production of *The King and I* and Sidney took over as director.

LIVE FROM NEW YORK

Even though he considered himself a "theater snob," steadfastly anti-Hollywood, Sidney did not find working in television to be a compromise or a comedown. New York television, especially, was full of possibility; it was live and risky and still quite close to theater and real theater people. In live television, every last detail had to be considered—every camera move, every placement of a microphone. Sidney loved that; he loved all the technical challenges, many of which drew on the knowledge of radio transmission and electronics he'd acquired in the Signal Corps. For starters, he had to figure out how to move the three cameras so the cables wouldn't tangle, because if they did, the cameras would get stuck; if a camera rolled over one of the cables, it would create a jolt in the image. In addition, when the cables slid on the floor, they made a scraping sound that the soundman had to struggle not to pick up. Sidney came up with the idea of running the cables up the wall and dropping them down from above, eliminating the noise and the tangling hazard. The old RCA boom microphones presented another problem because they picked up everything. Soon small directional microphones were developed for live broadcasts and hidden all over the set—sometimes as many as sixteen of them at one time. "From a technical point of view, anything we wanted to try, we could try," Sidney reminisced.

The infant television industry held many attractions for Sidney: directors, writers and those in charge of programming had creative freedom as they scrambled to fill airtime. The work was fluid, improvisational, fast-paced and well paid. What's more, it was populated with his crowd: actors, writers and directors with similar roots, ethnic, professional and cultural, sometimes all three. Of those working for CBS on *Danger* in the early 1950s, writer Walter Bernstein observed, "Marty [Ritt] and Sidney [Lumet] and I all came from the same kind of background—New York, Jewish. Sidney and Marty had both acted in the Group Theatre . . . we all came out of a certain naturalist thirties tradition. . . . We tended to relate to the same kind of material." Indeed, typically the shows explored the struggles, financial and social, of the ethnic urban working class. To watch Sidney's live dramas is to travel down the road not taken by American television, as nothing on current TV draws from this period or style of storytelling. According to Bernstein, writing drama for TV meant "making up stories with unhappy endings."

And Sidney was delighted to recruit young actors from the world of New York theater. Among the hundreds of up-and-coming actors he hired were Joanne Woodward, Rod Steiger, Kim Stanley, Tab Hunter, Walter Matthau, Leslie Nielsen, Grace Kelly, Sal Mineo and Anthony Perkins; James Dean appeared as the man who killed Jesse James, and Paul Newman was featured in a toga, playing Plato; Robert Preston, soon to become famous as "The Music Man," played a social worker trying to save a cocky juvenile delinquent played by John Cassavetes. Young actors jumped at the chance to do TV. As Sidney recalled, "If you worked on our show five or six times a year, it would pay your rent for the year."

Within eight months of starting out, Sidney became one of the biggest directors at CBS. He was running multiple television shows simultaneously and loving every second of it. Sidney recalled that "the pressure was wonderful"; he was totally absorbed and right there in the moment, spontaneous and creative, getting everyone on the same wavelength and being forced to respond to ten different problems at once. Using different parts of his mind and making full use of his powers was what he loved. One actor recalled, "He was a lot of fun. A situation on the set, because of the tension, would make things a little more tense, and he'd throw a donut at you or something like that, or trip you, something to break the tension. . . . He'd never get mad at anybody."

What he may have lacked in movie-star looks, he made up for with charisma, dynamism and an oft-noted sex appeal. Actress Phyllis Newman, who, with her husband, lyricist Adolph Green (*Singin' in the Rain, Peter Pan, Bells Are Ringing*), would become lifelong friends of Sidney's, recalled the time she first met him when she was seventeen or eighteen years old; he cast her as a secretary in one of his shows. She told me that she very quickly developed a "big crush" on him. Throughout her scene she was directed to keep typing, and, while performing on live television, she typed a love letter to Sidney. "I remember that it was on blue paper because white didn't read well on TV," she said. After the show she gave that letter to Sidney. What did he do when he read the letter? "He said 'OH!' That was all."

THE COMMERCIALS

As with most creative endeavors, there was also that other thing to consider: money. "There are no Lorenzo de' Medicis out there," Sidney once remarked. So instead of an aristocratic patron, he had

Amm-i-dent, the Ammoniated Toothpaste, and Py-Co-Pay tooth-brushes, the sponsors of *Danger* from 1950 to 1955. Sidney counted himself lucky that he worked directly with Mel Block, owner of the Block Drug Company. Sidney and Mel liked each other, and in the third year of the show, when Lumet wanted to do "more esoteric interesting things, less shoot-'em-up bang bang," he suggested to Block that "we do two for you and one for us." Block agreed, giving Sidney room to try new things.

Still, the commercial advertisements had to be squeezed in; they were part of the job and earned the director a little extra cash. For a thirty-minute show, commercials came at the opening, at the halfway mark, and at the end of the program. The commercials were filmed live, only a few feet from the set. After a brief pause during which the screen might go black or blank, the camera would find a man attired in suit and tie seated at a desk holding a product in his hand. He might begin by commenting on the drama, glancing unconsciously to the set at his left—"Well, that's certainly a difficult situation for those people . . ."—and then turn to his commercial script.

As TV gained in popularity, more money was at stake; sponsors and ad men, who had always had final script approval, were paying even closer attention. Keeping them happy might mean cutting the word "lucky" from a script if the sponsors were Marlboro or Chesterfield, eliminating even a subliminal reference to competitor Lucky Strike.

So much planning went into every live broadcast, yet things did not always go as planned. Stories of live-television bloopers abound. (Most of these moments are lost because the shows, going out live, were not usually recorded, except sometimes on fragile kinescopes, a pre-video technology.) One of Sidney's friends from that period, actress Maria Riva, daughter of Marlene Dietrich, recounts a classic mishap. Playing the scorned lover of Riva's character, Rod Steiger was scripted to pull out a gun and shoot her in the final scene, but when he pulled the trigger nothing happened—no sound, nothing. He pulled the trigger again, still nothing—then, in desperation, he yelled, "BANG!" and Maria Riva fell to the floor.

Sidney, too, reminisced about slipups: "On *Danger* I was doing an intense melodramatic card game at a round table; cameras were to dolly in to get a close-up of a hand." A moment too late, Sidney realized that he couldn't back up without catching the other cameras, so two cameras and the cameramen made a fleeting television appearance. And on Sidney's biggest hit series, *You Are There*, which employed the curious device of reporting on significant historic events as currently breaking news stories, the script called for Joan of Arc to go up in flames. As it happened, they had to use real flames. As Sidney put it, "There were special effects . . . and we had no special effects." So they decided just to give a glimpse of Joan burning and then cut away to another actor who was supposed to be hundreds of miles away, kneeling in prayer. But when they cut away, black clouds of smoke were choking the actor—despite his being "hundreds of miles away."

Sidney directed this series, *You Are There*, for two years. It was a great popular and critical success, winning two Emmys and a Peabody Award for outstanding achievement in education. Episodes were shown in schools all around the nation. Real reporters from the highly respected CBS news department featured regularly on the show to interview key players; Walter Cronkite was the commentator who opened and closed each episode. Ultimately the show was moved by the network to Hollywood, where it did not do as well.

Figuring out how best to costume the reporters for *You Are There* took some thought. It didn't work to dress Cronkite in toga and tights or medieval armor to fit an episode's historical context but having him appear in a modern suit was equally awkward. Finally, Sidney worked it out that Cronkite would introduce the story seated at a news desk, and thereafter they'd keep him off-camera while he or another reporter asked questions. The interviewees—Marie Antoinette or Madame Curie or Cleopatra—would stare into the camera as if talking directly to the reporter who was out of sight. Actors found it challenging to talk directly into the camera without slipping out of character. Sidney understood that their Method training centered on connecting with other actors, so he worked carefully with them on keeping a human connection with the camera lens.

The show's topics ranged widely, from "The Death of Socrates" to "The Secret of Sigmund Freud." Set designer Bob Markell recalled, "I had to create everything from the Oklahoma land run to Genghis Khan." Sidney insisted that the scripts draw on primary sources and include actual quotations. He explored themes that were important to him, such as conformity and bigotry in all its manifestations. And he especially liked stories that dealt with intellectual, political, and artistic freedom, which were not so hard to come by, as many of his writers were victims of the House Un-American Activities Committee blacklist.

Sidney directs "The Death of Socrates," an episode of *You Are There*. Paul Newman is standing to the left.

Sidney pushed the new medium about as far as anyone could. And there was something courageous about these solemn early TV dramas. In J. D. Salinger's novella *Franny and Zooey*, composed of stories written in 1955 and 1957, he gave a nod to shows such as Sidney's. Zooey is a TV actor. Commenting on a script sent to him by his friend Dick, he remarks to his sister Franny, "In Dick's thing, I can be Bernie, a sensitive young subway guard, in the most courageous goddam offbeat television opus you ever read." Franny responds, "You mean it? Is it really good?" and Zooey replies, "I didn't say *good*. I said *courageous*."

An episode of *Danger* that perhaps matches Zooey's characterization tells the story of "a mentally slow guy who loved music," who has a special attachment to Edith Piaf's song "La vie en rose." Miraculously, the man finds himself dancing with a beautiful girl to the French tune playing on a drugstore jukebox; the plot turns when he is wrongly accused of molesting her. It's a difficult episode to watch, and difficult to imagine how the advertisers felt about being associated with such downbeat material. One likewise wonders how, some time later, Sidney managed to convince Alcoa, the giant aluminum corporation, to let him direct the teleplay *Tragedy in a Temporary Town*. Written by Reginald Rose (who had also written *12 Angry Men*), the piece reaches its climax when a lynch mob descends on an innocent Puerto Rican laborer after a white girl is assaulted at a construction camp. Only one man, played by Lloyd Bridges, opposes the vigilantes. When Bridges, immersed in the reality of the situation, unexpectedly ad-libbed, "You goddamned stinking pigs!" the NBC switchboard lit up with more than five hundred calls, mostly decrying the profanity. This was at a time when a dog having puppies on-camera was considered obscene. Still, his performance gained Bridges an Emmy nomination.

In a different vein, Sidney developed an episode of *You Are There* with the blacklisted Academy Award–nominated screenwriter Abraham Polonsky (*Body and Soul, Odds Against Tomorrow*) called "The Emergence of Jazz." Set in 1917, the episode featured Louis Armstrong playing King Oliver and pianist Billy Taylor as Jelly

Roll Morton. Cronkite set the story in context in his intro, which mimicked a conventional period attitude toward jazz:

> *Our featured story today will be a new fad that's making war-time New York sound like a French battlefield.*
>
> *But first a roundup of the important headlines of the month.*
>
> *The big news is still Russia, and today Premier Kerensky announced the near collapse of the Bolshevik Revolution. In Petrograd, Leon Trotsky was greeted with taunts and laughter when he came to take over for the Reds.*
>
> *On the battlefront, the Germans have again defeated the Italians . . .*
>
> *In Washington, President Wilson is still being besieged by the suffragettes . . . demand[ing] votes for women.*
>
> *As if to forget their troubles, New Yorkers are going crazy over the music called jazz. War years always bring on new fads and tastes . . . and the strangest excitement has been generated by the musical noise called jazz. This strange music has been accused of everything, including the present decay in morality, the bad weather, and the desire of the women for the vote.*
>
> *We take you now to a musical recording studio in New York where some of this wild music is being recorded for posterity. All things are as they were then except . . .* you are there.

The episode recounts the northward movement of jazz from New Orleans to New York, when the whorehouses in New Orleans were shut down to protect the morals of soldiers passing through the city on their way to fight in the trenches of Europe. In a terrific sequence, Billy Taylor plays Jelly Roll Morton's "Tiger Rag" while explaining the tune's roots in an old French quadrille, a music lesson from a great musician.

In 1955 Sidney tried something unprecedented. With writers Reginald Rose and Rod Serling he created a show called *The Challenge*, underwritten by a private fund for original work on racial discrimination, blacklisting, academic freedom, and "the legality of loyalty oaths." The series' pilot centered on a beloved school bus driver (played by Jack Warden) who is fired for refusing to sign a loyalty oath. After the bus-riding children refuse to attend school to protest the firing, the community gathers for a meeting where voices are raised for and against the oath. The comments are substantive on both the left and the right, although the avid anti-communists express themselves with more heat. The scene opens with a liberal-minded woman proclaiming that the loyalty oath is "un-American and unconstitutional." A man identified as a professor challenges her: "There's a growing tendency in this world to call anything a person doesn't like un-American." She replies, "That's your opinion. Bill Whitman's [the bus driver's] opinion is just as good as yours, but he's lost his job because of it." When Whitman is asked to explain why he refused to sign the oath, he says:

> *If a man walked up to me on the street and asked me to sign*
> *a piece of paper saying I wasn't planning to rob a bank, well,*
> *I don't know what kind of right he had to figure I'd do such a*
> *thing. . . . I don't think anyone has the right to make me swear*
> *I'm innocent. You've got to prove I'm guilty.*

Another man wonders aloud what kind of workingman would stand on a principle if it meant losing his job. Things reach an emotional climax when a woman stands up and, in an effort to shame the bus driver, invokes her dead brother, killed in the Korean conflict. No one asked her brother, she exclaims, to prove his loyalty with a signature: "They asked him to prove it with his life!"

The show's most surprising feature, unlike anything done before on TV, was that the story's resolution—whether or not the bus driver would get his job back—was left to the viewer. The final voice-over intoned, "Don't go. You too have been in this room. You too will be counted. The issue is yours to decide. How will you vote? That is *the challenge*." At this very time, CBS had caved in to right-wing pressure and introduced a loyalty "questionnaire" that all employees had to sign.

No network was willing to pick up the controversial show, but the videotaped pilot episode found audiences with trade unions, civic organizations, and the American Civil Liberties Union. Cowriter Rod Serling soon went on, four years later, to create *The Twilight Zone*, with its complex messages delivered in his surreal and supernatural stories.

THE TELEVISION BLACKLIST

Most courageous of all was Sidney's quiet defiance of the network blacklists. He and producer Charles Russell risked everything by se-cretly employing blacklisted writers for more than two years and ninety-five scripts. Working especially closely with Abraham Polon-sky, Arnold Manoff, and Walter Bernstein, they juggled and intrigued to protect others working on the shows, including Walter Cronkite, from knowledge of what they were doing. "We worried about Sidney," Bernstein remembered. "He was doing something very good for us and we didn't want him to get into trouble. I would say, 'Be careful.' And he would say, 'Fuck them.'"

Because the ad men and network executives often wanted to speak directly with the shows' writers, Sidney and Charlie had to arrange surrogates or "fronts" to stand in for them. During one rehearsal, Sidney recalled, one of these stand-ins interrupted him repeatedly with suggestions and advice. Truly puzzled, Sidney called Charlie Russell aside to ask, "Is he for real or is he a front?" Charlie told him the guy was a front, and that they had to bear with him in order not to expose the real writer. As Charlie Russell remarked, "So we had to live with another irritant, a disease of another kind."

Another problem for Sidney and many others was an anti-communist tract, *Red Channels*, which had listed 151 suspected communists believed to have infiltrated the entertainment industry, and specifically radio and TV. The introduction to *Red Channels* in-veighed that:

Several commercially sponsored dramatic series are used as sounding boards, particularly with reference to current issues in which the [Communist] Party is critically interested: "academic freedom," "civil rights," "peace," the H-bomb, etc. . . . With radios in most American homes and with approximately 5 million TV sets in use, the Cominform and the Communist Party USA now rely more on radio and TV than on the press and motion pictures as "belts" to transmit pro-Sovietism to the American public.

Sidney's name didn't turn up on this list, but it did turn up in *The American Legion* magazine in an article about subversives and fellow travelers. His primary sponsor, Mel Block, "didn't knuckle under"; he stood by Sidney even when right-wing Laurence Johnson, owner of a supermarket chain in central New York, removed Block's products from his shelves and influenced others to do the same. Anxious that things could get worse, Block asked Sidney to meet with Dan O'Shea, who'd been hired by CBS head William Paley to do, as Sidney put it, "the Inquisitor's work." O'Shea was no right-wing fanatic, and the meeting was cordial, but having been assured that he was in the clear, Sidney could not refrain from asking O'Shea, "How can you, a decent and rational man, do what you are doing?" His reply: "Better one of us than one of them." Sidney never forgot O'Shea's words; he heard in them the kind of institutionalized moral injury that he would later explore in his police films, *Serpico, Prince of the City, Q & A* and *Night Falls on Manhattan.* Sidney felt the taint of this encounter; he called it "the second great humiliation I'd accepted in my life."

Hoping to erase any shadow of doubt, Mel wanted Sidney to also meet with Harvey Matusow and Victor Riesel. Matusow was a former Communist Party member and paid FBI informer. Riesel was an anticommunist syndicated columnist and McCarthyite who had been blinded by acid in an attack outside of Lindy's restaurant after writing an exposé of racketeers in the garment union. He had reported that both Sidney and Rita Gam had been present at Communist

Party meetings. Sidney often told the story of his storming the six blocks to Mel Block's Park Avenue apartment for the meeting, unsure whether he would "behave well," which to him meant not conceding anything no matter what they threatened. "I remember wishing a car or taxi would make the decision for me as I crossed the street," he writes. His anxiety and fury exploded as he entered the apartment shouting and calling Riesel a son of a bitch. Riesel, from his seat on the couch, patted the air and told him to calm down; he "wasn't the guy"—that is, they had no beef with him after all. In his memoir, Sidney adds this detail: as he and Matusow rode down in the elevator together, he turned to Sidney and said, "I've got a car. Can I give you a lift?" In some of Sidney's later films, such small, awkward and perplexingly humanizing gestures would add texture. As it turned out, two years later Matusow "found god," as Sidney put it, and began "unnaming names of people he'd blacklisted." The government was "terrified he'd recant his testimony on the Communist leaders, who were presently in jail." Sidney never tired of thinking about the untidiness and unexpectedness of human motives.

For years—forever, really—Sidney expressed relief that he had "behaved well," although he felt he'd never faced the really tough choices others had.

Sidney and his producer, Charlie Russell, found other ways to take swipes at McCarthyism. Whenever possible they coordinated their shows about historical persecution to line up with Edward R. Murrow's courageous jabs at Joe McCarthy. Given CBS's loyalty questionnaire and their in-house investigator, it is no surprise that Murrow once asked Charlie Russell, "How do you get away with what you do?" meaning with such politically risky stories. Sidney shared Russell's hopeful surmise that their show had encouraged Murrow to make his famous 1954 stand against McCarthy with "A Report on Senator Joseph McCarthy," which helped turn the tide of public opinion. In Murrow's words:

> *The line between investigating and persecuting is a very fine one, and the junior senator from Wisconsin has stepped over it*

repeatedly. His primary achievement has been in confusing the public mind, as between the internal and the external threats of Communism. We must not confuse dissent with disloyalty. . . . We will not be driven by fear into an age of unreason, if we dig deep in our history and our doctrine, and remember that we are not descended from fearful men—not from men who feared to write, to speak, to associate and to defend causes that were, for the moment, unpopular. . . . This is no time for men who oppose Senator McCarthy's methods to keep silent.

THE CRAFT

Sidney often reflected that his television years taught him the craft of directing; he learned multiple camera techniques, noting that "sometimes we had forty camera cuts a minute." Sidney used to indicate a camera switch by snapping his fingers, a habit that continued through the years. "Technically he was perfect," recollected actor Fred Scollay. "He'd say, 'Cut two seconds.' Or, 'We've got to cut four seconds out of this scene.' He had a mind like a clock." "Physically he flew and his mind flew," remembered actress Lee Grant. "He thought at twice the intensity of anyone else." Actor Fritz Weaver (*Fail-Safe*) recalled Sidney's fearlessness, adding, "But, you know, the pressures you were under with live television in those days—it was like going over Niagara Falls in a barrel."

Contemplating how exhausting it had been "in our little factory," Sidney reminisced, "When you're doing two shows a week, you're carrying eight shows up here [pointing to his head]. You were working on the script of the show that came up three weeks later; working on the sets and costumes of the show that came up two weeks later; working on the casting of the show that was coming up next week— plus your two shows coming up this week." This mental workout gave him the skills that earned him the reputation of a movie director who got things done on time and within budget. "*Nothing* was too complicated after that."

Early television was a legendary training ground, a film school for countless writers, directors, and actors. Television directors, then as now, were not as well known as the writers—who in those days included Paddy Chayefsky, Horton Foote, Rod Serling and Reginald Rose. But many of the directors went on to significant careers in the movies; the list of people who made the switch includes Robert Altman, George Roy Hill, Arthur Penn, Sydney Pollack, Blake Edwards and Robert Mulligan, as well as John Frankenheimer, who got his start as Lumet's assistant director on *You Are There* and *Danger*. "Meeting Sidney changed my life," Frankenheimer recalled. Sidney gave the future director of *The Manchurian Candidate* his first steady gig, as Yul Brynner had done for him. "Lumet is a fairly short individual," Frankenheimer reminisced, "and I'm six foot three. But he was *fast*. It was a funny sight, me running behind him—I never let him get more than a foot in front of me." During the making of *12 Angry Men*, the crew tied a pedometer to Sidney and discovered that he'd covered eleven miles on the set in one day.

When all this TV work commenced, Sidney, like most of his friends, had been drifting a bit—still figuring things out, directing small theater productions while teaching drama. He knew that without leading-man good looks, he'd be pushed further and further into the background. That meant less scope for his energy and artistic power. His daughter Amy once observed that her father was someone who needed more control over his life than actors have. Sidney worked steadily in television from 1949 to 1958, from ages twenty-five to thirty-four, directing hundreds of live and, ultimately, filmed shows.

12

MARRIAGE TAKE TWO:
MR. AND MRS. MOUSE

We try to choose our life . . .
— "Heart's Needle" by W. D. Snodgrass

It was no coincidence that Sidney and Gloria were both invited to a soirée for Grace Kelly at Richard and Doe Avedon's Beekman Place town house that evening. The Avedons were friends with Sidney and Gloria separately, and Richard was convinced that they "would have a lot to offer one another." Gloria recalled the evening perfectly, even what she wore: "I had little sleeveless short dresses made of satin in an array of delicious colors, long-waisted, in an F. Scott Fitzgerald mode, with pumps dyed to match, and that night I picked the *framboise* to wear." When she arrived at the party, "there he was, waiting for me."

She remembered dancing with Sidney, how he enfolded her in his arms "like a teddy bear." "I could feel the energy of his heart and soul going through me like warm honey," Gloria wrote. At a certain hour, Sidney, Cinderella-like, looked at his watch and said he had to leave to meet an agent at Sardi's, promising to return. Gloria felt panicky, fearing that was that. Considering the men in her life thus far, it stood to reason that she doubted Sidney's word. But he did come back, bearing a red rose for her, and they soon left the party together. "From that moment on we were glued to each other," Gloria recalled, "so glued that our friends found it hard to be around us."

Gloria Vanderbilt was eager and happy to share her memories of Sidney with me when we spoke on the phone; her voice was crisp and musical, her tone was warm and open and her memories were vivid. At moments she became tentative and introspective, rethinking aspects of their story. She allowed me to visit her studio, which was packed with personal treasures, along with her vibrantly colored and enchanting paintings, recent ones and ones painted years ago. Leaning against a wall in the kitchen stood a life-size photo of her son, Anderson Cooper, holding a Happy Mother's Day sign. Her assistant showed me to a comfortable settee, before which stood a large seashell-covered box that, she explained, had been brought down to the studio from Gloria's bedroom where it was kept. It contained notes and letters from Sidney, carefully tied in bundles with ribbons.

Gloria, like Sidney, had already lived many lives and survived many highs and lows when they met in the spring of 1955, both age thirty-one. Sidney, shaken by the failure of his first marriage and never good at being alone, was finding comfort and distraction among his wide circle of friends. His divorce from Rita Gam had not yet come through, and although he was on the lookout for someone new, he had no intention of getting involved with another actress. Gloria was recovering from the breakup with her second husband, the legendary conductor Leopold Stokowski. She'd found a welcome but not too promising distraction in an intense affair with Frank Sinatra, and she had recently discovered a new passion in acting.

Despite Sidney's conviction that actresses were out of the running, he could not resist Gloria. She was so open and curious and beautiful and responded so hungrily to Sidney's authenticity. ("Sidney was always Sidney," his friends would say.) And he wasn't so sure she *really* was determined to be an actress. Maybe she was just exploring. She had a book of poetry on the way to publication; she had long been serious about her painting and drawing and had kept a studio for years. Perhaps it was just a phase. It did turn out to be a phase, but one that lasted through their marriage.

They shared their stories. She could really talk to Sidney in a way that had not been possible with her previous husbands, and her passionate attentiveness to him took him by surprise. Unlikely as it was, their accounts had a crazy kind of rhyme. As small children, both had been moved around constantly, Gloria from one European palace to another, Sidney from one New York City tenement to another. Gloria was famous before she was old enough to understand or have a say, and, in his small way, Sidney also experienced a certain celebrity as a tiny child put onstage before he understood what was happening to him. Each knew the complex pull of fame, of feeling both special and uncared for. They were both in most ways parentless and exploited, and they both wondered, deep down, if those who cared for them cared more for the livelihoods they provided. Gloria's beloved Irish-German nanny, Dodo, was her only mainstay ("She *was* my mother, really," she said), and Sidney had only his sister, Faye; both caregivers were in some sense "paid for." Sidney and his father had had a seven-year estrangement over money; Gloria and her mother had been out of touch since Gloria gained control of her inheritance at age twenty-one and decided not to continue supporting her mother, a decision (later regretted) that catapulted her back onto the front page. They both felt they had been "saved" by their creative work.

Sidney and Gloria were born in the same year, 1924. That meant they knew the lyrics to the same popular songs. It also meant that when ten-year-old Gloria was at the center of "the trial of the century," as it was known, with her picture plastered on the front pages of every one of New York's twenty or so daily newspapers with the moniker "the poor little rich girl," ten-year-old Sidney was seeing the headlines. In some odd way, little Sidney may have identified with this quasi-orphaned heiress—her father died when she was eighteen months old—at the center of a custody battle between her remote, beautiful mother and her well-intentioned but icy aunt, Gertrude Vanderbilt Whitney, founder of the Whitney Museum. The headlines, mid-Depression, of family troubles among the highest and mightiest gripped the public imagination, and the scandal heated to the boiling point when a maid testified that she'd discovered Gloria's mother in bed with another woman. *Tout de suite*, Gloria was sent to live with Gertrude on her vast, lonely Long Island estate. Years later Sidney would remark in a letter to Gloria that, despite "starting so widely apart, [we share] the ridiculous and wonderful similarity of experience."

At age seventeen, Sidney had found a way to join the war effort; Gloria at seventeen had fled finishing school to take up residence—accompanied by a chaperone—in Los Angeles with her unreformed mother. As she recalled it, all she wanted was to date movie stars: "As a child I was obsessed with movies and movie stars. I thought that's how it will be when I grow up." She meant the romance and simplicity, but she also had some half-formed fantasies of becoming a movie star herself. "Of course my idea of it was nothing like it really is," she reflected. Her fame, wealth and beauty opened every door. Before she knew it, she was dating men she had girlishly worshipped: Errol Flynn, Van Heflin, Ray Milland and the millionaire aviator and movie producer Howard Hughes.

In almost no time, a stern letter from Aunt Gertrude—"You're being talked about"—pushed Gloria to seek a reprieve from the family watchdogs at the marriage altar. From among her many suitors, she chose a handsome and charming—in the style of singer-actor Dean Martin, as Gloria recalled him—Hollywood hanger-on who was sometimes employed by Howard Hughes, named Pasquale (Pat) DiCicco. Still seventeen years old, Gloria gave no thought to the fact that DiCicco's first wife had died under suspicious circumstances and no one had ever been charged for her possible murder. The abuse against Gloria began almost immediately, and, in the pattern of countless abused women, she dutifully carried on. She moved with DiCicco to an officer training camp in Kansas, where he blackened her eyes and banged her head against the wall. Ashamed, she told no one and stuck it out for three years.

At age twenty-one, while Sidney was making his way to Calcutta with the Signal Corps, Gloria married the famed conductor Leopold Stokowski (today known to many for his role in Disney's *Fantasia*). Stokowski, forty years her senior, turned out to be a tyrannical husband of a different kind, controlling, judgmental and jealous. Many years after their divorce, Gloria learned that the imperious Leopold, the father of her two sons Stan and Christopher, born in 1950 and

1952, had invented an identity for himself as the son of Polish nobility. In fact, he was from an English working-class family; his brother was a car salesman in London.

Breaking away from Stokowski proved difficult; Gloria always needed someone or something to run to. A brief fling with Marlon Brando helped move things along. She'd been smitten watching his film performance in *A Streetcar Named Desire*, and such was her confusing power in the world that within forty-eight hours of watching the film in New York City, she was dining alone with him in his Los Angeles home.

But it was Frank Sinatra who disentangled her from Stokowski. She had begun tentatively to pursue a career in acting while still in the marriage, but Stokowski had little respect for that art form, or for what he called its attendant "vanity fair." In open rebellion, she had begun studying with Sanford Meisner at the Neighborhood Playhouse, where her classmates Steve McQueen, Peter Falk, Joanne Woodward and Sydney Pollack inspired her. She loved the classes, and she had success in an out-of-town production of a play called *The Swan*, in which she played a princess. Theater and film agents responded instantly: she was a hot property, the celebrity child-turned-actress. Sinatra became curious about her and showed up where she was rehearsing a revival of Saroyan's *The Time of Your Life*, directed by her teacher, Sanford Meisner. In no time, Gloria and Sinatra were "involved" and he had signed her to a three-movie contract to work with him. She met Sidney before the shooting was scheduled, while Sinatra was on tour in Australia.

The last thing Gloria's friends knew, Frank Sinatra had been sending Gloria flowers and candy. "She seemed radiantly happy," Carol Saroyan wrote in her diary. "But only a few weeks later Sinatra was gone and Gloria announced she was in love with Sidney Lumet, a young director who was just breaking into films from TV."

Gloria, emerging from two complicated marriages—one to an abusive rageaholic, the other to a loving but domineering "fraud"—saw in Sidney the "warmest, the most loving person, the most open, unedited person I had ever met." And decades later she confirmed that assessment in our conversation: "I've never known a man in my whole life so completely honest, so completely *there*." Up to that point in her life, she had been famous for being famous. Gloria believed she might begin to own her fame, to *earn* her fame, on the stage. It wasn't calculated in a scheming way, but for Gloria in this moment, Sidney's profession was not entirely irrelevant. And despite his doubts about marrying another actress, and about Gloria's gift for acting, he was full steam ahead.

Although it wasn't to last long for Gloria, her attraction to the theater had much in common with Sidney's. "I loved starting the rehearsal of a play," she wrote, "the feeling of belonging to what I imagined a family to be like (temporary though it was), knowing that as in a family there would be altercations, fights, romance . . . but nevertheless we'd hang in, sticking together at least until after the play closed and the 'family' broke up. But after that there'd be another opening, another show, and with it, another family." Sidney shared this feeling of being nourished by an intense common endeavor, finding a temporary family in the work, first as a child in the theater and later as a movie director. In certain ways they clung to each other (as Sidney had to his sister)—again, like orphans in a storm.

Gloria had found a soul mate, a peer, not a father figure like Stokowski. Their relationship could be reciprocal, and she believed she could salve some of Sidney's wounds. For his part, he thought what she needed was to be loved unwaveringly, and he felt he could love her forever. And if what she really wanted was to become an actress, he could, unselfishly, make her one. Perhaps she sensed that Sidney held a more reliable magic wand than any of her previous lovers.

When, not long after Sidney and Gloria had become an item, she flew off to make *Johnny Concho* with Sinatra, Sidney determined to stay out of it, to say nothing, despite his anxieties about her reunion with Sinatra. Daily, or twice daily, Sidney's letters reached Gloria at her cottage at the Beverly Hills Hotel from his lonely East 66th Street apartment. In one letter he expresses his frustration at their telephone conversations; he felt rushed, and his "thoughts and feelings come

Sidney and Gloria marry at the home of Sidney's dear friend, playwright Sidney Kingsley. *(Courtesy Everett Collection)*

tumbling and pushing out, all trying to get to you, and the mouthpiece of the phone is too small an opening for them all to fit into. It's like too many people trying to get through too small a door." In another letter he laments, "Such a day of mummies, Egypt, comedy pacing . . . comedy is such work. The things I've had to cope with (Eva [Marie Saint]'s fighting with the leading man, the script is too long but we can't cut it, things that seemed funny aren't, etc. etc.) It all adds up to exhaustion." Meanwhile, Gloria was unhappy with the script of *Johnny Concho*; it was far from the vehicle she had hoped for. She felt it was "a trashy western, not in the same league as *High Noon* as I had been led to believe." After a week, she was back in New York with Sidney.

Before either of their divorces had come through, Sidney had purchased two gold bands engraved with their names. On August 27, 1956, they were married by a judge in a private afternoon ceremony. It took place at the home of Sidney Kingsley, Sidney's old friend, in the famed Dakota apartment building on 72nd Street. Kingsley had authored the first Broadway show Sidney had appeared in at age ten, *Dead End.*

MR. AND MRS. MOUSE

Just waking up in the morning, you know, it's an attitude, an attitude of what Fitzgerald called "romantic readiness."

—GLORIA VANDERBILT

When Sidney moved into the penthouse Gloria and her sons had lived in with Stokowski, the couple "breathed new life into it," as Gloria recalled. As part of that revivification, the apartment would require redecorating, a favorite pastime of Gloria's. Her oldest son, Stan, recalled a couple of his mother's decorating projects at that time: she covered a bathroom wall with seashells, and one of the bedroom doorways had a Romanesque arch. "Why was it there?" Stan wondered. "I don't know. It was too small for an adult." A notable contrast, Stan recalled, was Sidney's contribution to the décor: "one of the first color TV sets . . . it was really big and heavy and sat right on the floor."

Sidney's friend, screenwriter Walter Bernstein (*Fail-Safe*, *The Front*), recalled dinner parties at what he referred to as "Gloria's house." "It was very pleasant, it was very nice, but I always had the sense that Sidney didn't quite know what he was doing there." To Walter, it was all a bit contrived. "I remember one party they did, a formal party, you had to wear a tuxedo. It was just strange, it was odd, you know." Greeting guests at the door, Sidney was fond of saying, "Welcome to my humble abode." Their home was said to have had "the enchantment of a film set." It would be a while before he began to take the high life for granted.

Gloria woke up each morning to a love note from Sidney left at her bedside before he skipped off to work. At age thirty-one, Sidney was one of a handful of master television directors, and he had returned to directing theater in 1955 with off-Broadway productions, including George Bernard Shaw's *The Doctor's Dilemma*, starring Geraldine Fitzgerald and Roddy McDowall. His first movie was also in the offing.

Busy as he was, he never omitted his morning ritual of jotting down a few romantic sentences about how beautiful Gloria looked in her sleep or how much he loved everything about her; often his notes— always on dark pink or bright yellow paper—were captioned illustrations advancing the charming adventures of "Mr. and Mrs. Mouse":

"Mr. and Mrs. Mouse skipping through a field of buttercups" or "Mrs. Mouse does a graceful figure eight while Mr. Mouse looks on appreciatively." Sidney signed some of the notes with the nickname "Jug," or with just a little drawing of a jug. Gloria recalled that Jug referred to the lyrics of Glenn Miller's hit "Little Brown Jug":

> *Me and my wife live all alone*
> *In a little log hut we're all our own*
> *She loves gin and I love rum,*
> *And don't we have a lot of fun!*
> *Ha, ha, ha, you and me,*
> *Little brown jug, don't I love thee!*
> *Ha, ha, ha, you and me,*
> *Little brown jug, don't I love thee!*

He worked hard to delight her, and to bring her oversized life down to a mouse-sized scale. Here and there a morning note indicates some discord, an apology or effort to clear up a misunderstanding: "I

(From the private papers of Gloria Vanderbilt)

called you at 11:30. Again at 12:30. . . . I didn't know about the publicity meeting."

As Gloria recalled it, Sidney's hardest work in the marriage was finding roles for her and working with her on them. "He really knocked himself out" to support her acting career, she said, casting her in several of his own productions on TV and on the stage. In an early letter he expresses his belief in her acting talent. He tells her he wants her career to advance, "not only because you want it but because it'll enrich and fill us, you, me, us." He goes on to say, "It's starting in me because I feel you loving me thru it (the work) and with it (the work), and I love you so." He wanted to convince her—and himself—that, unlike Stokowski, he supported her acting career and didn't view her ambition as selfish, as he had come to view Rita's.

Sidney put a lot of effort into getting backing for a movie he thought was just the right vehicle for Gloria, an adaptation by Walter Bernstein of the 1926 F. Scott Fitzgerald story "Rich Boy." It had done well as a television drama directed by Delbert Mann, starring Grace Kelly, who again pops up as a star whose career presented a model for Gloria to emulate. It is the story of an old-money playboy who falls in love with a nice, socially appropriate girl, but he goes astray and realizes too late that he has wasted his life without her. Sidney had wanted Montgomery Clift to star with Gloria. Walter Bernstein recalled that he and Sidney had lunched with David O. Selznick to discuss the project, but Selznick wanted it for his wife, Jennifer Jones, and nothing came of it. Some celebrated lines of Fitzgerald's from this story might have resonated with Sidney in one way or another:

> *Let me tell you about the very rich. They are different from you and me. They possess and enjoy early, and it does something to them, makes them soft where we are hard, and cynical where we are trustful, in a way that, unless you were born rich, it is very difficult to understand.*

Unlike Sidney's other wives, Gloria felt Sidney put his own work second; their life together came first. "He turned his life over to me," she said. This may account in part for the two weaker films that followed *12 Angry Men*: *Stage Struck* in 1958 and *That Kind of Woman* in 1959. Gloria's recollection was that he directed these two movies strictly for the money: "We were living pretty high off the hog." It would seem that although they lived in "Gloria's house," Sidney was paying at least some of the bills.

At home, their life was full, with a lot that was new. Sidney enjoyed Gloria's two small sons tremendously and spent a lot of time with them. Stan remarked in later life that, when the marriage ended, it was "hard when Sidney left." Their penthouse was the perfect setting for Sidney's crowd of show business friends, Gloria recalled:

> *When Jule Styne arrived at our parties he would always head straight to the piano to play the songs he had composed over the years. It would be Judy Holliday or . . . Marilyn Monroe singing as she tried to remember the lyrics to "Diamonds Are a Girl's Best Friend." Lena Horne with Harold Arlen at the piano playing his [and Yip Harburg's] "[Somewhere] Over the Rainbow," Adolph Green singing Captain Hook songs from his musical* Peter Pan *or he and Betty Comden singing "Just in Time" from* Bells Are Ringing *along with Judy Holliday, while Truman Capote spooked around for something to write about.*

Gloria was glad to host Sidney's friends; she wanted him to be surrounded by people, *his* people; she felt he thrived on that. Other luminaries in regular attendance included Elizabeth Taylor, Sammy Davis Jr., Cecil Beaton, Carl Van Vechten, Gordon Parks, Richard Avedon, James Agee and Stephen Sondheim. Gloria recalled without bitterness that, with the exceptions of Harold Arlen and Jule Styne, who had given her singing lessons when she was a little girl, Sidney's friends "went with him when we divorced."

In quiet times, Sidney and Gloria buzzed around town in his red MG, and up to their Connecticut retreats, first one they rented from writer and director Joshua Logan (*South Pacific*, *Bus Stop*, *Camelot*), then one they bought together that they called Faraway House. When they were driving, Sidney would urge Gloria to sing; he loved to listen to her "wavery" voice. They took rustic walks together, even did a little skiing in the wintertime; in summer they gathered wild raspberries and cooked steak on their charcoal grill, all scenes lovingly portrayed in Sidney's "mouse" drawings. One such sketch features the two mice, one with a book in hand, standing atop a hill, and the caption reads, "Mr. and Mrs. Mouse study nature's greatest spectacle, the night time sky."

A garden party at their place near Stamford in Connecticut was memorable to Gloria's friend Carol, who at the time had recently married actor Walter Matthau:

> *Everybody sat around the pool. And Gloria had everything done up; it was like a fairy tale. Each little table with its Porthault tablecloth and a bouquet of flowers, and the wood-block cutting board, and all the fantastic food. It was a perfect, warm, fall afternoon. . . . The usual gang was there: Jack Warden, E. G. Marshall, the Avedons, Adolph and Phyllis Green, along with a few of the society crowd like Judy Peabody and the Eberstadts.*

Walter, who was new to this crowd and not feeling too comfortable, sat down on the edge of a glass-topped table—and it broke, leaving him embarrassed and bleeding. As Carol recounted, "Sidney took over immediately and got him into their car and drove with them to their doctor down the road." Many of Sidney's friends remarked on his take-charge instincts; some said he made people feel safe.

COMPLICATIONS

From the very beginning, Sidney and Gloria were both open about their vulnerabilities, attempting to work through them together. He strove to sustain her trust in the durability of his love and to bolster her confidence in her acting. And he did not disguise his own insecurities, writing in a letter to her, "Of course there are areas I need belief in too, and, my heart, you're working on them so beautifully." Gloria didn't recall him sharing much about his mother, but she was aware of the tensions with his father, Baruch, whom she met only once: "Sidney gave no indication that he wanted him to be part of our lives."

It was after the first and only meeting between Gloria and Baruch that Sidney jotted down some lines of doggerel, undoubtedly written when Sidney was in his cups:

Wasn't Dad Nice (alas)
Wasn't Dad nice
Though we put him on ice?
He gets so stinking
On sociable drinking
Was he really so bad?
Did he act like a cad?
He just childishly flirts
When he looks up your skirts . . .
He acts that way cause he's gettin' old
Why often before
He'd pee on the floor
That's why we moved
So you see he's improved.
Wasn't dad nice,
Wasn't dad nice last night.

Sidney references the family's frequent change of residence in his childhood, suggesting that it was Baruch, not his mother—as his father claimed—who repeatedly fouled their nest.

Gloria had her challenges as well. While Sidney was working on his fourth film, *The Fugitive Kind*, starring Marlon Brando and Anna Magnani, Gloria was going through a custody battle with Stokowski for their two sons. She recalled the very moment the summons had been served: she had been walking on Madison Avenue when a man shouted "Gloria" from across the street; when she turned, he dashed over and "jabbed papers into my hands." Stokowski wanted full custody, and, Gloria recounted, "because of my experience as a child going through the custody case between my mother and aunt, he thought I would never have the guts to fight him. How little he knew me!" Her story concludes:

> *I was awarded full custody. That night Sidney told me that*
> *when he arrived on the set the day after, the crew had taped on*
> *his camera a full-page headline from the* Daily News: GLORIA
> WINS WHERE HER MOTHER FAILED.

Sidney, no matter how busy he was with the film, was a "tremendous force in supporting me through this," Gloria emphasized. She also noted that her relationship with Brando, whom Sidney was directing, had "resolved long before I met Sidney," and that she did not recall Marlon's name ever coming up between them.

The two supported each other and shared enthusiasms for both a glamorous social life and simple family pleasures. They seemed to triumph where their parents had failed, with only some small fore-shadowing of the strain that was to come.

13

THE MAKING OF *12 ANGRY MEN*

He was great at melodrama with character—a lot of that came out of Yiddish theater—a lot of geshreying, *two people in a room. . . . He liked situations where actors could come at each other.*

—WALTER BERNSTEIN, FILM AND TV SCREENWRITER

Here's this guy who is thinking about this idea . . . some kind of larger question about the attainability or unattainability of justice. Can you ever obtain what is somehow floating out there? It's out there and can you grab it?

—JENNY LUMET,
MULLING OVER HER FATHER'S MANY FILMS
ABOUT THE CRIMINAL JUSTICE SYSTEM

In the photographs of Sidney directing his first movie, *12 Angry Men*, he looks like a young beatnik, slouching, smoking his Camels. He sports a series of hats: a fez, a top hat, a cowboy hat, a visor, a beanie with a pom-pom, a panama, a Sherlock Holmes cap. His friend Walter Bernstein suggested this might have been Sidney's way of dealing with his self-consciousness about being a movie director for the first time. Gloria Vanderbilt disagreed, protesting in an email that Sidney had no anxiety about assuming the helm: "NO insecurities

EVER," she asserted; "He was ALREADY a PRO" by this time, a master at making his actors "feel GREAT." Sidney and Gloria were married the summer the movie was shot, 1956. Occasionally, years down the road, a funny hat would turn up on Sidney's head on set. Maybe it was for luck.

With this film Sidney was making his transition from TV to movies, and so was the story he was directing. *12 Angry Men* took shape in 1954 when television writer Reginald Rose found himself serving as a juror on a manslaughter case. In the delib-

On the set of *12 Angry Men*, Sidney, unlit cigarette in mouth, stands behind director of photography Boris Kaufman, looking with him through a lens.

erations, during the struggle to arrive at a decision about another man's fate, "we got into this terrific, furious, eight-hour argument in the jury room," he recalled, and he saw in it the makings of a television drama.

The drama of the jury room hadn't been explored before on TV or film. Some courtroom dramas had left their mark, but the deliberation of the jury had always occurred offscreen. Rose wrote it as a teleplay for CBS, and it won him an Emmy. Henry Fonda, the great stage and screen actor, happened to catch the drama on television. His imagination was caught by this story of a single juror holding out against eleven others who were all too ready to convict a young defendant of murder. He wanted to play that holdout juror; he was convinced it would make a fine movie. Fonda reached out to Reggie Rose. Rose's original teleplay had been cut almost in half for the television production, so he restored some of the material, developed and polished the characters, and expanded it to movie length.

Fonda and Rose soon ran into a wall, though. With no women,

no Technicolor, a story set almost exclusively in a single dreary room, and without even a flashback, the film was a hard sell to a studio. The two men ended up producing it themselves, budgeting the film at about $340,000, less than the cost of mounting a Broadway musical at that time. The actors would each earn a modest $3,600.

Sidney had helped Rose get his first script on the air and just recently had directed Rose's powerful 1956 *Tragedy in a Temporary Town*, about a lynching narrowly averted. Rose suggested Sidney to direct. Fonda knew Sidney's TV work, and as he later explained, "I hired Sidney because he had a reputation of being wonderful with actors. We got a bonus that nobody counted on. He also had incredible organization and awareness of the problem of shooting and not wasting time."

In hindsight, "not wasting time" seems like a wry understatement, given his reputation for speed. On the set of his final film, *Before the Devil Knows You're Dead*, when Sidney was eighty-two years old, the joke, reported by Ethan Hawke, was that across town an identical film, with an identical crew, was being made, and the two were racing to see who would finish first.

Sidney delivered *12 Angry Men* right on budget, as he would with pretty much every film to follow, and he managed to complete the shooting two days ahead of schedule. As for organization and efficiency, Sidney's philosophy was that all the acting and setup work had happened in rehearsal, so the actual filming should take very little time. He was famous—some actors would say notorious—for doing no more than two or three takes. His work in live television involved planning every bit of everything before the cameras rolled, including "your dramatic selections," as Sidney put it. He saw that the supposed advantage of film is that you can "do a thing 97 different ways," but he believed that could also be a deathtrap.

Money was saved by efficiency, by an absence of overtime, and also by his parsimonious use of film footage. "In *12 Angry Men* I exposed a total of 63,000 feet of film," he recalled. "Now, this is insanely small. That's not even printed. I only printed about 17,000 feet, and the picture ran about 11,000 feet." In contrast, Hollywood directors typically printed eight to fourteen times the amount of footage they would eventually use. Sidney printed less than twice what he included in the film. Of course, now that films are shot digitally, this issue has become moot.

Sidney was thrilled to be working with Henry Fonda, and he knew the movie was right up his alley. He would line up the best New York character actors, whom he'd been working with for years. The scale of the piece, a story set in one room in continuous time, didn't worry him; he'd turned out dozens of live TV dramas from a single studio. Still, Sidney was nervous about Fonda—he didn't want to displease or disappoint him.

The two men hit their first and possibly only collision point when Fonda, entering the studio on West 54th Street for the first time, was alarmed by the painted backdrop outside the jury room windows. "They look like shit," Fonda complained. They compared poorly to the fabulous painted backdrops Hitchcock had used for *The Wrong Man*, the film Fonda had recently completed. Sidney had indeed opted for a cheaper designer, but he reassured Fonda that their brilliant cinematographer, Boris Kaufman, had a way to light them that would make them work, and they did.

THE NITTY-GRITTY

You have to cast your camera the way you cast an actor.
—Sidney Lumet

Sidney had brought on the renowned Polish-born cinematographer, Boris Kaufman, to help him figure out how to work the claustrophobic setting to their advantage in telling the story. Kaufman had filmed Jean Vigo's gorgeous classic French films, *Zero for Conduct* and *L'Atalante*; he'd worked with Jean Renoir, and had recently won an Oscar for Kazan's *On the Waterfront*. Most famous for expressive light and shadow, he likely contributed to the three-part lighting structure of *12 Angry Men* that establishes its three moods: bright and hot; darkened by the rain; and then, when Martin Balsam's Juror no. 1 switches on the lights, the more defined, intimate, inside-feeling light. Kaufman may also have had a hand in designing the compositions, the slowly increasing use, as the tension mounts, of two-shots and four-shots (framing that includes two or four people), and powerful ensemble frames, looking down the table at several men at once. Kaufman was the younger brother of the celebrated Soviet filmmaker Dziga Vertov (born David Abelevich Kaufman), director of the Soviet avant-garde masterpiece *Man with a Movie Camera*. Boris would go on to become an important collaborator with Sidney on seven of his films.

Sidney ran rehearsals for two weeks, as he had typically done for his television dramas. The rehearsal room was in Steinway Hall, at 113 West 57th Street in Manhattan. "Dear lads" was what he called his dozen actors, a jovial group who could turn their characters on and off in a moment. His soon-to-become-legendary "long-table reads" took place at a table very much like the one in the film. The routine was two full run-throughs every day. A *Herald-Tribune* reporter sitting in on an early rehearsal recounted these words from Sidney, who, sitting on the far end of the table, enjoined his ensemble:

> *Some people have suggested that the picture needs jazzing up . . . somebody had the idea that we should explain that all the regular jury rooms are occupied and have this in the basement, where we could show the exposed pipes and maybe the furnace in order to provide pictorial contrast. But we threw the idea out. Somebody else thought it would be great to have a glass top on the jury table to permit trick camera shots, but that too was vetoed. There's going to be no artificiality in this. You are going to be the whole picture. This is not a tract. This is not a pro-jury or anti-jury thing. It's just a thing about human behavior. No glass tabletops. No basement room. Just you and the fullness of your behavior. It's right in your laps.*

Adding to the no "jazzing up" ethos, Sidney asked the actors to wear their own clothes during the filming rather than be costumed. He would do the same years later for *Dog Day Afternoon*. He was after something, not only for the actors' performances but for the look of the films. Finding ways to authentically represent everyday people on film without quaintness or condescension was a lifelong pursuit. It was personal for him, to represent and attest to the weight and complexity of ordinary lives. Perhaps nothing moved him more than stories of ordinary people trying to cope with something bigger than themselves.

Shooting the film took nineteen days. In a piece for *Life* magazine that coincided with the film's release, Sidney commented on some of the challenges of the shoot. He explained that since they were shooting out of sequence and often only a few of the actors were on the set at a time, it was a mental puzzle to figure out who was looking where and at whom. Often the person the actor was looking at or speaking to was not actually there. Sidney spent long nights pondering the problem and turning his script into a maze of diagrams. He noted:

> *The camera went around the table, shooting chair by chair. Once lights and camera were pointed at a chair, then every speech, no matter its order in the movie, was shot. That meant that often you had only two or three actors in or near chairs, talking and arguing across the table with actors who were not there. You had to figure out where the nonexistent actor's eyes would be, so that the existent actor could stare him down.*

Sidney joked about getting the "sweat right" for each of the characters. Some jurors were meant to perspire more and some less. "The little bank clerk sweats very little," Sidney explained. "That is in character." Other jurors were meant to frequently wipe their damp foreheads. "With every scene we stood before the actor with an atomizer trying to figure out whether or not to squirt, and just how much to squirt."

Sidney, sporting his Sherlock Holmes hat, consults his diagrams, as Henry Fonda awaits direction.

Throughout the shoot, Sidney's admiration for Fonda, who was already one of his favorite actors (along with Spencer Tracy and James Mason), only deepened. Fonda's focus and technical perfectionism impressed Sidney. He recalled: "If the script girl said [he] took a puff of the cigarette on that word and he said no, it was two words earlier, he was always right." It surprised Sidney that Fonda "was too shy" to look at rushes, which, as the film's producer, he was obliged to do. He stopped in on the first night, squeezed Sidney on the shoulder, said it was "magnificent," and never came again. Years later Fonda, who was highly self-critical, observed that he felt this was one of his three best performances.

DISTRIBUTION MADNESS

United Artists agreed to distribute the film. Two years earlier they'd had great luck with *Marty*, also a remade TV drama, this one set in the Bronx. *Marty* was made for under $350,000 and pulled in

$3 million, plus four Oscars, including for Best Picture. *Variety* observed at the time, "If *Marty* is an example of the type of material that can be gleaned, then studio story editors better spend more time at home looking at television."

Even with this precedent, the promotion of *12 Angry Men* went way off course. The original trailer for the film seemed to be advertising a horror movie, with its splashy matrix wipes, dissonant chords and an ominous voice-over that warned, "Watch them and pray, for someday you may become one of them, twelve men with the smell of violent death in their nostrils . . . twelve men turned into twelve clawing animals."

Another blunder was scheduling the debut at the Capitol Theatre in New York, precisely the wrong venue for a picture Sidney thought of as leaning toward art house. The theater had a stage show and seated about four thousand; there was no way this black-and-white drama was going to pull in that kind of audience. It lasted there less than two weeks. Overall, it made "no money" in the United States, only $1 million in its first year.

At the time, Sidney was more concerned about the damage this poor return had on Fonda than on himself. Fonda had ventured into the producer's role for the first time with *12 Angry Men*, and he quickly discovered he hadn't much taste for producing. Sidney explained a few years later in an oral history he made at Columbia University: "Hank Fonda? Well, you see, the fact of the matter is that *12 Angry Men* wasn't successful enough for United Artists to put up the money for another picture with Hank . . . because in their terms, unless the profit is in the millions, you don't get the second crack at the next picture with your own company." What Fonda lost in money and opportunities to produce, he made up for in the prestige the film gained when it first appeared on television. It was an event with wide appeal; it touched a nerve up and down the social ladder. Discussed in diners and at dinner parties, the movie began its ascendance.

Sidney would fight throughout his career for more control over his films, including advertising and promotion, aspiring to establish his own production company so he would not have to play by studio rules. On his first two films, *12 Angry Men* and *Stage Struck*, he did most of the editing himself. He wanted final cut and ultimately would get it seventeen years later—a privilege few directors are able to negotiate, wherein no changes can be introduced by the studio.

Sidney had attempted to establish an independent production company in 1953, in hopes of making a film in Mexico that would feature Rita Gam, his wife at the time. He had purchased rights to a play called *Bullfight*, by Leslie Stevens. He had made plans to take a leave from CBS, where he was directing the hit show *You Are There*, and even named his independent company Fiesta Productions. It came to naught, perhaps because Rita was off to Marrakech to shoot her first leading role.

Sidney didn't believe good movies needed to cost so much to make or earn such big profits. He liked Fonda's model on their film: taking his share at the back end, no salary but ownership on the percentages. For *12 Angry Men*, Sidney figured that Fonda wound up making $300,000 (1958 dollars). Sidney quipped at the time, "Well, you know, if you watch your restaurant tabs carefully and don't tip too heavily in the cabs, you can struggle along on that for a year." Less film, less time and Sidney's final ingredient for reducing costs: less greed. Ultimately, though, Sidney did not want to get bogged down raising money, placating investors, or thinking too much about the business end, although he had a good head for it. He eventually suspended the idea of establishing his own production company, but inevitably, for some of his projects, he would have to apply himself to raising money.

Despite tanking in the American market, the film did well with the critics and was nominated for three Academy Awards: Best Picture, Best Director, and Best Screen Adaptation. It lost in all three categories to David Lean's magisterial *The Bridge on the River Kwai*. Sidney is one of a handful of first-time directors to receive a top nomination. The movie was warmly received overseas with both audiences and critics, taking home the British and German Oscar equivalents. And it drew the attention of the *Cahiers du cinéma* crowd, canonizing him on their list of the best films of 1957, along with Buñuel, Chaplin, Fellini, Bergman, Fritz Lang and Nicholas Ray, making him an American favorite in France for years to come.

WHAT MAKES *12 ANGRY MEN* A CLASSIC?

Familiar to moviegoers across generations, *12 Angry Men* is not the likeliest of Sidney's films to achieve the status of a classic, as it features a dozen mostly middle-aged white men in a room, doing nothing but talking.

Nevertheless, the movie has been subtitled, dubbed and celebrated around the world. Adaptations of the film have appeared in Germany, Norway, India, Russia, France, and China, with more still on the way. The film is sufficiently iconic to have been affectionately parodied on *The Simpsons*, *Saturday Night Live*, *Family Guy* and elsewhere. A 1991 Japanese spoof, *The Gentle 12*, opens with eleven members of a cheerful, smoothie-sipping jury instantly voting to acquit; the one holdout unsuccessfully attempts to sway the jury to convict. Oddly, this film was made before Japan introduced jury trials. When in 2006 Japan was preparing to adopt a jury system, a theater group performed *12 Angry Men* in local communities; their aim was to help future jurors overcome a cultural reluctance to express opinions or argue in public.

Doubtless much of its familiarity is attributable to its frequent use as a teaching tool. In 1956 the movie was previewed at every state bar association before it opened in theaters. The American Bar Association soon honored it for "contributing to greater public understanding and appreciation of the American system of justice." It remains a favorite in high school classrooms, an aspirational civics lesson on the principle of innocent until proven guilty and on the duties and responsibilities of American citizenship. It admonishes bigotry and bias and examines how our judgments are inflected. What's more, the film insists that a single person who stands up for what he or she believes *can* make a difference.

12 Angry Men has had a second life in recent years, becoming a favorite at corporate conferences of all kinds. For those in business management, the movie provides examples of leadership skills. Attendees learn from Juror no. 8 (Henry Fonda) the importance of allowing open inquiry, establishing equality among team members and recognizing that varying experiences and backgrounds are assets and conflict may be necessary to achieve objectives. Communications experts draw pointers from the film about how to get buy-in for your ideas by attending closely to Fonda's body language, his open-ended questions, the importance of eye contact and his fluctuations between soft and hard sell. They emphasize how attentively he listens, his use of visual aids and word pictures, and they note that the most influential jurors are those who maintain a calm disposition, while the hotheads in the jury room who attempt to impose their views fail to persuade.

And group psychologists note the influence of social norms on the jurors' behavior, observing that such influence often remains outside awareness until we are forced to question what feels normal in our world or defend why we think what we think. Asked why he is so sure the defendant is guilty, Juror no. 2 (John Fiedler) can offer no explanation beyond, "I just thought he was guilty." When Fonda requests a secret ballot early in the film, psychologists explain, he is successfully weakening the influence of the group. A course in negotiation at Harvard Law School finds in the film lessons in behavior-change initiatives.

Apparently one of the film's most salient attractions is that almost any lesson can be drawn from it.

For teaching purposes, the film is most frequently shown in film schools around the world. For starters, there is no better example of the use of camera lenses and angles to increase visual variety and convey mood. At first the walls are visible and the setting has a path of air around it. Gradually shifting to longer focal lenses, Sidney created the sense that the jury room is closing in on the characters, increasing the viewer's feelings of claustrophobia. He also repositioned the camera's angle on the actors. At the beginning, the characters are shot from above eye level; at the end, most are filmed from below eye level using telephoto and wide-angle lenses, shortening the depth of field, emphasizing the increased tension among the men. Close-ups grow increasingly insistent as the tension rises, as do powerfully jammed ensemble frames. Sidney has been acknowledged as ahead of his time in crafting his lens plots and lighting arcs, the purely technical changes he charted to be woven through his films. Years later Sidney observed: "You'd think that shooting in a tight space would be the easiest thing in the world, when in fact the easiest thing to shoot is a cattle round-up! Just put six cameras on it and all the footage will be so marvelous you won't know what to choose because the action is so terrific."

Composition and choreography are beautifully demonstrated in two scenes Sidney was justly proud of, and which took hours of rehearsal time to get right. The first is a six-minute crane shot near the beginning of the film, assembling the cast in the jury room. The camera moves in and out among the men, picking up their brief exchanges. As they mull and arrange themselves around the room, they begin to emerge as recognizable characters. Fonda recalled that lighting the scene turned out to be a phenomenal problem, taking from eight thirty in the morning until four o'clock in the afternoon to set up.

The second scene occurs when Juror no. 10 (Ed Begley) explodes in a racist rant: "You know what those people are like." One by one the other jurors rise from their seats and turn their backs on him. "Pulling the camera back and doing it in one shot saved the scene from sentimentality," Sidney said. It would have been ruined by breaking it up with reaction shots, registering each character scowl. He notes that Henry Fonda's Juror no. 8 is not the first to get up, suggesting a decision had been made not to portray him as always in the lead, or perhaps not as the period's textbook liberal. Some critics have seen in Fonda's character some traces of the academicism of presidential candidate Adlai Stevenson, for whom Fonda was stumping while shooting the film. Students also notice that roughly half of the edits take place in the last twenty minutes of the film, another technique for creating a sense of climax.

A TIME CAPSULE OF THE 1950s

12 Angry Men has become a popular script for high school theater productions; the title, however, has been changed to *12 Angry Jurors* to allow for mixed-gender casting. Why was the jury all male in the original anyway, since women had begun serving on juries in New York State in 1937? New York was the twenty-second state to empanel women. The 1937 law granted that women were permitted but not *required* to serve; they were granted automatic exemptions because of their "special obligation as the center of home and family life." Hence an all-male jury was more or less the norm. It was not until 1975 that the U.S. Supreme Court held that it was no longer tenable that women could be given automatic exemptions based solely on their sex.

It's likely that Sidney didn't give much thought to the gender issue in the film. Most of the people he worked with, besides actresses and "script girls," were, at this point, men. This would change later on. Indeed, outside the home, the world belonged to men. A large share of Sidney's oeuvre would focus on men, mostly on men at their jobs, contending with one another under duress. Friction between men, far more than friendships, was his theme. But for all the male-centeredness of his work life, Sidney was not really what you'd call a guy's guy. He was a schmoozer and had great fondness for many men, but he rarely grew close to them. Even the people he loved to work with, his closest working relationships, stayed at work. Some of his friends complained of this in their recollections.

It's interesting to consider how the presence of even a single woman would have altered the world of that jury room.

Along with the single gender of the jury, the solid whiteness of its members would have surprised no one in the 1950s. New York in that period was not the diverse, multicultural city it has become. Throughout the 1940s the city was overwhelmingly white, with only

7 percent of the city's inhabitants of non-European descent. As big a factor as demographics might have been, a bigger one was that, then as now, prosecutors deliberately excluded African Americans and other minorities from juries. These exclusions required no legal justification. More to the point, television and film rarely represented people of color. When they did, typically midcentury white liberal values prevailed in stories where people of color were cast as victims of bigotry, defended by white protectors or vindicators.

Rose's screenplay largely follows this pattern, although to his credit we never learn whether the defendant is innocent. Juror no. 8, Fonda's postwar liberal hero, also follows a pattern: a man belonging to the professional class (he is an architect), a rational man who uses reason instead of his fists, earns respect by respecting others. Gregory Peck's 1962 portrayal of Atticus Finch in *To Kill a Mockingbird* is the liberal hero's apotheosis. His antitype is Lee J. Cobb's Juror no. 3, bullying and hollow at his core.

When Juror no. 8 says of the defendant, "This boy's been kicked around all his life. You know, living in a slum, his mother dead since he was nine. That's not a very good start," he might have earned, among some viewers, the label "bleeding-heart liberal," an expression of conservative scorn coined in 1938 in a newspaper column castigating liberals in Washington for a bill directed at punishing those responsible for lynchings. Today the young man's background would be called mitigating evidence, and it would be presented to the court at the sentencing phase of a capital trial. Film critic Manny Farber noted in Fonda's performance a "mild debunking of the hero" as the consummate liberal, in his aloofness from the other jurors, and in the small moment when, in the washroom, he takes his time drying each of his fingers, showing himself to be "unusually prissy."

The screenplay indicates that the defendant belongs to an unspecified minority group, and in Rose's script, the viewer never gets a glimpse of him. Sidney, however, felt the viewer should see him, perhaps in order to raise the viewer's emotional stake in the outcome of the deliberations. He cast a vulnerable, fragile-looking actor for the part. The camera finds the young man holding back tears as he

The camera shifts across the courtroom to take in the fear and sadness of the young, presumably Puerto Rican defendant, as the solemn notes of Kenyon Hopkins's score are first heard. *(Moviestore Collection Ltd / Alamy Stock Photo)*

watches the jurors file out. Sidney used a slow dissolve (rare in his work) to superimpose the young man's fear-filled face over the empty jury room. This image holds for the seconds before the opening credits come up.

By current standards, a weakness of the film is its reliance on the pathos of racial victimization. But in its time, the exposure of behind-closed-doors racism was medicinal and rare in a mainstream film.

Audiences of the 1950s would have taken for granted that, as Juror no. 1 puts it, "If we find the accused guilty, we have to send him to the chair; that's mandatory." The era of the electric chair in New York State lasted longer than one might suppose, from 1890 until 1963. In New York alone, 695 people were electrocuted over those years. The highly publicized horrific dual execution of the Rosenbergs in 1953 would have been vivid in popular memory, as would the danger of standing up for your rights and the countless unscrupulous pronouncements of guilt in the McCarthy years, 1950–1954. *12 Angry Men* has become a cultural touchstone, a time capsule of American justice on the eve of the civil rights era.

Reginald Rose would go on, in 1961, to create the TV series *The Defenders*, which starred E. G. Marshall (who played Juror no. 4 in *12 Angry Men*). Unlike *Perry Mason*, a popular TV courtroom drama, *The Defenders* focused not on solving a whodunit, but on serious legal questions of the day: cases about capital punishment, abortion, no-knock searches, the insanity defense, immigration quotas, the Hollywood blacklist and cold war visa restrictions.

And of course Sidney went on to direct many films centering on courtrooms and cops, most famous among them *Serpico*, *Prince of the City*, *The Verdict* and his TV series *100 Centre Street*. *12 Angry Men*, nevertheless, would remain Sidney's calling card.

14

CAREER MOVES

This picture was filmed entirely in New York City.
—T<small>EXT APPEARING BEFORE THE OPENING CREDITS</small>
<small>OF</small> S<small>IDNEY'S SECOND FILM,</small> *S<small>TAGE</small> S<small>TRUCK</small>*

After the Oscar nominations and critical acclaim for *12 Angry Men*, the offers came rolling in. "I was being offered everything in the world," Sidney recalled. "The bank accounts in Switzerland, with the corporations registered on a ship that was going through the Panama Canal, the whole works."

He felt some pride in not taking the Hollywood bait. When a major studio head told him, "I'll tell you what I'm looking for, Sidney, I'm looking for a young Lewis Milestone" (*All Quiet on the Western Front*, *Mutiny on the Bounty*, the original *Ocean's 11* and nearly fifty other films), he responded, "What's the matter with the old Lewis Milestone?" and walked out. Sidney's agent stated his terms unequivocally to the studios: "Lumet wants to keep himself free and sees no reason for making commitments in advance."

The studio system turned Sidney off on several counts. The factory-like production was entirely alien to how he'd learned to run the show in television. Out there in Hollywood, "there were thirty-two heads of departments—I'm not exaggerating." Sidney exclaimed, "The head of the camera department had the right to come to the lot and talk to my cameraman about whether he liked the picture or not. The head of the art department, the head of editing—all these strangers. There was no way I was going to do that." The directorial control he was used to was unheard of in Hollywood. Even A-list directors were assigned movies they wanted no part of.

Sidney's objections to Los Angeles were, at that period, pretty comprehensive:

> *That place has no reason for being. . . . I'm not the most erudite person in the world—but all the great centers of art have been centers of other things. They've either been a geographical center of the country or they've been a seaport . . . they've had other functions. The life of a place has been connected to the mainstream of life of that nation, of those people. An art came as a flower of that. Now, Los Angeles [laugh], I'm sorry, it's not a seaport, it's lousy land for farming, it's got no reason for being. . . . It seems to me that it's very difficult for any creative work to latch itself on to an unorganic place. . . . I don't mean that Hollywood kills work; I just think it makes it tougher to do good work.*

He wanted to stay in New York and he wanted to make movies at a time when New York was home to theater directors and live-television directors but movie directors worked in Los Angeles. Over the next several years, during his marriage to Gloria Vanderbilt and beyond, Sidney did what he needed to keep working without leaving home.

If at this moment in his life his distaste for Hollywood, his need to stay close to Gloria and his cultural roots were anchoring him to New York, he turned these potential constraints to good purpose. He began developing an idea about being a New York movie director before that term meant anything. It would take some time for him to figure out what kind of New York story he wanted to tell, but in the meantime he would begin a lifelong effort to build up the movie industry in New York, while keeping his hand in directing for the stage and even returning to directing for television.

ANCHORED TO HIS CITY

Sidney's life with Gloria was absorbing; it could have been a full-time job in itself. He had his hands full finding acting work for her. Just a few months after they met, in the summer of 1955, Sidney featured Gloria in an out-of-town production he directed of William Inge's 1953 hit play, *Picnic*. Over the next few years, Sidney helped get her cast in a dozen or so television dramas, including one he directed where she played a Jewish refugee from Nazi-occupied Europe. Their household was a constant flurry of activity. With acting lessons and TV appearances, two young boys and hosting much of the artistic and entertainment elite of the era, Gloria still found time for one of her favorite pastimes, redecorating. Indeed, Sidney was in love with their penthouse life, their weekends at their place in Connecticut and spending time with Gloria's very young boys.

Gloria's eldest son, Stan Stokowski, told me quite simply that he had loved Sidney very much, that Sidney had been a wonderful step-father to him from when he was about six to thirteen. He shared a delightful pageant of memories of being with Sidney at their country home—"Faraway House, we called it"—with its castle-like tower at the top. He described the "pretty good-sized river" that ran along the property and poured into a pool with a waterfall where they swam together. "Sidney had a lot of boyish pleasure in doing stuff." He re-membered a photo of Sidney running around their swimming pool with him and his brother, all three of them wearing towels as super-hero capes. For Stan's eighth birthday party, Sidney had rented and projected *The Fly*, a horror movie that had only just been released (1958), and that delighted Stan's friends but terrified him. He recalled that Sidney "used to write Chris and me letters and cards when he was away. Very sweet. I still have some of those." Once, when he was about five, he'd given Sidney a card that read, "Will you be my Valen-tine?" "I didn't really know what the Valentine thing was all about," he laughed. And he recalled watching *The Wizard of Oz* on television with Sidney, the two boys "lying in that classic pose, heads resting on arms," on the carpet in the library in front on their large color television set that Sidney had bought for the family.

Going places with Sidney, driving the country roads in his white Lincoln convertible with its leather seats, was a treat for the boys. Stan had memories of being taken along once to scout a location, "on a walking bridge over the Harlem River," and of attending a rehearsal of *Caligula*, a play Sidney was directing. Most of all, and so revealing of their shared happiness at the time, "I never saw him in a bad mood," Stan said. "He was always either enjoying things or taking it all in. And there was something about his honesty, his frankness, that was very refreshing and made me feel comfortable."

Sidney was intently focused on giving Gloria and her children the attention and love he felt she and they had never truly known from a man. He worked hard at this marriage, and one thing was for sure: he wasn't about to leave for long stretches. He was not going to risk it.

NEW YORK AND THE MOVIES

He may have been driven by circumstance, but Sidney had ideas for changing the New York–Hollywood equation. In October 1957 he headlined a panel of directors and producers at the Museum of the City of New York to spotlight "factors favorable to New York's again becoming a major film-producing center." He established a workshop to encourage Broadway producers and directors to adapt their hit shows to film and, most vitally, to produce them in New York City instead of sending them to Hollywood. The workshop, held at Gold Medal Studios in the Bronx (where D. W. Griffith had made his films beginning in 1908), included among its faculty Elia Kazan, screenwriters Budd Schulberg and Walter Bernstein, Sidney's cinematographer Boris Kaufman and several art directors and technicians. Sidney understood that a certain number of movies had to be made in New York per year to cover the cost of producing them at all, and that the initial setup of technology, sets, transportation and housing of cast and crew would be so costly that several productions would need to share the overhead for New York location shooting to make sense financially. Later Sidney would become instrumental in supporting the restoration of the Astoria Studios in Queens that had become defunct when the army stopped making films there after the war.

Sidney's nascent vision of a New York director was in some ways sui generis; it didn't align with that of the cadre of young independent filmmakers who were emerging in this period and through the 1960s, people like Shirley Clarke, John Cassavetes and Michael Roemer. Unlike these mavericks, Sidney wasn't drawn to the French New Wave, although the French were big fans of his work. He wasn't interested in experimenting with storytelling or creating a more spontaneous or documentary style. He liked working with movie stars and deploying the technical expertise TV and Hollywood had developed, and he was a fan of many great Hollywood directors. What he wanted was to achieve those things in New York.

Sidney's agent at William Morris, Leonard Sitomer, made it clear to interested producers in Hollywood that Sidney wanted to stay in New York. Hence, legendary producer Hal Wallis (*Casablanca*, *Dark Victory*, *The Maltese Falcon*, *True Grit*) at Paramount Pictures had been sending Sidney scripts of stories set in New York City. Sidney was looking for something in a script, but he wasn't sure what it was. One script, called *Night Man*, was too noir-ish; another, *Danny Fisher*, was a boxing picture, a weaker version of John Garfield's 1947 *Body and Soul*. Another, *Girls of Summer*, was a quaintly risqué adaptation of a Broadway play about two New York sisters struggling with their sexual inhibitions. He was yet to find the New York film idiom he was looking for, something that felt authentic. He'd gotten excited about Herman Wouk's *Marjorie Morningstar*, about a young Jewish woman, set in 1930s New York and surroundings; he'd flown out to talk with Jack Warner about it and, at a meeting with Warner and the production designer, he was shown sketches of the Jewish resort in the Catskills where much of the movie would be set. Sidney immediately made his objections clear: the sketches looked more like Beverly Hills than anything he'd ever seen in the Borscht Belt. The production designer—Richard Sylbert, a longtime colleague of

Sidney's—fumbled for a response. As Sidney recalled in his 1995 book *Making Movies*:

> *At this point Jack Warner jumped in. "You see, Sidney," he said, "we don't want a picture with a narrow appeal. We want something more universal." I said, "That means we don't cast any Jews, right?" I was on the three o'clock plane home.*

BACK TO THE THEATER

Not finding what he was looking for in a script, Sidney returned to his first love, the theater, where, alas, he would never have much success as a director. He had begun directing plays off-Broadway as early as 1949, when he was still running his theater workshop and teaching high school. A rehearsal of his 1955 production of George Bernard Shaw's *The Doctor's Dilemma* was fondly recalled by Michael Lindsay-Hogg (*Brideshead Revisited*), son of the show's leading lady, Geraldine Fitzgerald. Lindsay-Hogg, a depressed fourteen-year-old who was spending a listless summer with his mother, decided to drop in on a rehearsal. Arriving at the Phoenix Theatre on Second Avenue, formerly a Yiddish playhouse, Michael found his mother sitting at a table on the stage beside an actor; both "were talking to a young man with dark hair and glasses with dark frames who was standing in front of them. After the conversation, the young man gave them both a hug." When his mother introduced him, Sidney shook his hand as if they were old friends and invited him to join the cast at the corner Jewish deli for sandwiches, pickles and tea in glasses, Russian-style. The teenager instantly fell in love with this theater world, where people "engaged with seriousness and good humor in a common endeavor." Sidney hired him to be on the book (serve as a prompter) for a dollar per day. Shaw's play, which takes up the moral predicaments doctors face because of limited resources, was promisingly reviewed in *The New York Times* as "one of the Phoenix's best," except, as critic Brooks Atkinson carped, it lacked G. B. Shaw's "sardonic crackle."

A year later, Sidney had an offer to direct a Broadway show, Arch Oboler's *Night of the Auk*, starring Claude Rains and Christopher Plummer. A science-fiction drama set in the year 2000—and written in blank verse—about a megalomaniacal millionaire astronaut returning from the moon who announces that he has claimed the moon for the United States, thereby setting off an endgame nuclear war with the Soviet Union. Unsurprisingly, the show ran for only eight nights. It would take a couple more flops before Sidney figured out how he might put across a social message he believed in while still keeping audiences entertained.

HIS SECOND MOVIE

Ultimately, Sidney signed a five-year two-picture deal with RKO and agreed to direct a remake of the 1933 film *Morning Glory*, about a loquacious, starry-eyed small-town girl who comes to New York to become an actress and ascends to Broadway stardom. The remake would be called *Stage Struck*, and Sidney would describe it as his "valentine to Broadway." Sidney had excitedly planned the climactic opening-night scenes, filmed not on a set but in the National Theatre on 41st Street. In his view,

> *The movie audience has been shown over and over what war was like on D-Day. But do they know the tension, the color, the anticipation and the excitement backstage on opening night? . . . I want to show what it's really like. No hoke, no propping, no music with violins backing it. The real thing.*

In a sustained shot of backstage technicians looking bored, one reading the newspaper as he routinely pulls levers and works the lights, we see that Sidney already knew how to give a feeling of "the real thing." The movie's slim sustained popularity lies with those who respond to the film's loving portrayal of Broadway's backstage atmosphere. It was, however, Sidney's treatment of the city, his first foray into the streets, to real locations, that was hailed by *The New York Times*:

> [They] photographed in vivid and lovely color nearly every nook and cranny connected with the theatre—from poetry-filled Greenwich Village bistros to swank penthouses. . . . [They] have captured the singular beauties of a veritable Baghdad-on-the-Hudson. Minetta Lane in the Village at dawn; the true colors and some of the sleaziness of Times Square in the glare of thousands of neon lights and the raucousness of its population; Central Park in a snowstorm are shining facets that point up the singular character of Our Town.

The juicy leading role of Eva Lovelace that had won Katharine Hepburn an Oscar had been updated and given to nineteen-year-old Susan Strasberg, daughter of Lee Strasberg, the famed Method acting teacher. She'd been widely praised as the lead in the Broadway production of *The Diary of Anne Frank*, but she would not have been Sidney's choice. He doubted she was strong enough to carry the picture, as the role demanded. Sidney "didn't dare" to watch the original version of the film, *Morning Glory*, until after he finished shooting his. He was pleased to work again with Henry Fonda—although many felt Fonda was miscast—and with Christopher Plummer, whom he had directed onstage.

As feared, the critics agreed that "Susan Strasberg was no Hepburn"; her performance was "stilted," "wooden" and "lacked passion." Some hypothesized that she'd been hampered by her father's presence on the set. Sidney mentioned that Susan frequently kept the crew waiting while, as he put it, "she and her mother [Paula Strasberg] studied acting in her trailer."

Following *Stage Struck*, Sidney had hoped to direct a film called *Career*, co-written by blacklisted screenwriter Dalton Trumbo, that depicted the destruction by McCarthyism of a theatrical group targeted as "subversive." But the film was to be shot in Hollywood, and Sidney wouldn't budge: "If ever a piece had to be shot here [in New

York], that was it. It wouldn't have been the truth, done on a back lot." Sidney had the power to say no to scripts, but he was far from being able to get a green light on pictures of his choosing. There were countless movies he yearned to make as the years went by that he could not get financed. Among other projects, he was unable to get funding in this period for a script by Reginald Rose called *Black Monday*, set in a southern town on the first day of school integration.

THAT KIND OF WOMAN

Sidney's first attempt to direct a female lead had fallen flat, but he felt blessed to direct Sophia Loren in his next film, *That Kind of Woman*. How it came about was that Carlo Ponti, Sophia Loren's mentor, agent, producer and husband, who had discovered her when she was fifteen years old, got interested in an award-winning short story by Robert Lowry, "Layover in El Paso," as a vehicle for her. The story, which would be radically revised for the film, was about the romance of a feckless woman and a much-younger furloughed small-town GI during World War II. Paramount had cast her in a series of movies that didn't suit her, and her career had stalled. Ponti wanted to improve Loren's profile as a dramatic actress; he asked Sidney to direct, recognizing his skill with actors. Sidney stipulated that the story had to be relocated from Texas to New York City. Along with his enthusiasm for working with Loren, Sidney liked the idea of a story set in New York during the war, as he hoped to capture the atmosphere of that time. New York suited the Pontis fine; they had tired of Hollywood, and their background in Italian neorealism attracted them to Sidney's plan for location shooting.

Sidney recommended his friend Walter Bernstein to rewrite the screenplay; he transformed the lead from a trite Texan prostitute to the sympathetic Kay, who is "kept" by a sophisticated New York industrialist and war profiteer. To play the GI love interest, Paramount, hoping to draw a younger audience, signed 1950s teen heartthrob Tab Hunter. Sidney had worked with Hunter in television, and he saw in him a good actor suffering from typecasting. Years later, Hunter wrote that this had been his best movie experience. He noted that Sidney's actors trusted him so much that if he said, "'I'd like you to lie down in the road and then this truck is going to drive over you,' you'd just ask, 'How do you want me to position my body?'"

Understandably concerned that Loren would overpower his performance, Hunter was glad to have two weeks of rehearsal to deepen his character and, he added, to make friends with Loren. They did become chummy, and during breaks in location shooting, Loren and Hunter sat in her air-conditioned limousine and sang along with the radio.

Loren wasn't keen on rehearsal, but Sidney was "supportive and encouraging," as Walter Bernstein recalled. Bernstein also remembered Loren fondly: "She was friendly and nervous. . . . She worked hard and took direction willingly. She had no airs. Everyone liked her." When the opening scene was shot at the Long Beach train station, made up to look like Miami in 1944, two thousand people showed up to catch a glimpse of her.

Sidney expected that Walter Bernstein would finally, after eight years on the blacklist, be able to write the screenplay in his own name, but two years after Joe McCarthy's death a subpoena was still out for Bernstein, tangling the film in delays. Ponti, impatient and confused by the whole matter, asked simply, "Who do we have to pay off, and how much?" As Bernstein put it, "Ponti had a Renaissance grasp of knavery."

The next hurdle would be the Motion Picture Production Code, Hollywood's in-house censor, administered by Geoffrey Shurlock. Sidney would have to contend with his oversight on his scripts through the mid-1960s, until the code's certificate of approval was traded for the system of labeling movies G (General Audiences), M (Mature Audiences), R (Restricted), and X. "As you know," Shurlock wrote, "the Production Code permits the telling of stories of illicit sex relations when they are shown to be wrong." Sidney was forced to cut a scene in a sleeper car between Kay and the male lead and

Sidney with Sophia Loren. He later said he had fallen in love with her. Rumors floated that they had a brief fling. *(AF archive / Alamy Stock Photo)*

make other adjustments to indicate a sober condemnation of Kay's immoral way of life.

Sidney later confessed to having "fallen in love with Sophia." Over the years he would become smitten with a few of his leading ladies, Julie Christie and Jane Fonda among them. It is not so clear what "falling in love" meant when Sidney used the phrase, but Loren's husband and Sidney's boss, Ponti, had gone back to Italy during the shooting. Gloria recalled Sidney remarking to Dick Avedon that fidelity in a relationship was "a step up the mountain."

The critics didn't buy the Loren-Hunter romance. And although Sidney had again made great use of the city, shooting all over town—on Sutton Place, in Saks Fifth Avenue, in the old Penn Station and in Angelo's of Mulberry Street—he was still treating the city as atmosphere, a "colorful backdrop." Here he inadvertently evoked the 1949 musical hit *On the Town*.

THE FUGITIVE KIND

There are not that many movies that border on the
fantastic. . . . [Brando's] character and Joanne's border on the
fantastic. . . . For me as a strictly realistic director, boy did
I learn a lot.

—SIDNEY LUMET, 2010 INTERVIEW

Tennessee Williams' *Orpheus Descending* had failed in a 1957 Broadway production directed by the Group Theatre's Harold Clurman, but Sidney was thrilled to be brought on to direct the film adaptation. He had directed three of Williams' one-acts for television and had been considered to direct a couple of his previous film adaptations. Marlon Brando was cast as the guitar-playing ex-gigolo who finds himself in a small Mississippi town engaging in a tragic affair with a middle-aged shopkeeper (Anna Magnani) whose husband is dying of cancer.

Sidney had considerable influence on the screenplay, renaming it *The Fugitive Kind* and working with Williams and Meade Roberts to bring Brando's character forward as the film's central focus while clarifying some elements of the story. Sidney suggested a new opening to the screenplay in which Brando's character, Val Xavier, talks his way out of a jail sentence following an arrest after a brawl. Sidney wanted the audience to be on this character's side from the start, and this sublimely delivered six-minute monologue before an unseen New Orleans judge does the trick, in spades.

The film's exteriors were shot in Milton, New York, not in Mississippi. Sidney commented twice on his reasons for not going south to film: "I had a mixed cast, and I didn't want to expose them to a segregated Mississippi . . . pre–civil rights, living in different hotels," he explained in a late interview. A few years earlier he confided to theater critic John Lahr:

I was very nervous about Southerners because, during the war,
my company was eighty per cent from Mississippi. I'm not

making up stories when I say that the first three, four days in the shower, I could see them looking at me. I thought it was some sort of sexual thing. I couldn't figure it out. Finally one of them told me: "We thought you had a tail. Jews have tails." (I was the only Jew, obviously) . . . It's one of the reasons I didn't go to the Delta to shoot.

Alongside these reasons, he also thought Anna Magnani, who did not enjoy being in the United States, would be happier in New York—and there was always the Gloria factor.

This was the only film that Sidney was not able to rehearse in his usual fashion before shooting. They had only two days of rehearsal before Anna said she couldn't go on with it. Seeing the floor marks on the set, she erupted, "What are these signs on your floor? I have to move where the signs are? I can't act this way. You must let me breathe." Altogether, Magnani was no picnic to work with. She would allow herself to be filmed only from one side, convinced that from the wrong angle she looked old. Sidney did his best to keep things on an even keel with her, but her edgy competitiveness with Brando was not making it easy. She claimed that when she did a scene she was pleased with, Marlon would intentionally blow his lines and ask for another take. She called him "a sadistic egocentric." From Sidney's perspective, Brando was the ideal partner in a scene:

Most actors when they are working with Brando are in hog heaven, because the surprises, the original way he does anything is marvelous for them to latch onto. It becomes an immediate focal point of concentration—your concentration locks right in—because you're so stunned at what he's doing you really start listening, really paying attention.

Sidney suspected she didn't want to rehearse because she was afraid to let Marlon know what she was going to do in a given scene; she wanted to be the surprising one. Likely adding to Magnani's irritability was that Brando was being paid a million dollars for the movie, the first time any actor had gotten that much. The root of the conflict, Sidney offered, was that the thirty-five-year-old Marlon had no romantic intentions toward the fifty-one-year-old Italian diva.

Sidney brought on Boris Kaufman. He knew Kaufman could create poetic lighting to match "the unreality of Williams' language," as Sidney described it. Sidney was never afraid of language, of "wordy" scenes or incredibly powerful emotions—the "geshreying," as Walter Bernstein described it. He knew that for the story to work, the internal life of the characters had to be on display at all times, and despite the challenges on the set, he was getting smarter and smarter about capturing great performances.

Sidney playing cat's cradle with Anna Magnani on the set of *The Fugitive Kind*. Always trying to make her feel comfortable, he called her "Anna Banana" on the set. *(Album / Alamy Stock Photo)*

Sidney added emphasis to the play's critique of the pre–civil rights South, its violence and bigotry. Primarily, though, for Sidney, this film that so powerfully blends the sacred and the profane was about "saving the sensitivity inside us . . . saving our poets." He felt all of Williams' work expressed this idea. Williams was on the set for much of the filming of *The Fugitive Kind*; he was enthusiastic and cooperative with Sidney, rewriting sequences when Sidney asked him to.

Over the years, Williams' opinion of the film and its director vacillated wildly. In 1965 he remarked, "I love what Lumet did. He is a great director." Six years later, after he and Sidney had done another film together, *The Last of the Mobile Hot Shots*, he expressed disappointment with *The Fugitive Kind*; and confusingly, in 1981, he proposed the idea that Sidney should direct a remake of *A Streetcar Named Desire*.

Tennessee Williams, Marlon Brando, Anna Magnani, and Sidney in a huddle over changes to the script. *(mptvimages.com)*

The first cut of *The Fugitive Kind* was not well received—screenwriter Meade Roberts said there were guffaws and boos at the preview. It was recut and shortened by twenty-five minutes, and that left some gaps in the plot. Sidney put on a brave face throughout, made light of the conflicts on the set, and bore up under the disappointment of the film's poor box office, the only one of Brando's films at that point not to make money. But even with its imperfections, *The Fugitive Kind* has grown in stature over the years. Recently remastered and released on DVD by Criterion, the film holds up as other Williams adaptations do not.

Marlon Brando taking direction from Sidney on the set of *The Fugitive Kind*. *(Associated Press)*

A LONG BUT NOT FINAL GOODBYE

In some ways Sidney was playing the long game, as he'd learned from the theater directors he most admired. They just kept working, show after show, hits or failures. Unlike many of Sidney's colleagues who were making the transition from television to movies, he had no problem returning to the small screen, even after the hoopla of the *12 Angry Men* Oscar nomination: "I'm ashamed to say I didn't go to the Oscars that year," he said. "Talk about the arrogance of the young! I had fallen in love with a new girl [Gloria] and she couldn't go. So we stayed in New York and watched it on TV at a party."

In the busy year of 1960, following *The Fugitive Kind*, Sidney turned out his most serious television work; it included *The Sacco-Vanzetti Story*, about the 1921 trial and wrongful execution of two immigrant anarchists; *John Brown's Raid*, about the 1859 slave revolt in Virginia; and an adaptation of Kurosawa's masterpiece, *Rashomon*, depicting conflicting accounts of the murder of a samurai. All of these productions were in one way or another personal to Sidney, but none more so than his 1960 direction of S. Ansky's Yiddish play *The Dybbuk, or Between Two Worlds*, based on a Hasidic folktale about star-crossed love, blasphemy and the possession of a young woman by the ghost of her former suitor. Sidney provided an introduction to the production; looking young (at age thirty-six) and self-conscious, Sidney spoke into the camera: "Hello, I'm Sidney Lumet. I'm the director of this production of *The Dybbuk* that you're about to see." He continued:

> *It's a play that's very close to me. My father appeared in it in I think it was 1927 [it was 1920]. It's the first play that I ever saw in the Yiddish theater. It's a beautiful story. It's essentially a love story and a tender one. But it's also a story about a people who essentially are no longer alive, a sect of Jews in Poland and Russia who lived about a hundred, hundred and fifty years ago, who never walked anywhere if they could dance there—they never said anything if they could sing it. The basis of their belief was that in a life of misery the best way to find God was through joy, and so they sang and they danced whenever they could. Thank you.*

Sidney made the surprising and dramatic decision to stage the final exorcism of the demon as a modern dance by the female lead, Carol Lawrence, who was then starring on Broadway in *West Side Story*. (She would play a leading role in his next film, *A View from the Bridge*.) The broadcast received ecstatic reviews, and, notably, although Sidney had staged the play through a secular lens, he offered no concessions to gentile viewers.

The Dybbuk belonged to a prestigious television series produced by Ely Landau, who would go on to produce Sidney's *Long Day's Journey into Night*, *The Pawnbroker*, and *King: A Filmed Record . . . Montgomery to Memphis*. The series included Sidney's greatest television production, Eugene O'Neill's *The Iceman Cometh*, starring

Jason Robards. *The New York Times* gushed, "To television has come a moment of enrichment and excitement unequalled in the medium's thirteen years, a theatrical experience that remorselessly envelops the viewer in the playwright's marathon documentary on doom." Lumet won an Emmy for the show, but more significantly he won the trust of O'Neill's widow, Carlotta O'Neill. She gave Lumet the future film rights to *Long Day's Journey into Night*, and within a year he was gathering momentum to direct a film adaption of O'Neill's extraordinary autobiographical family drama, unproduced in O'Neill's lifetime.

TURNING A CORNER

One of the great hells of [theater] work . . . is the lack of control over the result. You're at the mercy of everything from what the actor had for breakfast that morning to what the critic had for dinner just before he came to the show. Literally. . . . The area where motion pictures compensate, for a director, is that it is his medium.

—SIDNEY LUMET, 1959

What Sidney was figuring out slowly was that he was not really a theater director, and that he could do a better job with great plays by filming them, as camera techniques could deepen and reveal what hadn't been seen before in the play. In that busy year of 1960, after making *The Fugitive Kind*, Sidney took on his final Broadway drama, *Caligula*, written by Albert Camus in 1938 and revised in 1944, about the depraved Roman emperor who is destroyed by his excesses. It had been a two-year hit in Paris at the end of the war, but Camus had withheld permission for a U.S. production until he saw *12 Angry Men*, at which point he stipulated that Sidney Lumet had to direct the New York staging. He felt Sidney could give the audience an *experience*, not treat the play as an intellectual exercise. According to *The*

New York Times, Camus planned to come to New York to attend rehearsals; he died in a car accident just weeks before the show opened.

Composer-musician David Amram (*Splendor in the Grass*, *The Manchurian Candidate*), who provided the music for the play, recalled the humorous side of rehearsals: Sidney had put out a call for well-built men to play the Roman soldiers. *The New York Times* picked up the story of the cattle call, where "an aura of embarrassment filled the stage of the theatre as the men stripped to the waist." Several were heard to remark that "now they knew how girls felt about showing off their legs or torsos." David Amram recalled that during a rehearsal, Sidney noticed that one of the soldiers was flexing his pectorals as he would in a bodybuilding demonstration. Rather than simply telling the extra to stop, Sidney called everyone together, and they had a long discussion about the play and its meaning, to good effect. The bodybuilders took a serious interest in the story and became more focused and committed. The show ran a relatively respectable thirty-eight days.

Sidney's final Broadway effort would be in 1962, a musical written by his friend James Lipton called *Nowhere to Go But Up*, and nicknamed after it bombed, "Nowhere to Throw But Up." Sidney was finally convinced that theater is the medium of writers and actors but movies belong to the director.

A VIEW FROM THE BRIDGE AND *LONG DAY'S JOURNEY INTO NIGHT*

This is the first movie of mine which I have been able to watch without wishing I had been captured by pirates in childhood and never heard from again. Indeed, as one who had very little to do with the making of it, and thus may speak without blushing, I think the adaptation and production are superb.

—ARTHUR MILLER,
AFTER SCREENING *A VIEW FROM THE BRIDGE*

In 1962 Sidney appeared on CBS's *Camera Three*, an intellectual roundtable covering topics "from Shakespeare to economics," to discuss his latest stage-to-screen adaptations, Arthur Miller's *A View from the Bridge* and Eugene O'Neill's *Long Day's Journey into Night*. He was receiving a new kind of recognition; *Long Day's Journey* had been one of only three U.S. films officially selected and shown at Cannes, and the film's four stars collectively were awarded best-actor citations, the first time an entire starring cast of a film was so honored at Cannes.

Smoking nonstop, Sidney spoke about his radically different approaches to the two films, made back-to-back. He had worked with Arthur Miller and screenwriter Norman Rosten to lengthen Miller's play for the film: "I wanted to see if I could understand Eddie a little better," he said. He felt that in the original version, the central character of Eddie (played by Raf Vallone) seemed "neurotic" and "muddied." Sidney saw him as functioning out of "primitive emotions" and "old-world mores," and he wanted that to come through more clearly, which it does in the film. Sidney sought also to emphasize how much Eddie valued his position as a well-liked and respected man on the docks, someone able to resolve conflicts. To emphasize Eddie's relationships in the workplace and the community, Sidney took the characters out onto the Brooklyn docks and elsewhere. For O'Neill's play, however, Sidney took the opposite approach, not revising it for the screen and cutting only eleven pages from the three-hour-long play. He wasn't interested in "breaking it out" or taking the characters to different locations; Sidney wanted, as he put it, "to go further in. I wanted to get into the pupils of the eye." He felt frustrated by reviewers who complained that the movie was "just a filmed play." "Talk about critics not being able to see," he remarked in later years. "I remember Pauline Kael attacking the shit out of it for not being cinematic."

Sidney's editor on this film, Ralph Rosenblum, who also worked with him on *The Pawnbroker*, recalled a cutting trick Sidney came up with for *Long Day's Journey*, one that Rosenblum said he'd never have thought of:

I had always cut dialogue scenes by carefully choosing whether to focus on the speaker or the listener. Lumet came up with an alternative approach, "mathematical cutting," in which we cut back and forth from one actor to the other in evenly matched but progressively shorter snippets of film.

He said that Sidney was "the only director I've worked with who could tell me cut-for-cut what he wanted in a scene." Of this film, Sidney quipped, "There's as much camera technique in *Long Day's Journey* as in the chariot scene in *Ben-Hur*."

A View from the Bridge was Sidney's first really international picture. Raf Vallone, an Italian movie star, had appeared in the Paris stage version; Jean Sorel, who played Rodolpho, was a French star; the two female leads, Maureen Stapleton and Carol Lawrence, were American. Because the film's producer, Paul Graetz, had money in both dollars and francs, they "used the dollars to film in Brooklyn and the francs to film in Paris."

New York Times critic Bosley Crowther assessed one character's despair and frustration as "almost too poignant to bear," and indeed the film, often compared to a Greek tragedy, propels the ensemble into pain and devastation as though fate itself had decreed it.

PROUDEST ACHIEVEMENT

The individual life is made significant just by the struggle.
—EUGENE O'NEILL

I remember seeing Sidney Lumet's black-and-white film adaptation of Long Day's Journey into Night, *which I still think is one of the best adaptations of anything—of a book, of a play—ever done.*

—SAM SHEPARD,
ON WHAT INSPIRED HIM TO BECOME A PLAYWRIGHT

O'Neill's autobiographical play, written in the early 1940s but not published or performed until after his death, contains almost uncanny refractions of Sidney's family story. James Tyrone, played by Ralph Richardson, like O'Neill's father and like Sidney's, was a frustrated actor who chose to believe that he'd sacrificed his talent for financial security (although Baruch never achieved financial security). Mary Tyrone, played by Katharine Hepburn, is a morphine addict, which Sidney's mother was not, but her mental illness, like Mary Tyrone's addiction, plunged their family into a hell of blame, guilt and remorse; the strange and "unnatural detachment" that the morphine lends Mary accords with Sidney's description of his "distant mother." One can imagine Sidney hearing echoes of his own mother in Mary Tyrone's complaints of never having a real home because of her husband's miserliness, of being left alone, and of the mistress he kept in the early days of their marriage (although Baruch was unfaithful throughout their marriage). The play suggests that James has for too long turned a blind eye to Mary's condition, has let it fester for his own reasons, again recalling Baruch's behavior in the face of Jenny's mental illness. And as in Sidney's family, a baby has died, and the guilt and blame circulated among them.

Sidney was "in sync with" the play, as writer Phillip Lopate observed; there were no unexplored moments. Pointing, for example, to Jamie's sing-song assault on his younger brother, "Mama's baby; papa's pet," Sidney commented, "Those moments are so blinding because out of those terrible moments come these bursts of revelation about all our behavior, about us, and about who we are and what we are and the way we are, and what we do to each other."

Sidney had known from the start that he wanted Katharine Hepburn, and no one else, to play Mary Tyrone. His first encounter with her, however, did not bode well:

When we first met on Long Day's Journey, *she was living in John Barrymore's former house in Los Angeles. I stepped through the doors of what seemed to me a fifty-foot living room. She stood at the opposite side of the living room and started toward me. We'd covered about half the distance when she said, "When do you want to start rehearsal?" (No Hello or How do you do?) "September nineteenth," I said. "I can't start until the twenty-sixth," she said. "Why?" I asked. "Because then," she said, "you'd know more about the script than I would."*

Sidney was concerned that Hepburn wanted to dominate the situation, and he had no interest in power dynamics with his actors. But when his producer, Ely Landau, asked him as they left the meeting whether he wanted to look for someone else, Sidney was firm. "No. She's magnificent. When Mary Tyrone falls, it's got to be like a giant oak falling." He'd find a way to work through whatever difficulties might lie ahead.

Years later, Sidney described how their relationship evolved during the four weeks of rehearsal. For the first couple of days he said nothing to her about Mary Tyrone's character. "I talked at length with Jason . . . with Ralph and Dean." On the third day, when they finished the run-through reading, there was a long pause. "And then, from Kate's corner of the table, a small voice called out, 'Help!'" Sidney recollected that from then on "the work was thrilling . . . she built that character stone by stone."

Once the filming started, Sidney's respect for Hepburn redoubled as she demonstrated her remarkable professionalism. Although she had always been in the habit of going to daily rushes, she informed Sidney that she wouldn't be coming. She explained, "If I go to rushes, all that I'll see is this," and "she reached under her chin and pinched the slightly sagging flesh," Sidney recalled, "'and this'—she did the same thing under her arms—'and I need all my strength and concentration to just play the part.'" Sidney noted in *Making Movies* that her explanation brought a tear to his eye; he'd "never seen such self-knowledge and such dedication, trust and bravery." It was the beginning of their lifelong friendship. After screening an early cut of the film, Sidney expressed to her in a telegram his feelings about her performance: "Great not the way the word is usually used but in a very true sense deeply happy and deeply grateful producers and wives all agreed love Sidney." Hepburn was nominated for an Oscar for her role as Mary Tyrone, one of twelve nominations she received in her lifetime.

Sidney found working with Ralph Richardson entirely different but equally unforgettable. One of Sidney's great strengths as a director was that he could adjust to the needs of each of his actors. At one point in rehearsal, Sidney took Ralph Richardson aside, feeling something was as yet unrealized, and talked with him for a long time about what made his character, James Tyrone, tick. Richardson's response has become legendary: "I see what you mean, dear boy: a little more cello, a little less flute."

To get the production off the ground, Sidney had formed a cooperative with his magnificent cast; Hepburn, Richardson, Robards, and Stockwell would all work for the same minimal salary—as would Sidney—and divide profits equally among them. The film was budgeted at $500,000. The musical score—a lone piano—was composed and played by Oscar-winning musician André Previn. For the movie's New York run, it was treated like a play: it showed at only one theater, with reserved-seating tickets purchased in advance.

This was the film Sidney remained proudest of through the years. He was especially proud that decades later the film was studied "as much as *12 Angry Men*" for the cinematic techniques that critics had originally failed to take note of. These included different lighting established for each of the characters. For the male characters, the camera began at eye level and the angle dropped lower as the story progressed. It was the opposite for Hepburn; the camera went higher and higher with "longer and longer lenses on her as she slipped into her dope-ridden fog." Sidney had also used "wider and wider lenses on the men as their world crumbled around them." In act 4, when Edmund (Dean Stockwell) and his father (Ralph Richardson) finally unleash their honest feelings about each other for the first time, Sidney noted, "the lenses get wider and wider, the camera gets lower and lower, the light harsher but darker, as the whole story of these people gets wrapped in night and the final, terrible truths are articulated."

Sidney was well acquainted with the details of Eugene O'Neill's life, including the two years of struggle the Nobel laureate committed to writing *Long Day's Journey* while battling Parkinson's disease. He knew about O'Neill's failed marriages and his alienation from his children, whom he cut out of his will. Sidney was keenly attentive to what he referred to as the play's "moments of self-hatred." In a 2005 interview Sidney spoke about what moved him most about the playwright: "The belief in art is what's so moving to me, the redemptive quality of art. This life of misery. We know what happened to the children, what happened to his wives, what happened to him physically . . . we're talking about hell. And if there had ever been a way of asking him, I don't doubt for a minute that he'd have said it's been worth it."

THE MARRIAGE FALTERS

Call her not wicked; that word's touch
Consumes her like a curse;
But love her not too much, too much
For that is even worse.
O, she is neither good nor bad,
But innocent and wild!
Enshrine her and she dies, who had
The hard heart of a child.

—ELINOR WYLIE

Gloria felt that Sidney had "turned his life over to [her]," that throughout their marriage she always came before his work. But as hard as Sidney tried—and he tried hard—things were changing between them as they themselves were each changing: she'd had her fill of acting and he'd had his fill of stage flops. Perhaps as Sidney advanced to *Long Day's Journey into Night*, he was no longer putting his work second.

Of course it was, as Gloria remarked, "a combination of a lot of things" that brought down the marriage that had made them both very happy for much of the seven years they spent together. There might have been a certain wear and tear on Gloria in socializing with Sidney's wildly successful theater friends, many at the very top of their game. Katharine Hepburn, an astonishing Mary Tyrone in the film version of *Long Day's Journey*, had been Gloria's "passionate role model ever since I saw her in the movie *Little Women*." Gloria recalled a missed opportunity when she was very young to approach Hepburn; they had been seated near one each other on a flight across the country. Gloria was too awed to speak to her. And this time, during the filming of *Long Day's Journey*, she kept putting off going to the set. She recounts:

> *After the wrap, a week or so later she came for tea to our apartment at 10 Gracie Square. Surely then. But I was para-lyzed—my studio door was to the right of the elevator and when time came for her arrival—on the dot—I stood behind the closed door. Sidney was waiting to greet her as she came off the elevator and I could hear their voices mingling together as he welcomed her. I went back and sat in my studio agonizing WHY wasn't I in our library having tea with them? After she left I marveled over bolts of tweed from Scotland she had brought Sidney as a gift to have a jacket made.*

In retrospect, Gloria viewed her own acting ambition as a destructive force in their relationship: "It brought out things in me I didn't like," she said. She was "restless and driven," and at the same time ambivalent about acting. Before too long she would conclude that she was temperamentally unsuited to being an actress, that "the solitary demands of writing and painting" were more in her nature. Gloria continued to appear intermittently on television until early in 1963, the year of the divorce.

Perhaps the avalanche of Sidney's love notes holds a clue. Sidney showered Gloria with affection, feeling that the motherless child in her needed these daily attestations. But how does one sustain that intensity for the long haul? The relationship may have had too narrow a bandwidth and depended too heavily on the image of their "charmed life." Neither of them may have trusted that they would be able to navigate the more grinding parts of marriage. In our conversation, Gloria puzzled over whether it had been a plus or a minus that Sidney was "very sensitive to my moods."

For Gloria, the notes might have conveyed not only his love for her but also a neediness that put her on her guard. The Elinor Wylie poem "Beauty" (excerpted in the epigraph above) was a favorite of Gloria's. It warns, "But love her not too much." She recalled feeling "conflicted about the fact that Sidney could not be alone." Eventually his sense that their feelings were out of balance became explicit: "You don't love me enough," he would say, and that made her feel unsuccessful, "because I felt I was giving him all that I had." Gloria recalled that she had once given him a watch she'd had engraved with the words FOR A LONG, LONG TIME, "and that upset him because it didn't sound like forever. I hadn't thought of that; I thought it was poetic." It is not a big leap to imagine that the unmothered child in Sidney was looking for the unconditional love he had tried to offer her.

Gloria wasn't sure why she kept putting off having children with Sidney, which she knew he very much wanted. She wasn't sure if it was because of her desire to be an actress or, as she wondered aloud decades later to her son Anderson Cooper, because, as Sidney suspected, she didn't love him enough.

The joy Sidney took in spending time with Gloria's sons doubtless contributed to his longing for children. But that was a wish that would not be answered until his next marriage.

In his drawing, Sidney dresses both figures in old-fashioned attire, perhaps to create a little ironic distance as he expresses his sincere wish for children. *(From the private papers of Gloria Vanderbilt)*

In the spring of 1963 Sidney and Gloria attended a small dinner party given by British actress Leueen MacGrath and her husband, Stephen Goodyear. At the table was a very charming writer from Mississippi named Wyatt Cooper. The connection between Wyatt and Gloria was immediate and intense—and devastating to Sidney.

How did it all finally come to an end? "I had an assignment from Helen Gurley Brown for *Cosmo*, to write about Italian women," Gloria explained. "I used that assignment to go away and think things out." From Rome, Gloria flew on to California, which was where Wyatt was living at the time. "That's when Sidney went out to the Hamptons and got involved with Gail," she recalled—Gail Jones, that is, who would in short order become Sidney's third wife.

There was one final wrinkle in the story of Sidney's relationship with Gloria in this period: Sidney and Gloria had both been seeing the same psychiatrist, a Dr. McKinney. He was among a handful of psychiatrists working with LSD as a therapeutic agent. Gloria had experimented with it under his direction and had what she described as "the experience of a lifetime." More than sixty years later she remarked, "I can remember every single minute of it." She urged Sidney to try it—this was after the breakup—and she agreed to be with him for the experience. By this time Wyatt was not comfortable with their continued connection, or with this particular plan; he gave Gloria an ultimatum and flew off unexpectedly to Los Angeles the day before Sidney's LSD appointment was set. Gloria "panicked" and jumped on a plane, determined now to marry him. Decades later, in our conversations, Gloria remembered feeling "terrible guilt that I had let Sidney down, hadn't been there for him. He asked Walter Bernstein to stay with him." Walter's recollections of that arduous night with Sidney include his many unsuccessful efforts to get Gloria on the phone.

Asked if Sidney had accepted the end of the marriage, Gloria replied, "No. He believed we would get back together. But I knew it was over." Their story didn't in fact end there, but neither would be ready for its next chapter until many years later.

15

MARRIAGE TAKE THREE:
MAYBE THIS TIME . . .

At the end of the summer of 1963, Sidney was staying alone in a recently rented apartment in Greenwich Village when he made a half-hearted attempt to take his life. The Mexican divorce from Gloria had come through on what happened to be their wedding anniversary. He described his suicide attempt as "seven vodkas, a Miltown [a tranquilizer] and idiocy." He telephoned the new woman in his life, Gail Jones, daughter of singer and movie star Lena Horne, to tell her what he'd done. She phoned the police, who found him unconscious on the floor and took him to St. Vincent's Hospital. He was embarrassed by the incident and annoyed that Gail had phoned the police. He said she was being "hysterical."

He and Gail had met the summer before, 1962, at a Fourth of July party in East Hampton thrown by Kermit Bloomgarden, producer of the ill-fated musical Sidney was directing, *Nowhere to Go But Up*. Sidney's friend James Lipton, the writer of the show, was aware that Sidney was struggling mightily with the slow-motion collapse of his fairy-tale marriage to Gloria. He pulled Sidney aside at the party and told him he was about to meet "the girl of his dreams."

Gail, a twenty-four-year-old Radcliffe graduate, fourteen years Sidney's junior, had recently returned from living in Paris. She was fresh and lovely and smart. Like Sidney, she had grown up around show business. She had recently dated the well-known composer Burt Bacharach, and still she remained a bit bedazzled by celebrities, which likely had its charm, and perhaps gave Sidney a certain kind of assurance.

EBONY

A JOHNSON PUBLICATION

WHO WILL GET
THE NEGRO VOTE?
By Carl Rowan

HIS TOUGHEST
ASSIGNMENT

LENA'S DAUGHTER
MAKES STAGE DEBUT

NOVEMBER 1960 35¢

Gail Jones, after her stage debut,
November 1960.

Gail had had a brief flirtation with the stage, performing in a 1960 musical called *Valmouth* at a little theater on New York's Upper East Side. It ran only a few weeks, but she hadn't enjoyed the nightly repetition, and, as she recalled it, she didn't like being "stuck in a job" during the precious evening hours when her friends were "going to dinners and socializing." She would call herself a "show business civilian."

Sidney must have been relieved that Gail had no ambitions as an actor, given his experiences with Rita and Gloria. According to Gail, she really had no ambitions at all at that time. Still, worthwhile things came her way. She was recruited to work on John F. Kennedy's presidential campaign, to join a speech-making tour talking to young black voters. Soon thereafter she found herself in a job advising and advocating for black applicants seeking scholarships to predominantly white colleges, work she liked a lot. It brought her into contact with members of SNCC, the Student Nonviolent Coordinating Committee, a cross-section of the South, black, white, rich and poor, working together on racial integration. She found them "the bravest people I ever met." Despite her attraction to the civil rights movement, she was mostly caught up in the New York social scene. In 1960 she was named *Esquire*'s Girl of the Year. The blurb read:

> *Gail Jones, counselor for National Scholarship Service and Fund for Negro Students. Daughter of Lena Horne. Home, New York. Diploma, Radcliffe. Acted off-B'way. Likes knitting. Loves parties.*

Although she later claimed she'd had no interest in knitting, she robustly acknowledged that "the iceberg of my social consciousness was still almost entirely submerged." She was out clubbing almost every night.

As he had with Gloria, Sidney found with Gail some poignant parallels in their childhoods, marked by upheaval and strife. Gail's parents' tumultuous marriage had broken up when she was three years old; she and her mother moved around a lot, and at times she was handed off to family friends and relatives while her mother pursued her career.

Gail's mother, Lena Horne, belonged to an established family in Brooklyn's middle-class black community who were admiringly referred to as "the Hornes of Brooklyn." She could trace her family back six generations to an ancestor named Sinai Reynolds, who was born into slavery in 1777 and ultimately bought her freedom by selling pies. Their family had belonged to the black middle class for generations. Lena's grandmother, Cora Calhoun Horne, had introduced a very young Gail to W. E. B. Du Bois and Paul Robeson. To pursue her famous barrier-breaking career as "the first Negro movie star," Lena had, as Gail put it, "left the quiet waters of the black bourgeoisie for the perilous open seas of 'white' life." Gail was born in a segregated Pittsburgh hospital.

At the time of her parents' separation, three-year-old Gail had received a phone call from her weeping mother, asking her "whom I'd rather live with, her or my father. I remember distinctly not wanting her to feel worse than she obviously did. 'You,' I said. And then I cried and cried." Her father, Louis Jordan Jones, refused to allow Lena to take their newborn son, Teddy. The siblings were separated for a time.

When her mother was under contract with MGM, Gail and her brother lived with her in Hollywood. They played with the children of other stars, including Gene Kelly and Frank Sinatra, but, she said, "Though I was a Hollywood kid I was not a Hollywood princess." She and her brother were the only nonwhite children at their private school. They lived "not *as* white people, but *like* white people."

Still, her Hollywood childhood had its delights. She was beguiled by the restaurants "in the shape of sombreros, bowler hats, and old shoes" and the dyed Christmas trees, "usually shocking pink, or gold." And she loved the movies, always. Among her favorites was anything with Abbott and Costello, especially Lou Costello, whom she once caught sight of dressed in a cowboy suit talking to kids at a movie theater on Hollywood Boulevard. She participated in the war effort as a small child, collecting newspapers and silver cigarette papers. Wishing to wear a uniform, she wanted to join the Brownies, but they were segregated and the black Brownies convened too far from her home.

When she was ten, her mother married composer-arranger Lennie Hayton, who would write the music and win Oscars for *Hello, Dolly!* and *On the Town*. The two were married in Paris in 1947, at a time when interracial marriage was still illegal in California. Hayton was white and Jewish. "I thought that we left home for fun," Gail later wrote. "We actually left home because of race and politics." They soon settled in a hotel in New York, where Gail "took to hotel life like a duck to water." She reflected that all kids love hotels, because of "all those corridors, elevators, and opportunities for solo missions . . . magic, freedom." In a different mood, though, she referred to her younger self as a "lonely child of hotel corridors."

An early memory of those New York years was eating at Lindy's, where she saw Walter Winchell and J. Edgar Hoover "cheek by jowl, plotting over their black coffee." Her mother explained that the two men were "villains." When Lena's increasing political activism required her to travel, Gail was taken in by a left-wing Manhattan family and sent to the progressive New Lincoln School. There she learned the leftist anthems like "Joe Hill" that she and Sidney could later bond over. She also spent some of her high school years at a Quaker boarding school in upstate New York before heading to Radcliffe.

COURTSHIP AND . . .

When Gail met Sidney in the summer of 1962, she had recently taken a job at *Life* magazine. He had just finished shooting *Long Day's Journey into Night*. Sitting with Gail in her bright, elegant Upper East

Side apartment where her mother had once lived, I asked her what had attracted her to Sidney. "I had only gone out with boys so I was flattered that he was interested," she said. "And I was impressed because I'd seen a lot of his movies." When asked what it was about her that Sidney had fallen in love with, she replied, almost startled, "*With me?* I have no idea. No idea. I was basically a happy-go-lucky person—and I think he liked that. I mean that's a sign of not being very bright. I wasn't very bright in those days. I wasn't a big thinker, let's put it that way." But later in our conversation she reconsidered, recalling that she and Sidney talked politics a lot: "I was very political then," she noted, and Sidney was "very opinionated," always bringing to bear his "1930s man-of-the-left perspective."

Throughout the early months of their relationship, Sidney was still hoping to salvage his marriage to Gloria. When the gossip pages picked up that he and Gail were dating, Sidney protested that they were just friends. He saw in Gail just what he needed: comfort and distraction. Her youth likely gave him a greater sense of control than he'd felt with Gloria, and, by her own description, she had less for him to contend with in the way of moods. In a letter to Katharine Hepburn, written several months into their relationship, Sidney wrote, "All's well except I feel too tired to fall in love again, and I hate not being in love." However, as the signals became clearer that Gloria was planning to marry Wyatt Cooper, Sidney pulled Gail closer. Indeed, he and Gail were married one month ahead of Gloria's marriage to Cooper.

WORK/LIFE

Sidney had good reason for being uncharacteristically tired. During the year running up to his marriage to Gail, he shot *Fail-Safe* and began prepping *The Pawnbroker* in rapid succession. These were two of his major films. *Fail-Safe*, Sidney's third movie starring Henry Fonda, was shot in May and June of 1963, but it wasn't released for a year due to a legal kerfuffle with Stanley Kubrick. Unbeknown to either director, the two were simultaneously directing films adapted from different books on the topic of nuclear annihilation. Kubrick drew first, threatening to sue the producer of both their films, Columbia Pictures, which was enough to persuade them to allow his satirical masterpiece, *Dr. Strangelove or: How I Learned to Stop Worrying and Love the Bomb*, to be released nine months ahead of Sidney's film. This was a source of no small frustration for Sidney; he'd been happy with how his own film had turned out, but, thanks to Kubrick's finesse, it would underperform in theaters. *Fail-Safe*'s thunder had been stolen by Kubrick's dark comedy.

Gail's mother had initially been opposed to Sidney and Gail's marriage because of their difference in age and because of Sidney's two prior marriages. But Gail "dug in her heels," insisting to her mother that "Sidney was the perfect older man." They set the date for November 23, 1963. It was to be a small private ceremony at Sidney's friend Walter Bernstein's apartment. Walter had written the screenplay for *Fail-Safe*. Sidney's father and sister would attend, as would Gail's mother and stepfather and her brother Teddy. The ceremony would be followed by a reception for friends at the Waldorf Astoria.

It would turn out to be anything but a joyous occasion, occurring on the day following the assassination of President Kennedy. Half the guests didn't show up; the music was canceled, and those present were led in a prayer for the fallen president. Sidney and Gail spent their honeymoon watching events unfold: the swearing in of LBJ, Jackie standing by in her bloodied dress, the killing of Lee Harvey Oswald by Jack Ruby and the funeral cortège. They sat "glazed in front of the TV," Gail recalled. (As a side note,

Sidney and Gail on their wedding day. Sidney's smile and embrace express a paternal air. (*Associated Press*)

the circumstances of this wedding were borrowed for a 2009 episode of AMC's *Mad Men*; the marriage of Roger Sterling's daughter, Margaret, occurs on the day after Kennedy's assassination with similar consequences.)

While the wedding plans with Gail were taking shape, Sidney turned down the tempting offer to direct *A Raisin in the Sun*, starring Sidney Poitier. He was still holding his ground about shooting only in New York and this film would be made in Hollywood. Meanwhile, Sidney's friend Ely Landau, who had produced *The Iceman Cometh* and *Long Day's Journey into Night*, had asked Sidney to shift from another of his projects, Carson McCullers' *The Heart Is a Lonely Hunter*, to direct a film that had been kicking around for a couple of years, *The Pawnbroker*. It was an adaptation of Edward Lewis Wallant's 1961 novel about a shattered and embittered survivor of a Nazi death camp, "encased in his own coldness," as Sidney would later describe him, whose wife and children had been killed.

It would be the first American film to take on the psychic effects of what was yet to be known as the Holocaust. This dark story of trauma, for which Sidney chose to return to black-and-white film, offered the viewer none of the reassurances or buffers of the two prior American films that had addressed Nazi atrocities, *The Diary of Anne Frank* (1959) and *Judgment at Nuremberg* (1961). Several actors vied to play the lead character, Sol Nazerman, including Rod Steiger, James Mason and, remarkably, Groucho Marx. Steiger would take the role and win an Oscar nomination for his performance.

Sidney signed on to direct *The Pawnbroker* for the union minimum salary, as did the film's lead actors. The deal included equally divided profit-sharing. This was the same arrangement he and his actors had made on *Long Day's Journey into Night* and *The Hill*, and that Sidney would repeat on a handful of future films he cared deeply about.

Sidney's father, Baruch, appears in the small but potent role of Mendel, a bedridden death-camp survivor. Baruch's authentic accent and his intensity on-screen are memorable, as are his lines expressing his contempt for the pawnbroker Nazerman: "You breathe. You eat. You walk. You make money. You take a dream and give a dollar. . . . A

On the set of *The Pawnbroker*, Sidney looks exasperated, standing beside his father, Baruch, who is mindful of the camera. *(Courtesy of the National Center for Jewish Film)*

coward's survival and at a price. No passion. No pity. . . . The walking dead." Sidney's somewhat cool rapprochement with his father was holding, as evidenced by his presence at the wedding. But the strains in their relationship were apparent to Sidney's longtime assistant director, Burtt Harris; he recalled that Sidney's efforts to direct his father were met by Baruch's dismissive wave of the hand, swatting his son away.

Finding a distributor in the U.S. market proved difficult because of the film's grim topic and a protracted conflict with the Motion Picture Production Code over the matter of bared breasts. It would not be released in the United States until April 1965. Sidney was taken entirely by surprise when the film turned out to be a commercial success, his first "big grosser."

Rod Steiger was nominated for best actor for his role as Sol Nazerman, but Lee Marvin won the award instead, for his role in the comedy western *Cat Ballou*. Steiger was frankly stunned by losing the Oscar; throughout his career he considered this his greatest performance. Such a disappointment did not surprise Quincy Jones, who scored the film, his first of several for Sidney, launching his career composing soundtracks for many others. "Hollywood has a funny sort of prejudice toward films that come out of the East," said Jones, "and since *The Pawnbroker* was really an East Coast production, the industry resisted everything about it."

This searing film is what Sidney was working on when he and Gail commenced their married life together in Sidney's Greenwich Village apartment. The post-production took months as Sidney worked with his editor, Ralph Rosenblum, on what became a breakthrough technique that built on the stunning final shots of *Fail-Safe* and expanded Sidney's visual vocabulary. In his novel, Wallant used description and lengthy italicized flashbacks to take the reader inside Nazerman's head. For example: "Suddenly he had the sensation of being clubbed. An image was stamped *behind* his eyes like a bolt of pain." To convey the intrusive character of triggered traumatic memory, Sidney introduced a series of flash cuts; he and Rosenblum tested eight-, six-, and four-frame flashes, the shortest being one-sixth of a second, to determine what length could be readable by the viewer, and then made them increasingly longer as the story unfolded. Alain Resnais' 1959 *Hiroshima Mon Amour* had been the first film to experiment with this kind of jump-cut flashback; Sidney built the technique in his own way, drawing, he said, on his own experience of intrusive memories. This technique has since become a standard part of cinematic language.

It is hard to imagine that Sidney wasn't bringing some of the darkness of his films home with him. Back-to-back, he'd made nuclear war and Nazi Holocaust films following the failure of his marriage to Gloria. He'd been seeing a psychiatrist and working nonstop as usual, trying to *work* his way into a new life.

HOMEMAKING

Before his marriage to Gail, Sidney had enjoyed furnishing his Charles Street apartment to his taste, after inhabiting Gloria's overwhelming sensibility. But what began as a rather simple way of life for the newly-wed Gail and Sidney would change dramatically over the years, with children, travel, and Sidney's mounting successes. The couple would soon purchase a stately brownstone on Lexington Avenue in the 90s, equipped with its own elevator. "The house was dark, wisteria-wrapped, and old-fashioned," Gail said. "It had a small garden with rambling roses and a tulip tree." Sidney had set his sights on that house years earlier, when it belonged to playwrights Ruth and Augustus Goetz, who wrote the screen adaptation of *Stage Struck*, among many other credits. "I will own that house someday," he promised himself. His nomadic childhood left him determined to establish a real home. His daughter Jenny told me of her father's love of the house, of everything connected with it, with keeping it up and fixing things. She remembered him spending a whole Saturday—sometime in the 1970s—scrubbing graffiti off the exterior of the house. Gail spoke of the importance for Sidney of home as a respite from the intensity of his work, a place "where he took off his shoes and watched football" in their floor-to-ceiling book-lined library.

Sidney didn't want to wait any longer for children. He'd waited and waited with Gloria, to no avail. Gail was pregnant three months after their marriage. With a real New York home established and a baby coming, Sidney grew adventurous. Unwilling to go west to Hollywood, he was quite happy to go to Europe for work. Things British were on the ascent, from the Beatles to *The Pink Panther*'s Inspector Clouseau. Films like Tony Richardson's *A Taste of Honey* and *The Loneliness of the Long Distance Runner* and the American expat Joseph Losey's *The Servant* were international succès d'estime, and the list of in-demand British actors was endless: Julie Christie, Vanessa and Lynn Redgrave, Peter O'Toole, Richard Burton, Laurence Olivier, Alan Bates, Dirk Bogarde, Peter Sellers, Ralph Richardson, James Mason, Trevor Howard and Sean Connery, for starters. Sidney would work with most of them.

"Swinging London" also had much to recommend it; just a few months into Gail's pregnancy, Sidney relocated them to England to make *The Hill* with Sean Connery. It would be almost a decade of back-and-forth between New York and London, or sometimes Rome or Stockholm, where Sidney would be filming.

Gail liked living in London. She'd lived abroad before at various times in her life. They took a luxurious flat in Knightsbridge. "Near Harrods; always near Harrods," Gail recalled with a laugh. They socialized with the expat crowd, people who'd left because of the McCarthy blacklist, and with English actors whom Sidney adored. He liked London too, but, Gail said, he was always working, so they didn't see much of London, only "went to the theater when we could."

When Gail was nearing the end of her pregnancy, Sidney was shooting *The Hill* in a desert in southern Spain. They spoke by phone every other day. He was back in London in time for the birth of their daughter Amy at King's College Hospital in November 1964. Gail delighted in recalling that Amy's birth had coincided with that of Lord Mountbatten's twin grandsons, an event that brought Queen Elizabeth to the hospital. Looking at the babies in the nursery, Gail recounted, the queen pointed to Amy and said, "That's the one I want."

They returned to New York in December for Sidney to begin work on *The Group*, his tenth film. It was the biggest movie Sidney had directed so far and the biggest film production shot in New York to date, with a budget of $2.6 million. It called for thirty-five locations, more than fifty sets on sound stages, and more than a thousand costumes. To get the job done, they needed to borrow technicians and builders from the commercial and industrial film worlds. Many in the industry saw the film as a test of New York's moviemaking capacity. Sidney didn't blink. He approached it as business as usual.

Gail and Sidney with their daughter Amy, photographed in England. (*PA Images / Alamy Stock Photo*)

Adapted from Mary McCarthy's "scandalous" 1963 bestseller, *The Group* follows the post-college lives of eight Vassar women—friends and rivals—of the class of 1933. With all the organizational challenges, Sidney still maintained his focus on the performances, giving attention to each of the eight young women actors. A story in *The New York Times* describes the filming of a wedding reception scene, for which the set, built in New York's Fox Movietone Studios on 54th Street, reproduced the 1930s elegance of the vanished Brevoort Hotel . . .

> . . . *complete with tables, waiters, red damask walls hung with pseudo-Constable landscapes, potted palms and plaster-of-Paris Cupid on a Corinthian column. There they were too, the seven Vassar girls . . . and their swains crowded around the punch bowl. . . . And, seated on the camera crane high above the scene, director Sidney Lumet and cinematographer Boris Kaufman, satisfied with the simulated festivities and gay chatter, signaled "action." Slowly the camera was wheeled toward "the group," whose dialogue was directed toward the sound booms. . . . "Here's to the bride and groom." Lumet, dressed in habitual worn blue jeans and blue tennis shirt, called a halt. "Jessica, baby," he said endearingly, "don't slouch, just hold the cup naturally. Okay, let's give it another try."*

Again challenging the Motion Picture Production Code, Sidney's script included intimate bedroom scenes, alcoholism, wife abuse, lesbians, breastfeeding and an unmarried woman going to a doctor to acquire birth control. Besides the Code, the film was up against the Catholic Legion of Decency, which had earlier condemned *The Pawnbroker*, hurting its box office. At the last moment a few cuts were made to appease the Catholic Legion, including a shot of a man's unwanted hand slipping around to fondle the breast of one of the women (played by Jessica Walter) before she shrugged it away.

Sidney again cast his father in a small role, as Mr. Schneider, a benevolent neighbor. It's likely that Baruch needed the work; he'd been appearing in a few TV spots and B films, including a low-budget horror film. Soon Baruch would take off for Dallas, Texas, with his second wife and her daughter, to establish an acting school. He sensed that in Texas there was "money but not too much culture." Movie star and sex symbol Jayne Mansfield would become a prized student of his.

As filming of *The Group* began, Sidney gave a young Pauline Kael, freshly arrived in New York, free access during the shooting of the film. He had liked her work and hoped she might gain an appreciation for how movies are actually made. He recalled years later, "She had just come from San Francisco, and I thought, poor kid—she's probably lonely as hell. Little did I know what I was dealing with."

Here began Kael's career-long assault on Sidney. She described him as "the director producers settled for when they couldn't get the one they wanted—everybody's second choice," and wrote, "Genius? Yes, the genius necessary to convince people he's a genius." Yet along with her caviling, she acknowledged that Sidney was skillful, sensitive and patient with the young leading actors, and she liked the movie, calling it "one of the few interesting American movies of recent years."

Soon after the film wrapped and well before Kael's essay on the film came out, Sidney invited her to dinner at his apartment. Other guests included Sidney's beloved friend, caricaturist Al Hirschfeld and his wife Dolly. They had had "a good dinner and a lot to drink," Sidney recalled, when Pauline and Al got into "an idiotic discussion about the function of the critic." Gesturing toward Sidney, Kael remarked, "My job is to show *him* which way to go." "You've got to be kidding," Sidney said. "No, I'm not," she replied, and Sidney responded, "In other words, you want the creative experience without the creative risk." Sidney claimed never to have read her article, "The Making of *The Group*," having heard "it was going to be butchery." He added, "If there's an unpleasantness to avoid, I avoid it." It's likely, though, that he did read it.

With *The Group*, Sidney attempted to tell a female-centered story; some have referred to the result as "the ultimate chick flick." *The Group* was the inspiration for Candace Bushnell's novel *Sex and the*

City and its later adaptation into a TV show. When *The Group* was in production, it was remarked that Sidney, a child of the Yiddish theater, was an odd pick for this window onto an elite WASPy world, but of course Sidney had had quite a crash course on the subject in his marriage to Gloria and he was married at that time to a Radcliffe graduate.

It was an advantage to Sidney that the film did not center on romance; it is a sophisticated treatment of eight women boldly setting out to make their mark on the world, though they are thwarted, mostly in ways that reflect the sexism of the age. The film followed hard upon Betty Friedan's consequential *The Feminine Mystique*. Like that book, the film takes seriously the lack of fulfillment in the lives of white college-educated women, when the idealism and camaraderie of college are replaced by deep dissatisfaction with the limitations placed on them—what Friedan called "the problem with no name." It is unsurprising that the film had—and still has—passionate proponents and detractors; it was nominated for a few domestic and foreign awards, but it was not a hit.

Whatever Sidney's sympathies and insights, or failures of insight, into women were, from Gail's point of view Sidney was very much the husband, who expected her to fulfill the duties of the wife. This is quite a different description of Sidney than those of his two former wives. Sidney seems to have approached each of his marriages, like each of his films, according to its distinctive demands and requirements. He misread Gail's seeming contentment with the comforts and excitement of their domestic and social lives. As Gail describes it, Sidney ran a tight ship at home. With Rita and Gloria, he had not been in control, and indeed things had gone *out* of his control. Perhaps this was the lesson he took from his two failed marriages. Finally with Gail, he hoped his marriage would provide stability.

Gail couldn't recall whether it was Sidney's father or Sidney's friend Alexander King, an author and talk show raconteur, who said, "Your work is the only thing that matters," but she felt that this was Sidney's creed, and that "home was where he went after work." And indeed he *was* productive, directing some twenty films in the course of their fifteen-year marriage. She expressed the feeling that Sidney held narrow expectations for her. "Home," she reflected, "had to be clean, neat, and a good meal." Then she reiterated, "And he was the husband."

LADIES WHO LUNCH

And here's to the girls who play wife . . .
—"THE LADIES WHO LUNCH" BY STEPHEN SONDHEIM

Gail and Sidney's second daughter, Jenny, was born in February 1967 in New York, while Sidney was shooting *Bye Bye Braverman*. Gail reflected that during these years she herself had been "a hopeless prisoner of the boring 1950s," when all that mattered was that your "eye shadow did not clash with your dress." "Somewhere people were protesting a war," she reflected. "Somewhere they were smoking marijuana cigarettes and wearing micro-minis. But I was wrapped up in Liberty smocking, Beatrix Potter and Dr. Spock."

Gail conceded that their live-in domestic staff of three left her with little to do. But something was not sitting right with her. In the first of the three books she penned in the years following her divorce from Sidney, she writes self-critically:

It was a "tough" life: breakfast in bed and a car to take me to Bergdorf's. My greatest activity, besides shopping, was needlepoint. I was a passionate dabbler. Ballet, yoga, tennis, jogging . . . transcendental meditation, and Mind Control. I received my Mind Control diploma, but that was the only course I ever completed.

She felt out of step with her own generation. "As Sidney got more and more successful, I would get fur coats," Gail remarked dismissively. She wrote a plaintive letter to her friend Baby Jane Holzer, a member of the Warhol crowd and jet-setter; Gail told her she missed "twisting" with her at the Peppermint Lounge in New York.

But there was a lot of hobnobbing and partying to keep her occupied. She hosted the kind of parties her mother gave, where there was piano playing and singing, where "famous people liked to let their hair down."

At their recently purchased "pretty, old-fashioned house in East Hampton," they socialized with "the artsy crowd," writers, painters, and filmmakers. Larry Rivers, a good friend then, painted a portrait of Amy and Jenny. The annual parties held at their beautiful beach-front home for Sidney's June birthday were remembered warmly by many of the family friends I spoke with. Longtime intimate, Oscar-winning designer Tony Walton recalled that at these events friends made humorous toasts or sang songs they'd written for Sidney. Sidney sang Yiddish versions of Irving Berlin songs, and he and his childhood sweetheart Ellen Adler invariably dished up a rendition of the communist anthem, "The Internationale," from their youth. Lena Horne's and Sidney's birthdays were both in June, so sometimes they were feted together.

In the city, they were regulars on the party circuit, among the glitterati who frequented Elaine's, the fashionable watering hole on the Upper East Side. Their names appeared on the society page, and they attended such events as a farewell party for Princess Margaret at the Four Seasons and countless Broadway opening-night parties. At their Lexington Avenue home they hosted the intimate wedding ceremony of Lynn Redgrave and John Clark shortly after Redgrave's star turn in the British hit film *Georgy Girl*. In quieter moments Gail made paella for dinner guests that regularly included Sidney's New York theater friends, such as Al Hirschfeld and Sidney Kingsley, the benevolent older men who served as Sidney's surrogate fathers.

Gail recalled one evening at Al Hirschfeld's home, a dinner at which Al, Sidney, George Balanchine and Alexander King began counting and realized that "among them they'd had something like twelve wives." They laughed and laughed, Gail recounted, but she didn't mention that she or any of the other current wives were laughing.

ON THE BRIGHTER SIDE

Gail's disgruntlement and frustration with herself that come through in her recollections were at the time obscured by the "wonderful new friends" they made in the "intense colleagueship of making a movie." The all-star cast and crew members of Sidney's *The Sea Gull*, filmed just outside of Stockholm in the summer of 1968, bonded with one another to an unusual and happy degree. This instant work-based community was Sidney's ideal, and he and Gail both loved that time; neither wanted the cast and crew ever to disperse. When Vanessa Redgrave had to leave early for another project, farewell banners were strung to send her off. Adding to the festive atmosphere, the cast wore their costumes day and night to break them in; they came to breakfast in costume and wore them through the evening.

Sidney described *The Sea Gull* as a story "about misplaced love" and "who destroys whom." Perhaps he'd found a new way to think about his failed marriage to Gloria.

Gail recalled spending precious days that summer, when Amy was almost four years old and Jenny still a toddler, with their friends Gen LeRoy and Tony Walton and their two girls, ages four and five. "It was children, children, children," Gail said wistfully. They made frequent and memorable excursions to Skansen, a charming open-air museum and zoo on an island a short ferry ride from where they lived in Stockholm. The kids were always on the scene, always at dinner, "being pains in the asses," Gen LeRoy smilingly recalled.

What, Gail must have wondered, could she possibly have to complain about?

BACK AND FORTH

While the children were still small, Sidney and Gail were able to keep moving between New York and Europe. After *The Group*, he returned to London to make *The Deadly Affair*, an adaptation of a John le Carré spy novel, with James Mason and Simone Signoret. He was back to New York for *Bye Bye Braverman*, then to Sweden for *The Sea Gull*, and on to Rome to direct *The Appointment*, with Omar Sharif and Anouk Aimée, about a lawyer who stalks his beautiful wife, convinced she is a high-priced prostitute. This surprisingly static film was actually booed at Cannes and was never distributed in the United States. Sidney made two films stateside, *The Last of the Mobile Hot Shots* and *The Anderson Tapes*. Sidney also worked with producer Ely Landau and director Joseph L. Mankiewicz on a tribute to Dr. Martin Luther King Jr., *King: A Filmed Record . . . Montgomery to Memphis*. Newsreel footage traces events from Dr. King's 1955 address to a church in Montgomery and the beginning of the yearlong bus boycott and concludes with his assassination in Memphis in 1968. The newsreel footage is intercut with short readings from the Bible and poetry by celebrities, including Harry Belafonte, Ruby Dee, Walter Matthau, James Earl Jones, Paul Newman, Joanne Woodward, Sidney Poitier, Burt Lancaster and Anthony Quinn. Sidney and Mankiewicz worked mostly filming these short interludes. Originally released for a single night in seven hundred theaters around the country, the movie raised money for the Martin Luther King Jr. Special Fund. It received an Oscar nomination in the documentary category and is now listed in the National Film Registry. Sidney never claimed any credit for his work on this project.

The family again returned to London, this time to make *The Offence*, the third of five films he'd make with Sean Connery. Connery, who had tired of playing 007, insisted United Artists make the film as a condition of his return to the James Bond franchise. *The Offence*, filmed in the spring of 1972 at Twickenham Studios, is a harrowing police drama about a detective "blighted by misanthropic rage." This story of corruption at the heart of law enforcement looks ahead to some of Sidney's greatest films. The family would return to London a final time for *Murder on the Orient Express*.

With the exception of *Orient Express*, the films he made abroad did not make money in the United States, although several did well with critics. Sidney didn't publicly gripe about critics (Pauline Kael

Sidney with Producer Ely Landau and Harry Belafonte, filming a narrative interlude for *King: A Filmed Record . . . Montgomery to Memphis*, 1970. *(Courtesy Everett Collection)*

excepted). He was never blind to the weaknesses in his own films. Sometimes he became aware early in the filming that the picture was not going to work, but he felt a duty to all involved to forge ahead. I asked Gail about his reactions when he had a flop. Unsurprisingly, she said that it upset him: "He felt so exposed."

PARENTING

Amy and Jenny were on the scene for *Orient Express*, attending an English school for a year. Jenny didn't remember much about it, except the desserts: "I hated the desserts. They were all custardy. That's what I remember—the desserts." Settled back in New York, the girls were placed in the elite, progressive Dalton School. The two would listen in on their parents' dinner parties, where the likes of Adolph

Green, Betty Comden and Bob Fosse talked showbiz and politics. Their conversation, Jenny recalled, "was very smart, fast, and loud." In this house filled with actors and talk about acting, little Jenny, watching a cartoon in which Bugs Bunny did a drag impersonation, was able to name the impersonated actress—but, apparently having seen none of her movies, asked with a puzzled frown, "Who is this Greta Garbo, anyway?" Particularly attuned to and curious about this odd thing in the world, *fame*, Jenny brought a surprising question to her grandmother, Lena Horne, who often came over to their house to watch TV with her granddaughters. As quoted in James Gavin's celebrated biography of Horne, she recounted:

> *My Jenny, when she was four or five years old, said to me, "Are you Lena Horne?" I said, "No, who said so? I'm your grandmother, don't you forget it." They heard that I was Lena Horne from Michael Jackson, 'cause he used to go up to their room and sing to them and act like a child with them, and play with their toys with them, and they just adored him. And Michael Jackson told them that their grandmother was famous.*

Looking back, Gail wrote that her top priority with her kids was to make them feel loved and secure, but it was also important to her that they have *fun*. "Naturally I overdid it. Even *they* admit that they were spoiled." She goes on to say, "I was not an *all*-bad parent, despite encouraging unreal expectations and avid consumerism. But I was certainly not good enough. . . . If I had to do it over again I would be more relaxed and I would not try so hard to be popular with my children."

Sidney thoroughly enjoyed the kids when he was around. "He never took them to the playground, and everything was very structured, but he adored them," Gail recalled. "He especially loved their fractured English when they first began to talk. He was sad when they finally could just speak." Others recalled that he enjoyed being with kids and was good with them. He would get down on his knees and play and would splash around with friends' children in the swim-

Daughters Jenny and Amy Lumet, the ultimate New York City kids, photographed in 1976.

ming pool in East Hampton. He was good at organizing them, getting them to do things, "getting them hopping." He talked to them like adults: "Hello my darling love . . ." Years later, Jenny described her father as a "very merry, silly, googly baby-loving, goofy kind of guy—in a lot of ways. Except when he was working."

But there was trouble ahead, especially for their elder daughter, Amy.

TIPPING POINTS

Living vicariously through Sidney and his films was bound to cause problems for Gail sooner or later. She was too thoughtful for the life she found herself living. In the turbulent 1970s, she felt more and more like a "sort of half-baked celebrity" wife and daughter. The heady distractions of dancing with Lord Mountbatten, "Dickie, the handsomest man in the world," chatting with Dame Agatha Christie, spending weekends with Sean Connery and the countless A-list events were wearing thin.

Friends allude to a dinner at the Russian Tea Room at which Gail slapped Sidney across the face; the circumstances are disputed, but everyone agreed that Sidney was not prone to expressions of anger. His daughter Jenny said she'd heard him raise his voice only once. As Sidney himself said, "If there's an unpleasantness to avoid, I avoid it."

Gail lost her beloved younger brother, Teddy, in September 1970 to hepatitis and what she called a "high-speed life"; his kidney failure was linked to his use of drugs. Gail described him as "a brown Prince Mishkin," full of charm, whose heroes were H. Rap Brown, Herbert Marcuse and Hermann Hesse. He was also a "a very angry young black man," she observed sadly. He was thirty years old.

This excruciating loss likely brought certain feelings into focus; it couldn't have helped that Sidney wasn't good with death. She later wrote that she had been at the time "as isolated from the black mainstream as I was from the white." She enrolled in a course in black literature and letters, spanning poets from Phyllis Wheatley to Langston Hughes, novelists and theorists from Ralph Ellison to Frantz Fanon and historians of black America from Herbert Aptheker to Howard Zinn. "I learned about *being* black, but I still did not know about *feeling* black."

In the autumn of 1970, Gail and Sidney hosted at their home a fundraising event for the Black Panthers' legal defense. Twenty-one members of the Black Panthers were on trial in New York for conspiring to bomb Manhattan department stores, the New York Botanical Garden, police stations, subway switching rooms and railroad tracks, and were each being held on $100,000 bail. One of them was a seventeen-year-old junior at Long Island City High School. Those in support of the defendants believed they were being tried for their political beliefs alone. At that time, the Black Panthers had become an object of public fascination, receiving a tremendous amount of news coverage, often including images of armed Panthers protesting police violence in Oakland, California.

A week after Gail and Sidney's fundraiser, their close friends Felicia and Leonard Bernstein hosted a similar event, and that's when all hell broke loose. Their guest list included too many New York elites and celebrities to go unnoticed, among them Otto Preminger, author Jean Stein, songwriters Sheldon Harnick and Burton Lane, civil rights leader Roger Wilkins, Barbara Walters, editor Bob Silvers and a host of "wives of": Mrs. Richard Avedon, Mrs. Arthur Penn, Mrs. Harry Belafonte, and Mrs. Sidney Lumet. The journalist Tom Wolfe skewered those who attended as "radical chic" and described what to him was a ludicrous scene of Black Panthers eating hors d'oeuvres from silver trays at the Bernsteins' thirteen-room Park Avenue duplex, while "mau-mauing" (intimidating) the other guests. Here is a taste of Wolfe's ugly tone as he mocks the "limousine liberals":

> Obviously, if you are giving a party for the Black Panthers, as Lenny and Felicia are this evening, or as Sidney and Gail Lumet did last week, . . . well, then, obviously you can't have a Negro butler and maid, Claude and Maude, in uniform, circulating through the living room, the library and the main hall serving drinks and canapés. But it's all right. They're white *servants*, not Claude and Maude, but white South Americans. . . . Sidney Lumet and his wife Gail, who is Lena Horne's daughter, have three white servants, including a Scottish nurse. Everybody has white servants.

Hate mail poured into the Bernstein home, and their apartment building was picketed for weeks by the Jewish Defense League protesting Bernstein because of the Panthers' anti-Israel stance.

In May 1971, the New York trial of the Black Panthers ended with acquittals on all counts. In 1975, a Senate investigation exposed FBI director J. Edgar Hoover's covert operations against the Panthers, including planting informants and agents provocateurs and influencing press coverage. Years later, the Bernsteins learned through the Freedom of Information Act that the FBI had churned out most of the hate mail they'd received, and that most of the picketers were FBI plants. Hoover's FBI was aggressively fomenting hostility between blacks and Jews.

Despite the Panthers' vindication, the fallout from these efforts was awful, Gail said, especially for how it had hurt her friend Felicia Bernstein. The topic was still too sensitive for Gail to discuss when I asked her about it.

In the middle of one night at their East Hampton home, Gail had what she described as a "religious awakening" that would eventually lead her to the devout Catholicism she continues to practice. I asked her how Sidney responded when she spoke about her religious feelings. "He thought I needed a shrink. He believed in shrinks. I can understand that. I don't blame him for the way he felt. He was entirely secular, a man of the left, 'opium of the masses,' and all that."

Their daily life continued, the lacuna widening. They exchanged presents at birthdays and Christmas; Gail liked to give him artwork; he would pick gifts for her himself, although he didn't much enjoy shopping. What did he enjoy? He liked to eat "Jewish food," Gail said, "gefilte fish, smoked fish, sour cream, deli, that sort of thing." And he liked wine, "drank a ton of it and never got drunk. I never saw him drunk in my life."

Gail was forty years old when their marriage ended, but she reflected that she had been "like a child," hadn't known who she was. She described herself as "part brown bourgeois, part Ivy League, part Hollywood brat." The divorce came in 1978, when Amy was fourteen years old and Jenny was eleven. There were rumors that Gail had had an affair. There were rumors about Sidney too, but they remain rumors. Gail's mother, Lena Horne, came to the conclusion that Sidney was at fault. To a reporter she referred to him as "that bastard," and, she said, "You can print it."

Gail later wrote, "It took both therapy and divorce for me to have the courage to examine my newfound [religious] conviction. When I did, I discovered that I had found myself." Five years later she married Kevin Buckley, a writer and prominent magazine editor. Her first book was published in 1986.

As I was leaving her apartment, the one that her mother had lived in, she conveyed her assessment of the marriage: "Sidney protected me. He was kind—always. He was a kind, good person."

16

MEN AT WORK

Everyone talks about the movies of the '70s now like it was this golden age. We had no idea at the time.
— SIDNEY LUMET, 2008 INTERVIEW

Oh Bobby, we can be men in so many ways; we don't get to see in movies all the different ways we can be men.
— SIDNEY LUMET TO BOBBY CANNAVALE, 2003

One particular and somehow representative memory lodged itself in the mind of Sidney's daughter Jenny, so much so that a version of it made its way into the warmly praised film she scripted, *Rachel Getting Married* (2008). She was about eleven years old when she observed director-choreographer Bob Fosse (*Chicago, Cabaret, All That Jazz*) and her father playfully squabbling in the kitchen after dinner:

> *Bob Fosse, in all his Bob Fosse-ness . . . a long and languid human being. The whole being ends in the cigarette. He was in all black, with his black cashmere sweater, and his goatee. He was just gorgeous. Next to him is my Pop, who was smoking hot, but completely circular in every aspect. My dad's loading the dishwasher and Bob Fosse is next to him with a cigarette and he says, "You know, Sidney, if you put the salad bowl and the*

containers in the top level, you'll have 10% more space in the dishwasher." And my Dad says, "Bobby, go fuck yourself."

And they continued facing off over the placement of forks, tines up or down, where to put the saucer lids, and so on. Jenny herself pondered why this exchange had made such an impression on her. It had to be memorable, these two directors exercising their male competitiveness in such an unlikely pursuit.

He didn't do buddy or band-of-brothers movies, but he was fascinated by the cultures men create, by male systems of obligation and affiliation and by the particularized allegiances, occupational, familial, racial and ethnic, they live by. It was in *Serpico*, his first cop film, that he found the rich vein he would keep mining.

SERPICO

I need one hit so I can get the money for three more flops.
—SIDNEY LUMET, 1973 INTERVIEW

There's a lot of me in Serpico. . . . I hope someday it's apparent that there is a lot of me in Serpico.
—SIDNEY LUMET

The story of the events leading up to the creation of the 1970 Knapp Commission hearings on police corruption that precipitated the biggest shake-up in the history of the New York Police Department became the first of Sidney's four torn-from-the-headlines movies. He'd been brought on to *Serpico* just four weeks before shooting was scheduled to begin. John Avildsen (*Joe, Rocky*) had decamped over a dispute about the focus of the story; he was more interested in the politics surrounding the Knapp Commission than the character of Serpico, and it all came to a head over a location Avildsen felt was "absolutely necessary to the realistic atmosphere of the film," Frank Serpico's actual boyhood home in Brooklyn. Producer Dino De Laurentiis didn't see it that way. Sidney's approach to both authenticity and budgets presented a contrast to Avildsen's that appealed to the producers, and to producers generally. "Some directors complain about restrictions," Sidney observed at the time, "restrictions on budget, restrictions on time. . . . Personally I love restrictions; they're stimulating, they make you go deeper."

With *Serpico* a number of things clicked into place at once; a lot of it had to do with Al Pacino. Pacino, who considered himself primarily a stage actor at this point, was thrilled that, despite the tight time frame, Sidney planned two weeks of rehearsal. Pacino had been working off Waldo Salt's *Serpico* script, adapted from the book by Peter Maas, and already knew his lines cold. But in the meantime, Salt's version had been revised by screenwriter Norman Wexler. Pacino and Sidney agreed that the new script, while structurally improved, had lost something in the dialogue. Together, actor and director drew the best from each version, revising as they went. "In rehearsal we put together a new structure with Waldo's dialogue," Sidney recalled. "I think that Al saw that I was open to him and not playing turf games and things like that." It's not that Sidney had never revised a script in rehearsal or while shooting, but this was something different, deeply collaborative and based on a shared vision. Nothing made Sidney happier.

The decision to shoot the film in reverse sequence was made to accommodate Serpico's facial hair. They agreed Pacino should have a real beard—no fakery—so they started with the scenes at the story's end when he had a full beard, then shot sequences with the mustache, and finally those when he was clean-shaven. Pacino's brilliant performance of the character helped Sidney advance his distinctive vision of his city: a tough place inhabited by vulnerable, emotionally exposed individuals, especially men. This would become one of his trademarks.

Sidney met Frank Serpico about three days before rehearsals started. Serpico and Pacino had spent a lot of time together and grown close. Sidney's impression of Frank was that "he was extraordinary. Very

Sidney and Al Pacino confer on a Brooklyn rooftop location for *Serpico*. (*PictureLux / The Hollywood Archive / Alamy Stock Photo*)

frantic, very funny, very alive, very busy, and filled with great fun." But as it got time to shoot, Sidney asked him to stop coming: "Al is going to be playing you—and he can't do that if you are right off-camera watching him. It would make him too self-conscious." Sidney feared Serpico had been hurt by his dismissal: "he thought he'd done something wrong." Part of the "brutality of movies," as Sidney put it, was that Frank was "just research."

But Sidney intended the film to do justice to this man whom he admired, which didn't mean turning him into a plaster saint. Sidney described Serpico as a classic pain-in-the-ass type, relentless, committed at all costs, qualities Sidney admired and identified with but knew well could be less than endearing. Emphasizing these disagreeable traits in the character was important to Sidney, who never wanted to promote the pure-of-heart, physically attractive and dauntless

Hollywood-type hero. With Serpico, an incorruptible hippie cop, Sidney was also drawing a pointed contrast to a different movie hero of that moment, the reactionary bad cops of *Dirty Harry* (1971) and *The French Connection* (1971). Unlike Clint Eastwood's Harry and Gene Hackman's Popeye Doyle, Serpico doesn't bang heads or draw his gun to be effective; he takes meetings with bureaucrats and politicians, complains, waits, grows jittery, wrecks personal relationships and "is stupid enough to get shot in the face." Sidney never glamorized the use of violence, even to achieve lawful ends. Without a trace of piety, he shows us that, for a million different reasons, it ain't easy trying to do good.

Easing Sidney's way for filming at dingy precinct houses and on city streets in the east Bronx and Williamsburg was John Lindsay's recently established Mayor's Office of Film, Theatre & Broadcasting. Sidney had long been frustrated by the bureaucracy that had limited location shooting, and it had been standard to budget for paying the cops $400 at each location. MOFTB opened the way for the wave of 1970s movies set in photogenic New York City. As Vincent Canby wrote in *The New York Times*, "The star that attracts the filmmakers to New York City—dirty, crowded, hot, frenetic, soaring, squalid and graffiti-covered as it is—is New York City." The police assigned by the new office to handle traffic and crowds on *Serpico* expressed appreciation for what they saw being filmed; a common refrain was, "That's what it's like."

After shooting *Serpico*, Al Pacino dashed off to film Coppola's masterpiece, *The Godfather: Part II*, but it was *Serpico* that made him a star and earned him his first Oscar nomination for Best Actor. As Sidney would observe of Pacino years later, "The talent is so deep. His ability to understand so many different kinds of life is so amazing to me. As you know he is not an educated man, very rough, *very rough* childhood, strictly Bronx-sewer upbringing, yet he knows so much about people." Years later, when learning of Sidney's death, Pacino remarked, "He was the kindest man I ever knew." Piedy recalled how he "sat and wept" at the memorial service for Sidney.

Serpico marked the beginning run of Sidney's greatest films, almost one after the next: *Serpico*, *Dog Day Afternoon* and *Network*, made within a span of three short years, with two other films in between, the beautifully crafted *Murder on the Orient Express* and the failed and forgotten *Lovin' Molly*. *Equus*, *The Wiz* and *Just Tell Me What You Want* would close the decade. Between 1973 and 1979 Sidney's films were nominated for a grand total of thirty-one Oscars, including twelve for acting. There were only two nominations for Best Director, which makes little sense and must have stung. Although there would be more nominations and awards, he would never again have a run like this one.

A FAUX PAS

It's hard to say what got Sidney to leave New York for Texas to make *Lovin' Molly*, a screen version of *Leaving Cheyenne*, Larry McMurtry's offbeat story about a love triangle carried on over decades. McMurtry's *The Last Picture Show* had been winningly adapted by Peter Bogdanovich a couple of years earlier. Likely Columbia Pictures offered Sidney a package, a movie with financing and stars ready to go and a nice salary. All this had become harder to turn down in those days, but Sidney knew he hadn't prepared enough for this one. Maybe he was already focusing on his next film, *Murder on the Orient Express*. If Sidney "doing Texas" is not sufficiently nonsensical, how about Anthony Perkins playing what is supposed to be a light-hearted role? Beau Bridges and Blythe Danner struggle along with him, trying to make sense of their characters and their Texas accents. It was released only three months after *Serpico* and quickly forgotten.

MURDER ON THE ORIENT EXPRESS

Sidney adored the script of *Murder on the Orient Express* and laughed out loud when he got to the surprise ending. Paul Dehn, who had adapted Ian Fleming's James Bond for the screen, had written a loyal and witty screenplay from Agatha Christie's 1934 chestnut. Sidney's "engine turned over" on the first reading: he'd pack the cast with big stars to play the thirteen passengers on the train. The film would be steeped in nostalgia—after all, wasn't Agatha Christie all about nostalgia? Although it would be a British production, he wouldn't do it in the style of British realism; instead he'd drench his stars in the Hollywood glamour of the 1930s, when the piece was written and set. The movie appeared to him like a vision, complete.

Plus, he'd been looking for the right comedy, wanting to figure out how to master the light touch he so sorely wished for, still lamenting the failure of *Bye Bye Braverman*, a film that, as he put it, "should have been a soufflé, but turned out to be a latke." He knew he could create laughter in a realistic situation, as he'd done in moments in *Serpico* and would do even more brilliantly in *Dog Day Afternoon*, but not in high comedy. Here was a chance to stretch.

He called his dear friend Sean Connery, knowing that if he got one big star the others would follow. The wish list included John Gielgud, Ingrid Bergman, Lauren Bacall, and Vanessa Redgrave; they all signed on without blinking. The only exceptions were Alec Guinness and Katharine Hepburn, who were otherwise engaged. Some of the cast said they signed on just to meet the other actors. They all agreed to $100,000 up front with points on the back end. Sidney was delighted that all the actors made good money when the film became a hit.

Gail had packed up Amy, age nine, and Jenny, age six, and off they went, back to London, where much of the shooting would take place at Elstree Studios. Resettling in posh digs at the Grosvenor House in Mayfair, Gail arranged a school for the girls and reconnected with old friends. Gail and the kids joined Sidney on the initial filming, which took them across Europe, from Paris to Istanbul. Gail relished the company of their dear friends and godparents to the girls, Gen LeRoy and husband Tony Walton; Walton was designing the film's remarkable costumes.

The casting had gone smoothly; the only surprise was that Ingrid Bergman, whom Sidney had wanted for the role of Princess Dragomiroff, told him she preferred the role of Greta Ohlsson, the awkward and rather unhinged missionary who exclaims, "I was born backwards. That is why I work in Africa as missionary, teaching little brown babies more backwards than myself." Sidney respected Bergman's judgment and agreed to the change. When it came time to shoot her big scene with Albert Finney, Bergman saw that Sidney was doing no reverse shots of Finney, which meant there would be no cutaways from her speech. She was so grateful that "she gave me a kiss on the mouth," Sidney reminisced. She won an Oscar for her role.

Sidney was charmed by what happened on the first day of rehearsal: the cast was seated around a table, as usual, for a read-through. After about ten pages Sidney stopped them and said, "I'm sorry. I can't hear anybody." It appeared that the actors were whispering their lines, apparently because they were intimidated by one another; as Sidney put it, "the stage actors were completely in awe of the movie stars, and the movie stars were completely in awe of the stage actors. . . . Everybody was afraid to let go."

Sidney, however, wasn't awed or intimidated. In his denim shirt, faded blue dungarees and denim jacket, he was, as always, entirely comfortable and at home in his role, like a sculptor examining his clay. Soon this roster of A-listers developed a warm esprit de corps that comes through on the screen, especially in the final scene, which Sidney added to the script, where one by one the conspirators raise a glass to the plot's mastermind, played by Lauren Bacall; their delight in one another is palpable.

London was abuzz with the production, a remarkable lineup of celebrities, five of whom were concurrently appearing on the West End stage, joining forces to do justice to Agatha Christie, England's eighty-four-year-old national treasure. Everything was extravagant about the film. Sidney hired an ambulance to pick up Albert Finney at his home each morning at 5:00 A.M. so he could remain prone and try to sleep while his makeup was applied; it took hours to turn him into the much older and peculiar-looking Inspector Poirot. All sorts of celebrities stopped by during what became legendary lunchtimes on the set. Memorable to Gail was the lunch party attended by the

Prince of Wales. The whole cast was there, Gail explained, except Vanessa Redgrave, who "at the time did not sit down with royalty."

Gail recalled that she and Sidney had spent almost no time alone in London or as a family. "He was the same in New York and London, with his crew, making his movies. No sightseeing. He was working from six in the morning until ten o'clock at night." When I asked more broadly about landmarks in their marriage, she immediately returned to the making of this film. "That was really fabulous: meeting Agatha Christie, the Queen coming to the opening, dancing with Mountbatten." Jenny, too, recalled it as a highlight of her childhood. "The timing was very right-on then for my consciousness: 'Ooh, this cool train!' Such a beautiful, glamorous, funny movie, with all these movie stars in these great costumes. That's fun, big moviemaking, and my sister and I would do all their voices." They were all swept up in the momentum of the film, but they were not exactly sharing the experience as a family.

This was the first picture on which Sidney had final cut, a result of *Serpico*'s box office success. The movie was nominated for six Oscars. Years later Sidney admitted to "being pissed off that we got so many nominations and I didn't get nominated."

DOG DAY AFTERNOON

What you are about to see is true—It happened in Brooklyn, New York, on August 22, 1972.

—*Dog Day Afternoon*

The day in question was Tuesday, August 22, 1972. The temperature was 97 degrees. I was driving out to Long Island on the expressway, and, as was my custom, I was listening lethargically to the endless repetitious news bullets on WINS. . . . Then suddenly there was real news of the most ridiculous kind. A bank was being held up in Brooklyn. The police had arrived. Hostages were being held. A state of siege was in force. Demands were being made. It was a familiar scenario, but with bizarre variations. One of the bank robbers demanded that his wife be brought to him, and, when the police complied, it turned out that the "wife" was a transvestite. I began to suspect that Andy Warhol and Paul Morrissey had staged the whole operation as a tasteless parody of the terrorism around us.

—ANDREW SARRIS, *VILLAGE VOICE*, SEPTEMBER 29, 1975

The day before shooting began on *Dog Day Afternoon*, Pacino got cold feet. As Sidney told it, "He asked me and the screenwriter, Frank Pierson, to come up to his house for some cockamamie reason." When they got there, Pacino was "crawling around on all fours, barking like a dog." Sidney's sensitive query: "Al, what the fuck is this?" Pacino responded that he was "out of control" and that he couldn't do the film. Pacino was panicked because his career had just taken off and he feared that this role would end it; up to that point no major Hollywood star had played a gay man. Sidney's strategy was not to try to calm Pacino down, but instead to relate Pacino's current state of mind to the character of Sonny, "what the character must have felt when he decided to rob the bank." Sidney was confident that "the actor part of him would be digesting all these feelings and saying, 'Hey, I can use that in the performance.'" Pacino showed up the next day right on time.

Pacino was in, but he required changes to the script regarding the relationship between Sonny and Leon, his transitioning wife. Footage of their wedding was cut, and a farewell kiss outside the bank was traded for the incredible farewell phone call between the two. Sidney too had worried about audience reaction to that kiss. The balcony reactions at the Loew's Pitkin in Brooklyn when he was a teenager were alive in his memory, the rowdy boys hooting and booing Leslie Howard, who appeared too effeminate for their taste. He didn't want anything to push those buttons.

Prior to shooting, Sidney had consulted with the Gay Activists Alliance and gotten a thumbs-up. For the filming, Sidney called upon members of the gay liberation movement to be the extras in the crowd, including a teenaged Harvey Fierstein, whom Sidney would later cast in *Garbo Talks*. The movie was warmly received in the gay press.

Casting Leon, the first openly transsexual character in a mainstream American movie, took some time. As Burtt Harris recalled the auditions, "We had every performer, every drag queen performer in New York, and all they ever did was Geraldine Page in *Summer and Smoke*. They almost were identical, until we got Chris Sarandon. His approach was: 'All I gotta do is be in love with this guy, want to marry him and get a sex change operation. Simple.'" And that fit with Sidney's idea to treat what could be seen as outrageous in a matter-of-fact manner, relatable. Not to milk it. His famous one-line direction to Sarandon: "A little less Blanche DuBois. A little more Queens housewife."

Sidney's characteristic consideration for the people who lived in the vicinity of his location shooting—including requiring silence of the crew when shooting at night and making sure the lights never got pointed at apartment windows—was ratcheted up since they would be on one Brooklyn block in Prospect Park West for weeks with a massive cast, sirens and a helicopter overhead. He offered neighbors the option of a paid hotel stay; or they were welcome to watch the shooting—heads out of windows would not be out of place.

And unique to this film was Sidney's use of improvisation. Sidney's enormous respect for writers had been one of the reasons he had steered away from this process in the past. This time Sidney had the actors improvise dialogue that he recorded and that he and screenwriter Frank Pierson would cull, shape, and give back to the actors. Pacino recalled the process:

> With Sidney, he would say, "Okay, we've got this scene, we haven't quite gotten it. Let's go work on this thing." Right there, right on the set. And he has me and the actor improvise. . . .

Mainly we were able to do it because we had been working on it for weeks, maybe months, so we know the people we're playing a little bit. We did three improvisations that he taped of the scene. He takes all the data on that, and he translates it and writes one scene from the three improvisations. You know, you don't do that with the whole script, but at that particular moment, it was a fifteen-minute scene, that's what he did. These are the kinds of things that come up . . . and sometimes you get gold.

Some of the most iconic lines in the film were improvised on-camera, including Sonny's galvanizing "Attica, Attica," which beloved assistant director Burtt Harris had whispered to Pacino just before the camera rolled. When Sal (John Cazale) answers Sonny's (Pacino) query about what country he'd like to go to with "Wyoming," Sidney had to slap his hand over his mouth to silence his laughter so as not to ruin the take. This was a thrillingly organic process, just exactly right for this great film that earned Sidney his second Oscar nomination for best director, along with nominations for Best Picture, Best Actor, Best Actor in a Supporting Role for Sarandon and Best Editing. Frank Pierson won for Best Original Screenplay.

When Sidney was asked about what Pacino had needed to achieve this astonishing performance, he replied with characteristic forthrightness: "The creation of the character is really Al's own. He understood something about that man that is irreplaceable, and I don't think a director can ever give—he understood him down to his bone marrow."

There is a little-known postscript to directing this movie: a few days after the film opened, Sidney was picking up a suit at a store in midtown. Walking out of the store, he encountered these events unfolding on the street: Police were cajoling a man who had taken hostages in a bank. The bank robber's demands included releasing Patty Hearst and bringing in singer James Brown to mediate. The bank robber shouted, "I'm afraid to come out—the goddam FBI'll shoot me. Did you see *Dog Day Afternoon*?" The officer in charge, who had seen the movie, responded, "That was the goddamn FBI, not the New

York City Police Department." The man eventually surrendered. Sidney went on his way, pondering unintended consequences.

NETWORK

The family was resettled back in New York, in their Upper East Side town house, this time for good. Sidney would do his best to get home for supper, served promptly at six thirty, to keep the family thing going, as Jenny put it. But the "family thing" was thinning, and Sidney was on too much of a roll to heed the warning signs. Amy loved to draw and paint and was showing real talent for it, and Jenny was funny and irreverent, but Gail's uncertainties about herself were a strain on her parenting now that the girls were beyond trips to the playground and the zoo. Adrift herself, she was struggling to set a course for her daughters. And meanwhile Sidney was getting revved to direct Paddy Chayefsky's remarkable screenplay, *Network*, which was having trouble getting studio backing, in part because the studios worried they wouldn't be able to sell the movie to any TV networks after its theatrical run, given its scalding of the industry. Ultimately a coproduction deal was arranged between MGM and United Artists.

Sidney's name had been the first one mentioned to direct the film, but as Dave Itzkoff reports in his terrific book *Mad as Hell: The Making of Network and the Fateful Vision of the Angriest Man in Movies*, Mike Medavoy, vice president of production at United Artists, immediately reacted negatively: "Are you serious? Sidney Lumet? To do a funny movie?" He reminded Chayefsky of the scene in *The Pawnbroker* when Rod Steiger impales his hand on the receipt spike. "That ain't funny," he said, at which point Chayefsky "took his matzo ball soup and it went, a little bit flying." Medavoy continues, "And I looked at Paddy and I said, 'You know what? If you feel that strongly, he's probably a really good director for this.'" And that was settled as far as Chayefsky was concerned. Meanwhile the studio continued to throw out names: Kazan, Coppola, Huston, Nichols, Scorsese, Kubrick, Fosse, Penn.

While the studio wrangling was going on, Sidney was agitated; he hated waiting. Known to spend most of his retail hours in hardware stores, Sidney was at home "stripping the windows to pass the time," his longtime production designer Philip Rosenberg recalled. The contract, when it came, included a special arrangement with Chayefsky: he would be on the set throughout rehearsal and filming, and he'd have a say.

Arguably, no one but Sidney could have managed this arrangement, with Chayefsky watching over and voicing his opinions. As Sidney noted, "His cynicism was partly a pose, but a healthy dose of paranoia was also in his character." But as it turned out, all was well on the set. Itzkoff quotes script supervisor Kay Chapin's diary jottings:

> *Sidney knows specifically what he wants and is very adept at communicating his intentions to actors. Paddy almost always agrees but if he doesn't he's specific about his objections. . . . It looks like it's a perfect combination all around: a terrific script; a director that totally understands the material; a writer who knows that he understands it, and actors that are perfectly cast and adore the script and director. . . . It's the first time I've experienced this kind of intermeshing—a rare experience.*

A hard-earned feature of Sidney's contract was that his recently established production company, Amjen Entertainment (named for Amy and Jenny), would receive 12.5 percent of the movie's net profits, which would turn out to be a very good deal.

Casting was also being done by committee, but one person on everyone's list was Faye Dunaway. (Chayefsky had nixed Sidney's pick of Vanessa Redgrave because of her sympathies with the Palestine Liberation Organization.) Dunaway would prove inordinately troublesome as the filming progressed. Sidney recalled his first meeting with her before offering her the part: "I went to see her at 300 Central Park West, which is where she was living at the time, the residence of the stars. The elevator opened directly into the apartment, and I walked directly across. She was seated on a very luxurious couch with pillows, looking absolutely ravishing. And as I walked toward her, I said, 'Faye, I know what your first question is going to be.' And she said, 'What?' And I said, 'You're going to ask me, "Where's her vulnerability?"' And I said, 'She has none, and if you try to sneak any in, I'll cut it out.'"

Sidney credits Chayefsky for certain adjustments to laugh lines, but Sidney demurred over one crucial scene, when Max (William Holden) tells his wife Louise (Beatrice Straight) that he has fallen in love with another woman. Sidney took special care with this scene, as Itzkoff notes, especially Louise's "winter romance" speech: "She gets the great winter passion, and I get the dotage." Sidney did nine takes before he was satisfied, far more than any other shot in the movie. At one point Paddy approached Sidney with a suggestion, but, as Sidney told it, "I held up my hand and said, 'Paddy, please. I know more about divorce than you do.'"

The extra attention Sidney gave to this sequence helped win an Oscar for Beatrice Straight, in the briefest supporting role to ever win. (Coincidentally, Straight was a cousin of Gloria Vanderbilt's.) The scene beautifully demonstrates Sidney's contention that the camera can add dimensions to an actor's performance. Here is a quick look at how it was done: The sequence opens in medias res with a quick shot of Max and his wife, Louise, locked in silent intensity. Lumet cuts to a long shot, the camera looking through the doorway at the husband and wife seated at the kitchen table of their Manhattan apartment. As she breaks the silence, asking him, "How long has this been going on?" we cut to a medium close-up of her. When Louise begins to lose it, to scream at Max, the perspective switches back to the doorway, as indeed Max is withdrawing from her. When she rises from her chair and starts pacing from room to room, the camera begins to move, following her tentatively, keeping a respectful distance, reinforcing the power of her struggle between restraint and fury. The shift from a stationary camera to a moving one underscores her need to break free of the moment. For part of her speech the camera watches Max's face as he reacts to her words, her movement now a blur behind him. His intense guilt and grief-stricken expression reinforces what we are learning about their dynamic, and sharpens the precision of Straight's performance. There are no two-shots linking them together in the scene; they look at each other as if across an abyss, although they are only a few feet apart, and in effect Max is already gone. When Louise grows quiet, after some quaking tears, we observe her, as Max does, only from behind. The camera approaches her again, but cautiously. Lumet provides in this scene an astonishingly dignified and honest portrayal of a middle-aged woman in a moment of deep humiliation and loss. It is one of his greatest treatments of a female character.

Sidney had put his heart into that scene. His third marriage was unraveling, but his attention was elsewhere. On weekends at their East Hampton house he took the opportunity to stay in bed. As a friend recalled, he "had a lot of time religiously set aside for snoozing and watching ball games." Gail remembered it this way too. When asked what he most loved to do, she said, "Watch football." Their marriage was on the back burner. Gail wondered at the end of our conversation whether she might have taken Sidney for granted, but perhaps it was the other way around.

Nevertheless, Gail made the trip with him to Hollywood for the 1977 Oscars. Both were trusting that *Network*, with ten nominations, would hit it big. Gail sat beside Sidney looking elegant in a black gown, but Sidney's focus was elsewhere. The film had already become only the second in history to win three awards for acting; Best Director was soon lost to John Avildsen for *Rocky*. But the worst for Sidney was when they also lost Best Picture to *Rocky*. Sidney considered it an embarrassment.

"Chayefsky was so prescient," Sidney recalled. "Everyone was saying we were going to take it all. And on the flight out to LA, he said, '*Rocky*'s going to take Best Picture.' And I said, 'No, no, it's a dopey little movie.' And he said, 'It's just the sort of sentimental crap they love out there.' And he was right." Gail was beside him but didn't have the knack for comforting or distracting him from this kind of gut punch. In his quasi-paternal role with her, he was more or less the one who answered needs, at least the needs he recognized.

EQUUS

With initial reluctance, Sidney took on an adaptation of a West End hit that had also been a smash on Broadway. Playwright Peter Shaffer based *Equus* on a real crime involving a seventeen-year-old stable boy who blinded six horses in a small town near Suffolk, England. He wrote it as a kind of detective story in which the child psychiatrist tries to solve what could have caused the boy's actions, while also exploring the doctor's failing sense of purpose. "For 18 months, I refused the *Equus* movie because the stage production is about as perfect as it could get. There was nothing I could add," Sidney explained. "Peter Shaffer came to my East Hampton place, we talked endlessly. I still didn't know how a movie could add something." Sidney had reservations about the story's negative portrayal of psychoanalysis, which was still an active part of his life. It was an incidental query from his friend Tony Walton that gave Sidney the breakthrough. Walton, a scenic designer, asked if Sidney would like a ceiling on the boy's hospital room set: "Because if you have one, you could try that thing where he's lying in bed, and a car passes outside and the windshield reflects . . ." Bingo! Sidney realized,

> *My God, that's what this movie is about! As a kid I'd never believe that that passing reflection was what I knew it was! I always let it be slightly frightening, mysterious. Suddenly I knew how the movie could reinforce something that mattered hugely in the play, thematically—the duality of everything! Nothing is quite what you expect it to be! That if* Equus *is about anything it is about duality, Jekyll and Hyde, Apollonian versus Dionysian thought, the double-edged sword we all carry! Creativity and its direct counterpart, our capacity for destruction.*

Sidney and Shaffer worked together for months on the screenplay. The original plan was to shoot the movie in Ireland, but when Tony Walton arrived there to scout locations he was greeted by police who worried that a movie crew could be a target of an Irish Republican

Army bombing. Between 1969 and 1998, a period of fierce conflict between Irish nationalists and British loyalists and troops over the fate of Northern Ireland, the IRA would carry out some ten thousand bomb attacks. Sidney's response was uncomplicated: "I'm not making a film about The Troubles. Where else can we find to shoot?" They moved the production to Toronto, which is where they'd had a good experience shooting some of the sequences in *Network*.

Sidney had hoped to land Marlon Brando or Jack Nicholson for the role of the psychiatrist. He was wary of Richard Burton, who had fallen into a boozy phase and was, Sidney felt, doing second-rate work. Sidney worked his magic, getting Burton beyond his plummy recitations to an Oscar-nominated performance. Also nominated were Peter Firth, who played the disturbed boy, and Peter Shaffer, for Best Adapted Screenplay.

THE WIZ

Everybody objects to the graffiti all over the city. I think it's beautiful. I don't understand what's so beautiful about a clean subway car.

—SIDNEY LUMET, 1978

The white oppressor in The Wiz *is an invisible, but still overwhelming presence. Who put that impossibly heavy "mammy" on top of Tin Man? Who buried the Lion underneath pounds of concrete? Who hung the Scarecrow from his cornfield post? We don't meet him, but I have an inkling as to who.*

—ALEX LANDERS, "HOW BLACK LIVES MATTER IN SIDNEY LUMET'S THE WIZ"

It was on the set of *The Wiz* that Gail informed Sidney that their marriage was over; she was moving out. Her decision to move out, not to ask him to leave her in their home with the children, suggests that she considered the house his, and perhaps that she wanted to find some ground of her own. Or perhaps she felt in some way at fault.

Word got around the set as to why Sidney's usual exuberance was just not there. Directing his first musical, he was in a state of despondency. He added crying jags to the script where none had been: "The Lion cries, and Diana Ross, and the Tin Man," Tony Walton recalled, "none of which was really in the script." There's a memorable scene in Sidney's subsequent film, *Just Tell Me What You Want*, in which Max (Alan King) is told by his mistress that she has just married another man. Max responds to the news with great casualness, chitchats for a few minutes, then tells her he needs to make a call. Once she leaves his office he sits down at his desk, carefully removes one contact lens and then the other, places them both in their containers and then commences wailing and sobbing hysterically. This controlled and delayed reaction comes to mind in imagining what Sidney had to do in order to direct the most ambitious and expensive movie ever filmed entirely in New York.

Universal's call to ask Sidney to direct *The Wiz* had come out of the blue. John Badham (*Saturday Night Fever*) had dropped out after Diana Ross was cast because he thought she was too old for the part at thirty-three. Sidney asked for twenty-four hours to think, during which he read the whole of Baum's Oz series, "all 29 or whatever versions of the book." He explained: "I'd never read the novel; at eight years old I read Karl Marx but not L. Frank Baum." As with *Equus*, a full-blown idea came to him for adapting this Broadway hit to film: "Wow, I have got a crazy way I wanta do this! It's gonna be an urban fantasy," he told producer Rob Cohen. He'd move the story from Kansas to New York. It would be about a Harlem schoolteacher who had chosen to never travel below 125th Street, being lifted by a snowstorm out of her comfort zone. She "crosses a self-imposed border, learns, and goes home, home being inside herself!" Sidney explained. The trick would be to transform New York into the land of Oz, and the challenge delighted him. After *Dog Day Afternoon*, he felt he'd gone about as far with naturalism as one can go. "There's nothing left to squeeze from realism," he reflected. "Stylization'd be an incredible release!"

Sidney began assembling the rest of the cast and crew. He lined up top stars Richard Pryor, Nipsey Russell and his soon-to-be ex-mother-in-law, Lena Horne, to play Glinda the Good. When I asked Gail how it happened that her mother was cast at this complicated moment in their marriage, she replied, "Sidney asked her and she said yes." She paused and added, "She was the only good thing in the movie."

Sidney summoned his friend and collaborator Quincy Jones to supervise and produce the music. The film's producer, Rob Cohen, wanted to bring on Michael Jackson to play the Scarecrow. Sidney and Jones were both skeptical. Sidney was thinking of Jimmie "J. J." Walker, star of TV's *Good Times*. He thought Jackson was "a Vegas act." Cohen arranged a meeting with the nineteen-year-old Jackson. Sidney and Quincy Jones were instantly convinced, moved by his sweetness and what Sidney saw as a "purity" in him perfect for the Scarecrow. This would be the beginning of a friendship between Sidney and Michael, and, more consequentially, of a collaboration between Jackson and Quincy Jones. Jones had previously dismissed Jackson's childhood work as amiable bubblegum, but on *The Wiz* he saw potential in Jackson for a fresh, more adult sound. Quincy Jones went on to produce Jackson's 1979 hit record *Off the Wall* and, a few years later, *Thriller*, which for decades has remained the world's bestselling album. During lunch one day on the set Sidney informed the oblivious former child star that women around him were "like ricocheting bullets all over the place."

The Wiz would be the first film to shoot in the reopened and re-named Kaufman Astoria Studios in Queens, the very place where Sidney's only movie appearance to date, in *One Third of a Nation*, was filmed in 1939. He had been a vital force in getting the studio back up and running, helping to raise money and its profile. Much of the movie, as per Sidney's vision, would be filmed around the city. The New York State Pavilion at the site of the 1964 World's Fair became Munchkinland, and along the yellow brick road Dorothy

would encounter homelessness, labor exploitation, heroin, prostitu-
tion, graffiti, garbage and political corruption. The movie was hugely
popular with black audiences and remains a cult classic. Audience
favorites include the scenes of the Tin Man pinned beneath a larger-
than-life "mammy" statue at an amusement park and the Scarecrow
convinced by a gang of crows that he "can't win." Michael Jackson
sings the "crow anthem" about how there's no way to win, no matter
what people say:

> *People keep sayin' things are gonna change*
> *But they look just like they're stayin' the same . . .*

Its box office was hurt by harsh reviews and by theater chains in
white neighborhoods that shortened the movie's run for fear of scar-
ing off white patrons. The NAACP awarded Michael Jackson, Lena
Horne and Sidney top honors at their Image Awards ceremony, and
the film received four Oscar nods, for art direction, costumes, cinematography and music. But financially it was disappointing, taking
in only $13 million.

Perhaps to cheer him up, his friend Bob Fosse asked Sidney to do
a cameo in *All That Jazz*, his remarkable autobiopic. Fosse wanted
him to play Paddy Chayefsky. Sidney was up for it, which was rare
indeed, but ultimately the scene was cut from the finished film.

It had been a tough year for Sidney, but soon things would be
looking up.

17

MARRIAGE TAKE FOUR: PRINT IT

*He said once to Marie Bonaparte: "The great question that
has never been answered, and which I have not yet been able
to answer, despite my thirty years of research into the feminine
soul, is "What does a woman want?"*
—ERNEST JONES, FROM *SIGMUND FREUD: LIFE AND WORK*

Those close to him insist that Sidney "didn't look back"—when a passage in his life was over, it was over. Likely that was what Sidney
wished for, to put the past behind him, and he could often achieve
it regarding professional irritants and disappointments. As Burtt
Harris put it, "He would shut off before he would let it bug him."
But that wasn't true of his deeper feelings, as testified by his long
years in psychoanalysis and by Gail's recollection that he often spoke
to her about his childhood. When his fifteen-year marriage to Gail
ended, he did indeed look—he reached out to two of his former
loves, Ellen Adler and Gloria Vanderbilt.

Ellen Adler had been Sidney's first "sweetheart" (her word). She
mentioned that she thought she would have married Sidney if she
hadn't fallen in love with Marlon Brando, whose startlingly handsome
face looks out from photographs placed throughout her beautiful old
Long Island farmhouse. In the intervening years she had had a rich and
storied life, not only in her relationship with Brando; she became an
artist, lived for years at a time in Paris, where she was close friends with
authors Marguerite Duras and Simone de Beauvoir and philosopher

Maurice Merleau-Ponty, among many others; she married and had two children with David Oppenheim, the musician and record producer who had previously been married to movie star Judy Holliday. Ellen's marriage had ended in 1976, not long before Sidney came knocking.

When I spoke with Gail Lumet about Ellen Adler, she muttered softly that she thought Sidney had always been in love with Ellen. It seemed that Ellen had not perceived their relationship that way at all, although she remembered that after his marriage with Gail ended, Sidney was "what you call the marrying type, we were gonna get together out here [in the Hamptons]. We were gonna try . . . and then he met Piedy"—Sidney's fourth and final wife.

It was obvious in our conversation that Ellen knew Sidney in a way few did. They had grown up around many of the same people from the old Jewish left and the Group Theatre, where she and Sidney first met in 1938. She, too, had roots in the Yiddish theater; her mother's parents, Jacob and Sara Adler, were the greatest stars of the Yiddish stage. She remembered Sidney "in knickers," going with him to see the Brooklyn Dodgers play at Ebbets Field, and strolling together in Washington Square Park. She recalled one time observing Sidney looking around the park to see if anyone recognized him from his movie appearance. "In the beginning he really enjoyed his success, but at the end I don't think it meant anything. . . . And he never acted like a celebrity." Our conversation was dotted with all kinds of details and observations about his life: how "inseparable" Sidney and his sister Faye were until after the war; how in love Faye had been with her "very handsome husband," Selwyn James; how she and Rita Gam, Sidney's first wife, went clothes shopping together and picked out identical outfits and "the blouses had a little bow"; how Sidney had taken great pleasure in living in Gloria's world. "Unlike Marlon," she said, "Sidney was at that age quite taken with other people's fame or their money." She was perhaps as close as anyone to being a witness to his life.

Ellen was also convinced that she would "never have ended up with Sidney." She felt what had kept them close over the years were the memories they shared—and convenience! They had country houses near each other. "He never cut off with me because we ran into each other here." Their friendship was not derailed by this failed interlude of "trying."

With Gloria Vanderbilt things went further. Gloria had recently lost her husband, Wyatt Cooper. When Sidney phoned her "as soon as things exploded with Gail," she said, it was only a few months after her husband's death in early 1978. Feelings flared up between the two. Early on she asked Sidney what he had done with his wedding ring when they had separated, knowing full well that he had left it in the drawer of the night table by their bed. He answered that he'd thrown it in the East River! Gloria suggestively replied, "No, darling, I have it."

Gloria recounts in her memoir, "When summer came, we sped back and forth between our houses in East Hampton and Southampton. Sidney couldn't be alone (most men can't), and he kept pressing forward." Sidney discussed with Gloria his plans to enlarge his East Side town house to make room for Gloria's two youngest sons, both well known to and liked by Amy and Jenny because they all attended the same private school. Gloria's son Anderson Cooper recalled what most registered with him from that period: Sidney had invited Gloria and her two sons to the premiere of *The Wiz*. He was eleven years old and seated beside Michael Jackson in a limousine on the way to the opening-night party at Studio 54. "I remember people chasing the car, which I thought was kind of funny," he recalled. "I remember watching him dance, and I actually remember turning to someone— this is going to sound insane—and saying, 'He's really good at this. He should pursue it.' I was always concerned about people's financial viability and career choices. I would always ask people how they could support themselves."

Sidney wanted to marry again immediately, even before his divorce from Gail had come through. "It was just too soon," Gloria said with a hint of regret. But one fateful conversation stayed with her, perhaps turning the tide for good. She and Sidney were sitting in his garden as evening was falling, awaiting the arrival of playwright Neil Simon and his new wife, Marsha Mason. Sidney was reflecting on the fact that "Doc" (Neil Simon) had married Marsha just weeks after the death of Simon's first wife. Gloria expressed her astonishment: "I can't understand that," she said. "How could he remarry so soon after?" To which Sidney replied, "Let the dead be dead." Gloria writes in her memoir, "The words stunned me. . . . It really got to me, and later I told him it would be best if we didn't see each other for a while." Sidney replied that maybe she was right—that he had never been alone, and perhaps it was a good idea for him to spend time alone in East Hampton and see what it was like. Gloria confided, "I wasn't ready, but I knew he would not stay alone."

JUST TELL ME WHAT YOU WANT

While actively in pursuit of a wife, Sidney was simultaneously directing the comedy *Just Tell Me What You Want*, his only film that centers on a male-female relationship. When I asked Gail if she'd ever seen the film, she said she hadn't. I couldn't help but wonder what she—and perhaps Ellen and Gloria—would have made of it, a most unusual *un*romantic comedy, wittily cynical about love and marriage. The film opens with Bones Burton (Ali MacGraw) in voice-over saying she wants "to tell you the story of how I got married." And then, as a scene unfolds on-screen in which her character encounters the male lead, Max Herschel, brilliantly played by Alan King, in the tie section of tony Bergdorf Goodman, and she proceeds to knock him to the ground and pound him, her voice-over continues with humorous sarcasm, "It's a very *romantic* story."

Screenwriter Jay Presson Allen (*Marnie*, *The Prime of Miss Jean Brodie*, *Cabaret*), who would go on to collaborate with Sidney on three subsequent films, had been shopping the script—adapted from her own novel—with no luck. She was delighted but quite surprised when Sidney said yes. He was doubtless partly drawn to it for its Jewish *shtick*, recalling *Bye Bye Braverman*, a film he always wished he could redo, but he also had to love the terrific whack it takes at romance and sentimental feelings, ones he was likely battling in himself.

In *Just Tell Me What You Want*, Alan King's Max Herschel is a self-made Jewish mogul, brilliant, petty, cutthroat. He is a bundle of paradoxes: he believes that everyone has their price, and that he can provide those in his orbit with exactly what they want in order to keep the upper hand, but he is also somehow lovable, not only because he's funny and a not-ungenerous provider, but because he isn't merely a user, he truly connects. In fact, Max Herschel has something in common with Sidney, a Jewish man who runs the show, attends to every last detail and, through his insight into people, keeps everyone happy and doing what he needs them to do. In an interview a year after the film came out, Sidney remarked, "I just really like making movies. I enjoy being king."

On the set of *Just Tell Me What You Want*, Sidney listens intently to screenwriter Jay Presson Allen as Ali MacGraw looks on. *(Warner Bros. / Courtesy Everett Collection)*

Vincent Canby wrote in *The New York Times*, "Alan King is the funniest, most destructive egomaniac to be seen in any movie since John Barrymore was Oscar Jaffe in Howard Hawks's screen adaptation of *Twentieth Century*." Sidney knew he wanted Alan King, but he wasn't sure about Jay Presson Allen's choice for the female lead, Ali MacGraw. "I'm not sure she can act," he said at the time, and, as Sidney told the story, Ali agreed with him, "Ali came down, and we met. . . . She said, 'Sidney, you know what? I can't act. I've never studied; I have no technique whatsoever. . . . Why don't you give me acting lessons for two weeks, and at the end of that time if you don't think I can do it, I'll have had a nice time in New York, and I'm a very pleasant person to be around, so you will have had a nice time.' Sidney took her up on her proposal, and, he proudly recalled, "Within five days I was convinced she could do it,"

Alan King's Max Herschel is a surprising character on many scores. One of them is that the dialogue between Max and Bones humorously inverts the convention of the fast-talking dame from 1930s and 1940s screwball comedies. Bones, who successfully runs an Emmy-winning New York–based television show, tries to persuade Max to let her have control of a Hollywood studio he plans to sell off for parts. Here he tries to talk her out of it:

> MAX: . . . I couldn't stand what would happen to you out there. They'd cut you off at the knees. For no reason at all except you're a smart broad. You know what happens to smart broads out there? They can't get laid.
> BONES: Oh, I expect I could get laid. Somehow.
> MAX: Five will get you fifty. *Stars* can't get laid! No female over eighteen gets laid! It's in the city charter! They're zoned against it, I swear!
> BONES: Oh, come on, Max . . .
> MAX: No, no, I swear! I swear to God! Middle age out there, it starts at twenty-four. I'm *telling* you.
> BONES: Herschel paradise.

Max, not Bones, is the fast talker with the laugh lines. In this world, romance is a business arrangement; Bones is Max's favorite among a stable of mistresses. The two of them are constantly negotiating the terms of their relationship in which love is never a point of discussion or an operative term. Marriage, in this story, is the biggest business deal of all. The film's "happy ending" shows them negotiating terms for marriage. Max says, "Let's hear what you want, darling." And in the background we can imagine Sidney wishing for the answer to that question too. Sidney, taking his crack at Freud's eternal question, "What do women want?" is looking for a straight answer: *Just tell me what you want!*

Alas, the movie never found its audience. The film would have especially disappointed Ali MacGraw fans looking for something on the order of *Love Story*.

In keeping with the film's humorous ironies, it was not long after Sidney completed this film that he found Piedy Gimbel and experienced an entirely new kind of love in his life. As Ellen Adler put it, "Piedy fell in love with him; I don't think he expected that."

PIEDY

Mary Bailey Gimbel, nicknamed Piedy, had crossed paths with Sidney over the years. She and her first husband, department store heir Peter Gimbel, had been invited to dinner at Gloria and Sidney's penthouse around the time that Peter Gimbel had made a name for himself as a real-life adventurer by diving the wreck of the SS *Andrea Doria*, the ocean liner that had sunk off the coast of Nantucket.

Through the years Sidney and Piedy had traveled in overlapping social circles, especially in the Hamptons. They had been on one another's radar and had dated briefly not long after her divorce from Gimbel in 1960, before Sidney married Gail. She recalled running into him years later at one of George Plimpton's July fireworks celebrations: "He said 'Hi!' so animatedly, then walked right by," she mused. Finally the timing was right one summer day twenty-five years after their first encounter, when they were both shopping at a seafood market in Wainscott, near East Hampton. One thing led quickly to another.

Piedy was born Mary Laird Bailey to a social register family; or, as Sidney put it, "Piedy's relatives came over on the ship after the *Mayflower*, because the people who came over on the *Mayflower* were a little too low-class for her family." In line with her social position, she kept a low profile over the years, especially in comparison to the other women in Sidney's life. Except for a cute society-page story about her 1952 elopement with Peter Gimbel, and a few other society items, her name did not appear in the papers.

Raised in New Canaan, Connecticut, she attended the prestigious Milton Academy in Massachusetts, where she was the first love of classmate Robert F. Kennedy. Years later she described him as a shy boy, "one foot resting on the other foot; hands way down in his pockets . . . very appealing. Funny, separate, larky; outside the cliques; private all the time." Her discretion and charm can be heard in these few sentences. She remained close to the Kennedy family in the years since. As her mother had done, she graduated from Smith College, where she studied literature and art history, following a requisite year in Paris.

Having been born into the 1940s American version of "the purple," she had not been expected to seek a career; rather, she had pursued interests and dedicated time to charities and social causes, now and then taking jobs in publishing ventures, including writing a book (uncredited) about the Beatles. She smiled as she recalled taking her two children to see the band perform at Shea Stadium in 1965.

Piedy and Peter Gimbel had two children, Leslie and Bailey, but the marriage hadn't lasted very long. When Sidney came into her life, she had been a single woman for twenty years. For a while she had dated the dashing novelist John Marquand Jr., a former beau of Jacqueline Bouvier. She said she'd had a good time in those years, although "it might sometimes have been hard on the children," who were about a decade older than Sidney's daughters. Clearly this winning woman had been biding her time, waiting for the right man.

Piedy had belonged to a largely literary crowd, but she adjusted with great simplicity to Sidney's star-studded work world. One evening early in their relationship she and Sidney received a call from Michael Jackson urging them to join him at a gala at the New York Public Library. Likely as not, Sidney had put aside that invitation; he was attending formal events more selectively at this point in his life. When they arrived, they were escorted through the crowd to the inner inner sanctum, where Michael Jackson, Brooke Shields, and other celebrities of the moment were surrounded by scores of photographers snapping wildly. While Sidney went to greet Michael, Piedy stood back and observed the two men chatting quietly, entirely unconcerned with the hundreds of flashbulbs going off. Many of these stars had been in the limelight since childhood, including of course Sidney, and she understood that this was just normal to them. Sidney enjoyed Piedy's outsider perspective and loved her calm aloofness from the hoopla.

Photos of Piedy don't capture the twinkle in her eye, nor of course the buoyancy and music of her upper-crust inflections or her distinctive way with words. Her appearance is that of a lean, cool blonde, but she is in fact whimsical and warm,

Sidney and Piedy on their wedding day. Photos of them often show them laughing together.

a generous listener, curious and open, who catches on quickly. I asked her if she agreed that of Sidney's four wives, she was the only one who had not had a difficult childhood, who wasn't, in a sense, recovering in one way or another. "Right!" she said. "I'm just here!" meaning, I thought, "I'm not complicated." Piedy mentioned that Sidney had liked her mother and father, whom she described as "ordinary people from New Canaan." She conveys the impression not of someone who's had a charmed life or dodged her share of sorrow and worry, but someone with resources and a faith in simple caring. She spoke of Sidney, her husband for thirty-one years, in a nonproprietorial fashion, and saw him with clear and loving eyes.

In their early days, she and Sidney were able to share their worries over their kids, as they each coped with a child who was having difficulties and creating difficulties. Piedy's son had been expelled from several boarding schools; Amy, now placed at the all-girls Spence School, had emerged as a talented visual artist, but she seemed to carry a dark cloud around with her. One friend suggested that Amy had "come into the world angry." For both kids, things would get worse before they got better.

Piedy moved into Sidney's East 91st Street town house after the marriage. She changed the staff and redecorated, leaving the towering bookshelves but including some touches of Pierre Deux fabric and blue and white toile. She recognized that Sidney's girls were not initially thrilled at the marriage; they'd hoped to have their father to themselves for a while. She conjectured that consistency and regularity would smooth the rocky transition. One friend described the family dinners as "ritualized." At six thirty promptly they arranged themselves in the formal dining room; Piedy had a discrete bell under the table to summon the maid. Jenny, who was briefly overweight, at least in comparison to her drop-dead gorgeous older sister who was already working as a model, would place a 64-ounce bottle of Tab in the middle of Piedy's beautifully arranged table, a humorous gesture of teenage contrariness.

In the Hamptons, Piedy gave up her cozy place in the exclusive hamlet of Wainscott and moved into Sidney's larger house in East Hampton, with its handsome lawn and pool overlooking the ocean. Friends reported that Sidney "calmed down with Piedy." She did a lot of gardening, and Sidney sat on the porch and read. "He was a big reader, always interested in a lot of things, not just the movies," Ellen Adler observed. And they would have people over for dinner; among their frequent guests at that time were Piedy's friends George Plimpton, author Peter Matthiessen, historian Arthur Schlesinger and his wife Alexandra and Sidney's buddies, director Gene Saks (*Barefoot in the Park*, *The Odd Couple*), playwright Herb Gardner (*A Thousand Clowns*), Sidney's legendary agent Sue Mengers, composer-lyricist Betty Comden and Alan King—who, incidentally, was the first cousin of Lena Horne's husband, Lennie Hayton. Sidney made hamburgers and steaks on the grill and they ate in the screened-in dining porch. "I do believe that Piedy was the real wife," Ellen said warmly. "She liked his Jewishness and he liked her goyishness. . . . That was his real marriage."

THE OTHER WOMAN

Another woman entered Sidney's life at this time, and she too would stick around for the next thirty years. Lili Jacobs would become Sidney's trusted right hand, and often his associate producer. Straight out of central casting, Lili is cracklingly smart and no-nonsense, a flavorful New York character, petite and wryly funny. At the point at which Sidney was looking for someone to run things in his office, Lili was working for producer Martin Bregman. Sidney's most trusted assistant director, Burtt Harris, thought Lili was perfect for the job; he joked with her: "You're shorter than Sidney. He'll love you."

That first year, Lili barely spoke to Sidney—"too intimidated," she said. "He handed me his book, then told me whose calls he would receive." But over time their relationship developed into one of absolute mutual trust. She learned the business inside and out, knew everyone and where to find them, and everyone knew and appreciated her.

Among Lili's duties was packing up the business office she and Sidney shared. Perhaps in the tradition of Sidney's father's attitude toward paying rent, he didn't like to keep up their business office when they were shooting or nothing much was happening, so they moved pretty routinely. Usually they were located somewhere in midtown; for a while they settled in the landmark Ansonia apartment building on the Upper West Side. Visitors to his office often commented on how spare things were: nothing on the walls, Sidney at a big desk with a few books and scripts on it. Lili had his movie posters framed and hung them in their different settings, but she acknowledged, "He would tell me I had too much shit on my desk. His desk was clean as a whistle." He'd complain, "Aren't you going to throw anything out?" And she'd brush him off: "Not your department, not in your way." To lighten their routine moves, Sidney would tell Lili to shred things. She had to protect casting and location lists and postproduction material from the shredder, knowing they'd be needed later on. Just as he loved putting a big red *X* through a scene on his script once it was shot, he liked eliminating what he could of the past.

Unlike other major New York directors, such as Woody Allen, Martin Scorsese and Spike Lee, Sidney didn't maintain a permanent production office. Sometimes they'd set up a work space at the Kaufman Astoria Studios or on a location. For the preshoot rehearsals, Sidney liked what he called a "raw rehearsal space," so the cast typically gathered for two or three weeks in the large second-floor hall at the Ukrainian National Home on lower Second Avenue, within quick reach of good Jewish deli and dairy restaurants and on the very street where he'd performed on the Yiddish stage.

Sidney and Lili enjoyed and teased each other, and occasionally confided. "He used to eat my sandwich off my desk," she said. "He went through all my love affairs, all my boyfriends," and "he told the worst jokes. One Christmas he gave everyone Henny Youngman joke books."

When they were shooting, she would be picked up before 7:00 A.M. in "the old station wagon," to ride along with Sidney and Burtt Harris; they'd meet up with the director of photography, Andrzej Bartkowiak, on his bicycle, which he'd throw in the back of the car, and they'd head off to Astoria in Queens or to a location, doing their "homework" on the way.

Lili described one particularly indelible image of Sidney. At the opening-night party for *Night Falls on Manhattan*, she walked in on a scene of Sidney talking with James Gandolfini, looking up at him, both arms straight, his hands on the much taller man's shoulders, and Gandolfini gazing down at Sidney "like looking into sunshine," Lili said.

It was on this shoot, *Night Falls on Manhattan*, that both Sidney and Lili finally quit smoking, a challenge they undertook together. Sidney chewed a lot of Nicorette gum for quite a long time, but he managed to drop his unfiltered Camels for good.

Though there were very few things Sidney and Lili disagreed about, the credits at the end of the film, which were part of Lili's portfolio, were a point of contention. She would list everyone who'd played a part in the production, even a minor part, then Sidney would cut the list down. They argued. Perhaps from his TV days he thought the end credits shouldn't run more than three minutes. She'd manage to slip a few names back in. "This is the cheapest way to thank somebody, just to put their name there," Lili explained. "Here," she would emphasize, "is where we *thank* somebody." There was one other point of dispute between the two: "Well, Sid thought he didn't have a big ego. I said to him, 'Are you crazy? Of course you do—a gigantic ego.' He just thought I was wrong."

Of the many stories Lili shared about Sidney, one typified a particular aspect of his nature and his daily life. "One of our offices was on 56th Street between Sixth and Seventh on the south side, near Carnegie Hall. There was a parking lot on the opposite side of the street. He would sit there and watch them park cars." Sidney would get lost in looking at the parkers rearranging the cars to make them fit in the small lot; he so enjoyed watching people solve problems. Lili's story continues: "One day he was looking out the window and Isaac Stern walked by. He opened the window and yelled 'Yitzchak,'" and so the incomparable violinist popped in for a visit. Sidney seemed to know and love just about everyone in the New York cultural scene. Lili was touched that Sidney introduced Lili to Stern with his nickname for her: "This is Lilya."

Lili said Sidney was the smartest person she'd ever met; he seemed to know about everything, and he could do everyone's job on the set, solve any problem. His Achilles' heel, she said, was the computer. "He didn't like any machine he couldn't take apart and put back together. He needed to understand how it worked before he would trust it." He stuck with his yellow legal pads and never used email.

"I do remember that once I said that some people get personal days and vacation days. He said, 'What are those?'"

18

ACQUAINTED WITH THE NIGHT

We're complacent about corruption. Tax frauds, kickbacks, padded expense accounts, political scandals . . . we take them as a matter of course. But we expect our police to plunge into the rottenest sector of society and come up clean.
—SIDNEY LUMET, 1981

I don't think it was about cops, or just about cops. Although the cops had no disdain for the film. I think it was about corruption, about how you slide into corruption, begin to feel entitled, in an environment where corruption is so easy.
—TREAT WILLIAMS, 2018

PRINCE OF THE CITY

Burtt Harris distinguishes between two kinds of people: those who read instructions and those who don't. "My wife doesn't, either," he said, helping me with the coffee machine in my hotel room in Montreal where I spoke with him. "Sidney," he noted, "did read instructions. He could explain the difference between a motor and an engine."

Burtt Harris worked as Sidney's assistant director on twenty of his films over the course of about thirty years. Burtt's job description goes on for miles, including making sure cast and crew members went to him with a question before going to Sidney; hiring locations, props and equipment; watching the daily budget; checking weather reports; keeping track of everyone on the shoot; and gathering phone numbers of girlfriends or boyfriends of the movies' stars in case he needed to locate them in a hurry. But he was even more than Sidney's right hand; Burtt had a lot of tricks up his sleeve. He knew whose palm to grease or how to negotiate with a gang leader to arrange a trouble-free shooting location in the South Bronx. He said of Sidney, "He was willing to get his hands dirty, but he didn't get his hands dirty."

Mentioning Burtt Harris's name draws a broad smile from anyone who worked with Sidney over the years, and it's easy to see why. He is fast and funny, warm and confiding. A former actor, Burtt enjoyed being handed small roles by Sidney, like Jimmy the bartender in *The Verdict* or Construction Worker 2 in *Garbo Talks*. Burtt had worked with everyone over the years, including Elia Kazan, John Schlesinger and Otto Preminger; he could rig explosives for a special effect and also advise Dustin Hoffman on how to make his eyes look like a dead man's for *Midnight Cowboy*.

At eighty-two years old, Burtt enters a room with a boom blast of energy; his bright blue eyes instantly get a bead on you. In another life he would have made a great cop; in fact, Burtt was often Sidney's conduit to the police. "They, the cops, trusted me because I was into that macho stuff." He had known "all the French Connection cops," meaning the real-life counterparts of Jimmy "Popeye" Doyle and Buddy "Cloudy" Russo (played by Gene Hackman and Roy Scheider), who busted an international narcotics ring in the early 1960s. "They didn't smack people around, they just petrified them," he said, adding, "All those guys wanted to get into the movies." Sidney, Burtt said, didn't "hang out" with cops at bars like Burtt did, "but he met with them and talked with them, and rode around with them some." He remembered being approached by a cop in a bar in Greenwich Village who knew what Burtt did for a living. "You should make this a movie," he said, handing him the book *Prince of the City*. The cop said he was one of the characters in the book, Bob Leuci's partner after Leuci got acquitted. "Everyone wanted to shoot him," he told Burtt, "bad guys and good guys. We had to keep our eyes on him all the time."

Burtt recalled screenwriter Jay Presson Allen "grabbing the book out of my hand." "Where'd you get this?" she asked. When she finished reading Robert Daley's account of Bob Leuci, the real-life NYPD narcotics detective whose decision to expose police corruption resulted in tragic consequences, including the suicides of two of his closest partners and the near destruction of his own life, she thought, "Oh yeah. This *is* Lumet!" When she showed it to Sidney, "he just flipped." It turned out the book had already been sold to Orion, with Brian De Palma as director and David Rabe as screenwriter. Allen told the studio that if the De Palma deal fell through, she and Lumet wanted it. They waited and waited to see if something would come of it. "Sidney was within twenty-four hours of signing up for another movie when we got the call," Allen recalled.

From De Palma's perspective, Sidney "stole that picture" from him. He and Rabe had spent months in meetings with Bob Leuci and had been in discussion with both Al Pacino and John Travolta about starring in it. De Palma acknowledged that they were moving slowly on the script, and maybe that was why they lost the movie—or, he acknowledged, maybe Lumet and Presson just carried more weight over there.

De Palma felt that the scales were balanced when a couple of years later Sidney handed him *Scarface* to direct. Sidney had originally given producer Martin Bregman the idea for a remake of the 1932 Paul Muni classic, rebooting the Chicago gangster as a Cuban refugee, newly arrived with the 1980 Mariel Harbor boatlift. It had been big news at the time: Castro's short-lived opening to Cubans who wanted to leave and the arrival of 125,000 Cuban refugees in Florida. Among them, it was believed at the time—and it is still disputed—were a number of criminals that Castro had quietly released from his prisons.

Sidney's was a smart, timely concept, and Oliver Stone was brought on to write the screenplay. When Sidney didn't go for Stone's script, De Palma got the gig. When I asked De Palma why, in his view,

Sidney hadn't liked the script, he said he thought it was "not political enough" for Sidney. I suspect the extreme violence may also have been a factor.

Jay Presson Allen had hoped simply to produce *Prince of the City*, not to adapt it. "It seemed like a hair-raising job to find a line, get a skeleton out of the book, which went back and forth . . . all over the place. . . . But Sidney said he wouldn't do it if I didn't write it." Sidney offered to take a stab at an outline and swiftly began to break down the book, using index cards. He was intrigued by the complexity of the characters, the ambiguities that real-life stories contain and that movies typically simplify. He knew the story wouldn't work if they forced it to adhere to a three-act structure, and that it would need to run long.

With Sidney's outline, Allen began to build the scenes, working for the first time with a story about living people. "I had right next to me—the minute I was stuck on anything—all those phone numbers to dial. I could dial the *real* characters and say, 'This doesn't sound right to me . . .'" She and Sidney also had the benefit of the actual recordings made when Leuci was wearing a wire. With Sidney's first effort at writing, he and Jay Presson Allen were nominated for an Oscar for Best Screenplay based on material from another medium.

CASTING AND SHOOTING

I became the kind of director who became whatever his actors need. . . . I think part of the job of directing is to not make the actors work your way, but for you to work as a director in any way that makes them comfortable.

—SIDNEY LUMET, 1988

Everyone looks to the director for the energy. He had a joyousness about him.

—TREAT WILLIAMS, 2018

Sidney had stipulated with the studio that he didn't want big stars or even familiar faces in this one. The studio pressed him to at least cast a major star for the leading role, but Sidney had another idea. He'd recently seen a young actor in Milos Forman's *Hair* (1979), and he spotted something in him "tough and naive" that he wanted for Danny Ciello, the Bob Leuci character.

The way Sidney put it to Treat Williams when they met was, "I'm thinking about you for this because you don't really give a shit what anyone thinks of you." Williams took Sidney to mean that he trusted him not to make Ciello more likeable than written. "But," Williams recalled, "Sidney said he needed to know whether I had the gravitas—I was twenty-eight at the time—to handle the darker repercussions of what the character did." As part of the audition, Sidney gave him a scene to play in which a drug dealer is brought in and Ciello is asked if he knows this man; when he says yes, the script indicates that the drug dealer spits in his face. In what Williams took to be a test of his training, Sidney actually spat in his face! "I thought, 'I'm gonna stay

Sidney with Treat Williams on the set of *Prince of the City*.

in character,'" Williams recalled, "'I'm gonna kill this little fucker, but I'm gonna stay in character.' And I think Sidney saw then that I would go wherever the work required."

In preparation for the part, Williams spent weeks with a narcotics unit in the Bronx, and then a solid month basically living with Bob Leuci, who had a kind of remarkable magnetism about him: as De Palma put it, he was "the most charming guy in the world; he could stab you in the back and you'd still love him." Williams was also struck by Leuci's distinctive way of carrying himself. "There's a looseness, a cockiness about a cop's walk. . . . There's no fear in it." Williams recalled Leuci putting in one specific request regarding his performance: "Don't cry. I didn't cry so much."

Before the three weeks of rehearsals started, Sidney, Burtt Harris and a teamster took Williams to see all the important locations—a small sampling of the 130 locations in the film—to give him a sense of the precise world his character inhabited. Williams laughed recalling Sidney telling the teamster who was driving them through Queens, "No, no. Take a left here." He said Sidney knew every inch of every borough. The cast included 162 speaking roles; Sidney brought on some Broadway actors, but also many others who had limited or no acting experience, including some retired cops—"sixty years served in the police force among the cast," Williams recalled.

Imagining Sidney issuing commands to dozens of men chosen in part for their tough exteriors, I asked Treat Williams how Sidney carried himself around all that testosterone. He laughed. "Every morning you'd get a kiss on the lips and 'Hello, Bubby,' but Sidney could be a tough bastard when it was called for, although I saw it happen only once." One of the actors showed up on set one morning in a bad state; he'd been up all night, doing who knows what. When a gaffer corrected him on how he'd angled the car he was driving in a scene, the actor went off on the crewmember. "Sidney got right up in the guy's face," Williams explained, "and Sidney was like two feet shorter than the guy—and he said, 'If you ever do that again, if you ever fucking talk to anyone like that, I'll throw you off the set and reshoot every scene you've done. Watch me.'"

Another newcomer to Sidney's team was Martha Pinson, who, at that time, was called "the script girl," one of the few women then on film sets besides wardrobe and makeup. Her job was to make sure that there was continuity in every detail in the movie's 275 scenes and in Treat Williams' 76 wardrobe changes. Her eye assured the editor that every detail, prop, and wardrobe element in every scene shot out of sequence would work when cut together. She recalled Sidney responding readily to her many questions on her first day. Then he said, "I know you're new, but you're going to be fine. There's no substitute for intelligence." She quickly understood his process and priorities:

He didn't want to rehearse, try to find the scene, while a hundred crew people were standing around. He also liked to make decisions when he could envision the film more as a whole. For him, that was before the shoot. He felt he'd be less objective when tired from getting up early, the grind of the shoot days.

Pinson worked with him on eight movies. As Lili Jacobs noted, Sidney always checked résumés to see if people had worked repeatedly with the same director, a sure sign that they were valued.

AN UNEXPECTED FAN

When the incomparable Japanese film director Akira Kurosawa visited New York in 1980 for a retrospective of his films, his hosts greeted him at the airport and asked what he wished to do in New York. He said he wanted to see Sidney Lumet's new film. That very evening he saw *Prince of the City* at the small movie theater that was located for about a decade beneath the Plaza Hotel.

The following night Kurosawa was feted at the elegant home of director William Friedkin (*The French Connection, The Exorcist*). The guests included Arthur Penn, Martin Scorsese, Elia Kazan and Norman Mailer. When Sidney arrived, "wearing brown cords, a heavy white turtleneck, a tweed jacket, and black-rimmed glasses," as Lillian Ross described him in her *New Yorker* piece on the event, he made a beeline to Kurosawa. Grinning, Kurosawa pumped Sidney's hands, praising his movie. Sidney was not big on being praised in person—he often became stiff around fans—but this was different, a moment to cherish. Speaking through a translator, Kurosawa remarked on the physical beauty of the cinematography and lighting and how skillfully they enhanced the story. According to Ross, Sidney looked like he was going to weep with joy. He replied:

> *For you to recognize these things . . . we worked so hard for!*
> *In the first third of the film, the people are separated from*
> *the backgrounds; the light is not on the people but on the*
> *backgrounds—the neon signs, for example. In the second third of*
> *the movie, the light is on both the people and the backgrounds. In*
> *the last third, the light is on the people in the foreground; walls*
> *are stripped bare, and the focus is fully on the people.*

Kurosawa, right with him, replied, "And in the last shot you have the sea of blue shirts at the Police Academy, and then you show just that one face, the face of Danny Ciello. Superb!" Even with a translator between them, the two men spoke the same language: *How-It's-Done.* Kurosawa wanted to know exactly how Sidney shot the realistic-looking rain scenes. "Impossible," Kurosawa said, "to shoot in real rain." Lumet explained, "We had four hundred-foot cherry pickers, with hoses and metal pipes extending for thirty-two more feet. Four pipes were crossed with spinning nozzles, and we let the natural wind carry it. We used tens of thousands of gallons of water."

When their conversation turned from technical matters, Kurosawa explained that he would not be able to make a film about corruption like *Prince of the City* in Japan; he would not be allowed to touch political topics, and since he could not say what he would like to say about the present, he preferred to make historical films. He acknowledged that he was often criticized for not making more "relevant" films, as well as for what some saw as the Western influence in his work.

Lumet asked, "Do they consider you a reactionary in Japan?"

"Yes," he sadly affirmed.

Sidney replied, "When you hold on to where you come from and what you are, it's impossible for young people to understand. Young people like labels."

"Yes," Kurosawa said, still looking sad. "I just keep on doing what *I* can do."

Sidney's identification with this kind of generational divide may have reflected what was brewing at home with his daughters. Or perhaps he was feeling out of step with the film students he'd recently taught at Yale, at this moment when the avant-garde director Jean-Luc Godard was at the pinnacle of his appeal in academia.

Years later Sidney observed of Kurosawa, "He never affected me in terms of my own moviemaking because I never would have presumed that I was capable of that perception and that vision. For me, Kurosawa is the Beethoven of movie directors. It's that recognizable full sound that Beethoven had that is so unmistakable."

Younger directors have recognized and been influenced by Sidney's perception and vision in *Prince of the City*. One example: Christopher Nolan and his director of photography studied the film when working on *The Dark Knight Rises* (2012).

THE VERDICT

What Sidney liked most of all was for the phone to ring with a job.

—PIEDY LUMET

The Verdict opens with a short wordless shot: Paul Newman, as Frank Galvin, playing pinball in a bar. Sidney added this sequence, which is repeated later in the story, to David Mamet's script. In his DVD commentary on the film, Sidney offers a surprisingly personal reflection: noting that the film is about a depressed man, he goes on to say:

> When I've had that kind of depression in my life one of the things I've done always: well . . . how are the fates treating me today? So I would get to a pinball machine or solitaire or any other game, and really hope that I could make a good score. . . . If I could, the day would be okay, if not I knew the day was going to be in trouble. That was the whole idea behind this opening shot.

More surprising than divulging his bouts with depression, about which Piedy said, "he behaved so well you'd have to be very discerning to see it," is his keeping faith with this childlike superstition about "the fates," especially given the many ways he maintained control of his life and work. This dialectic of fate and self-determinism—not an overt theme in his movies—played a hidden role in his life. Unlike Frank in *The Verdict*, Sidney never had a drinking problem, but the AA serenity prayer applies in some respects to Sidney: he knew he had the courage to change some things in his life, sought to accept the things he couldn't change and tried hard to know the difference.

As usual, Sidney kept a lot of balls up in the air. He had recently made a cultural exchange trip for the State Department to Soviet-controlled Eastern Europe, his first time in that part of the world. Visiting East Berlin, Budapest, and his parents' city of Warsaw, he was impressed by the sophistication of the filmmakers and students he met and mindful of the constraints under which they worked. He found it sobering to compare the challenges he faced in bucking studio pressure and his "neurotic fear" of never getting another job to the political repression those directors endured.

In early 1982, the year he made *The Verdict*, he had been trying to get two other projects off the ground. One was about television evangelists called *The Kingdom*, which foreshadowed the lurid scandal and fraud conviction of televangelist Jim Bakker. The other project,

David Mamet's script of the life of Malcolm X, was far more controversial. Lili recalled threatening phone calls coming into the office as word got out that Sidney was hoping to direct this story. Sidney understood the sensitivities aroused by a white director proposing to handle this material; still, he felt he knew the era, especially the 1940s, and he hoped to get Richard Pryor, with whom he'd worked on *The Wiz*, to play Malcolm X. It would have been a remarkable leap of faith on both their parts, but the story would have to await Spike Lee's direction a decade later.

When Sidney received the phone call about directing *The Verdict*, he was ripe for an already green-lighted project. It came to him when the producers at Twentieth Century–Fox, Richard Zanuck and David Brown, had grown tired of waiting on Robert Redford and Sydney Pollack, who had unsuccessfully hired several different writers to take a stab at adapting Barry Reed's novel. Sidney liked the version David Mamet had written that had been shelved by them early on. He told them he would do the film if they used that one.

Unlike *Prince of the City*, *The Verdict* is a melodrama, a tidy three-act redemption story. Mamet took the basic plot from Reed's novel, but he injected his own themes into it and wrote all of the brilliant speeches. Sidney wasn't big on redemption stories. I'm not sure he believed in redemption, for himself or anyone; what takes the film beyond formula is that it doesn't just show us that story but manages to arouse the yearning in all of us to believe that we might in some small, uncompromised fashion serve a just cause. This was material close to Sidney's heart. As Galvin puts it to the love interest, Laura, played by Charlotte Rampling:

GALVIN: You see, the jury wants to believe. They're all cynics, sure. . . . I have to go in there tomorrow to find twelve people to hear this case. . . . And every one of them, it's written on their face, "This is a sham. There is no justice . . ." but in their heart they're saying, "Maybe . . . maybe . . ."
LAURA: Maybe what?
GALVIN: (beat) Maybe I can do something right.

The lines Galvin delivers in his closing argument to the jury seldom fail to move viewers:

Well . . . You know, so much of the time we're just lost. We say, "Please, God, tell us what is right. Tell us what is true." The rich win; the poor are powerless. We become tired of hearing people lie. And after a time we become dead, a little dead. We think of ourselves as victims—and we become victims. We become weak; we doubt ourselves; we doubt our beliefs; we doubt our institutions; and we doubt the law. But today you are the law. You are the law, not some book, not the lawyers, not a marble statue, or the trappings of the court. See, those are just symbols of our desire to be just. They are, in fact, a prayer, I mean a fervent and a frightened prayer. In my religion, they say, "Act as if you had faith; faith will be given to you." If we are to have faith in justice we need only to believe in ourselves and act with justice. See, I believe there is justice in our hearts.

On the set of *The Verdict*, Sidney tilts Paul Newman's head, while Charlotte Rampling keeps her focus. *(Daniel Simon / Gamma Rapho / Getty Images)*

The look of this film was unlike any of Sidney's others: "Because it's about people, especially Paul's character, who are trapped in the past, there's nothing new in it. There isn't a modern building or a modern piece of furniture in it . . . as if time stopped for them a long while ago." Regarding the lighting and colorscape in the film, Sidney continued, "We sat down with Caravaggio's paintings." He asked Andrzej Bartkowiak, the brilliant young Polish cinematographer he'd found for *Prince of the City*, to break it down for him. "We spent a whole day analyzing the way Caravaggio was treating background, the way he was treating foreground, where light came from, the way he was treating surfaces. Then we applied that to the picture, and the result is just extraordinary."

The film brought another five Oscar nominations, including for Best Picture and Best Director. But no wins. Frustrated, Sidney observed, "It wasn't a conventional enough script to win. It's like the difference between *Network* and *Rocky*. *Rocky* is handed to you like a roast pig at a Christmas dinner. *Network*, and [*Prince of the City*], you have to work a little."

Oscars aside, Sidney, now entering his sixties, had been the recipient of countless awards around the world, but the first-ever award from the American Museum of the Moving Image, in November 1985, gave him some real *nachas*, real happiness, raising money for the construction of the nonprofit's headquarters at the Kaufman Astoria Studios in Queens, a place Sidney had also done so much to revive. Sidney's friend Alan King was the master of ceremonies at the Waldorf Astoria gala, attended by 550 guests who had each contributed $500 for a seat, "And there are very few freebies," Sidney noted. King's remarks included, as *The New York Times* reported, jokes about Mr. Lumet's height, lineage and marital history, noting that the grosses for *Garbo Talks*, Sidney's latest movie, "were less than the alimony he pays every month."

As *The New York Times* noted, as of the mid-1980s, Sidney had "made 25 of his 31 movies here, and no other filmmaker—not Woody

Allen, nor Martin Scorsese, nor John Cassavetes—can come anywhere near that record." Of the thousands of locations where he'd shot around the city, Sidney had repeated a location only once, at a bar on Avenue B and 10th Street (a favorite of Burtt Harris') that appeared in both *Prince of the City* and *The Verdict*.

19

PARENTS AND CHILDREN

Nothing of him that doth fade,
But doth suffer a sea-change
Into something rich and strange . . .
—WILLIAM SHAKESPEARE, *THE TEMPEST*, ACT I, SCENE 2

In December 1992, Amy Lumet, Sidney's older daughter, then age twenty-eight, published an article in the conservative *National Review* titled "A Call to Arms: Baby Cons of America, Unite." The subtitle read, "You Have Nothing to Lose but Your Parents' Guilt." In a glib takedown of the "government as evil stepmother," with its imposition of "busing, rules in advertising, college quotas, low income housing projects in our neighborhoods, don't do this, don't say that, no smoking on planes or trains," Amy celebrated a recent rise in registered Republicans aged eighteen to twenty-nine whom she dubbed Baby Cons. She wrote, "One Baby Con put the problem very well: 'The creeping socialism manifest in the expansion of government threatens the only valuable right in the Constitution—the Fifth Amendment right to private property.'" She added, "I love this statement."

This apple had fallen very far from the tree. Her politics, which to this day land on the extreme far right, followed hard upon her partying years. In 1990 she had married conservative author and satirist P. J. O'Rourke, seventeen years her senior and a legendary hellraiser, known for such quips as "I remember thinking cocaine was subtle . . .

until I noticed I'd been awake for three weeks and didn't know any of the naked people passed out around me." O'Rourke later explained their brief marriage: he was headed to the Middle East to cover the Gulf War, and on the chance that he'd be killed he thought it "would make everything simpler if we had been married. It seemed much simpler to be a widow than a girl with a dead boyfriend." Together they worked in Republican circles, contributing to campaigns. The marriage ended in 1993, but Amy's political conversion had been cemented.

Amy's move to the opposing political camp from that of her father and mother would, in subsequent years, be attended by several other cultural leaps, including moving to Los Angeles, becoming a competitive body builder, and finding a community among far-right Zionists and Donald J. Trump supporters.

FATHER AND DAUGHTERS

Sidney was forty years old when Amy was born. He had been eager to become a father, though like many men of his generation, parenting wasn't something he thought a lot about. He never saw his role as the disciplinarian, even when the girls were young. His daughter Jenny said she had heard him raise his voice only once. He was mindful not to load a lot of demands or expectations on his daughters, as his father had on him; perhaps it would have been better if he had. Of course there wasn't the need; their experience was too different from his. When asked about the girls, he always smiled broadly and said they were "just great," although he knew his elder daughter Amy's antics had earned her a reputation among their crowd. Only Sidney's closest friends ever heard him express his worry or frustration.

At fifteen, Amy was featured on the cover of *Seventeen* magazine, the picture of health and beauty, but the image was deceiving. While modeling regularly throughout high school, she had, according to family friends, fallen into the extravagant 1980s drug scene. Unlike her mother, she wasn't doing the twist at the Peppermint Lounge;

she was hanging out at cocaine-saturated nightspots like Area, the hottest dance club in town, and she was gaining a reputation for being wild and a little crazy.

Her artistic talent lent hope that she would find her way. It was likely Piedy's idea to give Amy a dog, a beagle called Penny the Dog, to tie her to some responsibility. Amy began college at the Rhode Island School of Design, but she dropped out pretty promptly and returned to the druggy New York club scene. Gossip pages picked up on a 1983 Studio 54 "second-generation" party Amy attended, in which guests were admitted with the phrase "Hi, I'm the child of . . ."; the guest list included Ben Stiller, Mario Van Peebles and Anthony Peck, Gregory Peck's son, with whom Amy's name was romantically linked for some time. A 1986 *Spy* magazine article described her as a "show business brat," and there's been speculation that she was the model for a character in Jay McInerney's 1984 hit novel, *Bright Lights, Big City*, a story about losing oneself in the elitist hedonism of 1980s New York nightlife.

Coming up behind her, Jenny, who'd been a good student at Dalton, had quietly, maybe even secretly, begun taking acting lessons in the Meisner technique. Sidney cast her in a tiny role in *Deathtrap* (1982) when she was only fifteen. He was likely thinking about how performing as a child had kept him off the streets and out of trouble and hoping it would keep Jenny from her older sister's path, although he knew the two were so different. Jenny began at New York University, but college lasted only briefly for her as well. Sidney tried to figure out what had soured for Jenny at school. He gave Lili the futile task of trying to get hold of Jenny's college grades. Like her father, Jenny loved learning, but also like him, she preferred to learn in her own way. She soon took a job at the hip downtown paper *Details*, which covered avant-garde art, music and fashion; the job drew her into another tribe of the night, different from her sister's uptown scene.

Looking back, Sidney observed that several of the films he made in this volatile period at home had been about parents and children, specifically, as he put it, "the price children pay for the passions of the parents." A triad of films, *Daniel* (1983), *Running on Empty* (1988) and *Family Business* (1989), explored the theme, each in its own way. *Garbo Talks* (1984) might also find a place in the family category, given its unusual mother-son relationship. These were Sidney's first take on family stories since his adaptations of *Long Day's Journey into Night*, *The Sea Gull* and *A View from the Bridge* in the 1960s.

Sidney remarked that the pattern that emerged in the films only dawned on him in retrospect. He had not been conscious of it at the time. Without fully registering it, Sidney had been revisiting sites of trauma from his own childhood, while also obliquely questioning what had gone awry with his own eldest daughter, something that he was having trouble looking into very much or directly. Close observers contended that Sidney never said no to Amy, perhaps as a way of ending discussion. Although she and her younger sister had a good understanding, and occupied dramatically different roles in the family, Amy was pushing away from and against all of them. Most of her rage was reserved for her mother, but she would find ways to hurt each of them.

DANIEL

The first of the family-themed film cycle, *Daniel*, was adapted by E. L. Doctorow from his novel, *The Book of Daniel*. It is the award-winning author's fictionalized account of the lives of Julius and Ethel Rosenberg, renamed Paul and Rochelle Isaacson, played by Mandy Patinkin and Lindsay Crouse, and their children, Daniel and Susan, played by Timothy Hutton and Amanda Plummer. The story begins in the radical 1930s and picks up in the late 1960s with the Isaacson children, Daniel and Susan, now young adults.

Sidney rendered with great tenderness the very young Isaacson children (Ilan Mitchell-Smith and Jena Greco), brother and sister clinging desperately to each other, much as he and his sister Faye had done; "orphans in a storm" was how Ellen Adler remembered them together. A scene set in the 1930s, depicting a Communist Party orator defending the Hitler-Stalin pact to a group of Jewish left-ists, was drawn from an early memory of Sidney's that he carefully reconstructed, including the clothing and posture of the listeners. When the story jumps forward in time to the young adult siblings, no longer anchored to each other but at odds, we get another glimpse into Sidney's connection to the material. Daniel, the embittered elder brother, is furious at his sister for her relentless pursuit of a righteous cause, and, more poignantly, for the fathomless vulnerability that will lead to her suicide. The rift between the siblings and the guilt that plagues the brother recalls Sidney's severed bond with Faye, as well as her mental illness and early death in her fifties. Indeed, one friend believed Faye's death was a suicide.

As Doctorow explained it to me, he and Sidney had disagreed at the time about Sidney's decision to put the children at the center of the story. It was years later, Doctorow said, that he recognized that Sidney was absolutely right, that this was the proper focus for this depiction of the horrific destruction of a family and the impossible legacy left to the children.

Doctorow spoke with warmth and some regret about how things had ended up between Sidney and himself. He emphasized that, de-spite this disagreement, Sidney and he were "truly partners" on the film. Sidney reshot scenes if Doctorow didn't like them, sometimes denting the budget by as much as $60,000. "He kept all his promises to me," Doctorow said—and Sidney was "amazing to watch on the set," wrangling hundreds of extras, horses, 1930s police cars and five or six cameras going at once, some hidden behind fire hydrants. Most of all, Doctorow said, "I was amazed at Sidney's depth. He was so smart." Unlike other directors Doctorow had worked with, Sidney "did not surround himself with yes men. There was just Lili and Burtt, and sometimes Burtt would step in."

Doctorow reminisced that he and Sidney became chummy, as people do who work together on a movie. He recalled fun dinners with Sidney's theater friends at their home in East Hampton. For his part, Sidney had been moved when, on the first day of shooting,

Doctorow stood on the side and wept as they filmed the rally where the frightened Isaacson children are handed, like political props, over the crowd to the stage.

The project had begun when Piedy read the novel and passed it along to Sidney with the idea that he might like it for a film. Sidney promptly began looking for backing. It was a risky topic and it took Sidney a very long time to pull together the seven or eight million dollars he needed to get things underway. As it turned out, this brilliantly acted and heartbreaking film ran into a political meat grinder at its release. It opened days before the publication of *The Rosenberg File: A Search for the Truth*, a book that drew on newly released documents under the Freedom of Information Act to argue for the guilt of Julius Rosenberg and the likely complicity of his wife. In this inflamed environment Sidney's film was interpreted either as a whitewashing of the Rosenbergs, an indictment of them, or, even worse, intentionally vague as to their guilt or innocence. He was shocked when, at a press conference for the film, he was asked ignorant and reactionary questions, like "Are you a communist?" He was equally stunned when *The New York Times* failed to interview Doctorow for the film's opening.

Unlike Doctorow's previous film adaptation, *Ragtime*, directed by Miloš Forman, *Daniel* underperformed at the box office. This disappointment hadn't troubled the friendship between Sidney and Doctorow; a few years later, though, when Sidney invited Doctorow to a screening of *Running on Empty*, another story about outcast political radicals and their two children, things went wrong between them. After the screening Sidney, sensing something, asked Doctorow why he had crossed his arms in apparent irritation at a certain scene. With sadness in his voice, Doctorow told me that at the time he had experienced *Running on Empty* as Sidney's apology for *Daniel*. Sidney acknowledged that this film was a simpler film for audiences than *Daniel*, but he was baffled by the accusation. Their friendship then cooled. Doctorow realized later that he was wrong about the film, and he was deeply sorry to have hurt Sidney. In hindsight he felt he'd taken his long-simmering resentment of the movie industry, and its terrible treatment of writers, out on Sidney. "Sidney didn't deserve that," he concluded.

Sidney's marriage provided refuge from all that ailed him. In a change from his previous marriages, Piedy was folded into his work, providing her opinion when asked and often attending rushes. Sidney "liked having me around," Piedy allowed. "He'd send a car and I'd sometimes sit in on the dailies, not next to him—he sat with the camera man—but in the back with the editor."

Sidney grew more committed to his weekends in East Hampton. He often flew by helicopter from the East Side heliport, or he paid a teamster to drive him. They had begun contemplating selling the East Side town house with its old-world elevator that Piedy had once gotten stuck in. She wanted the change, felt she was living in someone else's home, in Sidney's prior life. The two occasionally attended parties. Piedy remarked that when she mentioned an occurrence from the evening before, Sidney often had no recollection of it. She marveled that he simply wasn't that curious about people.

Together they traveled pretty regularly, adding a vacation in southern France or Italy to a trip to receive an award or make an appearance at a European film festival. "He liked to go to any European country that was honoring him. He loved an honor in Lucerne, so he could take Piedy on a trip on their dime—break out his ties and his one suit," Jenny's first husband, Bobby Cannavale, lovingly recalled. Sidney and Piedy shared a deep affection for Rome, and Sidney made it a point to get there in a different month every year.

GARBO TALKS

Like so many of Sidney's films, *Garbo Talks* has its particular and passionate following. It is a Jewish mother-son story, and also the story of a broken marriage and an ex-husband who still somehow loves the wife he found too much to handle. Estelle (Anne Bancroft) is not the stereotypical Jewish mother: she refused to cross a picket line to attend her son's wedding, and routinely gets arrested staging her own private social protests; she buys her dinner from a food truck. Seemingly a light comedy, the movie takes you by surprise, calling up deep feelings in unlikely moments. Familiar from many of Sidney's films is a male character with an unshakeable commitment to a task; here it is Gilbert, played by Ron Silver. When his mother is diagnosed with terminal brain cancer, she asks him to fulfill her fondest wish, to meet her screen idol (and famous recluse), Greta Garbo. On his search for the elusive star, Gilbert, a beleaguered accountant, canvasses the outer reaches of show business and encounters a series of has-beens, also-rans and wannabes. Each is given a touchingly real life, with dignity and pathos. The hunger for recognition, to be seen and known, is everywhere in the film. When finally Gilbert locates Garbo (played wordlessly by Sidney's close friend, lyricist Betty Comden) and persuades her to spend a few minutes with his mother in her hospital room, Estelle reports that she truly has been seen by her idol; as she gushes to Gilbert after the visit, "She told me we are very much alike."

This film is often considered an expression of the softer side of Sidney Lumet. There is a simple tenderness in this family and in many of the characters we encounter, and Sidney also renders the glamour and fantasy of old Hollywood with great affection, including a gorgeous black-and-white clip from Ernst Lubitsch's *Ninotchka*. Perhaps this film expressed the same side of Sidney that his daughter Jenny spoke of when I asked her if her father was ever sentimental. She hesitated. "There was a lot of sentiment . . . I'm having a hard time articulating it because it wasn't like other people, but yeah, we would watch *Dumbo* and bawl. And bawl and bawl." Many people noted that Sidney cried openly and was never embarrassed by tears.

Years later Jenny would portray this trait of her father's in the award-winning film she wrote, *Rachel Getting Married* (2008), which is partly a portrait of her family. Rachel's wedding brings her sister home on furlough from rehab. As Jenny described the germ of the story, "I had an image of a bride getting ready for this big moment and she's in a room by herself in her wedding gown alone, and then her sister bursts into the room and is either destroying a moment or creating a moment." Jenny's original title for the film was *Dancing with Shiva*, a reference clarified when the returning sister, Kym (Anne Hathaway), rises to make a toast at the rehearsal dinner and introduces herself: "I am Shiva the Destroyer and your harbinger of doom for this evening." Kym follows this with a narcissistic display that leaves the room—and the audience—stunned and embarrassed.

The father in the film is unmistakably based on Sidney. In fact, the film's Oscar-winning director, Jonathan Demme, tried to enlist his friend Sidney to play the role. Understandably, Sidney declined, and Tony winner Bill Irwin instead portrayed the loving and worried father who endeavors ineffectively to keep the peace.

Through Jenny's conception of Kym, the attention-grabbing sister fresh from rehab, we see a brilliant portrait of an addict, and the film grants her a share of insight as she gives voice to her frustration with the family dynamic, and to being constantly under scrutiny, even as the family pretends to normality. As Jenny put it in an interview, Kym seems to want "a sock in the jaw . . . to be punished," but instead her father attempts to paper over past and brewing disasters. He doesn't call her out or express anger for what she has done to herself and her family, and when the situation ultimately explodes, he sits helplessly and weeps.

When asked about the autobiographical content of her film, Jenny was careful to say she drew from friends and family alike, and to point humorously at her father's real-life habit, echoed in the film, of making sandwiches for anyone who came within his ten-foot radius. But the fraught family scenes, with their exchange of hurt, disappointment, and sibling competition for fatherly attention, all comport with stories of the Lumet family's struggles. The girls' remarried mother (played incandescently by Debra Winger) is pained, brittle, and aloof. When the film premiered in Los Angeles, where Amy lives, she did not attend the opening.

Rachel Getting Married captures a feature of family life that Jenny aptly describes: "It never works out like 'this shit's all resolved, and we're all fine, and every holiday it's going to be like this with all of us cooking . . .' No, for this half hour, it's amazing, and then God knows what's going to happen the next time we get together for Thanksgiving."

POWER & THE MORNING AFTER

Power (1986) had a lot of promise, because of its outstanding cast, including Julie Christie, Richard Gere, Gene Hackman and Denzel Washington, and its potent and what would turn out to be its prescient message regarding the manipulation of the political process by marketing research and advertising. Coming two years before Lee Atwater's infamous Willie Horton ad, credited with felling a Democratic presidential candidate, the film centers on media consultant Pete St. John (Richard Gere) and his coldly strategic and amoral packaging of a millionaire candidate. Notably, the film opens with St. John operating in an unnamed Latin American country, directing a TV spot for a socialist candidate; his work is not confined to U.S. elections. Indeed, American media consultants were already helping foreign heads of state, including Prime Minister Giscard d'Estaing of France and kleptocrat Ferdinand Marcos of the Philippines. "The point of the picture is that it doesn't matter if you believe in your client or not," Sidney observed at the time. "The whole political process has become dehumanized, part and parcel of everything else . . . even movies look as if they were put together by a polling organization." Indeed, pulling back the curtain on the making of political ads, the film reveals exactly how film footage can be cut and sequenced to deliver any desired message. Sidney pushed through making the film, but he wasn't able to bring it to life. As one critic put it, the film "crackles with a kind of moral static." One can only imagine that Sidney's mind was elsewhere. Notably, while making this film, Sidney received a Bill of Rights Award from the American Civil

Liberties Union. At the tribute at the Ambassador Hotel in Los Angeles, Sidney's films were extolled as "a continuing testament to freedom, justice, and understanding."

That same year Sidney took on *The Morning After*, mostly, he said, for the chance to work with Jane Fonda, whom he adored. A sexy Los Angeles–based thriller co-written by Jay Presson Allen, it co-stars an endearing Jeff Bridges. The movie calls up memories of *Klute*, the great 1971 Alan Pakula film, with Fonda this time playing a washed-up actress caught up in a murder. It's the only film Sidney ever shot in Los Angeles; and he plays with the bright sunshine and the brightly colored buildings of the city, giving the film a different look from any of his others.

Piedy joined Sidney in LA for much of the shoot. While they were there they socialized with Barbra Streisand, among others, and checked in with Sidney's father, Baruch, who was now living in comfortable retirement, largely provided by Sidney. Piedy also reached out to Sidney's niece, Faye's elder daughter, Lisa James, who had become an actress. Sidney had seen her only once since her childhood, following her mother's death.

RUNNING ON EMPTY

Someone told me that the only love story that ends successfully in separation is that of a parent and child.
　　　　　　　　　　　　　—NAOMI FONER, SCREENWRITER

The film *Running on Empty* (1988) brought Sidney back into focus. Judd Hirsch and Christine Lahti play two 1960s radicals who have been living underground for two decades, with their two sons. Conscience had led them in 1970, at the height of the Vietnam War, to blow up a napalm lab; the explosion had blinded a watchman they had not accounted for. The link between this film and *Daniel* was the theme of the offspring paying mightily for their parents' passions and commitments. The story explores what happens to isolated members of a movement when the world has moved on, and to a nuclear family who have only one another. The plot turns on the maturing of the elder son, Danny Pope, played by a seventeen-year-old River Phoenix, whom Sidney would come to adore, as would the entire cast, and whose life ended five years later of a drug overdose.

Phoenix's Danny is a promising pianist who has been accepted to Juilliard, but he is deeply conflicted because if he leaves the family, their connection to him will necessarily be severed. In an unforgettable scene, Annie Pope (Christine Lahti) meets briefly with her wealthy, conservative father at a New York restaurant to ask him to take Danny in so he can attend Juilliard. They have not seen each other in eighteen years. In this scene we see how the cost of passions and commitments can deliver heartbreak not only to offspring but to parents as well. We can also see the enormous care Sidney put into building up to this scene between a father and his estranged daughter, a situation about which he had a lot of feelings, and that he would reprise years later in "Kids," an episode of the TV series *100 Centre Street* he wrote and directed, about the reunion of a father (Alan Arkin) and his troubled daughter (Amy Ryan). In the scene in *Running on Empty*, the pain felt by both father and daughter is sharpened by the father's contempt for her life choices. Weeping silently, Annie hesitatingly beseeches her cold, bereft father, "Tell Mom that I love her . . . and that I think of her . . . and you . . . all the time." The screenplay was written by Naomi Foner, mother of Maggie and Jake Gyllenhaal, who as small children sometimes joined their mother on the set. Sixteen years later, Maggie Gyllenhaal would appear in one of Sidney's final productions, *Strip Search*.

Jenny, too, was on the set; Sidney cast her in a small speaking role. That year she also appeared in a Run-DMC vehicle, *Tougher Than Leather*. She had appeared on the legendary La MaMa stage and was growing ever more serious about acting.

SIDNEY'S POST-1960s POLITICS

*Lumet's politics have irritated critics on the lookout for
sentimental leftism, and that may partially explain their
animus.*

—DON SHEWEY, FILM CRITIC, 1982

*I don't know whether it's true [that I'm losing that audience],
but I feel it's true. I feel I'm talking to a smaller and smaller
group.*

—SIDNEY LUMET, INTERVIEW 1986

Film curator Gavin Smith took the release of *Running on Empty* as a
good opportunity to query Sidney on his views of the 1960s politics
that the film recalls. While the film underwrites many '60s values,
Sidney expressed mixed feelings about the era, revealing his old-school
leftism: "Because it was a young movement and coincided with the
normal adolescent revolt, it also revolted against its own father
which was the old left." He felt that rock 'n' roll drug culture
hadn't "contributed to what one does about economics . . . about
very important forces in our lives," and he expressed disappointment
regarding the movement's lukewarm commitment to racial justice:

*The sixties "rebels" united with the blacks and then abandoned
them. . . . The only lasting influence was the black liberation,
which came about largely through the efforts of blacks themselves,
and mostly among southern whites. . . . That was largely
black-achieved, black-led, and white-supported at the beginning,
but as soon as the situation got a little sticky they pulled in their
horns. God knows, it's as racially a divided country now . . .*

But he recognized the achievement and expressed admiration for the
movement that had stopped a war. The '60s generation, he concluded,

succeeded at something he described as very romantic, but when it all didn't go their way, he believed they ran out of gas.

When the interview moved on to the current moment, the presidential elections of 1988, Sidney observed that the United States no longer had a left wing. "I was a Jackson supporter during the primaries," he noted, "but will happily vote for Dukakis." Sidney here referred to Jesse Jackson, the first black Democratic candidate to get a serious shot at the presidency, winning eleven primary contests and caucuses, and to Michael Dukakis, the Democratic candidate who ultimately lost the election to George H. W. Bush.

Sidney underwrote his liberal-left politics with yearly contributions to the American Civil Liberties Union, the Southern Poverty Law Center and Amnesty International. One of the few times he openly expressed his anger at Amy was when she asked him for some money, which she then proceeded to donate to a right-wing cause.

Running on Empty had multiple meanings for Sidney; it was, arguably, a parable of one aspect of his career and reputation. Like the two antiwar activists who have never left the politics of the late 1960s, Sidney was a political filmmaker whose politics in the 1980s seemed to be out of step not only with his elder daughter but with the times. His genius for rendering political complexity was lost on the Ronald Reagan decade, which favored simpler stories of the triumph of good over evil, *Ghostbusters* and *Back to the Future*.

Family Business was the third in the family triad, a misfire of a comedy wherein three generations, grandfather (Sean Connery), father (Dustin Hoffman) and son (Matthew Broderick) join forces to pull off a heist. As the *New York Times* reviewer observed:

> *If you can believe that Sean Connery and a Sicilian wife could be parents to Dustin Hoffman, and that this same Dustin Hoffman and a Jewish wife could be parents to Matthew Broderick, then you should read no further than the next paragraph. Drop everything and rush to the theater nearest you to see Sidney Lumet's new comedy.*

Again one imagines that Sidney's attention was elsewhere or he was not in the mood to be funny. Friends recalled that there was a period during these years when Sidney stopped listening to music. This great lover of classical music, whom Leonard Bernstein had lauded for his deep knowledge, tuned it out and stopped attending concerts because, as friends explained, "it made him too sad."

20

MAKE IT PERSONAL

The city is always changing and always remains the same, and that's what I hope about myself.

—SIDNEY LUMET

Everyone who worked with Sidney knew about his naps. Usually he took a little siesta during lunch, after eating his ham and tomato with mayo on lettuce (no bread). He'd sleep for half an hour or a little longer. He had no trouble falling asleep no matter what was going on or where they were on location; he said he "learned to do that during World War II."

In his fourth decade as a movie director, Sidney slowed down—by his standards, that is. He directed only six movies between 1990 and 1999, two of which he adapted for the screen. He directed a play for the first time in decades, based on Cynthia Ozick's *The Shawl*, and he also snuck in writing a book, *Making Movies* (1995), which has become a classic for filmmakers, film students and movie lovers. Four of the six films of this decade take up his cops-corruption-and-courtroom themes and fall into a category Sidney called melodrama, in that they are plot- rather than character-driven. But in each of them Sidney found something new, something to learn from and something personal.

A few projects that Sidney had been more or less counting on had fallen through. He and Budd Schulberg, who wrote the screenplays for *On the Waterfront* and *A Face in the Crowd*, had been working on an adaptation of Schulberg's 1941 novel, *What Makes Sammy Run?* It's the story of a Lower East Side kid, Sammy Glick (formerly Glickstein), who claws his way out of the ghetto and up the Hollywood ladder, becoming ever more venal and ruthless along the way. For decades, Hollywood had quashed efforts to adapt the novel for the screen; it was widely denounced as both anti-Semitic and anti-Hollywood. When Warner Bros. got interested in reviving the project in 1990, Schulberg brought the script to Sidney, who was game, noting its timeliness: "Budd says when he goes around on the college lecture circuit now, they think Sammy is a hero, which is an interesting generational difference." Sidney was eager for the challenge of a period piece. "We're going to start him [Sammy Glick] in 1936," he said, and he thought Tom Cruise could be good for the leading role. "I will be fascinated to see what people will draw from it," Sidney noted, adding tartly, Sammy Glick "may turn out to be the biggest hero since 'Star Trek VI' for all I know." But the project fell through.

Coincidentally, Sidney was offered another script about a Hollywood mogul: *The Player*, written by Michael Tolkin, a dark satire about a studio head who gets away with murder, literally. Sidney spent several weeks on the project, but his vision for the film was too expensive, and his salary demand, at $2 million, was too high. It's likely he wanted that hefty compensation for all the time he'd need to spend in Los Angeles. Robert Altman was brought in for less money and with a tighter budget; it proved a comeback for Altman, and the film earned three Oscar nominations, including Best Director. Lili Jacobs ruminated on how great it would've been if they'd each directed the script, leaving us with a Lumet and an Altman version of *The Player* to compare.

Q & A

Q & A was personal for Sidney for several reasons. One was its unabashed focus on racism in the police force. Indictments of racial prejudice had a place in Sidney's work from the beginning, but nowhere as stingingly as in *Q & A*, which Sidney adapted from a 1977 novel by Edwin Torres, a former Manhattan assistant district attorney who went on to become a judge, reputed to be conservative and tough. This was Sidney's first solo go at writing a screenplay: "What I saw in the book," he said, was "a story of racism, and how it is built into the warp and woof of the justice system. . . . Everyone—the Irish, the Italians, the Puerto Ricans—makes decisions, places trust, nurses antagonisms along racial and ethnic lines, consciously and unconsciously." Indeed, the New York Police Department is to this day broken down into fraternal organizations that provide insurance funds for widows and scholarships for kids along strictly racial and ethnic lines: the Columbia Association is for police of Italian extraction; the Steuben Association for those of German and Austrian heritage; the Shomrim Society for Jews; the Guardians Association for African Americans; the Asian Jade Society for Asian Americans; and the biggest one, the Emerald Society, is for police of Irish descent. Ethnic tribalism had in some ways benefited immigrant groups, as Sidney well knew, but it always had a dark side. The film explores its dire effects on the culture and daily functioning of the police.

Racism had taken on added personal significance for Sidney as his daughters got older and ventured further into the world. Jenny, who had been trying to gain some traction in her acting career, had also become politically engaged as a result of the racial tensions boiling over in New York in the late 1980s. Some of the headline-grabbing stories the family absorbed included the 1986 attack by a dozen whites on three black men in Howard Beach, Queens, that led to the death of Michael Griffith; the racially motivated murder of Yusef Hawkins, a black sixteen-year-old in Bensonhurst, Brooklyn, in 1989; and the "Central Park jogger" attack of 1989, in which a white woman was raped and severely beaten and five black teenagers, who were repeatedly called "a wolf pack" in the press, were wrongly convicted of the crime. (At the time, Donald Trump took out full-page ads in four of the city's daily newspapers calling for the boys—all of whom would later be exonerated—to receive the death penalty.) But it wasn't only the news reports that troubled Sidney; "It was largely the observations of racism that my children brought home that made it all the more urgent to me," he said. "Their awareness became my awareness."

Deepening his personal stake in *Q & A*, he cast Jenny, age twenty-three, in a leading role. As she told the story, when she asked her father if there was a role for her in the film, he said, "Ummm . . . there's a girl but I think . . . no. You're not right for it"—and, Jenny noted, "he said this for a year." But when she finally read for the part, Sidney said, "Okay. Come back and read again." Sidney worried that he'd face the charge of nepotism that Francis Ford Coppola had recently received for casting his daughter, Sofia, in *The Godfather: Part III* after Winona Ryder dropped out. Sidney didn't want to put Jenny through that, and he worried over it throughout the filming, but in the end the press never went in that direction at all, or almost never.

Jenny plays Nancy Bosch, a woman of mixed race whose romantic relationship with a young Irish police officer, Al Reilly (Timothy Hutton), ends in a split second when he sets eyes on her father, whom he didn't know was black. Gail Lumet Buckley, Jenny's mother, observed of the film that it was "a modern version of the so-called tragic-mulatto theme," where the heroine is rejected by her white lover once her "mixed blood" is revealed. The update in *Q & A* is that it is not the white man who breaks off the relationship; rather, Nancy, seeing the expression on Reilly's face upon meeting her father, rejects him and soon takes up with a Puerto Rican drug kingpin, played disarmingly by Armand Assante. When Sidney was asked if a single look could really kill a relationship, he replied, "No black person who ever read the script questioned it for a minute. For black people, it [is] a part of their experience: they can tell in an instant." An important part of Reilly's story is his belated recognition of his own racial prejudice. Regarding this character, Sidney said, "What I hope I'm going to get out of the movie is an acknowledgment on the part of just one character not that he is a racist but that, somehow or other, he is not a free man."

Detective Mike Brennan (Nick Nolte) is at the center of *Q & A*, a corrupt and racist cop whose violent character seems also to draw on the trope of repressed homosexuality. Al Reilly, having become

Jenny Lumet posing for a publicity shot for *Q & A*. (*Courtesy of Regency Enterprises*)

a district attorney, is investigating a cold-blooded murder Brennan committed in what he claims was self-defense. Reilly has to choose between his loyalty to Brennan as a fellow Irish cop and his commitment to the law; but although Reilly makes the right choice, ultimately justice is not served because of political exigencies within the district attorney's office. Doing the right thing doesn't necessarily have a payoff.

As in Sidney's prior police films, his lead actors spent time riding with real New York City cops. As Burtt Harris recalled, "Nick Nolte was very prepared; he found this guy [a detective] and disappeared for a couple of days, went out on cases with him." And Burtt remembered Timothy Hutton returning with a story of being on a rooftop "when guns came out." Getting the cops right was always a priority with Sidney. One of his drivers in this period was an ex-policeman. The film's dialogue is rife with racial epithets—accepted station house banter. Largely because of this language, the film was heavily edited for broadcast television; it was so cut up, in fact, that Sidney took his name off it, replacing it with the conventional "directed by Alan Smithee," the common pseudonym for directors whose work is altered or recut against their wishes.

The film's representation of New York tribalism extends to the Jewish characters, Leon Blumenfeld (Lee Richardson), a bureau chief in the DA's office, and Preston Perlstein, a disreputable lawyer played by Fyvush Finkel, who, like Sidney, had been a child actor on the Yiddish stage. Sidney enhanced the roles of the Jews beyond their original portrayal in Torres's novel; or rather, he enhanced their expressed Jewishness. Sitting at a bar with Reilly, Blumenfeld drinks scotch and ponders why Jews of his generation drink, given that their immigrant parents did not: "My parents, they came over from Poland. They used to sing this song," and then he sings a verse in Yiddish of "Shiker Is a Goy," which he attempts to translate for Reilly—"'A drunk is a gentile.' And then I forget. . . . He has to drink, because a gentile is a drunk." It's hard to say why Sidney injected this moment into the story; perhaps in Blumenfeld's indulgent nostalgia for his parents' simpler, uncorrupted world, Blumenfeld forecasts the shattering moral compromise he will later display. Neither of the Jewish characters comes out smelling like a rose in this film, but the Jews in his next film, *A Stranger Among Us*, would get an altogether different treatment.

A STRANGER AMONG US

The closed world of Brooklyn's Hasidic community is the setting for this melodrama starring Melanie Griffith as a cynical cop who goes undercover to solve a murder and along the way falls in love and is changed by her contact with this world of believers. Seeing in *A Stranger Among Us* a Jewish version of Peter Weir's 1985 film *Witness*, about a Philadelphia policeman played by Harrison Ford who enters the closed world of the Amish to protect a witness to a murder, critics redubbed Sidney's film with titles like "Witness on Rye" or "Vitness."

The Jewish world portrayed was far from Sidney's experience,

although he identified an indirect connection: "The Hasidic movement came from shtetl life—the small towns outside the big cities
where the very poor Jews resided. They weren't farmers [but] it was as
close to rural society as the Jews ever achieved in Europe. Small town
life, but very poor. My father came from one of those towns, about
eighteen miles outside Warsaw. So culturally I knew quite a bit about
it. Theologically, nothing; well, a little, but it amounted to nothing."
When asked what drew him to this project, Sidney conveyed a strong
personal motive; he made the film, he explained, partly in response
to the rise of anti-Semitism in Europe and the United States. "I'm
not a religious Jew," Sidney asserted, "but I become a fierce religious
Jew when I find anti-Semitism. And I'll tell you the God's honest
truth. My feeling was, you think you've seen Jews? Wait, I'm gonna
show you Jews."

Sidney did not, however, approach the Hasidic community for their
cooperation in the filming. "I thought it would be almost insulting,
disrespectful to ask them, to invade them," Sidney said. Instead he
found a neighborhood in Queens where the crew could refashion
stores to look like the Brooklyn neighborhood where the story is set.
The other major location was 47th Street in Manhattan, the dia-
mond district. Sidney's script supervisor, Martha Pinson, noted the
meticulous preparation that went into filming the forty-eight setups
for an action sequence they had to complete on that block in one day.
She marveled that they managed to finish by two in the afternoon.
In *Making Movies*, Sidney writes about the challenge of shooting on
47th Street, dealing with the elaborate private security network that
protects stores and vaults containing incalculable millions of dollars'
worth of merchandise:

> *When we first went scouting locations, there were four of us. We
> found out later that the private security people had spotted and
> photographed us the first day we walked down the block. Four
> guys walking slowly up and down both sides of the street, stepping
> in front of each store and talking, taking a picture and then
> moving on—that's not a welcome sight on Forty-seventh Street.*

Melanie Griffith, who had been the studio's choice for the role, ultimately received much of the blame for the film's failure; as one critic grumbled, "Griffith waxes and mugs tough, and singsongs through the station house . . . she's no more convincing than an extroverted second-grader play-acting." But Sidney defended her performance: "In my view, you always cast the third act. You cast the final truth of the character. And one of the things that has always moved me in Melanie's work is how open she is. It's extraordinary—the degree of vulnerability and openness in it." Nevertheless, in hindsight she does appear as one of a very few actors who didn't shine under Sidney's direction. One crew member I spoke with recalled that Sidney hadn't had such an easy time with her and that she could be difficult on the set. But Griffith is not the film's only problem; the plot is weak, and, as the *New York Times* reviewer put it, "the Hasidic characters, though vividly rendered, are diminished by the kind of sweeping generosity that makes each one a wise, kindly paragon." Indeed, the male lead, Ariel, played by Eric Thal, is a saintly figure, beautiful to look at, and a gentleman and a scholar ("what Mozart was to music, Ariel is to Jewish scholarship," his friend announces). Griffith's Emily sets her worldly sights on him, and he has his hands full resisting her. Protective of the innocence and purity he saw in Thal's performance, Sidney put out "an edict," as one crew member described it, that there was to be no flirting with him.

Despite its shortcomings, the film movingly conveys the impact on Griffith's Emily of the embrace of a spiritual community; the downsides of such a community, though—insularity, rigidity and the constraints on women—remained unexplored.

Despite the film's negative reviews, Sidney was proud of his re-creation of the Hasidic community. They'd had a Yiddish and religious adviser on the set who advised Sidney and worked diligently with the actors. "We are perfect in every detail," Sidney boasted, noting the irony that "having made such a perfect duplication, the only people who would ever know that won't see the movie."

GUILTY AS SIN

*What happens next. . . . Melodrama is a heightened
theatricality that makes the implausible plausible.*

—SIDNEY LUMET

Sidney had what he called his "brain trust," the small group of intimate friends whom he invited to screenings of early rough cuts of each of his films. His dear friend Phyllis Newman recalled those occasions as "rituals"; typically included were Betty [Lauren] Bacall, Adolph Green, Tony Walton, Gen LeRoy, Walter Bernstein and of course Piedy. Sidney writes in his book that he didn't need to hear a word—he could tell what they thought by the look in their eyes when the lights went up. Nevertheless, they would all head out to a restaurant afterward to talk it all over. "And we'd talk about it, offer lots of suggestions, but," Phyllis smilingly recalled, "Sidney never took one single piece of advice!"

I can imagine the surprise on the faces of Sidney's brain trust when the lights went up after the screening of *Guilty as Sin*, a courtroom drama, sort of, but with several film-noirish twists. "Zestfully trashy" was how one critic aptly characterized the film featuring Rebecca De Mornay as a lawyer of questionable ethics and Don Johnson as a sociopathic gigolo. Shot in Toronto, where Sidney had filmed *Equus* and a few scenes in *Network*, the city doubles for the story's setting, Chicago. The film has a slick look reminiscent of the glass-and-steel design of Sidney's 1986 film, *Power*. Notably it lacks the urban textures and background details of his New York films. Also absent are the distinctive lineaments and voices of minor characters we look for in his films, with the exception of the contributions of character actor Jack Warden, who seems to temper his usual warmth to fit the film's cold ambience.

Guilty as Sin was scripted by television and B movie writer-director Larry Cohen, known in for his outlandish imagination and guerilla filming tactics—regularly shooting on Manhattan streets without permits. His many films include blaxploitation films, campy horror films, and the 1976 *God Told Me To,* which involves a city cop in pursuit of an otherworldly Christ figure who is the instigator of a series of killings and who has—notably—a vagina located near his rib cage. Some consider this cult favorite as the horror film answer to *Dog Day Afternoon.* Cohen was thrilled when Sidney, one of his "great heroes," took on his script, but he felt that Sidney had lost enthusiasm for the project when he couldn't cast his first choice, Paul Newman, who declined because he felt too old for the part. This film was surely a departure for Sidney, and not such a successful one, but it's likely that the challenge of doing and learning something new kept him in the game.

LIFETIME ACHIEVEMENTS

Sidney had received a long list of awards over the years, but the D. W. Griffith Award, the highest honor from the Directors Guild of America, presented to him in 1993 by Martin Scorsese and Milos Forman, meant more than other awards. It came from his peers, and it put him in the company of such previous recipients as Ingmar Bergman, Billy Wilder, Orson Welles, John Huston, David Lean, Alfred Hitchcock and Akira Kurosawa. It was a nice consolation following the critical neglect and drubbing his most recent films had received.

The following year, Sidney celebrated the marriage of his daughter Jenny to actor Bobby Cannavale. The newlyweds were both struggling with their careers at that point. As Jenny later reflected, "It's an excruciating profession. I don't know if I was unhappy because I couldn't get a job or I couldn't get a job because I was unhappy." After *Q & A,* Jenny appeared in two other films, *Assassination* and *Dodgeball,* before deciding to channel her creative energies in new directions.

A MEETING OF MINDS

Sidney also found himself moving in a new direction during this period. He directed a play for the first time in over thirty years, Cynthia Ozick's part-adaptation, part-sequel to her unforgettable stories published under the title *The Shawl*. She was a writer whose work Sidney had long admired, and he was intrigued by this play about "people living in various illusions," as he described it. Set in the late 1970s, the play concerns an elderly former inmate of Auschwitz, Rosa; her niece, Stella, who survived the camp with her; and a seductive stranger who will turn out to be a Holocaust denier who pursues survivors, and, by pretending to assuage their grief, gaslights them into doubting their memories and disbelieving their death-camp experiences. Rosa, played by Dianne Wiest, is haunted by the ghost of her baby, murdered at Auschwitz. She imagines that daughter has grown up to become a doctor whom she conjures at will and to whom she recounts memories of her well-to-do childhood in Warsaw. This facet of the story may have evoked Sidney's memories of his delusional mother, who spoke of her own affluent childhood in Warsaw.

Working closely with Sidney, Ozick found her first theater experience "intoxicating," attending the six-hour daily rehearsals. "I can't keep away," she said. "It's like Mars to me. I sit in that rehearsal room, and they lead me to discoveries in the play that I didn't know were there. I believe that Sidney Lumet is a genius."

Sidney shared Ozick's concern regarding the risks entailed in creating any representation of the Holocaust, of trivialization or exploitation. Sidney said he agreed with Elie Wiesel that "artists should leave the Holocaust alone." Of his film *The Pawnbroker* (1964), about an embittered survivor living out his life in New York, Sidney said that the script called for real newsreel footage of the Nazi death camps, "and there was no way I would have done that. That would have been the final obscenity." He felt that Ozick's play was "about what is going on in the world today," by which he meant the rise of Holocaust denial. "It's amazing to me that people are totally unaware that [Holocaust denial] is a respected opinion all over the world. I once spoke to

Steven Spielberg about it, and he feels the same way." This was when Spielberg was using profits from his Oscar-winning *Schindler's List* to create the Shoah Foundation, sending camera crews around the world to record Holocaust testimony from survivors for posterity. Indeed, this period, the mid-1990s, was seeing the return to Europe of ethnic cleansing in Bosnia, as well as a rise in Holocaust denial. "There's a kind of insanity sweeping the world," Sidney exclaimed, "and there's no logical rebuttal for it. . . . Would you get into a discussion about whether the world is flat?"

The staging of Ozick's play began in the summer of 1994 at the Bay Street Theatre in Sag Harbor, which was run by Emma Walton Hamilton, the daughter of Sidney's dear friend Tony Walton and his first wife, English actress and singer, Julie Andrews. Two years later, after Sidney completed the filming of *Night Falls on Manhattan*, Ozick's play, considerably revised and now titled *The Blue Light*, had a brief run in Manhattan. Sidney said that returning to the theater was "like getting into an old pair of shoes," but the reviews were not what they had hoped. Here was another lesson for Sidney about how important the camera was to his art, a lesson that came at a timely moment, as Sidney took a turn down a new path.

THE BOOK

When I asked those close to him why Sidney decided to write *Making Movies*, the answer was always the same: he wasn't working; he didn't have a script he liked. He wrote the book by hand on a legal pad. "He'd come in to the office, and if he wasn't reading a script he would sit and write," Lili Jacobs recalled. He asked her to type it up, and here or there she offered a suggestion. It took him about three months to write the full manuscript. "Basically, it just flowed out of him," Lili said.

After having recently taught a film course at Yale, he was ever more convinced of what students needed to learn in order to answer the simplest question: Where do I put the camera? He said he "was so tired of the theory," by which he meant the French psychoanalytically inflected film theory that was, and generally remains, popular with graduate students. And he "was amazed at the ignorance of the students," by which he meant their lack of knowledge about how movies are actually made. He wanted to write a book that would become part of film school curricula, and that's exactly what he achieved. He admitted to being perennially clueless about what would make a hit movie (he remarked once that only Walt Disney and Steven Spielberg possessed an innate sense of what audiences would love), but he knew exactly how to aim his book to land where he'd intended. "And," Lili laughed, "he wanted the residuals." It seems odd that many of the younger readers of *Making Movies* have never seen a single one of his films.

He was pleased with how the book turned out, later marveling, "it's so simple, clear, direct, so non-bullshit." It is indeed a work of demystification that nevertheless increases the reader's sense of the magic of movies. And it's practical; he explains a daily call sheet, entry by entry, and he generously reveals many tricks of the trade, like "doing a Groucho," when an actor lowers her body before sitting to avoid angling the camera too far and shooting into the lights; or a "banana," which involves an actor arcing slightly away from the camera as she moves left to right; or explaining where body mikes are hidden. His enthusiasm for every aspect of the job—with the possible exception of sound mixing, which he found tedious—comes through in the dynamism of his prose. And we get glimpses of Sidney himself, speaking unselfconsciously as a man who gets up in the morning to do his job:

> *My alarm will go off at seven. I'll get picked up at eight, so I have an hour for coffee, a bagel,* The New York Times, *and getting my head ready for the day's work. . . . I've laid out my blue jeans, shirt, socks, sneakers in another room so that I don't disturb my wife. With my coffee I scan page 1. The object is to get as quickly as possible to the crossword puzzle, so that I can empty my mind completely and start the day fresh. A second cup*

of coffee, and I'm ready to open my script and look over the scene or scenes scheduled for the day.

In *Making Movies*, Sidney observes that it is important to make each project *personal* in one way or another. Writing this book about his work was of course very personal to Sidney. It was, though, entirely unlike his effort to write the memoir he began soon after this book's great success. The memoir took him to such dark places that he could not continue with it. Work was where he was safe; it was a story he could tell with ease and joy. The book went through eight printings while still in hardcover; it has been translated into at least a dozen languages and remains a key text for aspiring filmmakers well into the digital era.

GRAY AREAS: NIGHT FALLS ON MANHATTAN

Look, . . . this picture is the most autobiographical in the sense that all I'm trying to do is the best I can in whatever the system is.

—SIDNEY LUMET, 1997 INTERVIEW

Shortly after completing *Making Movies*, a tantalizing script came Sidney's way, a retelling by Paul Schrader (*Taxi Driver, Raging Bull*) of the 1970 Italian black-humor crime drama *Investigation of a Citizen Above Suspicion*. Sidney was eager to do it, but the financing collapsed, and the film was never made. It was a disappointment, but as always, he kept moving forward, by developing the next project, *Night Falls on Manhattan*.

Sidney returned to familiar territory with *Night Falls on Manhattan*; it's about an idealistic DA and former cop, played by Andy Garcia, who runs into the buzz saw of city politics, corruption and compromise, some of it involving his beloved father. Sidney adapted it from the novel *Tainted Evidence* by Robert Daley, who also wrote the book on which *Prince of the City* was based. The story was in-spired by the 1988 trial of large-scale drug dealer Larry Davis for a shootout with the police that left six cops wounded. Davis' lawyer, the controversial, grandstanding attorney William Kunstler, who was known as "the most loved and hated lawyer in America," contended that Davis had fired in self-defense, fearing that the police intended to murder him because they had been in business together and he knew too much about payoffs and drug dealing in local police pre-cincts. Sidney altered Daley's novel in substantial ways; he changed Daley's central character, the young DA, from a woman to a man, and he created a central father-son relationship between the DA and one of the cops wounded at the scene. Another poignant detail was added to the Kunstler character, played by Richard Dreyfuss: he has lost his fifteen-year-old daughter to a drug overdose. When Garcia's character, Sean Casey, asks him why he is so invested in nailing "dirty cops," Dreyfuss replies, "You know when your kid dies before you . . . it's not the natural order of things." Sidney builds up personal motivation and family connections in the story, and we can see a con-nection to Sidney's contemporaneous concerns over the threat that drugs posed within his own family.

Sidney saw this one as a comeback picture. He changed things up, hiring Oscar-winning cinematographer David Watkin, who'd shot *Chariots of Fire*, *Out of Africa* and the Beatles' *Help!* Wynton Marsalis created a beautiful score. Sidney cast Andy Garcia, trusting what he called "his purity"; he was intrigued that Garcia had seri-ously considered becoming a priest, and Sidney tried, when around him, to tone down some of his typically colorful language. He gave a juicy part to James Gandolfini, who had played a minor character in *A Stranger Among Us*; Sidney adored Gandolfini and praised and nourished his talent. The male leads and several supporting parts were multilayered, but Sidney's screenplay, alas, did not give his fe-male lead, Lena Olin, much to work with.

Sidney ran into trouble filming the final scene. It wasn't working. "I had reached this perfect moral dilemma and I couldn't find a reso-lution," Sidney said, referring to the choice Sean Casey faced between adhering to the letter of the law by letting a killer go free, or making a shady deal to keep him in prison. "The first ending I wrote was a scene on the beach where Andy quits the DA's office. But that isn't what I set out to do. So I reversed it. I shot it again, but that was so gung-ho I couldn't stand it. Yecch—it really looked as if we were just trying to make a happy ending." Sidney decided to call upon a playwright he admired, Jon Robin Baitz (*Other Desert Cities, The Substance of Fire*), to help him with Casey's final speech. "We had supper and I showed him the scene," Sidney said. "He came up with my favorite lines about working as a prosecutor," spoken by Garcia's character to a new crop of young assistant district attorneys: "If you are in it for the hustle, you'll find a case you really care about and you'll lose it and it will break your heart. . . . If you are in it because you think you're a saint, you'll find you have to make a deal and you'll win it and it will break your heart." He tells them that they will not spend their careers in the black or the white, but rather in the gray.

You need to be an attentive viewer of Sidney's police corruption films—*Serpico, Prince of the City, Q&A, Night Falls on Manhattan*—to tease out the different emphases in each of them. In *Night Falls*, Sidney explicitly addresses what is implied in the others: how police corruption often operates on a smaller scale than the corruption higher up the food chain. In dialogue written by Sidney, Sean Casey's father, played by Ian Holm, talks about the drug protection money a dozen of his fellow cops divided among themselves:

Six hundred thousand dollars a year? Six hundred thousand dollars a year? How many can resist that? How many doctors, lawyers . . . the bastards who put the gas tanks in the wrong place? Those fucks that buy boats with other people's life savings. Tell me, who can resist six hundred thousand dollars? I'll tell you who: twenty-seven thousand other cops on the force, that's who. Or maybe it's twenty-six thousand or twenty-five thousand. Or maybe it's twenty thousand. But it's more than the rest of the goddam country.

Like *Prince of the City*, *Night Falls* highlights the entanglements that compromise our actions, but in all but this last film the main character leaves the system, in one way or another. Sidney again explores the disillusionments and moral injuries that wear away at ideals and morale, and how little good intentions matter when struggling against a corrupt system—but his hero, nevertheless, does not quit.

At the opening-night party for *Night Falls on Manhattan*, held at the 21 Club, Mayor Rudolph Giuliani was scheduled to officially declare Sidney Lumet Day in New York City. (Giuliani's wife at the time, Donna Hanover, had a small part in the film as a TV newscaster.) Among the guests, along with the film's stars, were fashion designer Calvin Klein, Hollywood mogul Barry Diller and the granddaughter of William Randolph Hearst and former kidnapping victim, Patty Hearst. When the mayor failed to show up, Sidney's friend Alan King was asked to do the honors by announcing the proclamation. "What kind of deal is this," Sidney joked, "I get my day declared at 10:30 P.M.?"

AND NOW FOR SOMETHING COMPLETELY DIFFERENT: CRITICAL CARE & GLORIA

"A no-budget black comedy" was how Sidney described *Critical Care*. Getting funding for a movie about death, dying and what's wrong with the health-care system was no easy task, but Sidney believed in the project and loved the script, written by Steven Schwartz, whom Sidney would later hire to write for his TV series *100 Centre Street*. On this project, Sidney worked for less money than usual, and the cast followed suit. He returned to Toronto to shoot the film because the production costs were lower. Doubtless for marketing purposes, Sidney compared the film to *Network*, and said he hoped it would do for health care what *Network* had done for television—expose it. But the film is really nothing like *Network* or any of Sidney's previous films. "It's hard to describe," he said of it. "It's so different from anything I've ever done or anything I've ever *seen*."

Much of the action takes place in an intensive care unit—designed by Philip Rosenberg—that has the feel of a space pod, bathed in heavenly white light. Helen Mirren plays a caring, witty nurse whose playful contretemps with James Spader, a young physician "on the make," are funny and, in the end, quite moving. Albert Brooks is Dr. Butz, dotty and besotted, in charge of the intensive care unit. Brooks' deadpan is hilarious as he voices the revenue argument in favor of keeping well-insured patients alive as long as possible, without regard to their suffering. When Spader's Dr. Ernst proposes they cancel a procedure to insert a feeding tube into a man who has been comatose for months and is close to death, Brooks responds, "You think just because someone's going to die soon, we don't need to feed them? I've news for you! We're all gonna die! So why should any of us eat?"

As Sidney observed, the film was "a difficult mix of drama, realism, comedy, and fantasy," and indeed it is, with Wallace Shawn as "Satan's little helper," appearing intermittently to a dying patient played by Jeffrey Wright, and Anne Bancroft as an angel-like nun, hallucinated by and spouting off to Dr. Ernst. As Sidney knew from his experience on *The Wiz*, fantasy is especially hard to get right, and he worried that the opening sequence, in which the camera follows Helen Mirren as she checks on each of her patients, might not signal to viewers that it was "alright to laugh" at the jokes soon to follow. Sidney called on his friend Nora Ephron for advice. In an inadvertent borrowing from the 1986 British miniseries *The Singing Detective*, Ephron suggested playing "Dem Bones" during the sequence, and Sidney chose a wonderful version by the Delta Rhythm Boys. Lili Jacobs recalled that Anne Bancroft's husband, Mel Brooks, had come up to Toronto; they had dinner together and Sidney may have picked up a few tips.

It is unabashedly a movie with a message, culminating in a scene where Spader, who has found himself in a compromised position, is confronted with hospital administrators and attorneys, the insurance companies' attorneys and the attorneys of feuding family members. He pleads with them to listen to the patient's wishes, and for ethical care—a worthy message, to be sure. It doesn't all come together, but the movie nonetheless contains much that is strange and artful; and it proposes, as the popular TV medical comedy drama *Scrubs* would do a few years later, that, amidst the hospital's sterility and technology, unseen spirits roam.

The film didn't find its audience, and Sidney complained that it had been "catastrophically distributed." He lamented that for "pictures like that, you need the *Times* . . . to launch you . . . and we didn't get the *Times*."

Unlike *Critical Care*, for which Sidney worked hard for funding, *Gloria*, a remake of a 1980 John Cassavetes film, fell into his lap when the prior director exited over "creative differences" just as the film was set to go into production. The producers offered too much money for Sidney to turn down. Sharon Stone had been cast in the role Gena Rowlands had played in the original, a former gangster's girlfriend who goes on the run to protect a six-year-old boy being chased by the mob. Besides his dread of not working, Sidney may have been drawn to the project because much of the action takes place at street level, in delicatessens, pawnshops and hotels. To his surprise, Sidney found the work arduous; he noted, "Although I'm associated with shooting in real places, the truth is that I don't like doing it anymore." Sharon Stone, thirty-four years Sidney's junior, also found the shooting strenuous. "Sidney's a killer," she said with a laugh. "He had us in the streets of New York for two months of real traffic and real people, instead of well-fed extras and picture cars. Life was all around us with chaotic, obtrusive, frenetic energy. It was throw and go. . . . You get out of the car, get a take and you're out of there. It was commando filmmaking." Sidney was challenged by directing six-year-old Jean-Luke Figueroa; it wasn't easy to get his energy going in the right direction. Sidney said that working on the streets, and specifically action scenes, were helpful in getting Figueroa connected to the story. Cassavetes fans balked at the film for its "sweeter" tones than the original, and critics complained that Sidney let some scenes sag. *Rolling Stone* called the film "a stink bomb."

Following *Gloria*, a great script arrived in the mail one day, an adaptation of the 1986 Polish novel *The Beautiful Mrs. Seidenman* by Andrzej Szczypiorski. Lili read it and handed it excitedly to Sidney. Set in Warsaw, where Sidney's parents came from, the screenplay told the story of a Jewish woman during the war who poses as the gentile widow of a Polish officer; it follows her story through the postwar communist era, during which time she gets a political foothold with all the benefits thereof, but soon she begins to fall apart emotionally from the strain of living a false life. The screenplay ends with her making her way to Israel. Sidney was gung-ho, but European producer Arthur Cohn (*The Garden of the Finzi-Continis*) and he could not agree on casting. Sidney wanted Angelina Jolie, but Cohn didn't know who she was and didn't think she'd draw a European audience. (The following year Jolie won an Oscar for her role in *Girl, Interrupted.*) They approached Isabelle Adjani and flew her to New York for a meeting, but the deal didn't gel. Sidney wasn't crazy about relying on foreign money, which had become more available in recent years, because it complicated casting and increased reliance on a narrower cadre of stars. So instead, Sidney decided to take a little break from making movies.

THE CHEESE

Sidney and Piedy had moved from their East Side town house to Manhattan's West Side, first to the landmarked Hotel des Artistes building on West 67th Street and then to a spacious apartment in another landmark building on Central Park West, one that was home to many theater greats, including their close friends, actress Phyllis Newman and lyricist Adolph Green. Their social life had shifted a bit with the happy presence of Piedy's daughter Leslie's children, whom Sidney enjoyed. Piedy showed me some family photographs, and among them were many of Sidney with the kids, beaming with what Jenny called his jack-o'-lantern smile.

In 1995 Sidney's first grandchild, Jacob Carlo Lumet Cannavale, was born to Jenny and her husband Bobby. Bobby shared with me his sweet memory of watching Sidney bathe the baby in the sink while he sang "The Farmer in the Dell," always emphasizing the line "The Cheese stands alone": "Jake had all these folds and wrinkles, and Sidney would love him and laugh at him. He adored him. He called him 'the Cheese.'" Sometimes Sidney would fall asleep with the baby napping on his chest. Lili Jacobs said that when Jenny brought the baby to the office, "he could have gotten into the carriage with him. . . . He adored him so; he adored all the grandchildren, Piedy's too."

Bobby and Jenny lived near Sidney and Piedy. "Sidney would be shooting a movie," Bobby reminisced, "and we'd come over to the house for dinner at six with Jake, and we'd be out of there by eight thirty so he could go to bed at nine thirty." Bobby recalled that he would often run into Sidney on the street; it meant a lot to Bobby that "Sidney knew how to do everything for himself, like a regular person, have friends who are regular people, be someone who knows how to go to a hardware store, to keep the bills." To Bobby, Sidney represented a family man par excellence: "He showed me that you can do both; you can be true to your art and your vision and be a person who can be with your family." Sidney had always loved children; with Bobby he was exploring a new part of himself, as father figure to a son.

"Sidney was like a father to me," Bobby said. When Jake was born Bobby was still just getting started as an actor, on stage and in television. "Sidney would say to me, 'Just say yes to everything, so that you're going to work in the morning as an actor. It doesn't matter if you have any lines or how bad the project is.' He was right," Bobby reflected. "I learned from watching everybody. I felt like a working actor, even if I had to supplement it bartending." Sidney cast Bobby, first in small roles, in *Night Falls on Manhattan* (1996) and *Gloria* (1999), and then in a major role in *100 Centre Street* (2001–2002), as the cocky, ambitious assistant district attorney J. J. Jellinek.

Jenny, Bobby and the baby often drove out to East Hampton to spend time with Sidney and Piedy. "He loved having us come," Bobby reminisced. He and Sidney sometimes sat together in his TV room upstairs, where "he had his chair, and all his films lined up next to the TV," and they watched movies together. "I would watch his movies with him. I remember the first time I saw *The Hill*. He wanted to show me, to show me the acting in it. He wanted me to see Ossie Davis and Sean Connery and how they worked together in that film. 'You see that performance of those two guys?'" Bobby quoted Sidney. "'That's rehearsal. They're very different, but by the end of three weeks of rehearsal they were one.'"

Sidney also played a mentoring role for an important film in which Bobby co-starred, *The Station Agent*. Bobby introduced Sidney to first-time writer and director Tom McCarthy. (McCarthy would later hit it big with his 2015 film *Spotlight*, which took the Oscars for Best Picture and Best Screenplay.) Sidney spent a lot of time with McCarthy, talking about the script and advising him about running a movie set. As McCarthy recalled:

> *I remember I was having a panic attack before* The Station Agent *and he said, "Look, if you know what a scene is about, it will block itself. You'll KNOW where to put that camera." He was right. I always find that when I don't know what I'm doing with the camera, it's because I don't understand the scene. We haven't been honest to the scene.*

McCarthy said he watched Lumet's *The Verdict* over and over in preparation for *The Station Agent* in order to emulate the feel of that film. In Bobby's view, though, Sidney's most important contribution to *The Station Agent* was impressing on McCarthy the value of rehearsal. "I think that's why people like that movie," Bobby said, "because they feel they know those characters, their relationships— that's from the rehearsals." He went on to recall that the morning after the film's opening, "I came to Sidney and said I wanted to sit down and have him tell me what he liked about the film. I wanted notes. He said, 'But you've already done the movie. What do you want notes for?' His approval meant everything to me." Bobby recalled some of Sidney's observations on his character in the film: "Oh, Bobby, that character just wants and wants and wants friendship so bad; he doesn't care how embarrassing it might be at times. That's really how it is, isn't it? And we don't get to see men do that with other men."

Most emphatically, Bobby talked about how Sidney showed his love, man to man; it was a welcome contrast, as Bobby's father had not been much on the scene when he was growing up. As Bobby recalled, "Sidney would hug you and hold the hug and tell you he loved you, looking you right in your eyes. I never had a relationship like that with another man." He continued, "When he looked at you and held your face in his hands you felt seen, really seen. There aren't many people like that in that world."

21

LIFE ALL AROUND

*It's never lonely . . . life all around. You are constantly
communicating with and dealing in feelings between yourself
and others. There's a sense of energy . . . actors are fun, and
always interesting, endlessly interesting . . .*
— SIDNEY LUMET, ON DIRECTING, FROM A 2001 INTERVIEW

100 CENTRE STREET

Around him you couldn't be grand—it didn't work.
— DAVID BLACK,
CO-EXECUTIVE PRODUCER OF *100 CENTRE STREET*

Sidney said that this TV series gave him the happiest directing experience of his life. He enjoyed the daily-ness of the schedule and the
sustained relationships that were built in the creating and filming of
thirty-one episodes over two seasons. Long before hotshot directors
were getting involved in television production, NBC approached
Sidney about doing a TV series, but Sidney didn't follow trends, plus
he'd been holding on to an idea for a show for almost ten years:

When I was doing research for Prince of the City, *I went
to night court. I couldn't believe the sheer drama of it: the
juxtaposition of the banal, with everybody bored, yet the fate*

*of people's lives is being decided. I sat there and thought, my
God, this is the most natural TV series I've ever seen. There are
so many stories, with so many fixed, regular characters—the
judges, and lawyers, and repeat offenders. And the cases were so
varied.*

NBC made him a handsome offer to write a pilot, and when they took
a pass on it, Sidney stuck it in a drawer, a little relieved because he expected that NBC wouldn't have let him do what he wanted anyway.
He didn't want to tell stories about solving crimes or showcasing
trials. He had a different idea about exploring this well-covered territory, and he was convinced that a network would not be interested
in featuring "a recurring plotline about Zen Buddhism . . . mak[ing]
one of the heroes of the show a lousy father," and allowing characters
to deliver four-page speeches.

When A&E came knocking, very few dramatic series had been tried
on cable at that point, beginning with HBO's *Oz*, which premiered
in 1997. Written by Tom Fontana, with whom Sidney would later collaborate, *Oz* was set in a fictional maximum-security prison; airing
on cable meant it could be edgier and contain more violence and
explicit language than anything on network TV. *Oz* paved the way
for HBO's runaway hit series *The Sopranos*, which featured Sidney's
friend James Gandolfini in his first starring role, and the success of
that show sent all the cable networks searching for original dramatic
series. In Sidney's estimation, if cable TV meant he could try something outside the broadcast norm, he was in. Clinching it for him was
being able to experiment with the new technology of high-definition
digital video, which so far had only been used for sportscasting. It
would allow him to return to a modified live-television style; he
would tape scenes with three HD cameras, without stopping for new
setups. "It revives a fifty-year-old trick I did as a child of live TV,"
Sidney said, and he was excited about this method "because of the
kind of energy that the live technique will provide for the actors." It
also cut down on time—and Sidney was always for that.

He loved the look of HD, the sharpness and detail, taking in twice the visual information as traditional video: "It gave me what my eye saw," he said. "I really feel this is the way of the future"—and he was right. HD is currently the standard format used for most broadcasts and movies. But initially it took a little getting used to. David Black, Sidney's co-executive producer on the show, recalled one day when they were shooting in an apartment on West End Avenue that Alan Arkin, who played Joe Rifkind, a night court judge, was standing in front of a window, and he was in perfect focus, but they soon realized that a man in a window across the street was also in perfect focus; they had to alter the setup to adjust to the new technology. The show has something of the look of afternoon soap operas, also filmed live-on-tape, except that Sidney brings depth and texture to the images. The show's title, *100 Centre Street*, is the actual address of the criminal court in Manhattan, and the series does a good job re-creating the grime and chaos of the place, as people are churned through the system night after night.

Sidney wrote and co-wrote several episodes, but he also worked closely with a host of writers, urging them to script the stories they most passionately wanted to tell. Among his writers were Bob Leuci, the former narcotics detective on whom *Prince of the City* was based, and novelist and screenwriter Rudy Wurlitzer. Sidney created the central character, Joe Rifkind, a liberal Jewish judge, with Alan Arkin in mind. And for the tough-on-crime colleague and friend, Attallah "Queenie" Sims, Sidney sought out LaTanya Richardson (the wife of actor Samuel L. Jackson). LaTanya recalled that when discussing the role, Sidney "shared some things about the character. You know she was gay, and at the time it was not a popular character to put on television, and he shared some personal information about a friend who is a judge, the one he was patterning her after. I did get to meet her."

Sidney wrote his friend and neighbor Phyllis Newman into the story as the wife of Judge Rifkind. Her appearance was initially planned as a one-off, but the chemistry between the two actors was so winning that she became a regular on the series. It made sense to enhance the story line of Rifkind's private life; Sidney wanted to explore "the cost [the job] has to take in terms of the judges—the kind of internal exhaustion that must come from having to take on somebody's life, and the responsibility for somebody's life." At the end of the first season, Sidney learned that Alan Arkin had an interest in Zen Buddhism. "So," Sidney said, "I invented the idea of a daughter who had been gone all of those years, and all of a sudden she's back in his life and she has been a part of [Zen Buddhism]."

Sidney was particularly proud of the show's racial makeup; it resembled that of the city more than any other show at that time. Many episodes followed an A, B, C plot structure, shifting among the public defenders, the DAs, and the two judges, presenting a range of perspectives on the criminal justice system. As David Black observed, the show was Talmudic. It had—and still has—its devoted following.

MENTORING

In the preface to his book, Sidney lamented that when he began making movies there were only two kinds of jobs open to women: editor and script girl. He noted that film crews still remained predominantly male, but he hoped that "people working in the movies today have been brought up in a far more equally balanced world than I was." He took the opportunity of the TV series to do something about it. He devised a plan to have the Directors Guild of America fund an apprenticeship for up-and-coming women directors.

Sidney had seen the film *Shadrach* (1998) by first-time director Susanna Styron, daughter of writer William Styron, who was a friend of Piedy's. Impressed by her work, Sidney invited Susanna Styron to participate in *100 Centre Street*, along with a group that included Liz Garbus (who later produced such documentaries as *Ghosts of Abu Ghraib* and directed and produced others like *What Happened, Miss Simone?*) and Siobhan Byrne O'Connor (who later became a television producer of shows including *Blue Bloods* and *Law & Order: Criminal Intent*). When the Directors Guild failed to come through with the money, some of the group decided to come along to *100 Centre Street* on their own time.

Susanna Styron shadowed Sidney for months, loving every minute of it. One afternoon he handed her a script and told her to be ready to direct a scene the next morning. Although she had directed a film before, she was worried about calling the shots with three cameras, a filming technique Sidney had been teaching her. She said she was so nervous that she broke out in hives. "But it was great," nevertheless. "I felt like Sidney believed in me, that he wanted me to succeed; he was behind me." Like so many others, she was amazed at the quality of his energy—"He was always very present, very *there*"—and his concentration: "Sidney did not multitask. His intense focus was on one thing at a time." Sidney encouraged Susanna to work up a script; she brought him an outline and later a draft on which they consulted, and soon she found herself directing what she'd written, an episode called "Bottlecaps," about a man whose unaccountably odd behavior with his lawyer and his family is discovered to have been caused by a brain tumor. Sidney was thrilled with her work, and he let her know that he wanted her to continue writing and directing for the series in the upcoming season. But much to everyone's surprise and sadness, A&E unexpectedly canceled the series before they began shooting season 3.

When I asked LaTanya Richardson why she thought Sidney had decided to mentor women, she said, "He saw the tide changing and made a choice; he could be an agent of change or not." And she added that he hired women who "looked like real women in that world. He wasn't interested in the American female ideal."

"And everyone on the crew loved him" was a common refrain among the many people I spoke with who worked on the show. The cast and crew shared an amazing outpouring of affection for Sidney: "He knew everyone's name"; "He counseled a crewmember who was going through a rough divorce"; "He was a happy bundle of energy"; "He was quick to laugh; he loved to be amused"; "It was a no-blame, no-shame set"; "Sidney was the opposite of anxious"; "On Sidney's shows, everyone had lunch with everybody; it just was not hierarchical the way it usually is"; "I never saw him berate an actor; if he didn't like what you did, he'd say, 'Darling, Darling, I'm not sure that's what we want' or 'Can we try it this way?'"; "He created a safe space where people could be as creative as they could"; and "He protected his people more than any other director I know. One time he finished a shoot three days early, and the studio threatened not to pay the crew for those three days. Sidney said, 'No. You don't dock people for being efficient.'"

For the first season, the show was shot at both 80 Centre Street, the building next door to where the show is set, and at the Kaufman Astoria Studios, where Sidney had worked as a child actor and where later he was instrumental in advocating for the studio's restoration. But Sidney wasn't so happy that the studio required you to use their equipment and caterer and pay them at a premium. He had noticed nearby an old coffee-processing plant that was no longer in operation. He leased it, and within a month he had it soundproofed and ready. It wasn't glamorous, and when the weather was warm the smell of coffee would permeate, but it did the job. It was—and still is—called Hellgate Studios.

SEPTEMBER 11, 2001

From the roof of Hellgate you could see everything, a clear shot down the East River to the Twin Towers. Inside the studio there were dozens of TV monitors, but none of them were hooked up. Everyone was standing around a radio in Sidney's office in stunned silence; "It was like a scene from a World War II movie," Susanna Styron recalled. People were getting emotional, and no one knew what to do. Sidney called everyone together into the studio's largest space, the courtroom set; they were about seventy-five people, lighting, electric, and sound crews, actors, costumers, makeup, editors, office staff, teamsters. No one recalled Sidney's exact words, but one crewmember said it was like listening to Jimmy Stewart in a Frank Capra movie. Sidney announced that the bridges were closed and the subway was shut down, but that anyone who needed to get to their family, and had a way to do so, should go. He went on to list the national disasters he'd lived through, and that it was his personal experience that when things were bad, work was what kept him going. Some recalled that he spoke about how people grieve in different ways. He said he was going to keep working—that if he went home, he would only sit and watch the television and fret. He reiterated that unless you need to be with your loved ones, you may want to stay and keep your mind occupied. Most people stayed, a few people left. Sidney ordered in cots, blankets, and food in case they needed to shelter in place.

Some were appalled that Sidney kept working on that tragic day, a day he called "a cataclysm." He was criticized for it in the newspapers. But he didn't think working was disrespectful. For him it was coping.

A few months later, when he was asked if he was planning to incorporate the events of September 11 into *100 Centre Street*, Sidney said, "I don't think we should touch it." He thought it would be exploitative.

GOLDEN YEARS?

Sidney was entering his eighties. He was not particularly interested in slowing down, but work was not the only place he was experiencing "life all around." Receiving ever more invitations to be honored here and abroad, Sidney continued to enjoy the travel and the hobnobbing. But home was also a lively, happy place. Piedy was youthful, spry, and playful; for Sidney she was the perfect mix of self-reliant and giving. Sidney accepted without complaint that she didn't much like to join him in watching television, preferring to read, and she refused to sit up front in the car when Sidney was driving; but she loved their jaunts abroad as much as she loved working in her East Hampton garden. Sidney's oldest friends, Tony Walton, Gen LeRoy and Phyllis Newman, among others I spoke with, lit up at the mention of Piedy's name—cherishing her friendship.

In 2004, Jenny's marriage to Bobby Cannavale came to an end. Sidney and Piedy were there for her. It was not a contentious divorce, but as Sidney well knew, the end of a marriage breaks hearts. He made more time for the family, enjoying his grandson, Jake, who was precocious like his mother and bursting with talent. Jake would make his first on-screen appearance at age ten, joining his father, Bobby Cannavale, in a project written and directed by John Turturro, *Romance & Cigarettes* (2005), that starred Sidney's friends James Gandolfini and Christopher Walken, and a host of other stars. When the family gathered at Sidney and Piedy's, it was a sizable bunch that might include, along with Jenny and Jake, Piedy's children, Leslie and Bailey—with their spouses and children—four belonging to Leslie and three to Bailey. Sidney loved to feed them all, and word was that his cooking kept getting better and better.

GLORIA REDUX

In 2011, shortly after Sidney's death, Gloria Vanderbilt published a small collection of stories, or, perhaps more properly, vignettes, memories, and commentaries, called *The Things We Fear Most*, which she dedicated "In loving memory of S. L." One of the stories is about her last encounter with Sidney. Its title, "My Little Mouse," refers to the playful morning drawings Sidney often left for her before he went off to work, portraying the couple as Mr. and Mrs. Mouse. She recounts the sudden urge she had to phone him one day, "asking to see him for there was something I urgently needed to tell him." She said that when he "materialized" at her door it was "as if in answer to a wish—from a genie out of a bottle." She apologized to him for how she had treated him those many years ago, emphasizing her regret that she had put off having children with him. She quotes Sidney as having said, "But I was never angry with you, pain, yes, but never anger, because I knew you were searching." They made a plan to lunch together, but as the day approached, Sidney put it off, then finally sent her a letter explaining that he thought it best that they not meet. Gloria quotes it: "There is nothing you could ask of me that I wouldn't give if I had it. So please think of me fondly, as I do of you. And forgive my desire for a peaceful time for the remaining years."

STRIP SEARCH

This controversial 2004 production for HBO was the brainchild of screenwriter Tom Fontana (*Oz, Borgia*). The idea for this didactic story arose, he explained, "out of my sadness, and deep concern about the eroding of our country's Bill of Rights, after September 11." With the passage of the Patriot Act and related legislation, he saw elected leaders convincing American citizens to surrender their most basic liberties. The script crosscuts between parallel narratives of an American graduate student (Maggie Gyllenhaal) detained for questioning in Beijing and an Arab graduate student (Bruno Lastra) detained in the same circumstances in New York. Both characters are held without being charged or given access to lawyers, and both are subject to intimidation and humiliating strip searches. The matter of their guilt or innocence is left ambiguous. The script in the two locations is virtually identical, hammering home the point that the FBI in New York, like the military in China, was following an authoritarian playbook.

Fontana had given the script to HBO, which then suggested sending it to Sidney. "I was stunned and immediately intimidated," Tom Fontana recalled. "So Sidney and I got on the phone and within moments he made me at ease with his warmth. And his confidence in my writing." Sidney told him, "I was around during the McCarthy years. This film could get us both blacklisted. So let's do it right."

Fontana recalled that Sidney read with all of the actors, including Glenn Close, who played the FBI interrogator, and Ken Leung, who played her counterpart in Beijing. Sidney said, "I want to look the actor directly in his eyes," an indication of his sense of the stakes for all the actors in appearing in this production. Maggie Gyllenhaal and Bruno Lastra had the challenge of performing a significant portion of the piece in the nude. HBO aired the fifty-six-minute show once and then pulled it—even though it was scheduled for multiple airings. Sidney was pretty confident that a very high-level person at Time Warner, HBO's parent company at the time, had pulled the plug. Fontana wanted to mount a protest, but Sidney counseled restraint: "Wait," he said. "The world will come around." In the week following the show's only broadcast in April 2004, the shocking revelations broke of prisoner torture and abuse by U.S. Army personnel and the CIA at Abu Ghraib prison in Iraq. The connection was not lost on Sidney or Fontana between the degrading, often sexual abuses and "enhanced interrogation techniques" perpetrated on Iraqi detainees and the chillingly sexualized behavior of Glenn Close's FBI agent as she abuses the Arab student she is questioning. For several years *Strip Search* was locked away, only to resurface on HBO fourteen years later.

AN ARIA ON THE LOWER EAST SIDE

Sidney always said that in New York he could find locations that could pass for almost anywhere in the world. In 2004 he shot an aria from a nineteenth-century French opera, set in fifteenth-century Germany, on Norfolk Street on Manhattan's Lower East Side, in a synagogue built in 1849 in the Gothic Revival style. This twelve-minute film, titled after the aria "Rachel, quand du Seigneur," is from Fromental Halévy's 1835 opera *La Juive* (The Jewess). In this short piece, Sidney's love and deep knowledge of music finds singular expression. It is notable and curious that only a handful of Sidney's films boast distinguished scores, suggesting that he may have been reluctant to combine his two passions.

Although written by a Jewish composer, the opera centers on Eléazar, a stiff-necked Jewish character often called the "Shylock of opera," an anti-Semitic staple who, like Shakespeare's Jew, is nevertheless given depth and complexity. Here he is performed by Neil Shicoff. The opera that Sidney turned his unwavering focus on had been popular and well known until it was banned by the Nazis in 1936. Its tortuous plot turns on Eléazar, the Jew, who has been forced to watch the executions of his two sons during a pogrom instigated by Count Brogni, a Christian cardinal. When Brogni's estate is later sacked, Eléazar secretly saves Brogni's baby, whom he names Rachel and lovingly raises as his own. Years later a Christian prince falls in love with her, and in order to win her, he poses as a Jew. Without knowledge of her own Christian blood or of the prince's deception, Rachel agrees to marry him, but when his identity is revealed, he, Rachel and Eléazar are all condemned to death for violating the laws against intermarriage. Eléazar considers saving Rachel's life by informing the cardinal that she is his own daughter, but he grows defiant when he hears voices in the street calling for the blood of the Jews. This is when Eléazar sings the aria "Rachel, quand du Seigneur."

> *Rachel, when the Lord entrusted*
> *Your cradle to my hands*
> *I pledged my entire life to your happiness,*
> *And it is I who now delivers you to the executioner.*
> *I hear a voice calling me: I am young, I want to live,*
> *Dear father, spare your child.*
> *Oh, Rachel, it is I, your loving father,*
> *Who delivers you to the executioner.*

Seeing the aria as "essentially a prayer," Sidney set the piece in the synagogue, adding to the staging some new elements: after Rachel materializes in her father's imagination, his torment increases. When no solution presents itself, "he feels that even God has failed him," Sidney explained, "and in a burst of violence he tears the Torah." This, Sidney continued, is "an unbelievable sin, beyond anything you can imagine, beyond murder, anything."

One wonders when Sidney had last been inside a synagogue, especially one located on the Lower East Side where his family would have observed. Shicoff, who revived the Eléazar role that Enrico Caruso made famous, recalled that Sidney's interpretation was unlike his own: Shicoff saw in the deaths of father and daughter a message regarding the price of intolerance; Sidney saw something different, that at the aria's end Eléazar has retrieved his faith and resolved that he wants to go to God. Shicoff noted, "Sidney felt that was the most important thing."

THE MIRACLE OF PERSONALITY

This story enchants me. How the government could fuck up so badly is beyond me. They had twenty defendants on seventy-six charges, and the jury throws it out in fourteen hours!
— SIDNEY LUMET ON *FIND ME GUILTY*

The story that would become *Find Me Guilty*, Sidney's forty-second movie, fell right into Sidney's sweet spot: a true story so good you couldn't make it up. This was a New Jersey story, but Sidney's New York sensibility was what attracted him to it, his fascination with bizarre or implausible behavior by everyday people, or what New Yorkers in Sidney's day reacted to with a shrug and the expression "Go know," shorthand for "Can you believe *this* now?"

In the longest-running federal trial in American history, twenty members of the Lucchese crime family were charged with seventy-seven criminal counts that included racketeering, criminal conspiracy, gambling, credit card fraud, loan-sharking, and sale and distribution of cocaine. The proceedings lasted twenty-one months and cost the government millions of dollars. After only fourteen hours of deliberation, the jury acquitted all twenty defendants on all charges. *The New York Times* reported a scene that Sidney wonderfully re-created:

The defendants here were clearly elated as they left one door of the courthouse, marched down the street cheering and went to another door, where the jurors were expected to exit. As the 12 jurors were escorted by Federal marshals to a waiting van, the defendants again applauded and cheered and thanked them. Some of the jurors waved back. Several cried, and one yelled, "Good luck!"

None of the twenty defense lawyers were credited with winning over the jury; it was Jackie DiNorscio, the only defendant who acted as his own attorney, diverting the jury with jokes ("I'm no gangster; I'm a gagster") and the sheer force of his personality, who, most agree, got all of them off.

"Fat Jack" or "Jackie Dee," with only a sixth-grade education, was, to Sidney's eye, a fabulous leading character: "A mob guy, cocaine dealer, liar, cheat, whoremonger—everything unpleasant—and yet there was something quite moving about him," Sidney remarked after meeting him shortly after DiNorscio was released from prison. He had a lot in common with Sonny in *Dog Day Afternoon*; he was charming, relatable, committed—and he felt driven to take care of others. Sidney said, "His loyalty to his 'family' was steadfast, and the humor he brought into the courtroom was remarkable." Later Sidney added, "He spent so much of his life in prison, but he was able to articulate such a funny point of view on life."

Sidney wrote the script with T. J. Mancini and Robert J. McCrea, taking much of it verbatim from the court transcript. In the actual trial, as in the film, the government's star witness was an admitted drug addict and alcoholic who had been convicted of shooting his cousin, Jackie DiNorscio, five times. Some were surprised when Sidney chose action star Vin Diesel to play Jackie Dee, but Sidney had seen him in a short film Diesel had written and directed, *Multi-Facial*, about an actor unsuccessfully making the rounds to auditions. As Sidney commented, Diesel "gets a chance to play five different characters. It's only a twenty-minute movie. . . . When I saw that movie, I saw a major talent." From Sidney's point of view, being an actor is "a rather desperate occupation," and you make it work for you whatever way you can, "by making yourself financeable." Sidney recognized that many people are prejudiced and snobbish about action stars, but, he pointed out, "look at Sean Connery and Clint Eastwood," who both got their start that way—"We should know better by now."

Vin Diesel's Jackie Dee is warm, outrageous, and intuitive. In his closing argument (largely borrowed from the transcript), he seals the deal with the jury:

*I know it's tough to decide who to believe in this case. . . . For
600 days you've been sitting here. . . . If you believe anything . . .
if you feel that the prosecutor was right then I beg you, please,
don't take it out on my friends here. If you have to blame
someone, then find me guilty. You heard me right. Find me
guilty, and let these men go home to their families. You see,
I already lost mine. . . . I'm not guilty, but I'm used to it.*

It was a stroke of genius to use the word "blame," which echoes the
prosecutor's righteous and vengeful tone—an attitude Sidney amplified in the screenplay for dramatic effect. Such a harsh sentiment
didn't match the jury's feeling toward the defendants, especially
toward Jackie. Diesel movingly persuades not just the jury but the
viewer too that for him, if his life isn't about love and loyalty, then all
of it is just too awful.

Sidney cast Peter Dinklage as the top defense counsel who advises
Jackie; he had gotten to admire and like Peter Dinklage while advising on *The Station Agent*, and they developed a great mutual affection. "I think of Sidney all the time," Dinklage said. Ron Silver, who
starred in *Garbo Talks*, plays the long-suffering judge, and Marcia
Jean Kurtz, who appeared in *Dog Day Afternoon*, plays a member of
the prosecution's team, which, in real life, was headed by Samuel A.
Alito, later to become a Supreme Court Justice.

Vin Diesel and Sidney became close. When they were in Berlin with
the film, Diesel was mobbed by screaming fans. He turned to Sidney
and said, "How'd you like to live like this?" and Diesel headed back
to his hotel to play video games with his bodyguards.

OSCAR

The day before the 2005 Oscar ceremony, Sidney called his eye
doctor's office to ask if his new glasses were ready. "I'm so sorry,
Mr. Lumet, they haven't come in yet," manager Alba Garcia answered. She had, the week before, fitted him for a new pair; he'd

finally agreed it was time to give up his 1970s aviator-style frames. The night after he called, she turned on her TV to watch the Oscars, and there was Sidney being honored, wearing his old glasses. "Why didn't he tell me?" she exclaimed. "We could've put a rush on them!"

New glasses or no, the Academy honorary award for lifetime achievement meant the world to Sidney. He drank in that long standing ovation from his peers and colleagues.

Sidney was famous, and there were perks, of course, to his fame; "It could be fun," Piedy said, remembering Sidney's special delight at receiving a police escort one year at Cannes. But he walked the streets and rode the subway without being noticed. He didn't have the face recognition that belonged to his leading actors. He was a little impatient with stars who complained that they couldn't go out in public—"Sure you can," he'd say. Sidney went about his business, not interested in calling attention to himself, and he was funny about fans. "He didn't go places to court them," Piedy noted.

I once found myself standing beside the couple, following a film event in midtown Manhattan; Sidney and Piedy were waiting for their chauffeur to pull up when a middle-aged man excitedly approached Sidney saying he was a big fan and reaching out to shake Sidney's hand. Sidney acknowledged him—not quite curtly, but coolly, and he did not engage in conversation. An acquaintance of Sidney's recalled the warmth and openness Sidney had expressed when introduced to the friend's grandson, enjoying talking to him until the boy ventured that he admired Sidney and wanted to be a director like him. Suddenly Sidney went cold, the surprised friend recalled. He seemed not distrustful but rather uninterested in the public's adulation. But it was a different matter entirely among his peers and colleagues; he warmly received their acknowledgment and affection. As for the Oscar, he'd been nominated for best director four times, and never won it—"and I wanted one, dammit," he later said. He was deeply grateful for the honor and the warm reception. And he knew he'd earned it.

Sidney wanted to keep things simple around the event, giving pride of place in the "family box" only to his immediate family, Piedy, Amy, and Jenny. But behind the scenes it wasn't so simple. Amy seemed more alienated from the family than ever, politically and culturally. She had in recent years taken up bodybuilding and had received some publicity from competing. The work on her body included recent breast implant surgery that garnered a lot of internet attention. When the four of them were in a very long limousine on their way to the event, Amy decided she wasn't happy with her dress; she pulled another dress from a paper bag and she proceeded to strip down to change. The driver almost had an accident. Sidney quietly looked away.

Piedy said Sidney always spoke off-the-cuff when he received awards, but this time he wrote out his remarks beforehand. Piedy wondered if it would've been better had he spoken spontaneously. In his speech, he joked that he'd begun fantasizing about making such a speech when his first movie, *12 Angry Men*, was nominated: "I was a real smart aleck, and I thought I would say something like, 'I don't want to thank anybody; I did it alone.' It wasn't true, but I thought it would be a way of getting a little attention." He acknowledged that he couldn't possibly thank all the people responsible for his standing there, and he wondered how he might go about thanking all the great artists who inspired him. He began, "How do I thank Spielberg . . ."—at which point he glanced down and saw Martin Scorsese seated in the front row; that night Scorsese had lost both Best Director and Best Picture awards to Clint Eastwood. Looking him in the eye, Sidney said, "and Scorsese." And he then went on to list many of his lifelong favorites: Jean Vigo, Carl Dreyer, Willy Wyler, Akira Kurosawa, and Buster Keaton. Sidney ended his speech, "And of course, the ones who've paid more dues than I have: thank you Piedy, Amy, Jenny. See you later."

Jenny was wiping away tears as she and Amy rose with the audience in applause. Piedy was intensely focused on Sidney's every word—connected to him, it seemed.

Jenny, Sidney, Piedy and Amy on Oscar night, 2005. *(Patrick McMullan / Getty Images)*

BEFORE THE DEVIL KNOWS YOU'RE DEAD

May you be a full half hour in heaven before the devil knows you're dead.

—Irish saying

If the actor thinks it or feels it, you *think it or feel it. That's what being an actor is.*

—Sidney Lumet

Sidney had some other scripts lined up beyond this one, movies he was planning to make, but it's likely he knew this would be his last film. *Before the Devil Knows You're Dead* has been likened to a Greek tragedy. Some see it as an O'Neill play, a painful family drama, with a crime story overlay. The narrative is stark, and Sidney gave it a deliberately stark look, seeking out "uninteresting" exteriors and creating what he described as "banal bourgeois backgrounds." With a few brilliant changes to the script, Sidney layered the crime plot into a family story, making the two robbers into brothers rather than co-workers. The brothers plan the robbery of their parents' small jewelry store. The scheme goes awry and their mother is killed. Their grieving father discovers that his sons are behind the crime, and he takes the life of one of them. The family dynamics that drive these events are brilliantly crystalized in the performances by Albert Finney, Philip Seymour Hoffman, and Ethan Hawke. Sidney thought his way inside each of the three major characters: the cold, ungiving father who loves his wife but has shown no affection to his elder son; the elder son, who is driven by vacuous desires, and who resents, manipulates and controls his younger brother; and the weak, desperate and trusting younger brother. The brothers, one with a heroin habit, the other an alcoholic, are both in failed or failing marriages.

Unlike Sidney's other films, which move forward chronologically, this story unfolds in pieces, flashing back and forth in time, presenting the perspectives of the three major characters. Sidney front-loads the narrative, opening the film in the middle of his most explicit sex scene, coldly observed, between the older brother (Philip Seymour Hoffman) and his detached, not too bright wife, played deftly by Marisa Tomei.

There is no warmth in the world of this film, barely any human relatedness, but the characters ring true. In a baleful sequence after the mother's funeral, the devastated father makes an effort to apologize to his elder son, Andy, played by Hoffman, for pushing him hard and for not having been able to express love for him. They do not look at each other, and Andy responds with cold resentment, asking his father, "Are you sure I'm your son?" His father replies by slapping his face. The viewer's feelings are held in check throughout, which is part of the unusual power of this film—it never entreats our sympathy. In the director's commentary, on which Hoffman and Hawke converse with Sidney, as this scene begins, Sidney, most remarkably, says, "Ah, this is such a classic father-son scene." It is as if Sidney released all the darkness inside him all at once, the parts of himself he'd been wrestling with and hiding throughout his life. This film is not a revelation of the "true Sidney," but it does belong to him.

Indeed, these toxic characters were hard to inhabit, as Ethan Hawke and Philip Seymour Hoffman tell it; they were both relieved to leave them behind. The exchanges between the two actors and their director on the DVD commentary strike many notes; at one point Hoffman praises Sidney for giving him "exactly what an actor wants, something active and specific." Sidney replies, "I learned that from Sandy Meisner; he was a great acting teacher. He used to say: verbs verbs verbs," to which Hawke responds, "Adjectives are for . . ." and Sidney finishes his sentence, "critics." And later Hoffman observed of Sidney, "He grabs your shoulder, your face, your hand. He wants his connection close and wants you to know that he's on your side. He doesn't play the withholding father type. He's direct, he's honest, and he's supportive."

HOW THE MOVIE FELL INTO PLACE

People put themselves in Sidney's hands.
—KELLY MASTERSON, SCREENWRITER
OF *BEFORE THE DEVIL KNOWS YOU'RE DEAD*

For the film's producers, Michael Cerenzie and Brian Linse, who'd been trying to get the picture made for six years, Sidney was an out-of-reach dream director. They had recently managed to interest Philip Seymour Hoffman in the project, and to approach Hollywood power broker Jeff Berg, inquiring if he could interest a director who is "a young Sidney Lumet." In an echo of something Sidney once said about Lewis Milestone, Berg replied, "What's wrong with the old Sidney Lumet?"

"People said we were crazy to hire Sidney," said Linse. "He hadn't had a hit in twenty years." But they loved his work; they wanted him. Berg sent Sidney the script, and a few days later, Michael Cerenzie recounts, "I get a call, and the guy says, 'Hi, this is Sid,' I said, 'Sid who?' He says, 'Sid Lumet.' I said, 'Yeah, sure,' and hung up. I thought it was one of my friends playing a joke. A few moments later he calls again, and this time I recognized the voice, its rhythms and timbre. He says, 'I guess we had a bad connection.' And I say, 'Well, you know how these cell phones are.'"

Brian Linse met with Sidney in his office on West 51st Street. "It was a small office," he recalled. "It gave you no sense that you were walking into the office of one of the greatest directors in the world. . . . It was just simple, a place where a lot of work was done—not a place to admire his trophies." Sidney told him the changes he wanted to make to the script, and things moved quickly from there. Linse was enthralled by Sidney from the start: "He was very kind and genuine, and not unaware of the impact he had on people." At age eighty-two, Sidney "was marking up the architects' plans like he's an architect," Linse said, and "if he wanted to make a note on the other side of the page, he began *writing with his left hand*. . . . He had an intellectual mastery of everything, including his own ego," which, in Linse's view, "was something that had to be tempered." And he added, "I adored him even more on the last day than on the first."

For first-time screenwriter Kelly Masterson, a former Franciscan brother who was working in a bank while the film was in development, the news that Sidney Lumet was directing his screenplay—and with that cast—was a shock, to say the least. Equally surprising was when, at one of the early film festival screenings, Sidney referred to Kelly Masterson as "she." When corrected by a member of the press, Sidney explained that he'd never met the writer. "After that, he was very kind," Masterson recalled. "He wanted me to know that he knew he'd hurt me." For his part, Masterson was sorry that Sidney hadn't called on him to work on the revisions, but he agreed that Sidney's changes "took my material into richer psychological territory. This gave the wonderful actors great stuff to work with in which the emotional stakes were very high." And he added, "When I am working on projects now, I ask myself the question: How do I get further into this character and really rock him?"

The film went into production in the summer of 2006, mostly on location in Queens and Yonkers, and at Hellgate in Astoria. "A couple of days that were blistering hot, we shot the exterior of the strip mall, and an extra fainted," Brian Linse recalled, and "Sidney was wearing what was clearly a woman's gardening hat." About those sweltering days, Sidney said, "I forget that I'm an old man"—but he was grateful that one of his grips didn't forget and followed him around with an umbrella to keep the sun off him.

HOW TO END IT?

They shot one ending with Ethan's Hank and Marisa's Gina together, living off stolen drug money. That didn't work. They tried using "cards," language on the screen saying that Hank had run off with the money and Gina had joined him. Still not good. Lili and others were urging Sidney to end the film with Albert Finney walking down the hospital corridor after killing Hoffman's older brother character, Andy. Sidney feared it was just too dark, and there was pressure coming from the financing company not to go that dark. Sidney weighed it for a while. It was his policy to listen to suggestions but only once in a while to take one, and only after consideration. He decided to go with the "thud" ending, the one, as Lili put it, "that you walk out of the theater thinking about."

The score was yet another point of discussion. Sidney had hired Richard Rodney Bennett, who'd done the magnificent score for *Murder on the Orient Express*, but most agreed that it wasn't sufficiently cueing the audience to what was happening emotionally in the characters. Linse recalled that it took some doing to convince Sidney to change the music, and when he did, they brought on Carter Burwell, who'd done music for Charlie Kaufman and most of the Coen brothers' movies. He was just finishing work on *No Country for Old Men* when Sidney reached out to him. Burwell recalled his initial conversation with Sidney: "Lumet does not slather on the underscore like most American directors. Indeed, as he reminded me, many of his best films have no score, like *Network* and *Dog Day Afternoon*." He said that Sidney felt he should not be shy about the melodrama, "and so the score sounds a bit overwrought at first—at least to me. The theme, which opens the film in the manner of a 'crime drama,' comes eventually to play the recriminations of the family."

Sidney got tremendous performances from all of his actors on this film—and the movie was warmly received by critics. It won seventeen awards, several for best ensemble cast. Sidney credited his digital multicamera method for the remarkable intimacy and truth of the performances he got. Regarding the work between Hawke and Hoffman, he explained, "neither actor had to read lines for the other person's side in a reverse shot. And because the actors know they're not in a situation where they're going to have to do their lines again for the other guy's setup, they can go for broke; there's not going to be a wasted take." He was thrilled by the response. "The reaction has been extraordinary," he said as he was making the film festival circuit. "When people ask questions about the film, what I find very interesting is that the picture has enormous personal resonance. The questions come from a really personalized source."

Throughout his final shoot, his energy never flagged. Albert Finney noted, "I worked with him thirty-two years ago [on *Murder on the Orient Express*]. He shoots just as fast now as he did then. He's still the same."

Following the film's release, Sidney had also been working on a script called *Getting Out*, based on a newspaper story Sidney said he had "read thirty years ago." It was about a prisoner desperate to escape who enters into a twisted mind game with his psychiatrist. Among his many ideas for projects was a TV series about a theatrical family like the Redgraves, and he was mulling over the idea of doing a remake of his 1971 caper film *The Anderson Tapes*; he wrote to Kelly Masterson to see if he had any interest in developing a script with him.

Jenny got remarried, to Alexander Weinstein, whom she described as "a nice Jewish boy," and together they had her second child, Sasha, a darling granddaughter for Sidney. While quietly toiling away writing unproduced screenplays, Jenny was teaching theater—mostly

Shakespeare—at a Manhattan private school. She told me about teaching the kids *Othello* and discussing it with her father. "I got a little obsessed with the character of Iago for a while. He [Sidney] said, 'Why?' We would talk about Iago. . . . I told him to read Cormac McCarthy; then we could talk about Iago." (Iago is often seen as a source for the character of Judge Holden in McCarthy's novel *Blood Meridian*.) Jenny continued, "Then he read Cormac McCarthy and had this great time reading Cormac McCarthy, and then he didn't want to talk about *Othello* at all, until he read all of Cormac McCarthy." Jenny said her father was always a bit surprised when she asked him for creative advice. "'There is no one answer' was his answer. It was, 'You make the road by walking.'" They talked about her work—not so much about his—and he always supported her in it.

When Jenny gave her father a draft of her latest screenplay, *Rachel Getting Married*, he was delighted by it. He sent it to his friend, director Jonathan Demme (*The Silence of the Lambs*, *Philadelphia*), with a brief note to the effect that his daughter had written a wonderful script and "you should direct it." Demme concurred. The film was a hit and was nominated for some sixty-four awards; Jenny won the New York Film Critics Circle Award for Best Screenplay. Sidney was thrilled; he joined her on interviews, promoting the film with her. In one interview she did with her father, Jenny joked, "I can definitely say that if you want to be in the film industry, it's really good to be related to someone famous. I would advise that."

Their relationship was playful and loving. I attended an event, not long after her film was released, where Sidney was on stage in conversation with Jonathan Demme. Sidney referred to Jodie Foster's character in *Silence of the Lambs*, Clarice Starling, as "a little chippie" in the course of praising the film, and from the audience Jenny rose to her feet and said, "Dad, first, nobody uses the term 'little chippie' anymore, and secondly, Clarice Starling is the protagonist and hero of that film." Sidney smiled at her and said, "See, that's what happens when you send your kid to progressive school."

In an interview, Jenny responded to a question about "a special place" she likes to write: "I have a fourteen-year-old son who has a

Jenny makes her father laugh, as she often did, during a joint interview they did following the success of *Rachel Getting Married* (2008), the film she scripted and that Sidney warmly supported. *(Reprinted with permission of* The Wall Street Journal, *Copyright 2009. Dow Jones & Company, Inc. All rights reserved worldwide.)*

death-metal band, and a one-and-a-half-year-old who runs around screaming. And I have a huge dog and a husband and live on Broadway." Sidney was thrilled to have them all close by. Having a creative family at work as well as at home, a large, real and loving family, must have been a source of boundless joy. Though there was also always the deep sadness that Jenny's older sister, Amy, was at so great a distance, in so many ways.

The first public signal of Sidney's failing health came in October 2007, when Sidney was unable to attend the Roma Cinema Fest with *Before the Devil Knows You're Dead*, due to illness. Sidney would know about, but not get to see, his grandson Jake kick off his career as an adorable, smart-ass and hurting teenager on the hit Showtime series *Nurse Jackie*. He would certainly have appreciated that the project on which a new generation of the Lumet family was breaking into the film and television business was shot at Kaufman Astoria Studios—the very same place where Sidney began his film career as a child actor nearly seven decades earlier.

22

ALL IN ALL

"Wouldn't you agree that of all the arts, music is the most satisfying?" Sidney asked composer and Juilliard School music instructor Scott Eyerly.

"Why do you say that?" Scott inquired.

"Well," Sidney said, "it's most rewarding because it's pure."

Sidney was no longer directing movies—no longer working. He and Piedy had been attending Scott Eyerly's lectures at Juilliard, first a musical survey course and then his courses on opera. Piedy told Scott that his class was one of the few things Sidney was eager to get out of the apartment to do.

"I remember this about Sid immediately," Scott reflected. "Any teacher knows when you're standing in front of a classroom, some are bored, some are listening intermittently. I'd look up from time to time, and Sid would be at the edge of his seat, leaning forward—he was latched on to me." He was still enthralled and still learning. What humility in that. Scott once asked Sidney if he'd ever directed opera. "He told me he was once going to direct a production of Verdi's *Aida* with Pavarotti, and Lorin Maazel conducting. Lumet's requirement was that Pavarotti shave his beard—for historical accuracy—but Pavarotti refused to shave and backed out."

In this period, Sidney had particularly loved one production at the

Metropolitan Opera, *From the House of the Dead*, by Czech composer Leoš Janáček, adapted from Dostoevsky's fictionalized account of his years in a Siberian prison. "The opera is rarely staged," Scott noted. This production by Patrice Chéreau had premiered in New York in the autumn of 2009. Scott remembered Sidney saying, "If they were all that good, then I would go every night." Janáček's opera has no real plot; the music conveys what *New York Times* critic Anthony Tommasini described as "the volatile mix of restless tension and crushing boredom within this oppressed environment." In the opera's final tableaux, Tommasini notes, "a group of tattered, ailing inmates in the prison hospital release a wounded eagle they have nurtured back to health, only to be corralled by guards into a quick march to the work fields."

For Sidney, opera had no restraints or inhibitions about feeling. Unlike most movies, the music had no fear of emotional peaks and abysses, no obligations to realism. Perhaps he found a connection in this to the Yiddish theater, where he had had his introduction to art.

Sitting with Sidney when he was wheelchair-bound, near the end, Piedy asked him what he thought were their best times. Without hesitating, he said, "NOW." Then he added, "The *tenderness*." Piedy's eyes filled with tears as she shared the memory of it.

Sidney died on April 9, 2011.

Jenny was the onstage host at Sidney's memorial service, held at Alice Tully Hall in Lincoln Center, on June 28—an event full of love and humor. She began by remarking that Sidney's "spirit is hovering over the whitefish section at Zabar's." The list of luminaries in attendance is long, including Alan Alda, Bob Balaban, Boaty Boatwright, Joan Didion, E. L. Doctorow, Lee Grant, Buck Henry, Peter Matthiessen, Al Pacino, Vanessa Redgrave and Treat Williams. Glenn Close sang "Bye Bye Blackbird," Phyllis Newman performed "They Can't Take That Away from Me," and there were testimonials from Lauren Bacall, Jeff Berg, Walter Bernstein, Marshall Brickman, Bobby Cannavale, Jonathan

Sidney and Piedy. *(Courtesy of Mary Lumet)*

Demme, James Gandolfini, Philip Seymour Hoffman, Marcia Jean Kurtz, David Mamet, LaTanya Richardson, Gene Saks, Christopher Walken, Tony Walton; and Sidney's longtime cinematographer, Andrzej Bartkowiak, his sound man, Chris Newman, and his editor, Tom Swartwout.

Sidney's old friend Walter Bernstein described their work together in 1950s live television: "He really did snap, crackle, and pop on the set. He was a rare combination of enthusiasm and organization." Walter recalled their days as pioneers of product placement: "If you mentioned Charlie the Tuna on the show, you got a case of scotch. It wasn't easy, but we were creative people." Ending on a more serious note, Walter said, "I was blacklisted most of that time, but I worked because of Sidney. A lot of us did. He was a mensch, which is better than getting an Oscar."

Sidney at about age thirteen.

FILMOGRAPHY AND SOURCES

SIDNEY LUMET'S FILMOGRAPHY

12 Angry Men, United Artists, 1957.
Stage Struck, Buena Vista, 1958.
That Kind of Woman, Paramount, 1959.
The Fugitive Kind, United Artists, 1960.
A View from the Bridge (also known as *Vu du pont* and *Uno sguardo dal ponte*),
    Continental, 1962.
Long Day's Journey into Night, Embassy, 1962.
Fail-Safe, Columbia, 1964.
The Pawnbroker, American International, 1965.
The Hill, MGM, 1965.
The Group, United Artists, 1966.
The Deadly Affair, Columbia, 1967.
Bye Bye Braverman, Warner Bros., 1968.
The Sea Gull, Warner Bros., 1968.
King: A Filmed Record . . . Montgomery to Memphis, 1970.
The Appointment, MGM, 1970.
The Last of the Mobile Hot Shots (also known as *Blood Kin* and *The Seven
    Descents of Myrtle*), Warner Bros., 1970.
The Anderson Tapes, Columbia, 1971.
Child's Play, Paramount, 1972.
The Offense (also known as *Something Like the Truth* and *The Offence*), United
    Artists, 1973.
Serpico, Paramount, 1973.
Lovin' Molly, Columbia, 1974.
Murder on the Orient Express, Paramount, 1974.
Dog Day Afternoon, Warner Bros., 1975.
Equus, United Artists, 1977.
Network, MGM/United Artists, 1977.
The Wiz, Universal, 1978.

Just Tell Me What You Want, Warner Bros., 1980.
Prince of the City, Warner Bros., 1981.
Deathtrap (also known as *Ira Levin's Deathtrap*), Warner Bros., 1982.
The Verdict, Twentieth Century–Fox, 1982.
Daniel, Paramount, 1983.
Garbo Talks, MGM/United Artists, 1984.
Power, Twentieth Century–Fox, 1986.
The Morning After, Twentieth Century–Fox, 1986.
Running on Empty, Lorimar, 1988.
Family Business, TriStar, 1989.
Q & A, TriStar, 1990.
A Stranger Among Us (also known as *Close to Eden*), Buena Vista, 1992.
Guilty As Sin, Buena Vista, 1993.
Night Falls on Manhattan, Paramount, 1997.
Critical Care, Live Film & Mediaworks, 1997.
Gloria, Columbia, 1999.
La Juive. Millennial Arts Productions, 2003.
Strip Search. HBO Films, 2004
Find Me Guilty, Yari Film Group, 2005.
Before the Devil Knows You're Dead, Capital Films, 2007.

THE FOLLOWING INTERVIEWS WERE CONDUCTED
BY MAURA SPIEGEL

Ellen Adler, telephone conversation, July 25, 2013
Ellen Adler, Water Mill, NY, July 17, 2013
David Amram, Beacon, NY, Nov. 9, 2015
Andrzej Bartkowiak, New York City, Jan. 17, 2013
Walter Bernstein, New York City, Nov. 4, 2013
Theodore Bikel, telephone conversation, July 9, 2012
David Black, New York City, July 22, 2013
Gail Lumet Buckley, New York City, June 20, 2017
Bobby Cannavale, telephone conversation, Sept. 19, 2018
Brian De Palma, telephone conversation, June 24, 2018
Scott Eyerly, telephone conversation, July 21, 2014
E. L. Doctorow, New York City, June 18, 2014
Tom Fontana, by email, July 10, 2013
Rita Gam, New York City, July 18, 2012
Burtt Harris, Montreal, PQ, June 26, 2014
Lili Jacobs, New York City, July 9, 2013; July 23, 2013; July 11, 2018
Lisa James, telephone conversation, July 2, 2014
Brian Linse, telephone conversation. June 14, 2016
Jenny Lumet, New York City, July 17, 2012
Mary (Piedy) Lumet, New York City, July 24, 2012; Sept. 20, 2017
Kelly Masterson, telephone conversation, Nov. 24, 2014

Claudia Mohr, telephone conversation, Sept. 22, 2017
Chris Newman, telephone conversation, June 6, 2015
Phyllis Newman, New York City, Aug. 22, 2013
Austin Pendleton, telephone conversation. Aug. 9, 2018
Martha Pinson, New York City, June 29, 2014
LaTanya Richardson, telephone conversation, Sept. 19, 2017
Amy Ryan, telephone conversation, Sept. 25, 2018
Theo Sable, telephone conversation, Feb. 2, 2018
Susan Scheftel, New York City, Mar. 18, 2017
Stan Stokowski, telephone conversation, Sept. 29, 2018
Susanna Styron, New York City, Oct. 4, 2016
Tony Walton and Gen LeRoy, New York City, July 11, 2017
Treat Williams, telephone conversation, Aug. 2, 2018
Gloria Vanderbilt, telephone conversation and emails, Aug. 5, 2017–May 19, 2018

BIBLIOGRAPHY

BOOKS

Allen, Jay Presson. *Just Tell Me What You Want*. New York: E. P. Dutton, 1975.

Anderson, Maxwell. *Journey to Jerusalem: A Play in Three Acts*. Washington, DC: Anderson House, 1940.

Ansky, S. *The Dybbuk: Between Two Worlds*, trans. S. Morris Engel. Washington, DC: Regnery Gateway, 1974.

Arad, Gulie Ne'eman. *America, Its Jews, and the Rise of Nazism*. Bloomington: Indiana University Press, 2000.

Baker, Fred, ed. *Movie People: At Work in the Business of Film*. New York: Douglas, 1972.

Bendersky, Joseph W. *The "Jewish Threat": Anti-Semitic Politics in the U.S. Army*. New York: Basic Books, 2000.

Bennett, Robert. *Deconstructing Post-WWII New York City: The Literature, Art, Jazz, and Architecture of an Emerging Global Capital*. Hoboken, NJ: Taylor and Francis, 2013.

Bernstein, Walter. *Inside Out: A Memoir of the Blacklist*. New York: Da Capo Press, 2000.

Blake, Richard. *Street Smart: The New York of Lumet, Allen, Scorcese, and Lee*. Lexington: University Press of Kentucky, 2005.

Bogdanovich, Peter. *Who the Devil Made It: Conversations with Legendary Film Directors*. New York: Ballantine Books, 1997.

Bowles, Stephen E. *Sidney Lumet: A Guide to References and Resources*. Boston: G. K. Hall, 1979.

Boyer, Jay. *Sidney Lumet*. New York: Twayne Publishers, 1993.

Brestoff, Richard. *The Great Acting Teachers and Their Methods*. Lyme, NH: Smith and Kraus, 1995.

Brynner, Rock. *Yul: The Man Who Would Be King*. New York: Berkley Books, 1989.

Buckley, Gail Lumet. *The Hornes: An American Family*. New York: Alfred A. Knopf, 1986.

———. *The Black Calhouns: From Civil War to Civil Rights*. New York: Atlantic Monthly Press, 2016.

Caplan, Debra. *Yiddish Empire: The Vilna Troupe, the Jewish Theater, and the Art of Itinerancy*. Ann Arbor: University of Michigan Press, 2018.

Clurman, Harold. *The Fervent Years: The Group Theatre and the Thirties*. New York: Da Capo Press, 1975.

———. *On Directing*. New York: Fireside, 1997.

Comden, Betty. *Off Stage*. Pompton Plains, NJ: Limelight, 2004.

Cooper, Anderson, and Gloria Vanderbilt. *The Rainbow Comes and Goes*. New York: HarperCollins, 2016.

Cronkite, Walter. *A Reporter's Life*. New York: Alfred A. Knopf, 1996.

Cunningham, Frank R. *Sidney Lumet: Film and Literary Vision*, 2d ed. Lexington: University Press of Kentucky, 2001.

Daley Robert. *Prince of the City*. Boston: Houghton Mifflin, 1978.

De Rohan, Pierre, ed. *Federal Theatre Plays*. 1: *Prologue to Glory* (E. P. Conkle). 2: *One-Third of a Nation* (Arthur Arent, ed.). 3: *Haiti* (William Dubois). New York: Random House, 1938.

Desser, David, and Lester D. Friedman. *American Jewish Filmmakers*, 2d ed. Chicago: University of Illinois Press, 2004.

Doctorow, E. L. *The Book of Daniel*. New York: Random House, 1971.

———. *Three Screenplays*. Baltimore: Johns Hopkins University Press, 2003.

Emery, Robert J. *The Directors: Take One*. New York: Allworth Press, 2002.

Gam, Rita. *Actors: A Celebration*. New York: St. Martin's Press, 1988.

———. *Actress to Actress*. New York: Nick Lyons Books, 1986

Gavin, James. *Stormy Weather: The Life of Lena Horne*. New York: Simon & Schuster, 2010.

Getz, Leonard, with a foreword by Leo Gorcey Jr. *From Broadway to the Bowery: A History and Filmography of the Dead End Kids, Little Tough Guys, East Side Kids and Bowery Boys Films, with Cast Biographies*. Jefferson, NC: McFarland & Co., 2006.

Goldsmith, Barbara. *Little Gloria . . . Happy at Last*. New York: Alfred A. Knopf, 1980.

Goodman, Wendy. *The World of Gloria Vanderbilt*. New York: Abrams, 2010.

Gordon, Mel. *Stanislavsky in America: An Actor's Workbook*. New York: Routledge, 2010.

Goss, L. Evan, ed. *Excerpts from the Unpublished Files of Muriel Oxenberg Murphy*. Bloomington, IN: Xlibris, 2008.

Gottfried, Martin. *All His Jazz: The Life and Death of Bob Fosse*. New York: Da Capo Press, 1990.

Gruen, John Jonas. *The Sixties: Young in the Hamptons*. Milan, Italy: Edizioni Charta, 2006.

Hannerz, Ulf. *Exploring the City: Inquiries Toward an Urban Anthropology*. New York: Columbia University Press, 1980.

Harris, Warren G. *Sophia Loren: A Biography*. New York: Simon & Schuster, 1998.

Hawes, William. *Live Television Drama, 1946–1951*. Jefferson, NC: McFarland & Co., 2001.

Hillier, Jim, ed. *Cahiers du Cinéma: The 1960–1968: New Wave, New Cinema, Reevaluating Hollywood*. Cambridge, MA: Harvard University Press, 1992.

Hirsch, Foster. *A Method to Their Madness: The History of the Actors Studio*. Cambridge, MA: Da Capo Press, 2002.

Howe, Irving, and Kenneth Libo, eds. *How We Lived: A Documentary History of Immigrant Jews in America, 1880–1930*. New York: R. Marek, 1979.

Itzkoff, Dave. *Mad as Hell: The Making of Network and the Fateful Vision of the Angriest Man in Movies*. New York: Henry Holt & Co., 2014.

James, Selwyn. *South of the Congo*. New York: Random House, 1943.

Jurow, Martin. *Seein' Stars: A Show Biz Odyssey as Told to Philip Wuntch*. Dallas: Southern Methodist University Press, 2001.

Kael, Pauline. *Kiss Kiss Bang Bang*. New York: Little Brown, 1968.

———. *Hooked*. New York: Plume, 1989.

Kahn, Roger. *The Boys of Summer*. New York: Perennial Library, 1987.

Kaufman, William I., ed. *How to Direct for Television*. New York: Hastings House, 1955.

Kazan, Elia. *A Life*. New York: Anchor Doubleday, 1988.

———. *Kazan on Directing*. New York: Vintage, 2009.

Kellow, Brian. *Can I Go Home Now? The Life of Sue Mengers, Hollywood's First Superagent*. New York: Viking, 2015.

Kemper, Tom. *Hidden Talent: The Emergence of Hollywood Agents*. Berkeley: University of California Press, 2009.

King, Alan, and Chris Chase. *Name-Dropping: The Life and Lies of Alan King*. New York: Scribner, 1996.

King, Alexander. *Is There a Life After Birth?* New York: Simon & Schuster, 1963.

Knopf, Robert. *Theater and Film: A Comparative Anthology*. New Haven: Yale University Press, 2005.

Koszarski, Richard. *Hollywood on the Hudson: Film and Television in New York from Griffith to Sarnoff*. New Brunswick, NJ: Rutgers University Press, 2010.

Lahr, John. *Tennessee Williams: Mad Pilgrimage of the Flesh*. New York: W. W. Norton & Co., 2014.

Leibman, Nina C. *Living Room Lectures: The Fifties Family in Film and Television*. Austin: University of Texas Press, 1995.

Lévi-Strauss, Claude. *The View from Afar*. Chicago: University of Chicago Press, 1992.

Levy, Emanuel. *George Cukor: Master of Elegance: Hollywood's Legendary Director and His Stars*. New York: William Morrow & Co., 1994.

Lewis, Robert. *Slings and Arrows: Theater in My Life*. New York: Applause Books, 2000.

Lindsay-Hogg, Michael. *Luck and Circumstance*. New York: Alfred A. Knopf, 2011.

Lippy, Tod, ed. *Projections 11: New York Film-makers on New York Film-making*. London: Faber & Faber, 2000.

Logan, John. *I'll Eat You Last: A Chat with Sue Mengers*. London: Oberon Books, 2013.

Lumet, Sidney. *Making Movies*. New York: Vintage, 1996.

Markfield, Wallace. *To an Early Grave*. New York: Simon & Schuster, 1964.

Matthau, Carol. *Among the Porcupines: A Memoir*. New York: Turtle Bay Books, 1992.

Meisner, Sanford, and Dennis Longwell. *Sanford Meisner on Acting*. New York: Vintage Books, 1987.

Merwin, Ted. *In Their Own Image: New York Jews in Jazz Age and Popular Culture*. New Brunswick, NJ: Rutgers University Press, 2006.

Metzker, Isaac, and Harry Golden, *A Bintel Brief: Sixty Years of Letters from the Lower East Side to the Jewish Daily Forward,* trans. Diana Shalet Levy. New York: Schocken Books, 1971.

Moore, Deborah Dash. *GI Jews: How World War II Changed a Generation*. Cambridge, MA: Belknap Press, 2006.

Morris, Jan. *Manhattan '45*. New York: Oxford University Press, 1987.

Morris, Oswald, and Geoffrey Bull. *Huston, We Have a Problem: A Kaleidoscope of Filmmaking Memories*. Lanham, MD: Scarecrow Press, 2006.

Munyan, Russ, ed. *Readings on Twelve Angry Men*. San Diego, CA: Greenhaven Press, 2000.

Nash, N. Richard. *The Young and the Fair*. New York: Dramatists Play Service, Inc., 1976.

Parker, John. *Arise Sir Sean Connery: The Biography of Britain's Greatest Living Actor*. London: John Blake Publishing, 2005.

Parks, Gordon. *Voices in the Mirror: An Autobiography*. New York: Doubleday, 1990.

Plimpton, George, ed. *American Journey: The Times of Robert Kennedy. Interviews by Jean Stein*. New York: Harcourt Brace Jovanovich, 1970.

———. *Truman Capote: In Which Various Friends, Enemies, Acquaintances, and Detractors Recall His Turbulent Career*. New York: Anchor Doubleday, 1997.

Plummer, Christopher. *In Spite of Myself: A Memoir*. New York: Alfred A. Knopf, 2008.

Rapf, Joanna E., ed. *Sidney Lumet: Interviews*. Jackson: University Press of Mississippi, 2006.

Reid, David. *The Brazen Age: New York City and the American Empire*. New York: Pantheon, 2016.

Reinhardt, Gottfried. *The Genius: A Memoir of Max Reinhardt by His Son Gottfried Reinhardt*. New York: Alfred A. Knopf, 1979.

Rigby, Ray. *The Hill*. London: W. H. Allen, 1965.

Rischin, Moses. *Promised City: New York's Jews, 1870–1914*. Cambridge, MA: Harvard University Press, 1977.

Riva, Maria. *Marlene Dietrich by Her Daughter, Maria Riva*. London: Bloomsbury Books, 1993.

Rosenblum, Ralph, and Robert Karen. *When the Shooting Stops . . . the Cutting Begins*. New York: Da Capo Press, 1979.

Rotté, Joanna. *Acting with Adler*. Pompton Plains, NJ: Limelight Editions, 2000.

Salinger, J. D. *Franny and Zooey*. New York: Little, Brown, 1991.

Salamon, Julie. *The Devil's Candy: The Anatomy of a Hollywood Fiasco*. New York: Da Capo Press, 2002.

Sanders, Ronald, and Edmund V. Gillon Jr. *Lower East Side: A Guide to Its Jewish Past with 99 New Photographs*. New York: Dover Publications, 2014.

Saroyan, Aram. *Trio: Oona Chaplin, Carol Matthau, Gloria Vanderbilt: Portrait of an Intimate Friendship*. New York: Simon & Schuster, 1985.

Sayler, Oliver M., ed. *Max Reinhardt and His Theater*, trans. Mariele S. Gudernatsch and others. New York: B. Blom, 1968.

Schoener, Allon. *Portal to America: The Lower East Side, 1870–1925*. New York: Holt, Rinehart and Winston, 1967.

Segaloff, Nat. *Arthur Penn: American Director*. Lexington: University Press of Kentucky, 2011.

Singer, Isaac Bashevis. *Day of Pleasure: Stories of a Boy Growing Up in Warsaw*. New York: Farrar, Straus & Giroux, 2012.

Smith, Wendy. *Real Life Drama: The Group Theatre and America: 1931–1940*. New York: Alfred A. Knopf, 1990.

Stapleton, Maureen, and Jane Scovell. *Hell of a Life: An Autobiography*. New York: Simon & Schuster, 1995.

Strasberg, Lee. *A Dream of Passion: The Development of the Method*. New York: Plume, 1987.

Strasberg, Susan. *Bittersweet*. New York: G. P. Putnam's Sons, 1980.

Sturcken, Frank. *Live Television: The Golden Age of 1946–1958 in New York*. Jefferson, NC: McFarland & Co., 1990.

Styan, J. L. *Max Reinhardt*. New York: Cambridge University Press, 1982.

Thumin, Janet, ed. *Small Screen, Big Ideas: Television in the 1950s*. London: I. B. Tauris, 2002.

Torres, Edwin. *Q & A*. New York: Avon Books, 1977.

Vanderbilt, Gloria. *It Seemed Important at the Time: A Romance Memoir.* New York: Simon & Schuster, 2004.

———. *Never Say Goodbye: A Novel.* New York: Alfred A. Knopf, 1988.

———. *Once Upon a Time: A True Story.* New York: Alfred A. Knopf, 1985.

———. *The Things We Fear Most: Stories.* Holstein, ON: Exile Editions, 2011.

Vidal, Gore. *Palimpsest: A Memoir.* New York: Random House, 1995.

Wallach, Eli. *The Good, the Bad, and Me: In My Anecdotage.* Orlando, FL: Harcourt, 2005.

Watkin, David. *Was Clara Schumann a Fag Hag?* Brighton, UK: Scrutineer, 2008.

Werfel, Franz. *Eternal Road: A Drama in Four Parts,* trans. Ludwig Lewisohn. New York: Viking Press, 1936.

Wermus, Henri. *Le temps de la déchirure.* Geneva: Editions Labor et Fides, 2004.

Wilk, Max. *The Golden Age of Television: Notes from the Survivors.* New York: Delacorte Press, 1976.

Wojcik, Pamela Robertson, ed. *Movie Acting: The Film Reader.* New York: Routledge, 2004.

Wood, Audrey, with Max Wilk. *Represented by Audrey Wood.* Garden City, NY: Doubleday & Co., 1981.

Zinnemann, Fred. *Fred Zinnemann: An Autobiography.* New York: Scribner, 1992.

PERIODICALS

"'12 Angry Men': The Everlasting Testament to Sidney Lumet and Reginald Rose's Filmmaking Prowess." *Cinephilia & Beyond,* n.d. https://cinephiliabeyond.org/tag/12-angry-men/

Andreeva, Nellie. "Lumet Heads 'Search' Party for HBO Movie." *Hollywood Reporter,* Apr. 14, 2003.

Archer, Eugene. "View from the Director's Chair." *New York Times,* May 8, 1960.

Atkinson, Brooks. "Saroyan's Highland Fling." *New York Times,* May 7, 1939.

Bart, Peter. "War Is 'Hill,' Mate!" *New York Times,* Jan. 10, 1965.

Beck, Marilyn. "Robert Redford Fired from 'The Verdict.'" *Evening Outlook,* Sept. 2, 1981.

Bell, Arthur. "Not the Rosenbergs' Story." *Village Voice,* Sept. 6, 1983.

———. "Prints of the City: A Talk with Sidney Lumet." *L.A. Herald-Examiner,* Aug. 23, 1981.

Bennetts, Leslie. "Celebrities Make the Scene: Lumet Casts the Famous in New Film." *New York Times,* Mar. 29, 1984.

Bernstein, Jamie. "The Time My Parents 'Took a Knee' for the Black Panthers."

Huffington Post, Oct. 18, 2017. www.huffingtonpost.com/entry/leonard-bernstein-black-panthers_us_59e6c200e4b08f9f9edb7b11

Blum, David. "Slave of New York." *New York*, Sept. 5, 1988.

Brantley Ben, "Huddling Beneath Memory's Burdens." *New York Times*, June, 21, 1996.

Buckley, Peter. "The Sea Gull." *Films and Filming*, Feb. 1970.

"The Bull Sheet," Sept. 4, 1943. www.cbi-theater.com/bullsheet/bull_sheet_103043.html

Burke, Tom. "Suddenly I Knew How to Film the Play." *New York Times*, July 24, 1977.

Callahan, Maureen. "A Streetwise Legend Sticks to His Guns." *Gotham*, May 26, 1997.

Caplan, Debra. "Advice from Sidney Lumet's Yiddish Actor Dad." Digital Yiddish Theater Project, Dec. 15, 2014. https://yiddishstage.org/lessons-from-sidney-lumets-yiddish-actor-dad

Chanko, Kenneth. "Sidney Lumet An Interview." *Films in Review*, Oct. 1984.

"China, Burma, India Pointie Talkie." www.cbi-theater.com/pointie/pointie.html

Coates, Steve. "Plimpton's Party." *New York Times*, Dec. 11, 2008.

Cook, Roger. "Charles Beard's Story: Radar Counter Measures in the CBI Theater." www.cbi-theater.com/radar/radar_cbi.html

Dobuler, Sharon Lee. "Lumet Pulls Together Celebs, Press for Film." *Hollywood Reporter*, Mar. 30, 1984.

Duka, John. "Can 'Deathtrap' Survive on Screen?" *New York Times*, May 10, 1981.

Dundy, Elaine. "Why Actors Do Better for Sidney Lumet." *New York*, Nov. 22, 1976.

Felchner, William J. "Fail Safe—The Ultimate Cold War Thriller." *Movie Collector's World* #632, June 22, 2001.

Flatley, Guy. "About Sidney Lumet." *New York Times*, Jan. 20, 1974.

"Footlight Juniors to Give Own Show." *New York Times*, Mar. 21, 1937.

Foster, Frederick, "Filming 'The Fugitive Kind.'" *American Cinematographer*, June, 1960.

Foundas, Scott. "Sidney Lumet's Long Journey." *LA Weekly*, Oct. 26, 2007.

French, Philip. "'The Offence' Review: Connery and Lumet's Starkly Naturalistic Police Drama." *The Guardian*, June 14, 2015.

Gentry, Ric. "An Interview with Dede Allen." *Film Quarterly*, Autumn, 1992.

Georgakas, Dan, and Leonard Quart. "Still 'Making Movies': An Interview with Sidney Lumet." *Cinéaste*, Spring, 2006.

"Gloria Vanderbilt Wed." *New York Times*, Aug. 28, 1965.

Goldstein, Patrick. "Dick Zanuck Reveals His Secret Recipe for Surviving Studio Turmoil." *Los Angeles Times*, Jan. 21, 1010.

Greenspun, Roger. "Screen: The Pilgrimage of Martin Luther King Jr." *New York Times*, Oct. 23, 1969.

Guilliatt, Richard. "Lumet's 'Q & A': Fact and Friction." *Time Out* (London), Apr. 3–10, 1991.

Heller, Nathan. "What She Said: The Doings and Undoings of Pauline Kael." *New Yorker*, Oct. 24, 2011.

Hill, Logan. "Dog Day Afternoons: Sidney Lumet." *New York*, Sept. 24, 2007.

Howard, Manny. "Lost Boy." *New York*, July 24, 1995.

Kael, Pauline, "Hot Air." *New Yorker*, Dec. 6, 1976.

Kaufman, Michael T. "How Truthful Was 'Serpico'?" *L.A. Herald-Examiner*, Feb. 3, 1974.

Kaufman, Stanley. "Stanley Kaufman on Films." *New Republic*, Mar. 9, 1968.

King, Susan. "Chris Sarandon Reflects on 'Dog Day.'" *Los Angeles Times*, Sept. 28, 2015.

Kissel, Howard. "Looking at 'Daniel' from Two Directions." *W*, Sept 9, 1983.

Koszarski, Richard. "Subway Commandos: Hollywood Filmmakers at the Signal Corps Photographic Center." *Film History* (*War and Militarism*), 2002.

"Judge Puts Some 'Garbo' Ads on Temporary Hold." *Variety*, Oct. 25, 1984.

Laney, Jenny. "Casting Couch." *Interview*, May 1990.

Langley, Lee. "Lee Langley Talks to Sidney Lumet." *The Guardian*, July 2, 1966.

Leff, Leonard J. "Hollywood and the Holocaust: Remembering 'The Pawnbroker.'" *American Jewish History*, Dec. 1, 1996.

Lombardi, John. "Lumet: The City Is His Soundstage." *New York Times*, June 6, 1982.

Lopate, Phillip. "Sidney Lumet, or the Necessity for Compromise." *Film Comment*, July–August 1997.

Lumenick, Lou. "Interview with Sidney Lumet." *New York Post*, March 16, 2006.

Lumet, Amy. "Baby Cons of America, Unite: You Have Nothing to Lose But Your Parents' Guilt." *National Review*, Dec. 28, 1992.

"Lumet Divorce Decree Final." *New York Times*, Sept. 5, 1963.

Lumet, Sidney. "It Must Have Been." *The Nation*, Apr. 18, 1981.

Mason, Deborah. "Daniel: Love and Protest." *Vogue*, Aug. 1983.

McGilligan, Pat. "Jay Presson Allen: Writer by Default." *Backstory 3*, 1996.

"Minotaur Gets Trial Run." *New York Times*, Sept. 3, 1957.

Moore, Gaylen. "On the Cutting Edge of Film Editing." *New York Times*, Dec. 14, 1996.

Nemy, Enid. "Lucille Lortel, Patron Who Made Innovative Off Broadway a Star, Is Dead." *New York Times*, Apr. 6, 1999.

Norman, Barry. "Sidney Lumet Comes in on Budget." *The Times* (London), Mar. 19, 1974.

"'Nudity' Legion of Decency's Sole Reason for Condemning 'Pawnbroker.'" *Variety*, May 11, 1965.

Pollitt, Katha. "Daniel." *The Nation*, Oct. 1, 1993.

Provenzano, Tom. "Truly an Actor's Director, Sidney Lumet Explores the American Justice System." *Drama-logue*, May 15–21, 1997.

O'Toole, Lawrence. "Fast but Not Cheap." *Marquee*, Aug.–Sept. 1983.

———. "Sidney Lumet." *Moviegoer*, Oct. 1983.

Penman, Leigh. "That Kind of Woman: Amy Lumet." *RxMuscle*, Oct. 10, 2010. www.rxmuscle.com/rx-girl-articles/2105-that-kind-of-woman-amy-lumet.html

"Radar During World War II." Engineering and Technology Wiki. https://ethw.org

Rausch, Andrew J. "'I Love Vulnerability': An Interview with Tab Hunter." *Senses of Cinema*, Dec. 2017.

Robbins, Jim. "Lumet Relying on Foreign Coin to Finance 'Q & A.'" *Variety*, May 15, 1989.

Roberts, Sam. "New York 1945; The War Was Ending. Times Square Exploded. Change Was Coming." *New York Times*, July 30, 1995.

———. "Robert Leuci, 75, Who Exposed Graft Among Fellow Detectives in '70s, Dies." *New York Times*, Oct. 13, 2015.

Rosenbaum, Ron. "The Weather Overground." *Vanity Fair*, Oct 1988.

Royal, Susan. "An Interview with Michael Cerenzie." *Inside Film Magazine Online*, n.d. www.insidefilm.com/michaelcerenzie.html

Saito, Stephen. "Five of Sidney Lumet's Lesser-Known Films Work Seeking Out." *IFC*, Apr. 14, 2011. www.ifc.com/2011/04/sidney-lumet-1924-2011

"'Sammy' Loses Lumet." *Los Angeles Times*, Jan. 27, 1991.

Sapoznik, Henry. "Brooklyn Yiddish Radio, 1925–1946." *Yiddish Radio Project*, www.yiddishradioproject.org/exhibits/history/sapoznik_essay.php3?pg=2

"Saroyan's Play Set for April 2." *New York Times*, Feb. 24, 1939.

Scott, A. O. "Urban Realist with a Humanist Streak." *New York Times*, Apr. 13, 2011.

"Selwyn James, PM Editor, to Lecture Here." *Red Bank Register*, Oct. 26, 1944.

Shewey, Don. "Sidney Lumet: Reluctant Auteur." *American Film*, Dec. 1982.

"Sidney Lumet Denies Taking Overdose." *New York Times*, Aug. 27, 1963.

"Sidney Lumet Was a Hit at Army Camp." http://historicpalmbeach.blog.palmbeachpost.com/2011/05/05/sidney-lumet-was-a-hit-at-army-camp/

Simon, Alex. "Sidney Lumet: The Legendary Director Speaks." *Venice*, May, 1997.

Stark, Steven J. "A Master Director Returns to the Small Screen Armed with a High-Def Camera and a History." *Hollywood Reporter*, Jan. 9, 2001.

Stevens, Dana. "Evil Philip Seymour Hoffman, and Other Joys of Sidney Lumet's 'Before the Devil Knows You're Dead.'" *Slate.com*, Oct. 25, 2007. https://slate.com/culture/2007/10/before-the-devil-knows-you-re-dead-reviewed.html

"The Sidney Lumets Separate." *New York Times*, Aug. 24, 1963.

Thompson, David, "The Fugitive Kind: When Sidney Went to Tennessee" *The Criterion Collection*, Apr. 26, 2010.

Travers, Peter. "Sidney Lumet: The King of New York." *Rolling Stone*, Feb. 21, 2008.

Tunison, Michael. "The Old Man and the Cinema." *Entertainment Today*, May 16, 1997.

Turan, Kenneth. "The Fugitive Kind." *GQ*, Sept. 1988.

"Two Black Orgs at Odds Over 'The Wiz' Hiring." *Variety*, Oct. 6, 1977.

"Universal Will Film 'Wiz' in NYC Starting Sept. 30." *Box Office*, May 9, 1977.

Van Gelder, Lawrence. "Checking In with Lumet." *New York Times*, July 21, 2017.

Verrill, Addison. "MGM Delayed 'Appointment' Pic; 50 Prints of Lumet's Cut Versus Ditto of Margaret Booth's Cut." *Variety*, Jan. 28, 1965.

Warren, Steve. "Director Sidney Lumet Talks About 'Dog Day Afternoon.'" *The Advocate*, Nov. 19, 1975.

Wolf, William. "Now Leaving for 1934 on Track 9." *Los Angeles Times*, Sept. 3, 1974.

Wolfe, Tom. "Radical Chic: That Party at Lenny's." *New York Magazine*, June 8, 1970.

Yakir, Dan, and Sidney Lumet. "Wiz Kid." *Film Comment*, Nov.–Dec. 1978.

"Yanks Magic Carpet: A Souvenir Booklet Specially Prepared for U.S. Army Personnel in China, Burma and India (Pre-censored for Mailing)." 1945. www.cbi-theater.com/magic/magic-carpet.html

Zunser, Jesse. "Arthur Miller Tells How 'View from the Bridge' Was Made into a Movie." *Cue*, Jan. 20, 1962.

ONLINE, TV, FILM AND RADIO INTERVIEWS

Anker, Daniel. *Imaginary Witness: Hollywood and the Holocaust*. Anker Productions, 2004.

Anozie, Lorna. *Spike Lee's "25th Hour": The Evolution of an American Filmmaker*. Touchstone Home Video, 2003.

Brownlow, Kevin, and Michael Kloft. *The Tramp and the Dictator*. Warner Home Video, 2002.

Buirski, Nancy. *By Sidney Lumet*. American Masters, 2016.

Burns, Ric. *Eugene O'Neill: A Documentary Film*. American Experience, 2006.

Courrier, Kevin. "Interview with Sidney Lumet." Critics at Large, 1988. https://www.mixcloud.com/CriticsAtLarge/interview-with-sidney-lumet -1988/

Davis, Nick. *New York at the Movies*. A&E Home Video, 2002.

Demme, Jonathan. *The Manchurian Candidate*. (DVD extras). Paramount, 2004.

Emery, Robert J. *The Films of Sidney Lumet*. Wellspring Productions, 1999.

Engleman, Ralph. "Sidney Lumet Interview," parts 1–6. Archive of American Television, Oct. 28, 1999. https://interviews.televisionacademy.com

Farrell, Sean Patrick. "The Last Word: Sidney Lumet." *New York Times,* 2011. www.nytimes.com/video/obituaries/1194838961597/lwlumet.html

Geisinger, Elliot, and Ronald Saland. *Wiz on Down the Road*. Universal Studios Home Video, 1978.

Goodwin, Daisy. "Sidney Lumet." *Omnibus Series*, BBC, Feb. 26, 1991. www.youtube.com/watch?v=ajp-D7vcC3k

Gross, Terry. Interview. *Fresh Air*, NPR, 1988, rebroadcast Aug. 28, 2017. www.npr.org/2017/08/28/546733177/celebrating-30-years-of-fresh-air-prolific-filmmaker-sidney-lumet

———. "A Director of Classics, Still at Work." *Fresh Air*, NPR, Mar. 10, 2006. www.npr.org/templates/story/story.php?storyId=5256247

Gurian, Jeffrey. Interviews with Philip Seymour Hoffman, Sidney Lumet, Marisa Tomei, Ethan Hawke. *Comedy Matters TV*, Feb. 21, 2014. www.youtube.com/watch?v=Jm0GBdM21k4

Kenny, Glenn. "Prince of the City." Directors Guild of America, Fall 2007. www.dga.org/Craft/DGAQ/All-Articles/0703-Fall-2007/Interview-Sidney-Lumet.aspx

Krakower, Louise, and Michael Tobias. *Sean Connery Close Up*. Blue Dolphin Film Distribution, 1997.

Levin, Marc. "Interview with Sidney Lumet." Directors Guild of America, n.d. www.dga.org/Craft/VisualHistory/Interviews/Sidney-Lumet.aspx

Lopate, Leonard. "Sidney Lumet, Ethan Hawke, and Philip Seymour Hoffman on *Before the Devil Knows You're Dead*." *The Leonard Lopate Show*, NPR, Oct. 25, 2007. www.wnyc.org/story/54722-sidney-lumet-ethan-hawke-and-philip-seymour-hoffman-talk-about-their-new-movie/

Macandrew, James. "Theatre on Film, Part I." *Camera Three*, Dec. 2, 1962. www.tv.com/shows/camera-three/theater-on-film-part-i-1320723/

Naylor, David. *Inside: "Dr. Strangelove, or How I Learned to Stop Worrying and Love the Bomb."* Columbia, 2000.

Rose, Charlie. Interviews with Sidney Lumet. *Charlie Rose*, Feb. 25, 1993 (https://charlierose.com/videos/27074); Apr. 14, 1995 (https://charlierose.com/videos/12385); May 14, 1997 (https://charlierose.com/videos/26243); Nov. 11, 1997 (https://charlierose.com/videos/29217); Mar. 21, 2006 (https://charlierose.com/videos/18347); Nov. 30, 2007 (https://charlierose.com/videos/11379).

Rosenbaum, Thane. "An Evening with Sidney Lumet." 92nd Street Y, Jan. 28, 2009. www.youtube.com/watch?v=XiJbpjCKURY

Rutkowski, Gary. "Maria Riva, Actress." *The Interviews*, Television Academy Foundation, n.d. https://interviews.televisionacademy.com/interviews/maria-riva#interview-clips

Schwartz, David. "Pinewood Dialogue with Sidney Lumet." Museum of the Moving Image, Oct. 25, 2007. http://movingimagesource.us/dialogues/speaker/127

Schwartz, Jeffrey. *Revisiting* Fail-Safe. Columbia TriStar Home Video, 2000.

Stuart, Jamie. "Sidney Lumet Talks Digital, Filmmaking & New York in 18-Minute 2007 Interview." *Eyes On Camera*, Nov. 19, 2014. www.youtube.com/watch?v=PrdEl2oOX2Y

Weissbrod, Ellen. *Listen Up: The Lives of Quincy Jones*. Warner Bros., 1990.

ARCHIVAL SOURCES

Baruch Lumet Papers. Unpublished Memoir by Baruch Lumet. Collection 1451, Department of Special Collections, Charles E. Young Research Library, University of California, Los Angeles.

Gore Vidal Papers. Sidney Lumet–Gore Vidal correspondence, 1968–1995, Box 467, Folder, Houghton Library, Harvard University.

Katharine Hepburn Papers. Sidney Lumet to Katharine Hepburn, Aug. 4, 1963, File 1067, Margaret Herrick Library, Special Collections, Academy of Motion Arts and Sciences.

Katharine Hepburn Papers. Sidney Lumet to Katharine Hepburn, Jan. 12, 1962, File 81, Margaret Herrick Library, Special Collections, Academy of Motion Arts and Sciences.

Luther Adler Papers. A Flag Is Born. Script, 1947, Box 2, File 11, New York Public Library for the Performing Arts, Dorothy and Lewis B. Cullman Center, Billy Rose Theatre Division.

Production Code Administration Records. Geoffrey M. Shurlock to Hal B. Wallis, July 30, 1956, File #2158, Margaret Herrick Library, Special Collections, Academy of Motion Arts and Sciences.

Production Code Administration Records. Stuart Millar to Geoffrey M. Shurlock, Jan. 18, 1957, File #2158, Margaret Herrick Library, Special Collections, Academy of Motion Arts and Sciences.

Roman Bohnen Papers. Roman Bohnen to his father, n.d., 1932, Box 2, Folder 4, New York Public Library for the Performing Arts, Dorothy and Lewis B. Cullman Center, Billy Rose Theatre Division.

GOVERNMENT DOCUMENTS

Center of Military History, United States Army. Washington, DC, 1991. *The Technical Services, The Signal Corps: The Outcome (Mid-1943 Through 1945)*. United States Army in World War II. George Raynor Thompson and Dixie R. Harris. https://history.army.mil/html/books/010/10-18/index .html

Library of Congress: "China-Burma-India: World War II's Forgotten Theater." *Stories from the Veteran's History Project.* https://loc.gov/vets/stories/ex-war -cbi.html

Office of the Chief of Military History, Department of the Army, Washington, DC, 1957. *The Technical Services. The Signal Corps: The Test (December 1941 to July 1943)*. George Raynor Thompson, Dixie R. Harris, Pauline M. Oakes, Dulany Terrett. https://history.army.mil/html/books /010/10-17/CMH_Pub_10-17.pdf

U.S. Office of War Information. *The Battle for China: The Flying Tigers and the Stilwell Road*. Narrated by Ronald Reagan. 1945.

BLOGS

Bordwell, David. "Endurance: Survival Lessons from Lumet." *David Bordwell's Website on Cinema* (blog), Apr. 21, 2011. www.davidbordwell.net/blog/2011 /04/21/endurance-survival-lessons-from-lumet/

Bowles, Stephen. "Sidney." *The Classic TV History Blog,* Apr. 22, 2011. https:// classictvhistory.wordpress.com/2011/04/22/sidney/

———. "Sidney Lumet: Memories from the Early Years." *The Classic TV History Blog,* July 18, 2011. https://classictvhistory.wordpress.com/2011/07 /18/sidney-lumet-memories-from-the-early-years/

———. "The World of Sholem Aleichem and the Dybbuk." *The Classic TV History Blog,* May 12, 2012. https://classictvhistory.wordpress.com/2012 /05/21/the-world-of-sholom-aleichem-and-the-dybbuk/

Grissom, James. "Sidney Lumet on 'The Fugitive Kind': Delighted and Challenged." *Follies of God by James Grissom* (blog). Dec. 9, 2012. http:// jamesgrissom.blogspot.com/2012/12/sidney-lumet-on-fugitive-kind -delighted.html

Jackson, Tracey. "Sidney Lumet: One of the Greats in Every Way." *Tracey Jackson* (blog), Apr. 9, 2011. https://traceyjacksononline.com/2011/04 /sidney-lumet-one-of-the-greats-in-every-way/

"Rita Gam." *Glamour Girls of the Silver Screen*, n.d. http://www.glamour girlsofthesilverscreen.com/show/100/Rita+Gam/index.html

ORAL HISTORIES

Frank, Robert and Joan Frank, "Reminiscences of Sidney Lumet." Transcript of an oral history, conducted 1959 by Robert and Joan Frank, Popular Arts Project, Butler Library, Columbia University, New York, 54 pp.

Wincelberg, Anita M., "Baruch Lumet: Interview." Transcript of an oral history conducted in Dec. 1976 by Anita Wincelberg, New York Public Library, American Jewish Committee Oral History Collection, Oral History Box 48, no.5., 271 pp.

SOCIAL MEDIA CONTENT

Amy Lumet, Twitter posts, Feb, 2009–Mar. 19, 2019. https://twitter.com /amylulu1

INDEX

Note: *Italic* page numbers refer to photographs.